AF601294

PRAISE FOR *THE LANSKY LEGACY*

"Meyer Lansky pioneered an international gambling empire that continues to this day. His grandson captures his legacy from a perspective only he can share, and no stone is left unturned."

—Louis Ferrante, internationally bestselling author of the Borgata Trilogy

"When asked which mobster I would like to have lunch with, my answer was Meyer Lansky—because of his organizational skills and mathematical genius in establishing casinos, but most of all his ability to work with the Italian Mafia to establish the National Crime Syndicate. This stellar book confirms my reasoning."

—Joe Pistone, former undercover FBI agent and author of *Donnie Brasco* and *The Bonannos: A Century of Murder*

"A riveting account of the birth, ascendancy, and decline of the Mob as revealed through the life and letters of Meyer Lansky and recounted by Lansky's grandson, who has established himself as one of the premier historians of organized crime in the first half of the 20th century. Both a fascinating story and an invaluable resource for anyone interested in America's criminal underworld. A must-read."

—Ed Falco, *New York Times* bestselling author of *The Family Corleone*

"This is more than the biography of a mobster. It's a chronicle of a bygone era that left an indelible impact on the ever-evolving American landscape."

—Phil Genovese, grandson of Vito Genovese and author of the award-winning novel *The Grandfather Clause*

"Meyer Lansky II gives us a revealing, intimate portrait of his grandfather through correspondences that reveal the ambitions, family values, philosophy, and heartbreak of the man who turned gambling into an industry and made the Mob 'bigger than U.S. Steel.' A must-read!"

—Charles Bufalino, author of *Bufalino*

"Provides a fascinating look into the very private life of America's smartest, most powerful mobster of the 20th century, illustrating how he impacted our society today. With new insights and shocking details, this is a riveting tale of how a Jewish immigrant from Eastern Europe launched an empire through a mix of criminality and sheer guile. A classic story of the best and the worst of the American Dream."

—Thomas Maier, author of *Mafia Spies*

"A detailed and highly personal look at the man who helped create the modern American underworld. Meyer Lansky was always in the room where it happened and was, more often than not, the guy making it happen."

—George Anastasia, *New York Times* bestselling author of *The Docile Don* and *Blood and Honor*

"Meyer Lansky was one of the most important figures in American organized crime, and also one of the most private. But now, his grandson pierces the shroud, using his private letters to his family members as the framework for an engrossing look at his world and dealings. It is a story of a cunning and tragic figure, a proud Jew, and in his way, a patriotic American who played a major role in the emergence of the US Mafia in the 20th century."

—Anthony M. DeStefano, Pulitzer Prize and Emmy Award–winning journalist and author of *Jimmy the Gent* and *King of the Godfathers*

"Through a collection of deeply revealing letters, *The Lansky Legacy* presents a rare and intimate portrait of the legendary Mob financier, illuminating the contradictions of an American family bound by love and fractured by reputation, while offering insights into his humanity that history books and Hollywood portrayals have largely ignored. For readers fascinated by organized crime, 20th-century American history, or family legacies shaped by controversy, this book is a poignant and essential read."

—Chris Enss, *New York Times* bestselling author of *Meet the Kellys*

"The first book I've read where Meyer Lansky is a real person. Through one-of-a-kind family letters and oral accounts that simply cannot be found anywhere else, he is brought to life as much as a stranger you might sit down next to and have a heartfelt conversation with. For both fans of crime and anyone who wants to have a better understanding of the 20th century."

—Jonathan Lang, author of the graphic novel *Meyer*

"Meyer Lansky never left a paper trail. Fortunately, this book does. It deserves five stars and an offshore account. The writing is well-researched and engaging, and even the endnotes feel like they're hiding something. Highly recommended."

—Malcolm Kushner, author of *The Official Book of Mob Humor*

"Forget what you think you know about Meyer Lansky. The authors peel back decades of mythmaking to reveal the man behind the headlines, supported by letters, records, and firsthand family insight and documentation to prove it. It's as engaging as a thriller—but unmistakably true."

—Everett De Morier, co-author of *In the Ghost Shadows*

"A brilliant and unique insight into one of modern history's most enigmatic characters with previously unseen detail. A must-read about a fascinating era."

—Francine White, arts journalist

THE LANSKY LEGACY

Books by
MEYER LANSKY II and S. J. PEDDIE

The Lansky Legacy:
The Life and Letters of Meyer Lansky

Bugsy and Flamingo:
The Tumultuous Life and Times of
Benjamin "Bugsy" Siegel and Virginia Hill

Books by
S. J. PEDDIE

Sonny:
The Last of the Old Time Mafia Bosses,
John "Sonny" Franzese

THE LANSKY LEGACY

The Life and Letters of Meyer Lansky

Meyer Lansky II and S. J. Peddie

CITADEL PRESS
Kensington Publishing Corp.
www.kensingtonbooks.com

CITADEL PRESS BOOKS are published by

Kensington Publishing Corp.
900 Third Avenue
New York, NY 10022

All Kensington titles, imprints, and distributed lines are available at special quantity discounts for bulk purchases for sales promotions, premiums, fund-raising, educational, or institutional use. Special book excerpts or customized printings can also be created to fit specific needs. For details, write or phone the office of the Kensington sales manager: Kensington Publishing Corp., 900 Third Avenue, New York, NY 10022, attn Sales Department; phone 1-800-221-2647.

10 9 8 7 6 5 4 3 2 1

First Citadel hardcover printing: August 2026

Printed in the United States of America

ISBN: 978-0-8065-4497-7
ISBN: 978-0-8065-4499-1 (e-book)

Library of Congress Control Number: 2026937378

The authorized representative in the EU for product safety and compliance is eucomply OU, Parnu mnt 139b-14, Apt 123, Tallinn, Berlin 11317; hello@eucompliancepartner.com

To my father, Capt. Paul Lansky, USAF (1932–2024),
and my wife, Dani Porter-Lansky.
—Meyer Lansky II

To Brian, Sean, and Bret.
—S. J. Peddie

CONTENTS

AUTHOR'S NOTE

MEYER LANSKY is a singular figure in American history.

With Charles "Lucky" Luciano, he established the 20th-century National Crime Syndicate. The two men corralled fractious rival gangs spawned during Prohibition into a single, unified organization by persuading them it was in their interest to work together. In doing so, they created a formidable criminal underworld that not only vexed law enforcement but was ultimately able to insinuate itself into every aspect of American life and grew internationally. Despite some law enforcement victories and cultural changes, the organized crime structure they created exists to this day.

An astute businessman, Lansky created the modern-day casino. Until he arrived on the scene, gambling had been confined to seedy carpet joints average citizens were loath to enter. He knew huge money could be made by broadening their appeal. Walk into a top casino today, and you'll encounter a self-enclosed world where every possible need is met. The best chefs at elegant restaurants, top-flight entertainment, shopping for designer goods, and even activities for children. The goal is to make it unnecessary for gamblers to leave. Every last detail has been considered, down to the lack of pesky clocks. With no reason to leave, gamblers stay at the tables longer and gamble more money.

And unlike most mobsters, Lansky moved comfortably among world leaders. He counted congressmen and presidents as friends.

This book is an intimate portrait of the life of an enigmatic man. It is based on thousands of pages of archived court proceedings; sworn court testimony; police reports, extensive FBI notes, letters, and memos; state and federal crime commission investigations; articles from forty-four publications from 1928 through 2007; telegrams; marriage licenses; naturalization papers; and letters from Meyer Lansky primarily to his son, Paul, as well as close friends. The paper records have been fleshed out by interviews with more than forty-five family members, friends, and associates; Meyer Lansky's own words shared with his family; and the memories of his grandson, Meyer Lansky II.

This is the first—and only—time the Lansky legacy will be fully and faithfully disclosed from the inside.

FOREWORD

By Antoinette Giancana

AS A CHILD, I didn't know that my father, Sam Giancana, was a powerful Mob boss. I didn't even know what a Mob boss was. I grew up on West Lexington Street in Chicago. I didn't know anything in grammar school. Then my parents sent me to a boarding school in Indianapolis. That was where I found out who my father was.

It wasn't exactly directly in front of me, in front of anybody. It was kind of, "Oh, you know your father is a gangster, don't you?"

I couldn't respond, couldn't say anything. Who understood the word *gangster*?

Sam tried to hide it from us. I was aware that boarding school cost my father a lot to get me there. It was an excellent school. That's where they threw me so I wouldn't find out. How could parents do this to their kids?

You always find out. No matter what.

I knew that Sam was different from other fathers because he went away to "college" sometimes. As I grew older, I noticed the trappings of my father's growing power when we moved to Oak Park, a beautiful suburb of Chicago. I saw the comings and goings of his business associates, like Rocco Fischetti and Paul Ricca, who were more like members of the family. I didn't know exactly what he did for business, but I remember hearing Sam say, "Meyer this, Meyer that."

Paul Ricca lived about a block away from us. He walked around like a king, and he *wasn't* the king. It was just his attitude, and his quiet walk, his mannerisms. When I would go to their house, Paul

Ricca would always get up, introduce us to the kitchen, and always go in to the refrigerator and make us each something to eat. What a spread he put up.

Sam once told me that Meyer Lansky was the man most responsible for all the money he made in Cuba. I still didn't know what the business was, but I knew Sam had shrimp boats there. I never went to Cuba, and I would assume the reason was that my father was a little on the rough side when he was down there. They're all men down there. No women went down with these guys that I'm aware of.

When I was a junior or senior, I started going to Las Vegas with my aunt and uncle. Sam would follow us there. You have no idea the fun we had in Vegas! I went here, there, everywhere with an escort, meeting all of these so-called gentlemen—and they were gentlemen. *Perfect* gentlemen. Quiet, reserved, spoke intelligently of topics we wanted to talk about.

We'd have our suite there at the Desert Inn. It was nothing ostentatious, because that would attract too much attention. The one thing that was elaborate was the service. Everyone would bow and scrape to us, trying to please Sam. So did Moe Dalitz.

I recall quite vividly being taken into Moe's private office. He was sitting behind a big horseshoe desk. He asked me how I spelled my name. I said, "Toni, T-O-N-I."

He smiled and said that was his wife's first name. I looked over at her and couldn't help but notice a beautiful pendant on her neck, with her name spelled out in diamonds. I said, "Oh my, those are beautiful."

Six weeks later, I received an identical diamond pendant from him. I still have it. I wouldn't give it up for anything.

I knew all these characters, I really did. And they were really so terrific. We went to all their dressing rooms just to say hi and whatever. It was not the usual circumstances. I'd have dinner with Frank Sinatra and the Rat Pack—Dean Martin, Sammy Davis Jr., Peter Lawford, and Joey Bishop. I mean, those guys were a delight.

Sam's business associates, these guys—and I use the word *guys*—were different. When they were with other people's daughters—especially me, who was so aggressive sometimes—they changed their tune. They calmed down. I don't remember them saying curse words. I'd hear them talking about Meyer Lansky. I remember seeing him once in Vegas when I was real young. He was like the other guys—a gentleman.

It was great and fun. I could not pay for what I have learned from the gang over there, the theater people, and those who owned the posh hotels. For me, it was a great education. They were all very sweet people. In the private way, the way we were whenever we got together with these guys; it was family.

In the outside world, they would be treacherous. I wouldn't trust them. But as long as they treated you well personally, it was all that really counted.

We all had fun with each other. They would poke each other and do little crazy things. But they all remained friends. This was something you couldn't take away from these guys—the love, the friendship, the camaraderie. They were all together as one organization, Black and white together.

The Kennedys were close to Sinatra. They loved hanging around him. Things changed when J. Edgar Hoover and the government went after organized crime. All of a sudden, the Kennedys wanted nothing to do with Sam. He was bitter about that.

It was around that time that the surveillance started. You saw all these damn cars parked outside your house. It was absolutely terrible. A horrible feeling. You'd wonder what all these guys were doing parked there.

I remember Sam watching the McClellan Committee hearings, which were televised. He snickered as his old friend, Tony Accardo, came before the committee and dodged questions. Sam's interest picked up as Robert Kennedy handed Accardo some photographs and asked him to identify them. There were photos of Meyer Lansky, Charles Luciano, Paul Ricca, and Sam.

Kennedy asked Accardo about his association with Sam, and Accardo declined to answer. Sam chuckled and said, "What jerks," before realizing I was in the room with him.

In the outside world, Sam would make comments. There were times when he was with his friends he spoke differently about them. These guys had two different personalities. You're one person with somebody and one person with another. They can turn.

I was summoned to testify at one of the last committees. My father put me in the hospital and wouldn't let me go to the committee to testify. I was one of their goats that got away.

Meyer II and I are the dearest of friends. We have a nice relationship. We met on a TV show. He was in New York; I was in New York. I was in a dressing room; he was in a dressing room. It was *Maury.* That's how Meyer and I met.

We both know people. It's kind of a homey type of feeling when we talk together. We understand things that other people don't understand. We also experienced some of the same things.

I usually forget who I am. When I'm out with people who remind me who my father was in the 1940s and 1950s, it throws me because I don't hear my father's name very often. I live kind of a cloistered life. It's *the* life.

When I die, I'm going to have my undertaker put little drops of mementoes in the casket. I want some of that stuff with me. I've got Frank Sinatra's picture. I've got the pictures that I want with me.

These days, just thinking about these guys puts a smile on my face. I wouldn't change my life, except maybe do it better.

Antoinette Giancana *is the daughter of Chicago Outfit boss Sam Giancana and the author of* Mafia Princess *and* JFK and Sam.

INTRODUCTION

THE DAY I WAS BORN—AUGUST 4, 1957—MY FATHER, Paul Lansky, was over the moon with excitement. He was an accomplished man. A West Point graduate, he had completed a master's in engineering, done one tour in Vietnam, and was a successful businessman. But none of that compared to having a son.

My grandfather, Meyer Lansky, felt exactly the same way. When my parents called to tell him, he shouted, "Hooray!" A bunch of his buddies immediately sent their congratulations.

For them, the birth of a son was the fulfillment of everything they believed was important.

My parents had been talking about what to name me. My mom, Edna, wanted to name me Phillip, after a professor of hers. My father had other ideas.

"I want to name him after my father," he told her.

She didn't love the idea. She knew what my grandfather's name meant to some people. Besides, Jewish families don't typically name their children after the living. But when she saw how excited my father was about the idea, she relented.

My father had a good relationship with his father but was sent to prep school at the age of eight. He found he liked being on his own. As a teenager, he just wanted to be independent. Even though he had always been proud of his family name, he hated some of the things that went along with it. And although both he and my grandfather often argued as adults—they were both very strong-willed—they had an unshakable bond.

As happy as my father was with the idea, my grandfather was the exact opposite.

"Don't do that!" he railed. "It'll be a burden to him."

He worried that I would be harassed, as he had been throughout his life. First by street thugs, then the FBI, and later, by politicians who were always happy to take his money in private while they denounced him in public.

He worried about something even more sinister: the threat of a kidnapping. He told my father that I "might not fare well throughout life" with his name. He urged my father to reconsider.

As I said, my father was just as iron-willed as his father. He refused to change his mind.

And so I became Meyer Lansky II.

Growing up in Tacoma, Washington, the family name didn't seem like a big deal to me. I had a pretty normal childhood. I played a lot of sports—football, wrestling, and baseball. I was a pretty good swimmer, too, and my grandfather and I would swim together when we visited him at his home in Hallandale, Florida. Sometimes, we would even race in the pool. He was in great shape.

Grandpa grew up on the East River and learned how to swim there. That's where he had some of his early confrontations with the Irish kids. They didn't want him there. There were always fights. They'd say, "You can't swim here."

My grandfather wasn't the type of guy to take that. Neither was his best friend, Ben Siegel. Ben would be the one who would be aggressive immediately. He'd put a stop to all that.

Grandpa loved to power walk, too. We walked all the time. If you couldn't keep up with him, he'd let you know.

Even though he lived all the way across the country, he kept in constant touch with phone calls and letters. I still have a lot of those letters. As a kid, I was more excited by the gifts he would always mention in those letters—like the $50 he'd slip in the envelope, telling my dad to buy something nice for the kids or the time he bought me a Sting-Ray bicycle.

He always wanted to know what I was doing. Around sixth grade, I started writing him letters. He always answered my letters, but he added his own special twist: He'd correct my grammar and spelling with a pen and send them back to me. Then he'd tell my father to work with me on that.

Naturally, I didn't like criticism. I felt frustrated by that. But my dad told me you have to do things this way. "He's right," he said. My letters were wrong.

I got used to it.

To me, he was just Grandpa. He wasn't anyone famous. Whenever he came to visit, he'd always greet me with, "Whaddaya say, Meyer?"

But even as a young kid, I started to pick up clues that Grandpa was different.

When I entered junior high school, the older boys liked to "initiate" the younger boys. I'd walk to school with my friends, and the older boys started to push us around. Out of the blue, one of the older kids pointed to me and said, "No, leave him alone."

I didn't get it, but I wasn't about to complain. I shrugged and said, "Whatever."

When I was eleven or twelve, I heard on the radio that my grandfather met with John Connally, who was the US Treasury Secretary at the time, when he visited Las Vegas. The next time I saw Grandpa, I excitedly approached him.

"Hey, I heard your name on the radio!" I said.

"You did?" he said, with a small smile.

Nothing more.

When I was a little older, I was in a band with some older friends. We'd practice at my house. When my grandfather visited, my bandmates would know. A couple of times, one of their fathers dropped by the house. They didn't normally do that, but they would show up, act casual, and say, "Oh, I'm just looking for my son."

Naturally, my father would introduce them to his father. They probably had all this history they were thinking about when they shook Meyer Lansky's hand.

I was impressed. It started to dawn on me that Grandpa wasn't like other grandfathers.

I knew that he cared a lot about world events. He read everything. He always told me to know my congressmen and senators. While driving me somewhere, he'd quiz me as I sat in the back seat.

"Who's your senator, Meyer?" he'd say.

If I faltered, he'd say, "Scoop Jackson! He's a friend of mine!"

He'd be terribly upset if I got it wrong. He'd say, "Oh, Meyer, you have to read more."

I loved it when he visited, and I loved visiting him. He always made sure that we had quality time. We went shopping and had dinners out.

Everything changed when I was fourteen.

My parents' marriage imploded. There had been tensions. When my mother discovered that my father hadn't been entirely faithful to his marriage vows, she was furious. She filed for divorce.

She decided she had to get away. She told my sister, Myra, and me that we were moving to California.

Although I was not happy about the divorce, I was pretty happy to get out of Washington. I remember walking to school one day and a clogged gutter burst. I got soaking wet. I remember thinking, "One day I'm going to move away to the sun and never come back!"

My mom wanted to break all ties to her former life. She decided to change her name. She became Malana Mason.

That wasn't enough for her, though. I had to, too.

She started talking about it after we got in the car and were headed down to California.

"That name has never done you any good," she said. "You always got the bad and not the good. I don't see any future in it for you. Why don't you pick a name?"

I wasn't so sure, but she kept at it. When we got to California, she said, "Pick out a name here."

I saw a street sign with the name "Bryant."

"I think I'll take the first part of that one," I told her.

And so my name became Bryan Mason.

We spent a great year in California. I loved it. After that year, we moved back to Washington because my parents settled their divorce. Even though I attended a different school, some people knew me by my birth name, Meyer. I felt kind of embarrassed by the name change.

Kids would say, "What are you doing? Why did you change your name?"

I didn't really have an answer. The name Bryan felt weak. It didn't have any of the cool connotations that my birth name did. People didn't associate me with my grandfather anymore. I started to feel weak.

I wasn't Meyer Lansky anymore.

My grades started to slip. I couldn't really focus on my studies. Finally, I went to a psychologist. He attributed my lack of focus to one thing.

"When you changed your name, you lost your whole identity," he said.

When I was twenty-one, I started working at the La Costa Hotel and Spa in Carlsbad, California. It was Mob-owned at the time. Moe Dalitz was one of the bigger guys there. My mom was like, "Hey, wait a minute." She wasn't sure she wanted me working there. I just wanted to tend bar and go to the beach.

I started to want my old name back. By 1986, I moved to Lake Tahoe and changed it back. Nobody knew me there as Bryan anyway.

I felt more confident. I felt more like myself.

I started to work at Caesars Tahoe. One day, I got called up to the office of Larry Wolfe, the general manager.

He started the conversation by saying that they had a bunch of Jewish high rollers in Los Angeles and needed someone at

Caesars Tahoe to be their liaison. I had only been there about six months, but he wondered if I was interested.

I was. But then he got to the real reason why he called me into his office.

"We've had some trouble back east," he said. "We rented a garage in Atlantic City. Behind the garage guys were some Italian guys. I just wanted to make sure everything's okay with you."

In other words, he was asking me if I was connected.

I wasn't. I can understand why he wanted to check, given the scrutiny of the gaming commission. I assured him I had a clean record. It was pretty comical. All his life, my grandfather wanted to protect his family from the criminal life.

With my name change, all sorts of attention came my way. Most importantly, it was how I met my wife, Dani. She was working at Caesars Tahoe in advertising and a mutual friend asked her if she wanted to meet Meyer Lansky. She said, "Heck, yeah!"

We met in the middle of a casino, but we were each with other people at the time. Then, fifteen years ago, we reconnected on Facebook. We've been together ever since.

I've worked hard to learn everything I can about the history of the Mafia and my grandfather's legacy. I know what rings true with what I know about my grandfather.

Along the way, I've met my fair share of imposters, poseurs, and hangers-on. They all have this revisionist history going on. They want to get their bit of fame by associating themselves with the Mafia. The worst are the ones who try to latch on to my grandfather's story.

I don't want to cut anyone down, but these guys missed the mark. My grandfather worked with world leaders and built casinos in foreign countries. He was a brilliant businessman, capable of juggling a lot of different things at the same time. He was always in control, even when things were chaotic. People wanted him to help with their problems, and he helped them when he could.

When I see the phonies acting like experts on a stage, it makes me mad. I want to set the record straight. My grandfather was the same way. He hated hypocrites.

That's why I wrote this book. I want to give people an inside look at what really went on, what the life was like. My grandfather was famous for keeping all his business deals in his head. Fortunately for posterity's sake, when it came to his family, he wrote it down.

What mattered most of all to Meyer Lansky was his family.

Even in the 1970s, he would say, "If people ask you questions, Meyer, don't talk to them. It's none of their business."

CHAPTER 1

A Hungry and Ambitious Young Man

MEYER LANSKY FILED his naturalization application in 1921. He believed deeply in the principles of his adopted country. Getting citizenship was important to him. And he figured it wouldn't hurt to give himself a little edge. He listed his birth date as the same day as that of the United States—the Fourth of July.

In fact, he was born on August 28, 1902.

Thanks to his naturalization application, the Fourth of July date followed him around the rest of his life and was picked up by various federal agencies. He didn't mind. He always celebrated his birthday on the Fourth of July anyway.

That was Meyer Lansky. He was always going to take charge of his destiny.

He was born Maier Suchowljansky in Grodno, Poland, a village at the border of Russia and Poland. Nearly half the population was Jewish, according to a Russian census at the time. Russians treated the village Jews with utter contempt. Not surprisingly, Jews chafed at their treatment. They pushed back at the abuses Russians inflicted. The tensions simmered but were treated as a fact of life. As World War I loomed, however, a surge of anti-Semitism swept Europe. Attacks on Jews burst out into the open. They became increasingly violent. To some, the only sensible option was to take their chances in America. Lansky's father, Max Suchowljansky, was one of them.

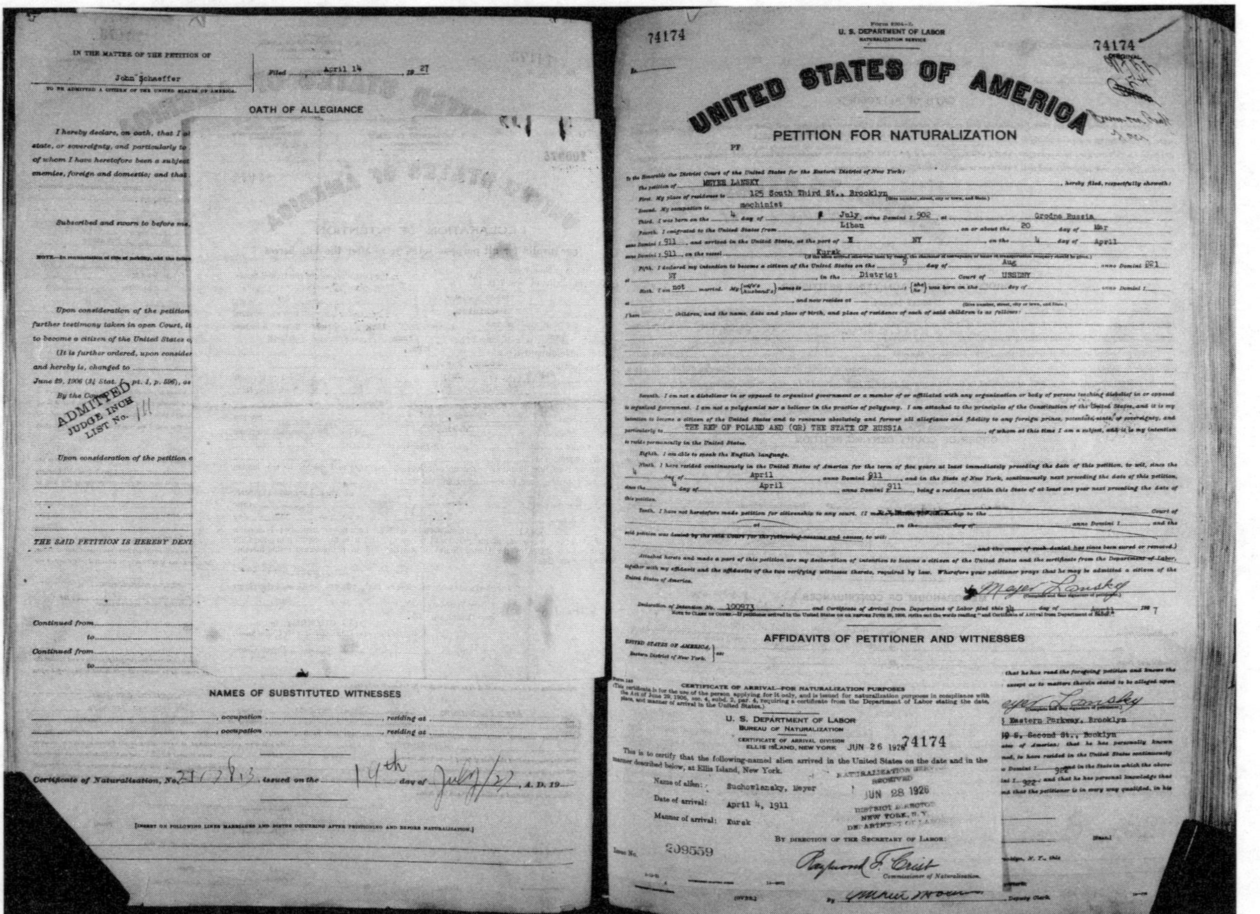

IN THE MATTER OF THE PETITION OF

John Schaeffer

TO BE ADMITTED A CITIZEN OF THE UNITED STATES OF AMERICA.

Filed April 14 19 27

OATH OF ALLEGIANCE

I hereby declare, on oath, that I a…
state, or sovereignty, and particularly to…
of whom I have heretofore been a subject…
enemies, foreign and domestic; and that…

Subscribed and sworn to before me…

Upon consideration of the petition…
further testimony taken in open Court, it…
to become a citizen of the United States o…
(It is further ordered, upon consider…
and hereby is, changed to …
June 29, 1906 (34 Stat. L., pt. 1, p. 596), as…
By the Co…

ADMITTED
JUDGE INCH
LIST No. 111

Upon consideration of the petition o…

THE SAID PETITION IS HEREBY DEN…

Continued from … to …
Continued from … to …

NAMES OF SUBSTITUTED WITNESSES

…, occupation …, residing at …
…, occupation …, residing at …

Certificate of Naturalization, No. 2172813 issued on the 14th day of July/27, A. D. 19…

74174

U. S. DEPARTMENT OF LABOR

74174

UNITED STATES OF AMERICA

PETITION FOR NATURALIZATION

To the Honorable the District Court of the United States for the Eastern District of New York:

The petition of MEYER LANSKY, hereby filed, respectfully showeth:

First. My place of residence is 125 South Third St., Brooklyn

Second. My occupation is machinist

Third. I was born on the 4 day of July, anno Domini 1902 at Grodno Russia

Fourth. I emigrated to the United States from Liban, on or about the 20 day of Mar anno Domini 1911, and arrived in the United States, at the port of N NY, on the 4 day of April anno Domini 1911, on the vessel Kursk

Fifth. I declared my intention to become a citizen of the United States on the 9 day of Aug anno Domini 1921 at NY in the District Court of USDENY

Sixth. I am not married.

Seventh. I am not a disbeliever in or opposed to organized government or a member of or affiliated with any organization or body of persons teaching disbelief in or opposed to organized government. I am not a polygamist nor a believer in the practice of polygamy. I am attached to the principles of the Constitution of the United States, and it is my intention to become a citizen of the United States and to renounce absolutely and forever all allegiance and fidelity to any foreign prince, potentate, state, or sovereignty, and particularly to THE REP OF POLAND AND (OR) THE STATE OF RUSSIA, of whom at this time I am a subject, and it is my intention to reside permanently in the United States.

Eighth. I am able to speak the English language.

Ninth. I have resided continuously in the United States of America for the term of five years at least immediately preceding the date of this petition, to wit, since the 4 day of April anno Domini 1911, and in the State of New York, continuously next preceding the date of this petition, since the 4 day of April, anno Domini 1911, being a residence within this State of at least one year next preceding the date of this petition.

Tenth. I have not heretofore made petition for citizenship to any court.

Attached hereto and made a part of this petition are my declaration of intention to become a citizen of the United States and the certificate from the Department of Labor, together with my affidavit and the affidavits of the two verifying witnesses thereto, required by law. Wherefore your petitioner prays that he may be admitted a citizen of the United States of America.

Meyer Lansky

Declaration of Intention No. 100973 and Certificate of Arrival from Department of Labor filed this … day of April 19 27

AFFIDAVITS OF PETITIONER AND WITNESSES

UNITED STATES OF AMERICA, Eastern District of New York. } ss:

CERTIFICATE OF ARRIVAL—FOR NATURALIZATION PURPOSES

U. S. DEPARTMENT OF LABOR
BUREAU OF NATURALIZATION
CERTIFICATE OF ARRIVAL DIVISION
ELLIS ISLAND, NEW YORK JUN 26 1926 74174

This is to certify that the following-named alien arrived in the United States on the date and in the manner described below, at Ellis Island, New York.

Name of alien: Suchowlansky, Meyer
Date of arrival: April 4, 1911
Manner of arrival: Kursk

NATURALIZATION SERVICE RECEIVED JUN 28 1926 DISTRICT DIRECTOR NEW YORK, N.Y. DEPARTMENT OF LABOR

By DIRECTION OF THE SECRETARY OF LABOR:

Raymond F. Crist
Commissioner of Naturalization.

Issue No. 209559

that he has read the foregoing petition and knows the … except as to matters therein stated to be alleged upon …

Meyer Lansky

Eastern Parkway, Brooklyn

… Second St., Brooklyn

Meyer Lansky’s naturalization application, approved June 28, 1926.

IN THE MATTER OF THE PETITION OF

MEYER LANSKY

TO BE ADMITTED A CITIZEN OF THE UNITED STATES OF AMERICA.

Filed April 14 19 27

OATH OF ALLEGIANCE

I hereby declare, on oath, that I absolutely and entirely renounce and abjure all allegiance and fidelity to any foreign prince, potentate, state, or sovereignty, and particularly to THE REP OF POLAND AND (OR) THE STATE OF RUSSIA of whom I have heretofore been a subject; that I will support and defend the Constitution and laws of the United States of America against all enemies, foreign and domestic; and that I will bear true faith and allegiance to the same.

x Meyer Lansky

Subscribed and sworn to before me, in open Court, this 27 day of September A. D. 19 28

Clerk.

ORDER OF COURT ADMITTING PETITIONER

Upon consideration of the petition of MEYER LANSKY, and affidavits in support thereof, and further testimony taken in open Court, it is ordered that the said petitioner, who has taken the oath required by law, be, and hereby is, admitted to become a citizen of the United States of America, this ______ day of ______, A. D. 19__.

(It is further ordered, upon consideration of the petition of the said ______, that his name be, and hereby is, changed to ______, under authority of the provisions of section 6 of the act approved June 29, 1906 (34 Stat. L., pt. 1, p. 596), as amended by the act approved March 4, 1913, entitled "An act to create a Department of Labor.")

By the Court:

ADMITTED JUDGE MOSCOWITZ LIST No. 500

USD, Judge.

ORDER OF COURT DENYING PETITION

Upon consideration of the petition of ______ and the motion of ______ for the United States in open Court this ______ day of ______, 19__, it appearing that ______

THE SAID PETITION IS HEREBY DENIED.

______, Judge.

MEMORANDUM OF CONTINUANCES

REASONS FOR CONTINUANCE

Continued from ______, 19__, to ______, 19__.

Continued from ______, 19__, to ______, 19__.

NAMES OF SUBSTITUTED WITNESSES

______, occupation ______, residing at ______

______, occupation ______, residing at ______

Certificate of Naturalization, No. 2517814, issued on the 27th day of Sept/28, A. D. 19__.

74175

U. S. DEPARTMENT OF LABOR
NATURALIZATION SERVICE

UNITED STATES OF AMERICA

2300

U. S. DEPARTMENT OF LABOR
NATURALIZATION SERVICE

TRIPLICATE

No. 155182

74174

UNITED STATES OF AMERICA

DECLARATION OF INTENTION

Invalid for all purposes seven years after the date hereof

State of New York, County of Kings, ss: In the Supreme Court of Kings County.

I, Harry Jaffe, aged 40 years, occupation Operator, do declare on oath that my personal description is: Color white, complexion fair, height 5 feet 4 inches, weight 138 pounds, color of hair Brown, color of eyes Blue, other visible distinctive marks ______

I was born in Rupeska Latvia on the 15 day of April anno Domini 1882; I now reside at 78 Wilson St. Brooklyn, N. Y.

I emigrated to the United States of America from Antwerp Belgium on the vessel Finland; my last foreign residence was Latvia; I am married; the name of my wife is Sadie; she was born at America and now resides at 78 Wilson Av Brooklyn. It is my bona fide intention to renounce forever all allegiance and fidelity to any foreign prince, potentate, state, or sovereignty, and particularly to The Republic of Latvia of whom I am now a subject; I arrived at the port of New York, in the State of New York, on or about the 17 day of August, anno Domini 1903; I am not an anarchist; I am not a polygamist nor a believer in the practice of polygamy; and it is my intention in good faith to become a citizen of the United States of America and to permanently reside therein: SO HELP ME GOD.

Harry Jaffe

Subscribed and sworn to before me in the office of the Clerk of said Court at Brooklyn, N. Y., this 28 day of May anno Domini 19 23

[SEAL]

William E. Kelly, Clerk of the Supreme Court.

By William J. Farrell, Deputy Clerk.

Isidore Geltzer, occupation Window Cleaner, residing at 1990 Coney Island Avenue Brooklyn

Ben Lash, occupation Window Cleaner, residing at 189 Rosa Street Brooklyn, N

each being severally, duly, and respectively sworn, deposes and says that he is a citizen of the United States of America; that he has personally known Harry Jaffe, the petitioner above mentioned, to have resided in the United States continuously immediately preceding the date of filing his petition, since the 1 day of April, anno Domini 1921, and in the State in which the above-entitled petition is made continuously since the ______ day of April, anno Domini 1921, and that he has personal knowledge that the said petitioner is a person of good moral character, attached to the principles of the Constitution of the United States, and that the petitioner is in every way qualified, in his opinion, to be admitted a citizen of the United States.

x Isidor Geltzer

Ben Lash

Subscribed and sworn to before me by the above-named petitioner and witnesses in the office of the Clerk of said Court at Brooklyn, N. Y., this 14 day of April, anno Domini 19 27

By Arthur Hitchins, Deputy Clerk.

(continued)

He left for America in 1909. After two years of working as a garment presser, he had saved enough money to bring his family over to America on the SS *Kursk*. In their new country, they became the Lanskys.

The family moved to a cramped apartment in Brownsville, Brooklyn. There were some farms and fields nearby, but it really wasn't much different from the place they had left. It was a tough tenement populated by Eastern European Jews. They followed the customs and traditions of the old country. Shabbat, a day of rest and prayer, began on Friday at sunset and continued until nightfall on Saturday. Yiddish was the language heard on the street. Families kept kosher. While it might have felt familiar to young Lansky, he hated the poverty.

"Homes weren't conducive to spend time in," he later recalled with his typical terseness. "Hot in the summer, cold in the winter."

He was a bright student, and he loved school. He loved learning, which became a lifelong passion. He read Shakespeare and could recite *The Merchant of Venice* by heart. He was fascinated by world history and memorized the *Gettysburg Address*. His education in America was so much more broad-based than the rabbinical teachings of his early years in Grodno. He reveled in the variety of subjects in public school: mathematics, science, poetry, and chemistry. He even told his family in later years that he appreciated the discipline the teachers exerted over their charges.

"Our teachers were strict. They didn't tolerate nonsense, and if you wanted to learn, you could learn very much," he said.

When he first arrived in the United States in 1911, he was placed in the first grade, but he moved up quickly, jumping to the sixth grade in three years. He was in a hurry. He later lamented that he would have read more, but they didn't have good lights in their apartment. Nonetheless, he got all A's and a couple of B's, according to an FBI report. But there was something else on his report card: chronic absenteeism. For a boy who loved to learn, he found himself spending more time on the streets than in school. The pull of the streets was simply too strong.

He didn't admit it to his family, but their poverty embarrassed him. He hated his family's cramped living conditions. There was no privacy within the apartment or beyond—the plywood walls of their apartment were paper-thin. Although his father worked long hours, his earnings didn't cover the needs of his young family.

"There were times that food was just enough to exist," Lansky recalled. The grinding penury felt endless, and Lansky found himself resentful of his father's failure to succeed financially. He was keenly aware of his second-class status in life, or as he put it, "third-class." Later, as an adult, when his own children asked him about his childhood memories, Lansky grimly shut down the line of questioning by saying simply, "It wasn't nice."

Public school had opened his eyes to the possibilities of the world, and for a time, he combined his education with street life. But it was clear to him that he needed money to take advantage of those possibilities. He was also very conscious of his responsibility toward his parents. He saw himself as a devoted son. To fulfill his duty as a devoted son, he needed to make money. That's what he told himself anyway.

By 1914, when Lansky was eleven years old, the family moved to Manhattan's Lower East Side. Lansky immediately joined the Seward Park Library. It was, quite literally, a magical place for him. His academic interests turned to sports, biographies, and mechanical magazines. He loved being surrounded by books. Home was a different matter. The Lower East Side was not exactly a step up. To Lansky, it was even more crowded and poor. It was a different ethnic mix, however.

"The Jews were locked in between Italians and Irish," he later recalled. That afforded him an entirely different education.

There, he found himself fascinated by the games of chance on the street, particularly craps. As he watched gamblers lose money, he figured out pretty quickly that the only winners were the ones who controlled the game. He set his sights on controlling the game. One way to do that was to calculate the odds, and it turned out that he had an uncanny ability to figure them out.

Later in life, Lansky's business associates marveled at his genius with numbers. Able to do complex calculations in his head, he never wrote anything down. As he learned more about business and making money on the streets, that talent became a crucial survival skill. Not leaving a paper trail made it harder for investigators to pin anything on him.

That skill had started on the streets. As kids, he and his brother, Jacob—known as Jack to his family—constantly called out numbers to one another. Then they'd each have to add them up or multiply them in their heads. It was a game both he and Jack played into adulthood, testing friends' children with columns of numbers. What people who played that game with Lansky remembered most was that he always got it right.

Lansky was never a big kid. He was small and wiry. One day, he was walking home from school and ran into one of the pitfalls of his new neighborhood. It was Charles Luciano and a group of Italian toughs. They surrounded him. They figured that Jews were an ideal target because they didn't usually fight back. At least, that was the prevailing sentiment among the streetwise kids of New York. The thugs would extort whatever money they could from them or deliver a beating. Sometimes, they'd pull down the kid's pants to see if he was circumcised, Lansky later recalled.

Lansky was no ordinary target, however. He might have been short, Jewish, and book smart, but he refused to take a beating without a fight. "Go fuck yourself!" he shouted.

That impressed Luciano. Years later, Luciano called Lansky the toughest guy he ever knew.

That's the greatest compliment a gangster like Luciano could give. Gangsters admire toughness. It's one quality that can't be faked. They know because they're always on the lookout for weakness, something they can exploit or leverage. Woe to the man in that life who reveals weakness. It immediately sparks derision. Or worse, it can be a death sentence. Intuitively, Lansky knew that.

Luciano and Lansky formed a tight, lifelong bond. They seemed to intuit what they were each thinking. They shared the immigrant experience, with Luciano—born Salvatore Lucania in 1897—hailing from Palermo, Sicily, and also being looked down upon as a second-class citizen by America's entrenched classes. Over the years, associates who saw them together would comment on their obvious ability to understand one another. Their trust in each other forged a friendship that not only mutually benefited them, but one that would have a profound impact on the history of organized crime.

When Lansky was in the eighth grade, he left school. World War I had been raging at a distance for several years, but in 1917, the US Congress voted to declare war on Germany. Although as a fourteen-year-old, Lansky was not going to be drafted, the world as he knew it was changing. He decided it was time for him to go out and make his own way. He got a job as a machinist in his cousin's tool-and-die shop, Lansky's Tool and Die. In some ways, it was a good fit because of his avid interest in mechanics. His foreman admired his skill, but the hours were grueling. He worked fifty-two hours a week at ten cents an hour.

"At my age, I should have worked no more than forty-eight hours," he later recalled. "No possible future for a machinist at that time."

It was a critical lesson. If he stayed in the machinist's job, his life would never change. Instead, he would be doomed to follow his father's failure. A grim determination set in. He would not let that happen. He had thought, even dreamed, of studying engineering, but once he dropped out of school, that dream was foreclosed. He never fully explained to his family why he didn't stay in school and do just that, saying only, "Circumstances didn't permit it."

There was something else, something he knew his devout and hardworking parents wouldn't approve of. It was the money to be made on the streets. He knew that with his extraordinary skill at mathematics, he could make a lot more money much more easily at a craps game.

About a year after he took the machinist's job, he saw Benjamin Siegel on the street—where else? Two rival gangs were fighting over turf. Someone dropped a gun. Siegel picked it up. As he did, a police whistle sounded. Siegel raised his arm to shoot the gun. Lansky stopped him.

"You're crazy!" he shouted, grabbing his arm. "Drop the gun!"

Siegel did, and the two ran off, eluding the police.

After they were safely out of sight, Siegel made it clear that he wasn't happy. He had really wanted that gun and he had wanted to win the fight. He asked Lansky, "Why didn't you let me kill that bastard?"

"If you'd been caught with the gun, you'd be in deep trouble," Lansky replied. "Only a schlimazel would shoot with the cops in sight. Use your head."

Although he was still barely a teenager, Lansky had already learned how to survive on the streets.

Although Lansky was several years older than Siegel, they clicked. Outwardly, they were dramatically different. Siegel was charming and gregarious but given to sudden violent outbursts when angered. Lansky was quieter and self-contained, much more inclined to analyze a situation before acting. Their similarities were more important, however. They shared a deeply ingrained sense that they were both outsiders. They were Jewish, the sons of immigrants, and trying to figure out how they would make their mark in the world that they knew wouldn't cut them any breaks. They decided to depend on themselves, and on each other.

Street guys often talk about loyalty. In reality, they demonstrate very little of it. Under pressure, they'll rat on their friends or worse, set them up to be killed. Lansky and Siegel weren't like that. They were the exception. Throughout their lives, they remained fiercely loyal to one another.

After their dramatic meeting, they decided to form their own gang of street guys. There was Lansky's brother (Jack), Meyer "Mike" Wassell, Samuel "Red" Levine, Irving "Tabbo" Sandler, and Joseph "Doc" Stacher. On the street, they became known as the Bugs and Meyer Mob.

"Bugs" was a reference to Siegel's nickname—Bugsy. A lot of guys called him that because he would "bug out" like crazy when he got angry. He hated the nickname, and Lansky never, *ever* called him that because he wouldn't do that to a friend. Other guys did, however, but always behind his back. Anyone who dared to call him that to his face was likely to face serious and violent repercussions from Siegel. Despite that very real threat, the nickname stuck.

Like his friendship with Luciano and Siegel, Lansky's early friendships from the streets lasted throughout his life.

The boys in the Bugs and Meyer Mob prided themselves on being tough. They wouldn't take any crap from the Irish or the Italians. On hot summer days, they'd swim in New York's Hudson River, often jumping off the piers. The river was hardly pristine. Sewage and blood from the nearby slaughterhouses flowed freely into it. But the boys sloughed it off. They had more consequential things to worry about—like turf. The local Irish gangs considered the river their territory. Lansky and his friends thought otherwise. Their gang—with Siegel leading the charge—never backed down. Fights were frequent.

In later years, Lansky minimized his activities with his crew as "playful and mischievous." It was something they turned to because there was no place to play. Occasionally, "a sour policeman would show his authority," he told his family, without elaborating. FBI files, however, show something a little more than that: two arrests in 1918, when he was all of sixteen years old. The first one, for felonious assault, was dismissed. The second one, for annoying and disorderly conduct around a woman, resulted in a conviction. The penalty was a fine of two dollars.

The details of those arrests are unclear, but the arrest for his conduct around a woman is particularly striking because throughout his life, he was known for being nothing but gentlemanly toward women in his company. Writer Robert Lacey speculated that that particular arrest might have been Lansky's attempt to be a pimp for prostitutes in the area. Pimping was not uncommon in

Jewish neighborhoods, so it was likely something with which Lansky was familiar. It was also true that Lansky was always looking for places where money could be made. But as he got more established on the streets, he eschewed rackets like drugs and prostitution, even though his buddy Luciano favored them. Lansky considered them dirty. After that youthful conviction for disorderly conduct around a woman, there never was another one.

His early arrests made one thing clear: His behavior was a little more than "playful and mischievous." He was an adolescent running with a tough gang on the streets. As much as he felt a duty to honor his parents, he had formed a tight, familial bond with the tough Jewish kids in his gang. After years of feeling like an outsider and resenting his lower-class status, he reveled in being able to take charge and do things his way. If that meant getting into fights or breaking laws that he thought were stupid, so be it. He felt no allegiance to the miserable poverty of his childhood. He was determined to make a success of himself, whatever it took.

As he entered adulthood in the 1920s, the stakes got higher. A fellow criminal, Daniel Patrick Ahearn, described two particularly violent incidents years later. Once, after a man refused to join a strike that Lansky had planned, he cracked his head open with an iron bar. Then, in 1928, there was the assault on another criminal, John Bartlett, who admitted stealing a few furs from a job Lansky and Siegel had run. He was taken for a ride, shot, and dumped. Whether it was done to scare him or kill him, Bartlett survived. He told a police detective that three men were responsible for the assault: Lansky, then twenty-six, Samuel Levine, and Joseph Benzole. All three men were charged with assault.

While Bartlett was recuperating at St. Joseph's Hospital in Long Island City, he received a meal of chicken as a gift. When his wife told him that Lansky had sent it, Barrett threw it out his hospital room window. His instincts were correct. The chicken had been poisoned with strychnine.

When it came time to appear before a judge on the case, Bartlett refused to sign the complaint against the three men. The detective implored the judge to give him some time to talk to his witness. The judge accommodated him and went through all his other cases for the day. At the end of the day, the judge called Bartlett before him. He continued to refuse to sign the complaint. He admitted that he had, indeed, named the three men as his assailants, but now couldn't be certain. Angered, the judge muttered, "I'd like to lock you up for perjury."

He didn't, however. The judge had no choice but to dismiss the charges.

The reporter who covered the hearing noted that when Bartlett left court, he did not get into the same car with the three men charged with his assault. Whether the story of the poisoned chicken was true or not, it was the kind of tale that would enhance a guy's reputation on the streets. Everyone knew that Lansky was a clever guy.

Smart criminals monitor word on the street very carefully, and word was spreading about the Bugs and Meyer Mob. Arnold Rothstein was one of those who heard about these tough kids. Rothstein was the ultimate fixer, the go-between for street guys and politicians. His friend, writer Damon Runyon, called him "The Brain."

Rothstein carefully crafted an image of sophistication and genteel wealth, even though his money came from grubby street crimes and backroom deals during the crazy days of Prohibition. He was famous for fixing the 1919 World Series in the notorious Black Sox Scandal, although it isn't entirely clear whether he fixed the series or merely capitalized on it. In any case, he liked to keep an eye out for useful talent. He preferred to bankroll the jobs he had in mind and let other people take the risks. Tough, young Jewish kids were the perfect kind of talent.

He met Lansky at a bar mitzvah of mutual friends in Brooklyn. They wound up talking for six hours at the Park Slope Hotel. That an adult with Rothstein's stature would spend so much time talking to a young street tough is remarkable. He clearly saw something in Lansky.

Lansky initially was in awe of Rothstein—this was the famous Arnold Rothstein, after all—but Rothstein put him at ease.

"It was a big surprise to me," Lansky said later. "Rothstein told me quite frankly that he picked me because I was ambitious and hungry."

In Lansky, Rothstein saw an opportunity: He needed someone to run his bootlegging business.

During Prohibition, the manufacture, sale, and distribution of alcohol was illegal, but the consumption of it was not. Rothstein had spent years cultivating the rich and famous. He knew what they wanted: top-shelf liquor. He wanted nothing to do with what he called the "rotgut whiskey" that low-level thugs were selling. He wanted only the best. For that, he needed to go to Europe. And he needed to set up a distribution system along the coast in order to transport the booze inland by truck. He needed someone who was smart and tough and who had good organizational skills. He saw all that in Lansky.

Rothstein opened doors for Lansky. He schooled Lansky and his friends on how to dress, table manners, and how to blend in with the crowd. There were introductions as well, like with Abner "Longy" Zwillman, a powerful New Jersey mobster who became a lifelong friend. He was the one who advised Lansky on how to keep the press happy (send them cases of liquor at the holidays). Another Rothstein introduction was to Frank Costello. He schooled Lansky on keeping up appearances so he was less likely to attract the attention of police. There was money to be made, and there was no need to get caught by the cops.

Bootlegging was big business. Lansky and Siegel were breaking in and making money. They became partners with Costello in the King's Ransom Distilling Co. Before long, Lansky and Siegel were known as the musclemen in the booze wars of the 1920s.

It seemed like an unbroken string of successes. Rothstein, however, couldn't sustain the same winning streak. He liked to gamble. Though there might be ups and downs while gambling, he prided himself on always winning in the end. He was too smart to lose. At least, that's what he told himself and anyone who would listen.

"I never played with a man I wasn't sure I could beat," he said. "I knew how to size them up. I still do. That's all there is to making money."

One secret of his cockiness was that he wasn't averse to cheating in order to win—or to lose, for that matter.

By November 1928, Rothstein had accumulated a staggering $322,000 in gambling debts—the equivalent of $5.9 million today. His debt was eye-popping. Even worse, he refused to pay it. He claimed he was a victim of cheating. That might have assuaged his considerable pride, but it certainly was not something his lenders wanted to hear.

It was a big mistake.

On November 4, 1928, Rothstein got a call at Lindy's, a Times Square restaurant where bookies, gamblers, and entertainers like Harpo Marx hung out. Rothstein liked to hold court there. After getting the call, he got up and left for the Park Central Hotel. He took the precaution of entering the hotel through the service entrance, but it wasn't enough to protect him. A shooter or shooters shot him twice in the abdomen in a hotel room. After walking some distance, he collapsed, bleeding. Police rushed him to the hospital and asked him who shot him. True to his code, Rothstein refused to say.

"You stick to your trade," he told police. "I'll stick to mine."

He died the next day.

For Lansky, Rothstein's death confirmed what he had already decided about gambling: "There is only one way to win, and that is not to play. Every player, even Arnie Rothstein—king of them all—loses in the end, whether it's the horses, craps, blackjack, roulette, or anything else."

The death of his mentor was a personal blow to Lansky, but he knew that he could make his own way. He was canny enough to know that his success—or failure—depended solely on himself and a small circle of people he trusted, like Siegel. But there was an upside to Rothstein's death. As often happens in the underworld, Rothstein's fiefdom had to be passed on to someone else. Lansky and Siegel were already primed. They immediately assumed control of his operations.

By the late 1920s, Lansky's naturalization application was still pending. At long last, he was able to schedule an interview. The process seemed straightforward enough. And, as he had done in filling out his naturalization application, he decided to edit the facts to ensure the best possible outcome. He conveniently omitted the fact that he had a criminal record—which normally would be grounds for denial—and the interviewer apparently didn't press the issue. And so, seven years after his naturalization application, Lansky took the oath of allegiance and became a citizen of the United States.

He was on his way. He was sure of it.

CHAPTER 2

Next Step: Marriage and Business

LIFE—AND DEATH—for a gangster in the Prohibition days of the 1920s were good.

When Francesco Ioele—commonly known as Frankie Yale or Frankie Uale—was gunned down in his new Lincoln coupe in the Fort Hamilton section of Brooklyn in 1928, New York newspaper tabloids reported every bloody detail of his murder. He had been a successful crime boss, running protection rackets in Brooklyn and supplying Canadian whiskey to Al Capone. He also served as a mentor to other up-and-coming street guys who worked for him, like Anthony "Little Augie Pisano" Carfano, Umberto "Albert" Anastasia, and Lansky's good friend and business partner, Joe Adonis. (Adonis's real last name was Doto. He changed it to reflect what he regarded as his dashing good looks.) Allegedly, Yale even pulled the trigger on James "Big Jim" Colosimo—first boss of the Chicago Outfit—at Johnny Torrio's behest, for shying away from bootlegging and its limitless windfalls.

Unfortunately, Capone suspected him—correctly—of cutting into his profits from booze.

While Yale's murder in broad daylight—on a Sunday afternoon, no less—shocked and titillated the good citizens of New York, it was his funeral that made a truly lasting impression on the public.

No fewer than 15,000 people crowded around St. Rosalia's Catholic Church, an imposing structure dedicated to the patron saint of Palermo. People lined the streets of Brooklyn for blocks. Whether they lined up to show fealty to a man whose influence they still feared or whether it was just to gawk, they were right. It was a good show. Thirty-eight cars carried the huge floral arrangements—many too big to fit into the cars and protruding over the cars' trunks.

Another 250 Cadillacs carried mourners to the church. The august *New York Times*, whose reporters would have much preferred covering a funeral for a respectable dignitary, could barely contain its contempt for the "tawdry" funeral and the "gaudy" floral arrangements. It also noted the "shining nickel-silver coffin" that had been paid for by Yale's "henchmen" with fifteen $1,000 bills extorted from local business owners and trade associations. That $15,000 would be the equivalent of more than $275,000 today.

The New York Times' disdain for the flashiness of the funeral notwithstanding, it was impossible to miss the fact that mobster Frankie Yale had been a resounding financial success. His death didn't mean that others couldn't reap the fruits of his success either. Adonis took over his operations.

Lansky undoubtedly knew Yale since they both ran booze shipments and knew the same guys, but it's doubtful he attended his funeral. Although he was a Jew, he had already formed deep friendships with Italians like Luciano, who wanted to expand the Mafia's ranks to use smart Jews like Lansky.

As Lansky entered his twenties, he had a pretty good idea of what worked for him and what didn't. Making a show of his criminal connections was not a good idea. He knew that the brazen killing of Yale had sparked a shake-up in the New York Police Department. It was too public a murder, something that never should have happened on their watch. Worse, Yale's lavish funeral was literally a celebration of his criminal life. Lansky was not a man to back down ever, but he was shrewd enough to understand that it was unwise to show up and, in effect, thumb your nose at angry and humiliated cops.

Besides, he had his own business to attend to. Rum-running was exceptionally lucrative, but also incredibly dangerous. He didn't have to worry too much about the Prohibition agents. They were largely outmanned and outgunned and often very open to payoffs. It was the other bootleggers who were the problem. They were criminals, after all, and they used whatever means necessary to steal their rivals' shipments. The men who had money on the line turned to Lansky and Siegel. They had become known as musclemen who came in handy when a particularly important shipment of booze needed to be protected. They were tough, fearless, and armed.

Siegel didn't limit himself to merely protecting shipments. He craved action. One time, he heard about a shipment of top-shelf whiskey coming in on the South Jersey Shore. When he learned the shipment belonged to Joe Masseria, a bitter rival, he leapt into action. He bribed one of Masseria's men and got critical information about where the shipment was coming in. He came up with a plan to steal it. He recruited Lansky and a few others to assist him. They decided to set up an ambush.

They cut down a tree and dragged it across the road. The convoy of trucks carrying the booze appeared exactly at the time the informant said it would. Upon seeing the fallen tree, the driver of the first truck got out and signaled to some of his men to help him move it. Bad move. At that moment, Siegel's men let loose a fusillade of bullets. Masseria's men shot back, but several of them succumbed to gunshots. It was over within minutes. Siegel and Lansky succeeded in hijacking a very valuable shipment.

That caper was just one of the many violent episodes common during Prohibition. Most of them didn't make the news. In 1929, the brutality of rum-running exploded into public view with the shocking Saint Valentine's Day Massacre in Chicago. Four men, including two wearing police uniforms and flashing badges, burst into a garage in Lincoln Park on the city's north side at 10:30 in the morning. They lined up seven members of the Bugs Moran gang against a brick wall. Then they opened fire with machine guns and summarily executed them.

The brazenness of the assault sparked headlines in newspapers across the country. The public outcry in Chicago was thunderous. People demanded answers as to who the culprits were. Capone seemed to be the likely instigator, given that the victims had been known to hijack his whiskey shipments, and he had eliminated the previous bosses of the North Side Gang, including Dean O'Banion in his flower shop headquarters in 1924 and his successor Hymie Weiss in 1926 outside the same location. Within days, Capone was summoned to a grand jury, but he demurred, saying he was too ill to attend. Police investigated the heinous murders, but they were never able to connect Capone conclusively to the case. He was never charged.

While the killing might have accomplished a strategic end, the resulting publicity was bad for business. Lansky took a cue from his mentor Rothstein and laid down strict rules for the guys working under him: He banned flashy clothes and loud talk. He told his men to be low-key, quiet. He wanted them to do nothing to attract attention. As strict as he was, he related to the guys working for him. He never held himself aloof from them. If they followed his rules, he gave them bonuses and paid them exceedingly well. It was a business model he would follow throughout his life.

In that sense, he was different from other gangsters who liked to keep the men under them on the edge financially because they knew that would keep them dependent. Lansky knew that real loyalty was more important. With that assured, he focused on strategic planning. He and Siegel ran a car and truck rental business on Cannon Street on the Lower East Side. It was the perfect cover for what they were really doing. An added bonus was that it was profitable in its own right. Lansky, drawing on his experience as a mechanic, built secret compartments in cars to smuggle the booze. They also did a steady business in stolen cars. Yet on paper, it looked legitimate.

Demand for the illegal booze grew. "I think the majority of the people never wanted it [Prohibition]," Lansky said years later. "It was a minority with political influence that kept it from being voted out. The power of influential women with the church brought it about."

To meet the demand, Lansky tapped his underworld connections—Moe Dalitz and Sam Tucker in Cleveland, Joe Adonis in New Jersey, and Al Capone in Chicago. They recognized that they could ship booze from Canada into New York. American consumers wanted whiskey and beer, and the good stuff came from Canada. With its unprotected border, it made perfect sense to smuggle in booze from there. The profits were eye-popping. They could make $100,000 to $250,000 on a single shipment. Everybody wanted in. Even small-time smugglers realized they could make a tenfold profit on the booze they smuggled. Ultimately, Dutch Schultz, a particularly vicious New York mobster, forced the small-timers out of business.

Rum, also in high demand, came from the Bahamas. They could smuggle it into the New York waterfront, where Italians ran the show, or via the 1,180 miles of Long Island coastline, with its countless inlets, beaches, and bays that were out of the way and difficult to police. There was a three-mile US territorial limit off Long Island, just outside the reach of the US Coast Guard. That was a perfect place, of course, to place vessels poised to sneak the booze ashore. The flotilla of vessels lining up there were dubbed "Rum Row." The sheer size of the smuggling operations was astonishing. Lansky later bragged that he and his friends were running the most efficient international shipping operation in the world.

"We coined the word 'underworld' during Prohibition," Lansky later told his family. "We should have said 'overworld.'"

That sentiment reflected his firm belief—one that he held throughout his life—that the real criminals were the hypocrites who imposed laws like Prohibition on the public.

The money flowed in. So did the deals. Before long, Lansky's younger brother, Jack, joined him. He had started out as a furrier, but when he saw the kind of money his brother was making, he wanted in. Like his brother, he had a head for numbers, but he was more amiable and approachable. Most of all, he was loyal. Lansky knew he would never let him down.

In a world of ruthless lawbreakers whose every inclination was to cheat and steal, Lansky gained a reputation for playing it straight. You could do business with him and not worry about getting burned. Word got around. He held court at Ratner's, a kosher delicatessen. He was picky about what he ate, demanding that his meals be prepared just so. Ratner's was more than happy to accommodate him because, unlike some gangsters, he always paid. And the deals kept coming.

He and Siegel were making money—lots of it. And they were enjoying their wealth. They dressed well, enjoyed daily manicures and shaves at the barbershop, and always kept a thick roll of money in their pockets. As much as they enjoyed the action and their nights on the town, however, they were both traditional Jewish boys at heart. They started to think about settling down. As with their business, they would do that together.

They had been double-dating two Jewish girls: Anna Citron and Esther Krakower. Though the girls were still teenagers, they were stylish and elegant. Anna, in particular, carried herself with a certain sophistication. Her father was a wealthy businessman, and she enjoyed a higher social status than Lansky. The foursome had a great time together, and the girls were drawn to the evident success Lansky and Siegel enjoyed. Lansky and Siegel had already earned a fairly notorious reputation among people in the know. The girls had no illusions about how their beaus made their money, but they didn't mind. These young men were on their way up.

Siegel—always one to act immediately on his impulses—got married first on January 27, 1929, at a brownstone in Crown Heights, Brooklyn. Lansky was his best man. Siegel was twenty-two, Esther, seventeen. Because she was so young, her father had to sign a consent certificate.

THE CITY OF NEW YORK.
DEPARTMENT OF HEALTH.

25-2050-27-B, 10 H

STATE OF NEW YORK.

No. of Certificate 10593

CERTIFICATE AND RECORD OF MARRIAGE

OF

NO MUTILATED CERTIFICATE WILL BE RECEIVED

(Groom) Meyer Lansky and (Bride) Anna Citron

Groom's Residence	6 Columbia st N.Y.	Bride's Residence	156 So. 9 st Brooklyn N.Y.
Age	26	Age	19
Color	White	Color	White
Single, ~~Widowed or Divorced~~		Single, ~~Widowed or Divorced~~	
Occupation	Auto Rental	~~Maiden Name, if a Widow~~	
Birthplace	Brooklyn N.Y.	Birthplace	New york city
Father's Name	Max	Father's Name	Moses
Mother's Maiden Name	Yetta Grotch	Mother's Maiden Name	Selma Landes
Number of Groom's Marriage	First	Number of Bride's Marriage	First

I hereby certify that the above-named groom and bride were joined in Marriage by me, in accordance with the Laws of the State of New York, at 437 Grand st New-york city (Street), *in the Borough of* Manhattan, *City of New York, this* 9 *of* May 1929

Signature of person performing the Ceremony: Rabbi Isaac, Leib Epstein

Witnesses to the Marriage: William Wiseman, Ben. Siegel.

Official Station

Residence 437 Grand st N.Y. city

WE hereby certify that we are the Groom and Bride named in this Certificate, and that the information given therein is correct, to the best of our knowledge and belief.

Meyer Lansky Groom

Anna Citron Bride

Signed in the presence of William Wiseman

and Ben. Siegel.

It shall be the duty of the clergymen, magistrates and other persons who perform the marriage ceremony to keep a registry of the marriages celebrated by them. * Every person authorized by law to perform the marriage ceremony shall register his or her name and address in the office of the Bureau of Records (Sec. **35**, Sanitary Code).

It shall be the duty of every person required to make or keep any such registry, of * * * * * * * marriage * * * * * * to present to the Bureau of Records a copy of such registry signed by such person * * * * * * * * * * * within ten days after the * * * * * marriage * * * * which shall thereupon be placed on file in the said Bureau (Sec. **33**, Sanitary Code).

N. B.—Sec. 1239, Chap. 532, Laws of 1905, makes the failure to report within ten days a written copy of the registry of the marriages provided to be registered a misdemeanor, punishable by fine or imprisonment.

Meyer Lansky and Anna Citron's marriage certificate, May 9, 1929. Ben Siegel signed as witness and best man.

Less than four months later, on May 7, 1929, Anna and Lansky would elope. Siegel served as best man. As was the case in Siegel's wedding, a rabbi officiated. Throughout his life, Lansky considered himself a secular Jew. But when it came to important turning points in his life, he always turned to Judaism.

Lansky was twenty-six, Anna, eighteen. The marriage lists "auto rental" as his business, a rather ironic notation, given what his business really was—a cover for his criminal enterprises.

Unlike Esther, Anna was legally of age and didn't need her father's consent. That was just as well because her father, Moses Citron, most certainly did *not* consent. Born in Moldova, he had very traditional views. He declared that she had violated Jewish law by marrying before her older sister, Sadie. He refused to give the union his blessing.

Her father's disapproval devastated Anna. She had always been close to her family and couldn't bear the thought of any kind of estrangement. But she was also in love. She couldn't let a catch like Lansky slip away. He was kind and gentle and exceedingly generous, and she basked in his admiration for her sense of style and her social status. She prayed that her father would come around.

The couple honeymooned in, of all places, Atlantic City. As he so often did in his life, Lansky combined his business and personal lives. The particular business at hand was a massive conclave of gangsters and rival bootleggers from all over the country. Luciano wanted to organize a national syndicate. He knew that if they could eliminate the petty rivalries, they could make much more money by joining forces. Lansky agreed and helped work out the details with Johnny Torrio, a gangster who, like Lansky, was known for his brains.

The primary goal of the conference—considered by historians to be the earliest summit of organized crime—was to strike some sort of truce among rivals because their violent warring over bootleg routes and booze were cutting into profits. The law enforcement crackdowns resulting from the Saint Valentine's Day Massacre had been costly. And because Lansky was always thinking long-term, he wanted them to discuss how to expand their illegal operations to offset losses when Prohibition was repealed. He knew it was just a matter of time before that happened. He wanted to be ready. He wanted to set up a nationwide gambling syndicate—something of particular interest to Al Capone—and state-of-the-art casinos.

Luciano, Torrio, and Frank Costello were considered the hosts. As usual, Lansky tried to stay in the background, but everyone knew he was right next to the top three bigwigs. The guests were a veritable Who's Who of organized crime. New York sent the largest contingent, including Ben Siegel, Joe Adonis, Albert Anastasia, Vito Genovese, Vincent Mangano, Gaetano "Tommy" Lucchese, Dutch Schultz, Owney Madden, and Frank Erickson, among others. Coming from Chicago were Al Capone, Frank Nitti, Jake Guzik, and Frank Rio. Philadelphia sent Waxey Gordon, Nig Rosen, Max Hoff, and Irving Bitz. Cleveland sent Moe Dalitz and Lou Rothkopf. Other delegations came from Detroit, Boston, New Orleans, Kansas City, and Tampa. It was truly a national conference unlike any other. They all knew it. Gangsters and their lady friends showed up in their finest clothes and grinned at the news photographers snapping their photos.

South Jersey crime boss Enoch "Nucky" Johnson provided the hotel accommodations. Not surprisingly, given the guest list, there were a few hiccups. The exclusive Breakers Hotel on the Boardwalk was just that: exclusive. It only opened its doors to white Anglo-Saxon patrons. When a sudden influx of ruddy-faced Italians started registering under Anglo-Saxon names, some were refused rooms. Capone, used to far more deferential treatment in his home turf of Chicago, exploded in a rage. Johnson rushed over to try to defuse the situation. He hustled Capone out the door to the more receptive Ritz-Carlton.

Lansky and his new bride suffered no such indignation. As guests of honor, they were given the Presidential Suite at the Ritz. He was in his element. At all of twenty-six years old, he was wheeling and dealing with connected guys from all over the country. Many of them were seeking his counsel. There were meetings in the hotel rooms and on the beach. There was no mistaking who truly was in charge.

They held one large meeting in a hotel conference room. Torrio opened up by saying that all the internal fighting had to stop. Then he introduced Costello, who took over the meeting.

"The reason we got to organize is that we got to put ourselves on a business basis. That is what we are in, a business. We got to stop the kind of things that's going on in Chicago right now," he said. "You guys are shooting at each other in the street and innocent people are getting killed, and they're starting to squawk. If they squawk loud enough, the feds get off their tails and start cracking down. And you know what that means."

After Costello finished, Torrio got up and dropped the bombshell: He told Capone he had to go to jail.

"We think you need a vacation, Al," he said.

Capone thought it was a joke, but Costello assured him it was not. "This ain't a joke, Al. We got too much invested for you to ruin the gravy train. Make it easy on yourself. Think of a way. But you need to be off at 'college' until things cool down."

The gangsters clearly meant business. (Capone did, in fact, manage to get himself arrested when he returned to Chicago. Given the scope of his criminal activities, it wasn't particularly difficult.)

The constant business meetings hardly seemed like a romantic honeymoon, but Anna and Esther enjoyed themselves relaxing poolside. Plus, there was an added perk for every wife and girlfriend accompanying a delegate—a brand-new fur cape. It all felt very luxurious and important. And it was.

Beneath the gaiety and newfound bonhomie, however, there were still simmering tensions. Two men were missing from the conclave: New York Mob bosses Giuseppe "Joe the Boss" Masseria and Salvatore "Little Caesar" Maranzano. That was no oversight. Luciano considered them "Mustache Petes"—that is, old-fashioned gangsters committed to outdated ways of doing things, mostly from the old country. They had allowed stupid vendettas to spark open warfare on the streets, leading to murders like Yale's, in what eventually became known as the Castellammarese War.

(Maranzano and his faction, notably his second-in-command Joe Bonanno, hailed from Castellammare del Golfo, Sicily.)

The killings and shootings were attracting too much attention and were bad for business. Luciano wanted to create a new world order, while they were just trying to get a piece of his rackets with offers that seemed too good to be true.

Lansky agreed with Luciano. He was wary of Masseria and Maranzano. Not only that, he knew these Mustache Petes would never be open to working with men like him—Jews.

He warned Luciano, "Once you accept such an offer, you'll find yourself under their total control. Neither will hesitate to kill you . . . You're a pawn in their game. Only it isn't a game. Our lives are at stake."

The conference concluded without any bloodshed. That was fairly remarkable, given the personalities involved. Somehow, Lansky, Luciano, Torrio, and Costello had persuaded the attendees that they could make more money and expand by working together, not against one another. It was a resounding success and a precursor to the nationalization of organized crime two years later.

Meyer and Anna returned to New York and settled into married life. They moved into an apartment building in Brooklyn. A little more than eight months after their elopement, Anna gave birth to their first son, Bernard Irving Lansky. They called him Buddy.

He was a bright, happy, easy baby. To Anna, however, things didn't seem quite right. He didn't seem to be developing physically the way he should. At six months, he couldn't sit up. She took him to doctors. They told her to be patient. Still, she worried.

Lansky, meanwhile, was focusing on business. An important opportunity opened up. Luciano had made his move, exhibiting the treachery that is the hallmark of the Mafia. As much as he disdained the gluttonous Masseria, he served as his bodyguard. On the afternoon of April 15, 1931, Luciano accompanied Masseria to his favorite restaurant, Scarpato's Nuova Villa Tammaro on Coney Island. As Masseria ordered some bread and wine, Luciano excused himself to go to the bathroom. The restaurant's owner, Gerardo Scarpato, took a walk. As Masseria played pinochle, a card game, four gunmen entered the restaurant and shot him to death. He took four bullets in the back and one in the head.

The gunmen were reportedly Anastasia, Genovese, Adonis, and Siegel. The hit had been sanctioned by Maranzano, Masseria's archrival.

A boss might be killed, but his rackets always survive. Luciano, conveniently enough, took over Masseria's profitable Little Italy lotteries. Maranzano got his bootlegging business.

Dividing the spoils should have quelled tensions, but it didn't. Maranzano deemed himself the boss of all bosses, emulating Julius Caesar, his Roman obsession. He demanded complete obedience from his underlings. Even that wasn't enough, however. He installed himself in a lavish office suite above Grand Central Station in New York City. For the men who had to kick up a lot of money to him, Maranzano's grandiosity and high-handed treatment of them sparked deep bitterness. Then, Luciano started to hear talk that Maranzano was going to have *him* killed, a not-unreasonable fear in that business. Maranzano thought Luciano was too ambitious, and he saw how readily he betrayed Masseria. He decided he had to be eliminated.

Luciano, a wily denizen of the streets, knew he needed to strike first. An ally tipped him that the Internal Revenue Service was going to Maranzano's office to audit his books. The IRS agents came to his office for several appointments. Each time, Maranzano told his bodyguards to ditch their guns for the day. He had to do it to maintain his guise of respectability, but it created the perfect opening for Luciano. Less than four months after Masseria's murder, four gunmen disguised as IRS agents burst into Maranzano's lavish suite. Within seconds, they shot and stabbed him to death. His bodyguards were of no use: Two of them took off running.

The gunmen did not appear to be Sicilian or Italian. Some believed the shooters were Jewish gunmen dispatched by Lansky. To be sure, they were not typical Mob assassins. They were dressed in suits and hats, looking very much like taxmen. It is said that Lansky was very much involved in the planning. He stashed the men in a safe house, taught them how to walk and talk like federal agents, and showed them Maranzano's photo. Some recorded histories believe them to be Ben Siegel, Red Levine, and Bo Weinberg, but Luciano and Lansky would have sent four unrecognized faces.

The Mustache Petes were in the ground, and all the racial and cultural obstacles removed. It was truly a diverse meritocracy. Maranzano's death cleared the way for Luciano's ascension and the death of the old order. It also solidified Lansky's alliance with the Mafia. Few people were closer to him than Siegel and Luciano. To all three men, the consolidation of their power would pave the way to a new era of organized crime. Luciano eliminated the title "boss of all bosses" and created a commission to assign territories and adjudicate internal disputes. Although he was distributing power among the families, it was clear to everyone who was in charge, in reality if not nominally.

And Lansky was right by his side.

CHAPTER 3

At the Top at Thirty

THE PHOTO IS literally arresting.

Six men, dressed in overcoats and fedora hats, lined up in front of a dark curtain. All look as if they'd rather be anywhere but there. Paul "The Waiter" Ricca, Salvatore Agoglia, Luciano, Lansky, John Senna, and Harry Brown. They each strike their own pose, but Lansky's pose stands out. With his hands clasped in front, he glares at the camera, as if he's trying to stare it down.

The photo was, in effect, a group mug shot in Chicago in April 1932. Luciano and Lansky had taken a train to Chicago. They had tried to keep their visit low-key, but local police immediately spotted them. They followed them to a nightclub on the South Side and then to their hotel room. Two cops checked into the adjoining room, where they could hear Luciano's phone calls. He received more than thirty phone calls in two hours. The topics of discussion included Detroit shipments, airplanes, and steamships. And the name of Joe Fusco, Capone's right-hand man, came up.

As Luciano and Lansky were about to leave their hotel for a 9:00 P.M. train back to New York, the cops swooped in. They arrested them and the four other men at gunpoint. Then they lined them up for the photo. Police couldn't hold them because they couldn't find any crime they committed. Reluctantly, they released them. But knowing how averse most mobsters were to publicity, they immediately leaked everything they knew to the Chicago papers. It was dubbed the "mystery trip" in the press.

Even though the Chicago police didn't figure out exactly what drew Lansky and Luciano to meet with men from the Chicago Outfit, their instincts to follow them were correct. Ricca was effectively running the Outfit while Capone was away in prison on a tax evasion charge, with Frank Nitti serving as the acting boss until his eventual suicide. Ricca's stature was such that Capone had served as the best man at his wedding in 1927. The fact that Lansky and Luciano were meeting with him was a sign of their trust in him. And that fact that all three men were meeting was a clear signal that the meeting was important.

The cops didn't know it, but Luciano and Lansky were there to broker a peace agreement. Too many killings had broken out over turf. They attracted too much attention in the press and from law enforcement. Peace was better for business.

Lansky, almost thirty years old, was operating within the very top echelon of organized crime.

On a personal note, he deeply admired Ricca. Nitti's underboss dressed elegantly, had the manners of a refined gentleman, and was quiet and low-key. A few years earlier, Ricca had saved Capone's life. He spotted some rival gunmen approaching and shouted a warning to him. It was enough for Capone to duck out of the way, but Ricca took a bullet in his left shoulder. When the police interviewed him about the shooting later, he gave them a phony name. That was exactly the kind of comportment that earns respect on the street.

Lansky so admired him that when Anna gave birth to their second son on September 22, 1932, he insisted on naming him Paul, after Ricca. Paul, like his older brother Buddy, was a happy baby. He was strong, and before long, was crawling and developing normally. That was a delight for his parents, but it also made them ever more aware that there was something terribly wrong with Buddy. As Paul took his first steps, Buddy was still crawling. In fact, Buddy couldn't walk until he was three years old. Even then, he was jerky and uncertain.

They took him to see more doctors. Finally, they received the devastating diagnosis: Buddy had cerebral palsy.

The news was catastrophic for Anna. She became convinced that Buddy's disability was a bad omen from God because her father had opposed her marriage.

Lansky said nothing. He simply left the apartment and didn't come back for days. He took refuge at the apartment of his close friend, Vincent Alo, known on the street as Jimmy Blue Eyes, who consoled him through the crisis.

Anna collapsed, alternating between hysteria and almost catatonic depression. Though she was still close with her sisters, who rallied to her side, she felt as if she had been left to handle everything herself. When her husband finally returned home, he simply wouldn't talk about it. That was his way of handling deep emotions and was typical for men of his time. It was clear to Anna, though, that his son's disability embarrassed him. He had worked so hard to create the perfect life for himself and his family.

Despite the crushing disappointment, Lansky rallied. He spared no expense in treating his son. There was nothing wrong with Buddy's brain. It was just his body that was failing him.

The couple decided to get a fresh start by moving. They had spent a few years in smaller apartments. It was time to trade up. They chose the Beresford apartment building on Central Park West in New York. It was an elegant and dignified twenty-two-story building designed by Emery Roth, a prominent Hungarian architect. Roth designed many of New York City's hotels and apartment buildings in the 1920s and 1930s.

The Beresford, across the street from the Museum of Natural History, as well as Central Park, was one of his more beautiful buildings. Built in 1929, its lobbies were each bedecked in marble and brass and with coffered ceilings inlaid with cherubs and mythological figures. Marble pilasters and brass sconces flanked the doorways, and fresh bouquets of flowers were placed daily on the entryway tables. It reeked of exclusivity. It was perfect for the elite residents who prized their privacy. The Beresford's doormen understood that. They made sure that only residents and approved guests entered.

With the move to the Beresford, the Lanskys had arrived.

The move was the perfect antidote to Anna's pain over Buddy's diagnosis. One of the first things she did was to hire her own interior decorator. After all, she had fifteen spacious rooms to bring up to her own exacting standards. She made sure that her husband had his own oak-paneled library, complete with a full set of the *Encyclopædia Britannica*, which he prized. For bookends, he had busts of Abraham Lincoln, because he had always admired the sixteenth president. His admiration for Lincoln was not surprising. He had, after all, brought the nation together after a civil war. To Lansky's mind, that must have been similar to the summit in Atlantic City.

As he did in childhood, Lansky often escaped to the library for solitude. He was a voracious reader. He read Greek philosophers and often committed their writings to memory.

The front hallway to the apartment was grand, tiled in black and white. That led to a beautifully appointed living room, where there was a grand piano. There was a butler's pantry and a separate room for a pool table. A wraparound porch afforded spectacular views of Central Park. As the children got a little older, they loved playing on that porch.

Lansky expected his wife to maintain the household, and he didn't stint on giving her the money she needed to do it. Their kitchen had the most modern appliances, but Anna didn't cook. She had a chef, maid, and nanny. Even though she was barely in her twenties, she felt at ease managing a household staff.

Anna was petite, with dark eyes and creamy skin. She always made sure she dressed in the latest fashions, which suited her. She strove to complement her successful husband, and she did. He, too, was a meticulous dresser. He wore only custom silk shirts. His standard suit order was 40 Short, navy, single-breasted. He had suits tailored at Barney's. He had taken Rothstein's advice to heart: If you dress with class, you'll attract customers with class.

Their home and personal style were perfect for a man determined to show the world he had made it. (Apartments at the Beresford currently sell for around $20 million and have housed the likes of Jerry Seinfeld, Mike Nichols, and the president of Columbia University.)

Not far from the building, however, was one of many shantytowns, or "Hoovervilles," that popped up after the Great Wall Street Crash of 1929. Families who had lost everything resorted to building shacks out of cardboard and tin for a place to live. One such Hooverville appeared on a vast field called Forgotten Men's Gulch that later would become Central Park's Great Lawn. The shacks were flimsy, small, and primitive, in stark contrast to the decorous buildings like the nearby Beresford. Some residents of the beautiful apartment buildings on Central Park West made a determined effort to ignore the shantytowns. For Lansky, they were a grim reminder of the tenements he had been so desperate to escape.

He considered himself a good son, but he did everything he could to shed his parents' life, including their Judaism. His sons did not get any religious instruction. The family celebrated Christian holidays like Christmas and Easter. The children did visit their grandparents for Passover, but that was the only time they tasted kosher food. Lansky's father, Max, was horrified at what a Gentile his son had become and told him so. Lansky ignored his father's remonstrances.

Lansky was often away from home, working on his many business deals. As he had predicted a few years earlier, Congress repealed Prohibition in February 1933, when he was thirty years old. He knew what that meant. He understood politics, particularly when it came to business. He knew the important politicians well. After all, he, Luciano, and Costello had traveled with the Tammany Hall delegation—the New York City political machine famed for graft and patronage—to the Democratic National Convention the year before.

As prescient as he was about the end of Prohibition, Lansky wasn't fully prepared for the financial hit he took as it ended. He had never worried much about saving money. He was supremely confident he could always make more. But when the spigot of money from Prohibition was shut off, he felt the squeeze.

One day, when Anna's older brother, Julius "Julie" Citron, ran into Lansky on the street, he asked him how he was doing.

Lansky replied bitterly, "I'm not making any money."

He was, in fact, making enough money to support his family's lavish lifestyle, Buddy's medical treatments, and his own parents, but it wasn't enough. Keenly aware of his outsider status as a Jew, he knew he had to make enough money to keep his Mob buddies fat and happy. His life literally depended on it.

Anna's father, Moses Citron, came through for his daughter's husband. Although he had disapproved of her marriage, he wouldn't allow her family to flounder financially. He helped Lansky become a partner in the Molaska Corporation, a company that supplied dehydrated molasses to the liquor distilling industry. Citron was the company's assistant treasurer. Given Lansky's experience selling alcohol during Prohibition, it seemed like a good fit. The fact that Lansky's experience was entirely illegal didn't seem to matter.

Lansky noticed the success of Samuel Bronfman and Lewis Rosenstiel, who had made their fortunes during Prohibition, as they went legitimate and turned their liquor businesses into respectable companies. But going straight wasn't for him. He loved figuring out the angles too much. He loved figuring out ways to beat the system. Though he stayed away from gambling money because he saw firsthand what it did to people, he was a gambler at heart.

He also loved the easy camaraderie he had with his fellow street guys. He often brought them home to his Beresford apartment to play cards, smoke cigars, and joke around. Frank Costello had "the voice of a lion," Paul later remembered. Ben Siegel was just fun, always ready to roughhouse with the boys.

One night, Lansky called Anna to tell her that he wouldn't be home for dinner. She was used to this, and besides, she didn't cook anyway. Her mother, Sarah Citron, came over to keep her company. So it was a surprise when her husband came home with his brother, Jack, and another friend and expected dinner. All she had were a few lamb chops to offer. She pulled together a last-minute meal, but Lansky was embarrassed. They started quarreling. In his anger, he picked up a hot potato and threw it at her.

His stupid stunt shocked and infuriated Anna. Her husband had never been abusive before. One of the qualities that had made her fall for him was his gentleness. This was completely out of character. But the damage was done. Something in her died that night. She decided to soldier on and make the best of her situation. After all, she had two small boys, including one who was severely disabled, to care for. She might have been a spendthrift and even a bit of a snob, but she was a devoted mother. Her children came above all else. But she never forgot that night.

Lansky, for his part, was an emotionally remote husband and father. He felt far more at ease with his pals, Siegel, Luciano, and Costello. As was typical of his generation of men, he felt he was doing what he needed to be doing by providing financially for his family. He loved his children, but rarely expressed it. He hardly ever took Buddy anywhere. That fell to his brother-in-law, Julie. He was the one who took Buddy and his cousins to ball games, always gently carrying Buddy around.

Lansky felt much more comfortable making deals. He began to eye both Florida and Saratoga Springs, New York. They seemed like good places to set up "carpet joints." A carpet joint was essentially a roadhouse with gambling. It was a step up from a "sawdust joint," which was the same thing, but with sawdust floors. Carpet joints were a little fancier—they had carpeting, hence the name. He knew they were a great way to make money.

Saratoga Springs made sense because Rothstein had already made inroads there with his "lake houses," essentially casinos on Saratoga Lake. Saratoga Springs was a small, bucolic city outside of Albany, New York, roughly 190 miles from New York City. It would seem like too quiet a place for street toughs like Rothstein and Lansky, but for the one thing: horse racing.

In the early 19th century, wealthy businessmen hosted horse racing trials there. Soon, they needed farms to support the trials. Before long, horse breeders, drawn by the area's mineral springs, open land, and peace and quiet, established sprawling horse farms and stables. Horse breeding is an expensive proposition. A single racehorse can consume twenty pounds of food and thirteen gallons of water a day. Only the richest of the rich can afford to do it—like Cornelius Vanderbilt Whitney, Harry Guggenheim, and August Belmont Sr., who established homes in Saratoga Springs. By going there, Rothstein was following another one of his rules: Go where the money is.

Rothstein knew, as did Lansky, that gamblers want nothing more than to keep gambling. The lake houses filled that need. After the gamblers finished their day at the track, they could come over to the lake house casinos to keep going. Lansky, by now very familiar with the accoutrements of wealth, made sure his first club there, the Piping Rock, had all the finest amenities. There was a casino and a cabaret, and guests were expected to don formal wear. The club served French champagnes, imported wines, and Scotch whiskies. The menu, designed by famed New York City chef Al Delmonico, was expansive. It led off with appetizers like lobster cocktail, entrees ranging from Frog Legs Provencale to Chateau Briand, and desserts like Baked Alaska and French pastries.

The entertainment was just as impressive. Two twenty-piece orchestras regularly performed there, as did stars like Joe E. Lewis, a famed American comedian friendly with Capone, and Sophie Tucker, an enormously popular singer and comedienne known as "The Last of the Red-Hot Mamas."

The Piping Rock, like other lake houses, operated in the summer and primarily in August, during horse racing season. The month of August was unspeakably hot and humid in New York City. Many residents with the means looked to get away then. Costello was Lansky's partner in the club, along with Adonis. Costello was also a silent partner in the Copacabana, so he made sure its staff worked at the Piping Rock in August. That ensured that the service, along with the food, was top-notch.

Security guards posted at the door ensured that only the right people got in. In other words, they kept the locals out. Lansky later told his family that he did that because he didn't want people who couldn't afford it to lose their money gambling. That may be true, but it also gave the club an irresistible air of a private club.

That wasn't the only place he employed security. When couriers tried to deposit cash at the bank, enterprising toughs frequently robbed and shot at them. The wild days of bootleggers, who smuggled their booze through Saratoga Springs to New York City, hadn't really faded, and that was bad for business. Lansky had to put a stop to it. He and his partners hired sheriff's deputies to ferry the cash to the bank at specific times. By setting up that agreement with the various lake houses, he was able to stop the robberies. The added benefit was that the sheriff's deputies, happy with their extra income, didn't bother to look too carefully at the illegal gambling going on. It was a pretty comfortable arrangement for all involved.

By 1935, the Piping Rock was the top club in Saratoga.

Meanwhile, Florida was experiencing a real estate boom. At the same time, the political powers were moving toward legalizing slot machines. Lansky knew a good business opportunity when he saw one. In January 1935, he and his friend, Vincent "Jimmy Blue Eyes" Alo opened up a carpet joint in Hallandale, Florida. It was a rural part of Florida then known as Hollywood-By-the-Sea. Lansky didn't know it then, but Hallandale would become an important place in his life.

Alo—a member of the Luciano family—and Lansky had met six years earlier after an unfortunate event. Alo had learned about a plot to kill a friend of his and take over his beer business. He warned his friend. The man, greatly relieved to have the information, asked Alo to tell his business partner. That partner happened to be Luciano. The Mob boss, ever wary, agreed to meet Alo. But he wouldn't meet him alone.

"When we met, he had this little guy with him. That was Meyer Lansky. I had never heard of him. But we were immediately attracted to one another. He was a man of principle. We could talk about a lot of things. I can't think of anyone that I admire more than Meyer. He really educated me," Alo recalled later.

Alo and Lansky became lifelong friends and business partners. They took over the Hollywood Country Club. Built in the style of Moorish architecture, it had a rooftop that slid back to reveal the open sky above the stage. They set about renovating it. To avoid annoying legal problems, they paid off local officials. They also made generous contributions to the Elks, Shriners, and area hospitals. That became a business practice Lansky employed throughout his career: Bribe the politicians and give to local charities. Whether he became a philanthropist to expiate some unspoken guilt or simply because he never forgot what it was like to be poor, he always gave.

For their grand opening, they brought in Xavier Cugat and his orchestra. Cugat was a wildly popular Spanish bandleader who grew up in Cuba. Desi Arnaz was a member of his group. Lansky brought his wife and family to Florida for the opening. Anna loved it. Even better, she hit it off with Alo's wife, Flo, just as Paul Lansky's wife, Edna, did years later.

Lansky was doing what he loved—making deals, building businesses, and raking in money, lots of it. His marriage seemed to have stabilized. Anna loved the getaways to Saratoga Springs and Florida.

But all the dealmaking wasn't enough to tamp down the underworld violence that was so disruptive to business. Despite his and Luciano's efforts to keep the peace, the National Crime Syndicate shootings and killings didn't stop. At the same time, the Great Depression had laid bare the huge divide between the rich and poor. A reformist zeal took root.

In July 1935, New York Governor Herbert Lehman was feeling the pressure. There was a loud public outcry over the shootings. Worse, people believed that the New York District Attorney,

William Dodge, was doing nothing to pursue Mafia corruption because he was corrupt himself. Lehman had no choice but to take action. He appointed a special prosecutor for the County of New York.

The man he selected was none other than the young, brash, and thoroughly incorruptible Thomas E. Dewey. A career prosecutor and staunch Republican with political aspirations for higher office, he was not one to shy away from the spotlight. He was also savvy enough to understand the power of radio. He appeared on a radio series called *Gang Busters*, which dramatized real crimes from NYPD police files. The public ate it up. Dewey declared that the operations of organized crime were effectively "a huge, unofficial sales tax" on the honest people of New York. He made a passionate appeal, urging citizens to come forward to help in the fight.

The public response was overwhelming.

It was a harbinger of things to come. Good for Dewey. Bad for Lansky and his friends.

CHAPTER 4
Luciano's Downfall

DEWEY WASTED NO time in setting his sights on a notorious New York racketeer and killer: Dutch Schultz.

Schultz, born Arthur Simon Flegenheimer, got his start in the business of crime—like many gangsters—as a bootlegger during Prohibition. On the street, he was known, feared, and admired as a bloodthirsty maniac. He had no compunction about murder, kidnapping, or torture to expand his illegal operations. His own lawyer once said of him that he killed friends and enemies "just as casually as if he were picking his teeth." As savage as he was on the street, he was savvy about the workings of Tammany Hall in New York. He took out some insurance—in the form of bribes to well-placed politicians. For years, it paid off, and he evaded prosecution.

Dewey, however, was picked for the job precisely because he wouldn't take a bribe. He actually took a substantial pay cut in taking the job because he thought it would advance his career. (He already had his eye on a Senate seat and even the US presidency.) Dewey empaneled a special grand jury to go after Schultz. Unlike other prosecutors who went about their business quietly, Dewey made a show of it.

Schultz was enraged. True to his reputation, he devised a plot to kill Dewey. He approached Albert Anastasia, a killer known for his own bloodlust—as attested by his monikers "Lord High

Executioner" and "Mad Hatter"—about his plan. Anastasia was highly attuned to the internal politics of the Syndicate and would never do anything to jeopardize his own career rise. He immediately ratted out Schultz to Luciano, who hastily called a Commission meeting and put the issue before its delegates, including Lansky.

Schultz made the case that Dewey was a threat to all of them. Luciano entertained the notion enough to task Anastasia to do some reconnaissance. Anastasia surveilled Dewey, as he emerged from his Fifth Avenue apartment for his daily routine, which was exactly that—a routine. Dewey, for all his caution with informants and witnesses, didn't vary his own routine. He'd leave his home every day at 8:00 A.M. and have coffee at a nearby lunch counter. Even though he had bodyguards, Anastasia felt it would be fairly easy to pick him off.

After receiving Anastasia's report, the Commission delegates deliberated. They responded with a resounding no. The last thing they needed was a war with a prosecutor who could rally an army of angry supporters to his side. It would be just too much heat. Schultz erupted in anger and berated Luciano and the others. Most were offended by his outburst. Lansky felt some sympathy for Schultz, but he was pragmatic. A gangland war with Dewey would destroy everything he and Luciano had tried to build.

The Syndicate bosses knew Schultz. He wasn't the kind of guy to go away quietly. He was a problem. Instead of authorizing a hit on Dewey, Luciano and the Commission authorized a hit on Schultz. That would make the problem go away. And with the cool, calculating efficiency the Mafia could employ in the 1930s, they did just that.

On October 23, 1935, three armed men burst into the Palace Chop House and Tavern in downtown Newark, where Schultz was eating dinner. He had gotten up to go to the men's room (an unusually popular location for such shootings), and a gunman mortally wounded him while the others finished off his bodyguards, though he would linger in delirium, babbling nonsensically before he finally died in the hospital.

His death solved a problem and provided an opportunity: Following a time-honored tradition among mobsters, Luciano took over Schultz's rackets. That dramatically expanded his own empire and, at the same time, his criminal profile.

Luciano focused on expanding his rackets even further. He loved power and money, and he loved living well. He had always patronized prostitutes, sometimes two at a time. He realized there was a great business opportunity there. He started charging them for protection. The scheme, as outlined in court papers, went like this: The women were charged $10 a week, essentially as insurance in case they got arrested. They were to pay the money to their bookers, who, in turn, were expected to kick up money to Luciano. If the women got arrested, they would pay half their bond, and their bookers would pay the other half out of the money they had already collected.

The money was not insignificant. A payment of $10 would the equivalent of $230 today. The women, understandably, didn't warm to the idea. They were already expected to pay their pimps a large portion of their earnings anyway. Most were too terrified to refuse. They knew all too well the violence that would be inflicted on them if they did.

But one woman, Joan Martin, did object. She loudly declared that she'd pay her own bond if she got arrested. Her defiance proved to be foolhardy. Chivalry wasn't Luciano's strong suit. He felt no compunction about hurting a woman if she defied him. He decided Martin needed to be taught a lesson. He directed one man to "pipe" her, or beat her with a pipe for refusing to pay up. He told another man to wreck her place. And they did.

Lansky watched his friend's business activities warily. He wanted nothing to do with a dirty racket like shaking down prostitutes. Luciano, firm in his belief that his leadership was solid, didn't worry. He held court at the Waldorf Astoria, often summoning his underlings to his suites there. And as always, he continued to enjoy the benefits of his position, particularly women. Everybody knew about his appetites.

That gave Dewey an opening. He launched a secret plan.

Dewey used an undercover detective to insinuate himself with Luciano's friends. The undercover told them that he operated a bordello in Boston. To establish his bona fides, he showed up one night with five prostitutes in tow (which duly shocked the prim Dewey). Luciano's buddies felt comfortable enough with him to share stories of their activities with the boss.

The undercover detective tapped a rich vein of information that amazed the veteran prosecutors. Other detectives actively interviewed witnesses and listened to wiretaps. Before too long, Dewey was ready to strike.

On February 1, 1936, he assembled teams of 150 detectives and patrolmen at precincts throughout New York City. Secrecy and precision were of the utmost importance. Each team got sealed envelopes that they were told not to open until 8:55 P.M. At 9:00 P.M., they swung into action. They raided forty houses of prostitution simultaneously. In all, there were sixty-eight madams, pimps, prostitutes, and bookies.

Normally, an operation that massive would attract news reporters and nosy spectators. Dewey couldn't risk that. Transporting them in paddy wagons to his headquarters in the Woolworth Building would guarantee that they would attract attention. Instead, he reserved a fleet of taxicabs to ferry the prisoners to an undisclosed location, where they would be held and questioned. Prosecutors told them they had a choice: cooperate or go to prison.

That night, Dewey's assistant, Murray Gurfein, went to a dinner party at the Fifth Avenue Hotel apartment of his former boss, Judge Julian Mack, and his good friend, Felix Frankfurter. Gurfein got a call and was told that the prisoners were ready to be questioned. He slipped out without saying a word. Frankfurter noticed. He turned to Gurfein's wife and said, "It was just for a bunch of whores he left us."

Eva asked what he meant. Frankfurter opined that the only reason her husband would have left the party was for something very, very important. "It had to be whores," he said.

Frankfurter was right. Although his comment was flippant and meant to be funny, he was right to infer that the case was significant. The Luciano case would result in completely upending the way the Syndicate did business and, at the same time, would make the ambitious Dewey a household name.

Dewey was notorious among his underlings as a cold and rigid man, but he took care to be kind to the women he planned to use as witnesses. He knew they were terrified of testifying because they knew the consequences, but he also knew that most of them had been starved of any basic human kindness for years. He fed them sandwiches and coffee during interrogations. He also had them treated for venereal diseases, and he helped them wean off their drug addiction. At the time, heroin was the main drug of addicts, and the withdrawal led to gut-wrenching sickness. Those who did agree to testify got to stay in comfortable hotels under guard.

Upon hearing of Dewey's crackdown on the Mafia, Luciano decided to leave town. He hid out at the Arlington Hotel in Hot Springs, Arkansas. Hiding out, however, was a relative term for Luciano. He was not one to deny himself creature comforts. He enjoyed the nightlife there—and women. Lucky's luck ran out when a New York detective spotted him near the Hot Springs bathhouses. On April 4, slightly more than two months after the raid, police arrested Luciano. They brought him back to New York City. His trial began May 11.

A top Syndicate boss, prostitutes, pimps—it was titillating fodder for the newspapers, and the public couldn't get enough of it. Letters poured in to Dewey. Most lauded him for taking on the vice racket and upholding the morals of a good and just society. Not all the letter writers were so concerned about society's morals, however. One writer, who signed his missive with "A. Sucker," complained that he got cheated by a $3 whore. "They hang out on south

COPY

New York City
September 28, 1935.

It is high time I got Jip. Properly. $3 whore 2 blondes. 142 West 46th Street, Apt. 22, third floor rear. One stout. One small, light, Helen.

They hang out on south side of 46th, near Broadway.

I sure was a sucker, now will squeal.

Do your work, get them.

A. Sucker

10/2/35

Jip me for $3, and how.

5 Ref. to Insp. Lyons

Letter by "A. Sucker" to Special Prosecutor Thomas E. Dewey during Lucky Luciano's 1935 trial.

side of 46th, near Broadway. I sure was a sucker, now will squeal. Do your work, get them."

Dewey had established himself as a crime fighter, the perfect profile for an ambitious politician. He understood the significance of the case, and he made sure the jurors understood it as well. He opened up the proceedings by appealing to their sense of duty: "You are not to convict—you are not here to convict. You are here to mete out justice."

And he let them know that they were participating in something very special: "Everything about the case is extraordinary."

He was right about that. There were nearly 100 witnesses listed in the court file. Each one had a colorful street moniker, like Cokey Flo Brown and Charlie Spinach. In addition to the madams, pimps, prostitutes, and bookies rounded up earlier, horse trainers, bartenders, waiters, and Waldorf Astoria employees were called to the stand. The latter were important because their testimony could tie Luciano directly to the crimes. Their testimony also offered a fascinating peek at Luciano's ostentatious lifestyle behind the scenes at the Waldorf Astoria.

Cokey Flo was one of the more damaging witnesses. She was a heroin addict who had gone through the horrors of drug withdrawal while in jail, but she managed to hold her own on the stand. She testified that she and her pimp met with Luciano when business matters were discussed. Another prostitute said she had sex with Luciano several times at his Waldorf Astoria apartment and said she heard him tell an underling to wreck Martin's apartment. The Waldorf Astoria employees testified that they had seen some of Luciano's codefendants visit him there.

They might have been a parade of mostly unsavory characters, but their testimony was compelling. Dewey didn't like the tawdriness of his witnesses, but he used it against the defendants in his summation: "What decent occupation do any of these defendants have?"

Luciano's defense attorney fought back. He said Cokey Flo "purred like a little kitten" and compared another witness to famous actress Sarah Bernhardt. And he took pains to ask how one woman, "an intimate of gangsters for years," got her "twenty-six dresses, dozen hats, innumerable sets of underwear."

But the defense couldn't refute the phone records and wiretaps Dewey produced as evidence. Defense attorneys almost always advise defendants not to take the stand because the risks of cross-examination are too great. Luciano felt he had no choice but to take the stand. Besides, he was convinced he could charm the courtroom. After all, he had wrangled a bunch of warring gangsters into a solid crime organization. He was sure that it wouldn't be that hard to persuade a courtroom of respectable citizens that he had done nothing illegal.

It was a rare miscalculation. Luciano floundered under Dewey's withering cross-examination. Dewey grilled him about everything from whether he paid his taxes to the dope deals he arranged. After he was done, any close observer would have concluded the Luciano was involved in an array of criminal activities.

After thirteen hours of closing arguments from the defense and seven hours of closing arguments from Dewey, the jury retired at 10:53 P.M. After five and a half hours of deliberations the next day, the jury announced its verdict: Luciano and his nine codefendants were guilty of sixty-two counts of compulsory prostitution.

On June 18, 1936, the judge sentenced Luciano to thirty to fifty years in Dannemora, the toughest prison in the New York State prison system. It was not only tough, it was located in the northeastern corner of the state, close to the Canadian border. Winters were cold, and the prison was difficult for friends from New York City to visit. It was a grim place.

As close as Lansky was to Luciano, his name never came up at trial or surfaced in any of the copious records or wiretaps. His caution about getting involved in such dirty rackets had been wise.

Luciano's conviction was a blow to Lansky. He was, after all, one of his closest allies. But there was more to his anger over the trial than the loss of a close partner. He complained to friends that the trial was "a fix." He knew all too well the "respectable" men who patronized prostitutes and gambling dens. The hypocrisy of it all gnawed at him. He decided he had to do something to help his friend. He introduced Luciano to another old friend of his, Moses Polakoff.

Polakoff and Lansky had both grown up on the Lower East Side of New York. Both were the sons of Russian Jewish immigrants, and both were bright young men with big ambitions. While Lansky made his life on the streets in organized crime, Polakoff kept on the straight and narrow. Polakoff attended a selective high school in the city, Townsend Harris. After graduating, he wanted to attend law school but couldn't afford it. He took a job wrapping fish for $1 a day, then became a trolley conductor and later a bank teller. With his day jobs, he earned enough to go to New York Law School at night. After graduating in 1918, he served in the Navy. He went on to work several years as an assistant US attorney before starting his own private practice.

Polakoff and Lansky remained close friends into adulthood, often discussing American history in Lansky's study in the evenings. In public, however, they behaved very differently. Lansky knew that his friend harbored dreams of becoming a judge one day, and he didn't want their friendship to jeopardize that. If they saw each other on the street, Lansky would avoid greeting him by walking on the other side of the street.

But Lansky knew his old friend was a good lawyer, and he felt that Luciano deserved the very best. Polakoff, for his part, fervently believed that everyone deserved a strong legal defense. He knew that taking on Luciano's case would not earn him friends in New York politics, but he was fiercely loyal to old friends like Lansky and even more so to the law. After reviewing the case, he became convinced that there was a basis for appeal. As he told his family years later, "Luciano did a lot of bad things, but not that," he said, referring to the allegation that he was a pimp.

As the appeal worked its way through the court system, big changes were in the offing for the Syndicate. Costello wasted no time in taking over as head of Luciano's New York crime family, the premier organized crime network in the nation. Though Lansky and Costello were business partners and even friends, there wasn't the same closeness that he had with Luciano. He was wary of Costello's interest in politics. Costello was a smart and adept leader, but he yearned for legitimacy and public acceptance.

"Frank Costello was drawn into politics by influential Italians," Lansky said years later. "Why they needed him, I don't know. Frank had no personal gain. He was a vain man and thought his only interest was to help Italians get their share of representation. He grew to like acting the part of a leader. I warned him sooner or later he will not be able to fulfill all the demands made on him, and he will become a bastard to them. That is just what happened."

Before Luciano went away to prison, Lansky approached him about investing in Cuba. Lucky liked it. He convened a meeting of the bosses at the Waldorf Astoria in New York to tell them all to kick in money.

"It was like dropping a bomb," Luciano later recalled.

Lansky then took over. He carefully explained the money that could be made in Cuba, far away from the prying eyes of the US government and Internal Revenue Service. Even better, Cuba was an exotic island where every kind of vice could be bought. Within a few weeks, he had collected $500,000 (about $12 million today).

He and his old friend, Doc Stacher, flew to Havana with the money in suitcases. They met with the Cuban military strongman, Fulgencio Batista, a wily politician who had risen up to the peak of power from the depths of poverty. Batista certainly wasn't averse to bribes, but he couldn't hide his disbelief at the amount of money they were bringing him. Lansky couldn't speak a word of Spanish, but before long, it became clear to Stacher that "Meyer and Batista understood each other very well."

By January 1937, the Cuban cabinet approved plans to place certain gambling operations under Batista's control. That was all Lansky needed. The floodgates opened for the Mob.

He loved Cuba. He loved its warmth, exoticism, and money-making potential. Rich American families owned vacation homes on the Cuban beach and started vacationing there in the early 1930s because liquor was cheap and plentiful. Those very same families could be enticed to play at high-end casinos.

He had hoped Luciano could join him there, but his hopes were dashed when the appeals court denied Luciano's bid for a new trial in May 1937. Polakoff had fought hard, even finding that three witnesses recanted their testimony, but it wasn't enough. Luciano would remain in prison.

Batista had worked as a laborer in a series of jobs before rising in the military. He craved power and money. He knew gambling was his ticket to riches. But in Cuba, virtually all games of chance were rigged. To attract wealthy Cubans and American tourists, he needed an operation that was professionally run.

Enter Lansky. His first foray into Cuban gambling was the Oriental Park Racetrack, a thoroughbred horse racing track and casino in Havana. Although it was located in a lush and beautiful tropical setting, the track had a bad reputation. Everyone knew the races there were fixed, so they simply didn't come. Lansky's friend, Lou Smith, whom he had met in his bootlegging days, came down to Cuba to clean it up. Among other things, he installed a photo-finish machine and even tested the horses for drugs.

Lansky ran the casino. Although he always hired locals at his businesses to engender community support, he knew he couldn't use the Cuban pit crews in the casino. They were known for cheating. He brought in his own. A typical casino had a "pit," or area where there were separate tables for blackjack, roulette, and craps games. Each pit crew consisted of dealers and a manager, who kept an eye on the floor to ensure everything went smoothly. On Lansky's orders, they also watched for something else—cheating. Even specially trained employees could succumb to the temptation of cheating. Lansky knew that nothing could drive customers away faster than a suspicion that a game was rigged.

Craps, the game Lansky learned as a kid on the streets of New York, was particularly popular among Cuban gamers. It's simple to play it—it involves rolling a pair of dice on a felt-covered table—but the number combinations for the odds that determine a win or a loss are complex. To run the craps tables, he decided he needed someone trusted among knowledgeable gamblers.

He brought in Al Levy. It was a smart move. In addition to being known by the high rollers they wanted to attract, Levy had his own ideas about bringing in gamblers. Lansky, ever the businessman, listened. The result was a special opening ceremony for the new casino. They invited Batista and presented him with his complimentary key to the place. Batista loved it.

Horse racing and casino gambling were a winter activity in Cuba. It was simply too hot and humid to race horses in the tropical summers. Lansky loved it when everything slowed down in the Cuban summers. It was the perfect antidote to his frenetic life. He loved the Cuban summers so much that he brought Anna and the boys down to the island for a month to spend time there.

The best part, to Lansky's mind, was the absence of a meddling US government. With Batista on board, he could operate unfettered and run his business the way he wanted to run it. The money poured in. There was enough to keep everyone, even the extraordinarily greedy Batista, happy.

CHAPTER 5
Fighting the Nazis

THE CUBAN IDYLL was good for the Lansky family. Back home in New York, they welcomed their third child, Sandra, in December 1937. Lansky loved his sons but was absolutely thrilled to have a daughter.

Lansky got a kick out of his sons, especially when they broke the rules, but he delighted in Sandra. Like her mother, Sandra was a girly girl. She loved the frilly frocks her mother dressed her in. She very much expected to be treated like the family princess, and in her father's eyes, she was just that. She had the prettiest bedroom and all the dolls she ever wanted. When she was just six years old, her father bought her a horse that she rode in Central Park. Sandra was spoiled, and she reveled in it.

Lansky was enjoying his life as a family man. During the summers, he would rent a cottage for a few weeks at the Jersey Shore. The children loved it because the Siegel and Adonis families rented cottages nearby, and all the children played together. At night, the fathers would smoke cigars and play gin rummy for a penny a point. They would laugh and argue and insult each other—basically, they had a great time.

At other times, the family would vacation in Saratoga Springs. Anna loved the elegant club dining and made sure her boys wore smart-looking suits and ties so they could eat there as well. She dressed stylishly—and expensively, of course—in four strands of pearls and beaded dinner shawls. She fit in perfectly with the rich crowds.

Lansky, a rabid Yankees fan, always had seats right behind the dugout. One day, he took his boys to a game. He had to step away for a few minutes but seemed comfortable with it because he knew the man sitting in front of them. A few minutes later, the man turned around and said, "You boys want a hot dog?"

It was singer Al Jolson, one of the country's highest-paid entertainers in the 1920s and 1930s and also one of the few openly Jewish entertainers. Casual celebrity encounters like that one were common for the Lansky boys.

When they were back home in New York City, the Lansky children stayed in the tightest of circles. They played only with family and the children of the most trusted friends. They were never allowed to bring home friends from school. Anna wouldn't allow it. It was simply too dangerous. She was terrified of what might happen to them. Later in life, the children heard from family friends about the death threats against them because of their father. As children, they never knew because their parents never discussed the threats with them.

Anna was still best friends with Esther Siegel and often had her over. The Siegel girls were okay outside at the Jersey Shore, but terrible hellions at home. They could be whiny. They often fought and ran around the apartment. Anna's sister-in-law detested them, calling them the "wild animals." Still, they were always welcomed in the Lansky home, partly because so few other children were, and, of course, because they were Ben Siegel's children.

Paul was a natural leader. Often, he was the instigator, cooking up escapades with his older brother and cousins. Paul's stunts exasperated Anna, and she disciplined her son. Meyer, however, was amused. Anna thought, for example, that the family should have liver twice a week. The boys hated it and would sneak in to tell the family chef to change the menu. Meyer loved it.

But when it came to their cousins, Lansky could seem a bit forbidding. Whenever they came over to play, Anna would urge them to, "Go kiss Uncle Meyer hello." They always felt a bit awkward because he never seemed to warm to them.

More often than not, Meyer would slip into Paul's bedroom and close the door so he could talk business with Siegel and others. That was fine with the children. Sometimes, Costello would stop by. The children weren't sure who he was, but they knew there was something special about him. He had a voice like a lion, Paul thought.

Where Siegel was animated and flamboyant and Costello was commanding, Lansky was rigidly self-contained. He rarely raised his voice and said little. For years, he worked to get rid of any Yiddishisms from his accent (though they returned when he was older). It was a source of embarrassment to him that his parents spoke only Yiddish. He wanted his voice to sound neutral and cultured. He wanted to fit in as an American, a rich and successful American.

Lansky's stubborn rejection of his Jewishness was anathema to his elderly and deeply traditional parents, Yetta and Max. He supported them financially and felt obligated to visit them, but often the visits were strained. Max never approved of Meyer's career choice, or that he had brought his younger brother, Jack, into it. He particularly disapproved of the fact that Meyer never sent his sons to religious school. It was a complete abrogation of his Jewish heritage and traditions. He railed constantly about it but had no effect. Lansky was determined to shed the old traditions and anything else that he thought could hold him back in America.

Lansky never spoke about his business in front of his children, but as often happens in households, children pick up on the unspoken as much as what is said. Paul, who was more like his father than either of them realized, grew to resent the hypocrisy he saw around him. In that, he mirrored his father's feelings exactly.

As comfortable as the family was financially, Buddy's disability cast a pall over everything. Anna was determined to find a cure. She finally found a doctor who was an expert in cerebral palsy. He was based in Boston, so the family moved there. They still kept their New York City apartment so Lansky could easily go back for business meetings and visit his aging parents.

Anna ran the household in Boston and managed Buddy's treatments. He had to wear painful leg braces. She did everything she could to soothe his pain, often staying up through the night to massage his legs. With her husband's frequent absences and her family and close friends in New York, it was a lonely time for Anna. But she felt it was the only way to give her son a chance at a normal life.

Lansky never stinted on spending money on Buddy's medical treatments or on making his family comfortable. He desperately wanted a cure for Buddy, but he didn't feel the need to stay close to his temporary home in Boston. There was too much going on in his various businesses. And in the world.

The 1930s were a turbulent time, particularly in New York. As Adolf Hitler rose to power in Germany, Nazi sympathizers—known colloquially as Brown Shirts, the Silver Shirts, and Friends of the New Germany—proliferated. Nazi sympathizers espoused virulent anti-Semitism at well-attended rallies. High-profile and respected American leaders, like industrialist Henry Ford and aviator Charles Lindbergh, gave speeches that embraced racist ideologies and promoted isolationism. Their views were not limited to adults. German Bund youth indoctrination camps opened up on nearby Long Island.

American Jews viewed these developments with dread and alarm. Judge Nathan Perlman decided he needed to act. A former congressman, he had been appointed as a New York City magistrate by New York Mayor Fiorello La Guardia. The mayor had no tolerance for the Brown Shirts. When the city was getting ready for the New York World's Fair, La Guardia declared that it should include a "Chamber of Horrors" from the brown-shirted fanatic who was menacing the world—in other words, Hitler. Because he was such a prominent politician, his criticisms were widely reported and reached Europe. The German government protested, and Secretary of State Cordell Hull apologized. La Guardia, however, didn't change his position, and American Jews were grateful.

Perlman was not the type of man who was accustomed to dealing with mobsters. But he was pragmatic. He had seen and read enough about the Nazi rallies to know that he needed to reach out to someone tough enough to take on what he was proposing. He also knew that La Guardia felt so strongly about the threat of Hitler that he had some latitude in what he wanted to do. He called Lansky. They arranged a meeting.

"They march in the street, and they are anti-Semites, and they think we are soft, Meyer," Perlman said.

Lansky agreed.

"It's a movement. Powerful men are openly making anti-Semitic remarks. Some of the newspapers and magazines are backing them up. Nazism is flourishing in the United States," Perlman said.

Again, Lansky agreed.

Then Perlman broached the delicate reason for his reaching out to Lansky.

"We Jews now have to demonstrate a little more militancy," Perlman said. "You got some boys who might want to punch a Nazi?" he said.

Perlman's question delighted Lansky. He considered himself a true American patriot, and despite his disavowal of what he considered to be old-fashioned Jewish traditions, he was a proud Jew. And he was supremely proud of being tough. For all his efforts to build a stable family life, the pull of the street was never far away. And here, a respected member of the judiciary was reaching out to him to fight for a noble cause. He leapt at the opportunity.

Perlman made clear that he couldn't condone anyone getting killed. Fisticuffs, baseball bats, and pipes were okay, but no killings. The point was to show that American Jews weren't soft.

Then he offered to pay Lansky.

Lansky refused. "I need no pay, Judge," he told him. "I am a Jew, and I feel for the Jews in Europe who are suffering. They are my brothers."

With that, Lansky was expressing his deeply held belief and evoking memories of his early childhood in Grodno. For all his desire to be seen as an American, his Judaism defined him.

But Lansky, ever the dealmaker, did have one request for the judge. He asked him if he had any influence with the press, particularly the Jewish press. Perlman said he did, indeed, have some influence.

"If we get caught, please, no bad ink," Lansky said. "I don't want anything in the Jewish press that my wife shouldn't read."

Perlman agreed. They had a deal.

Not long afterward, Lansky got word of an upcoming rally in Yorkville, a neighborhood on the Upper East Side of Manhattan that was heavily populated by German Americans. He immediately rounded up fifteen guys—including, of course, Ben Siegel—and went there. Swastikas and photos of Hitler lined the stage. The restive spectators were awaiting a speech by Fritz Kuhn, considered the American Führer. When Lansky arrived with his gang, he lit firecrackers and threw them into the auditorium. As the Brown Shirts reacted in shock and confusion, his gang went in with clubs and bats. The resulting chaos was enough to stop the rally. Kuhn never got to the stage to give his speech.

A pretty good outing for his gang. There were other rallies and other skirmishes. Those were merely preparation for the big one: a celebration of Hitler's forty-ninth birthday on April 20, 1938. It was scheduled at the Yorkville Casino at 210 East 86th Street in Manhattan. Despite having "casino" in its name, it really was just a social hall for German Americans. The national headquarters of the German American Bund was just around the corner on 85th Street. A crowd of about 3,500 people gathered there, expecting not only speeches, but a parade.

This time, Lansky used more sophisticated tactics. He and his group gathered a few blocks away. Lansky had a box of brand-new hats with American Legionnaires logos on them. He passed them out and told everyone to say that they were patriots and veterans. It was a savvy move, not only because of the disguise, but because newspapers had reported that top US officials had exhorted American Legionnaires to wage war on Nazism at their convention at Madison Square Garden in New York. Lansky and his gang were no Legionnaires, but they were certainly tough enough to carry off the ruse.

It was the perfect subterfuge, and it was pure Lansky.

Lansky's small group divided into three teams: One went inside the ballroom where the rally was being held, one stayed outside, and the third team climbed a fire escape to get into the building through an upstairs window. Lansky and Siegel were with the first team. There was no way either one of them could allow themselves to stay outside. They had to be where the real action was.

They were sickened by what they saw: a huge photo of Hitler on the stage flanked by swastikas and the American flag. The first speaker, Otto Wegener, got up and praised, in German, the German seizure of Austria as a "birthday gift by Chancellor Hitler" to Greater Germany.

A man, who said he was a veteran, stood up in the crowd and shouted, "Is this an American or German meeting?"

A man jumped up and slugged him from behind.

Shouts erupted in the audience. Several Nazi storm troopers moved toward the man who had interrupted the meeting. But the men sitting near him—others in the crowd said there were about 100 of them, when actually, there were just a handful of them—stood up, put on their Legionnaires caps, and moved toward the stage. The outside group pushed past the guards at the door, and the guys upstairs ran down to back up their friends. A free-for-all broke out.

The Bund organization's chairman ran to the center of the stage to try to restore some semblance of order, but when he saw he was not getting anywhere, he ordered the band to play. As the music played, Lansky's gang pulled out blackjacks and bats. The Nazi storm troopers pulled off their belts and swung the buckles as weapons. Chairs were thrown.

The Nazis outnumbered the phony Legionnaires, but they weren't nearly as tough or impassioned. When they saw what was happening, many of the Nazis ran out the doors, bloodied and terrified. Around 9:30 P.M., someone yelled out the window: "Help! Police! Immediately!"

The men in Lansky's crew managed to fight their way to the doors of the hall. Finally, Lansky's crew and the Nazi storm troopers who were left wound up outside on the street, shouting to picketers and bystanders about what happened. The crowd surged toward the hall, but a detail of twenty-four police officers held them back. Fights broke out on the street. Fearful of the fights spreading, New York Police Department Captain Edward McDonald called in an additional fifty police officers.

With the additional reinforcements, police managed to restore order after about half an hour. At least seven men were badly injured. Others had contusions and broken bones. Four men were arrested on minor charges.

Lansky, Siegel, and their crew were nowhere to be found. They had managed to slip away amid the confusion.

Years later, he described what happened: "The speakers started ranting. There were only fifteen of us, but we went into action. We . . . threw some of them out the windows . . . Most of the Nazis panicked and ran out. We chased them and beat them up."

He concluded, "We wanted to show them that Jews would not always sit back and accept insults."

The Yorkville riot did more than that. Because it was so bloody, it became something of a rallying cry for groups fighting the Nazis. They mobilized to fight Nazi propaganda, even planning a "Germany-in-exile" exhibit at the World's Fair the following year.

As Lansky had hoped, his name and those of his friends didn't show up in the New York press coverage of the melee. Ironically, however, the Jewish papers had a little more insight into what actually had happened. They quoted the rabbi who had attended the meeting between Perlman and Lansky. He described the "Bund busters" as a bunch of Jewish gangsters.

To the rabbi, it was a matter-of-fact statement, but the description deeply offended Lansky. Worse, he felt Perlman had reneged on his promise, something he would never do. Years later, he vented his fury:

"They wanted the Nazis taken care of, but were afraid to do the job themselves. I did it for them. And when it was over, they called me a gangster."

As satisfying as it had been to fight the Nazis, Lansky was fed up with the hypocrisy of his fellow Jews. He decided to go back to Cuba. Business was going well there. He proposed taking Anna and the children to the Caribbean getaway for ten weeks.

Buddy and Paul loved the idea. They thought it would be a great adventure. It was. Just getting there was exciting. Air travel was far more primitive in the 1930s than it is today. The planes traveling from Miami to Cuba were practically "puddle jumpers," and Paul remembered the thrill—tinged with a little trepidation—of seeing the sea spray on the plane windows when they landed.

While their father managed the casino, the boys attended the American School in Havana for a year. Away from New York, they got to let their hair grow and wore shorts all the time. They loved the Cuban food and were treated practically like royalty by Cubans. At school, the teachers had a tough time pronouncing Buddy's name and called him "Bodey." Children of other American casino employees—like casino manager Dino Cellini—attended the same school, so they had a built-in set of friends.

The tropical weather was a refreshing break from the cold and dreary winters of New York City. It was just easy to be in Cuba, and they saw the difference in their father. He seemed so relaxed there. He loved the island.

The boys didn't know it, but there was another reason Lansky loved Cuba. Havana was considered an open city. In other words, anyone in the Syndicate could operate there. There were no worries over territory. Anyone with the smarts could invest and make money there, and Lansky had the smarts.

Then, in April 1939, reality intruded. Lansky's father, Max, died at the age of fifty-nine. The family held a funeral and had him buried at Mount Carmel Cemetery in Queens, New York. Lansky, at thirty-six years old, was now head of his family. It was a responsibility he took seriously.

For years, Max Lansky had worked long hours in the sweatshops of the garment district of New York City. It was hard work, but honest work. He died deeply disappointed in his oldest son's choice of occupation.

As always, Lansky said little about his father or how his death affected him. He remained devoted to his mother, Yetta. He set her up in a luxurious apartment on Ocean Parkway in Brooklyn.

At home with Anna, it was clear that she was feeling overwhelmed by her brood. Paul, so much like his father in his intelligence and self-discipline, was becoming increasingly irritated. He didn't like his younger sister at all. She would shriek and scream at the slightest provocation, managing to turn minor things into dramatic, tear-filled scenes. They always ended up with Paul, not Sandra, getting punished.

One day, out of frustration, he bit Sandra. As always, she screamed and cried as if she had been mortally wounded. Anna was at her wit's end. She insisted to her husband that they had to do something.

A lot of the Lanskys' friends were sending their sons to military school. It was the upper-class thing to do. And so, at eight years old, Paul was sent off to the New York Military Academy, more than an hour away in Cornwall, New York.

Being sent away from his family so young, wounded Paul, but it also toughened him. Like his father, adversity only made him more resolved. As he later told his wife, "I cried about it, and then I went to military school, and I never cried again."

As it turned out, he loved military school. He loved the discipline and organization, and he loved his uniform so much that he wore it even when he returned home for vacation. But his feelings about his sister never changed. For the rest of his life, he wanted nothing to do with her.

CHAPTER 6
The US Goes to War

ALTHOUGH HE ASSIDUOUSLY tried to avoid publicity, Lansky was becoming known in certain circles. Word was spreading about his business acumen. He was seen as the guy with the Midas touch, and he was seen as trustworthy—an unusual trait in his world. Opportunities came his way from all over the country.

In 1941, he went to—of all places—Council Bluffs, Iowa, a small city in the southwestern corner of the state. A few years earlier, the state of Iowa decided to hold a Centennial Exposition in honor of its upcoming 100th year of statehood in Council Bluffs. It was a flop. The fairgrounds built for the exposition now stood empty. A host of local businessmen lost a lot of money, and they wanted to be made whole. They began looking for investors. Iowa was a largely agricultural state, and the small city of Council Bluffs was hardly a magnet for outside investment.

Enter William Syms, an old friend of Lansky's. He had run a dog racing track with him in New Jersey. He turned to Lansky with the idea of opening a dog racing track there. Council Bluffs seemed like an unlikely location for a couple of streetwise guys from New York and New Jersey, but Lansky saw its potential. The city of Council Bluffs was located just across the Missouri River from Omaha, Nebraska, a much larger city. Lansky knew that the right setup would easily attract players from Omaha.

In the 1940s, greyhound racing was hugely popular. It was relatively inexpensive to set up. Greyhound dogs cost far less to keep than horses, and the race tracks themselves were simple. Basically, the dogs were linked up on a track and chased a lure—typically some kind of wind sock—across the finish line. At the same time, the returns for the right operator could be highly profitable.

During the summer months, Florida was deemed too hot and humid for comfort, and many people cleared out. Lansky shut down his Florida track during that time. One thing Lansky knew for certain: Gamblers wanted to gamble year-round. A dog racing track in Iowa could satisfy their needs.

The location served another critical need: It allowed his East Coast bookies to take bets. With his Florida tracks idle in the summer, this new dog racing track would give the bookies business. It would also help Lansky achieve another goal of his: to set up a nationwide system of betting.

He and Syms got a five-year lease on the fairgrounds. They agreed to pay $1,000 a week for a minimum of five weeks a year. That was exceedingly generous and appealing to the Iowa creditors, because they would quickly earn back all the money they had lost. As usual, Lansky went big. He and Syms spent between $50,000 and $100,000 renovating the fairgrounds. They built a new track and small stadium.

Lansky, according to the FBI, "maintained excellent local public relations." Throwing money around is always good public relations. With the exception of a few key people, he hired all local people. And he made a point of running a clean track. There would be no cheating, no rigged races. He and Syms lived and spent their money at the Chieftain Hotel, the city's most elegant hotel, during the eight weeks of racing season.

"They spent money lavishly and tried to get along with everyone, obviously to keep anyone from complaining," one citizen told the FBI.

The Lansky FBI files are filled with such observations. There was no crime in maintaining good public relations, but the observation was a good insight into how Lansky operated. Agents needed to understand how Lansky conducted himself in order to understand any crimes he might be committing. Unfortunately for them, he was extremely self-disciplined and never showed his hand.

They opened in July 1941. Crowds flocked to the track, eager to watch and bet on the greyhounds racing. The daily crowds numbered between 2,500 and 5,000 people, with half the people coming from Omaha. It was good business for Lansky and Syms and good business for Council Bluffs.

There was one small problem: Gambling was illegal in Iowa.

That might have deterred other people, but not Lansky. As usual, he found a way to get around that niggling problem. At a typical racetrack, bettors are given betting slips to fill out. At Lansky's dog racing track, people coming up to the cashier's window were given something called "option slips." Instead of placing bets, spectators were allowed to buy options in each dog running a race. If the dog won, they could sell the option back to the track at a profit because the dog's value had increased. (Coincidentally, that was just liking winning a payoff on a bet.) If the dog lost, it was considered worthless, and they simply lost their money.

It was a thinly disguised betting system, and the customers loved it. So did the city fathers, because their municipal debt was getting paid off.

As popular as the track was, some people disapproved. This was Iowa, after all, where much of the public hewed to a strong streak of conservative values. On July 22, 1941, just eleven days after the track opened, a local farmer, Joe True, filed suit to stop the track. "I'm still a pretty good farmer, and I would like to sink a plow in the middle of that track," he told the Omaha newspaper.

His lawyer stated the obvious: The option system was just a "subterfuge" and a violation of Iowa's anti-gambling law.

By September, True's case was headed to the Iowa Supreme Court. Normally, that would be a big problem for the track's owners, but not everyone was eager to see the track closed.

"Although the racing season has been closed a week, nothing but compliments—except in the pending civil suit—have been heard concerning the operation and personnel of the Dodge Park

Kennel Club," racing writer Frank Lane noted in *The Council Bluffs Nonpareil* newspaper.

By October, True—for reasons that are not particularly clear—dropped his lawsuit. "I am not convinced the enterprise (dog racing) is a gambling institution nor a racket," he told the Omaha newspaper.

Given who was involved with the track, it was perhaps not surprising that True changed his mind.

It had been a successful racing season. It was so successful that Lansky and Syms were persuaded to do it again the following year. That summer, instead of staying in the hotel, they rented the home of a local doctor, who was away in the service at the time. Syms and Lansky each had a woman staying with him, and a Black housekeeper tended to both couples. The doctor's home afforded them the comfort and privacy they wanted.

For Lansky, it was a familiar pattern. Often, when he was away from his home and family for an extended period of time, he'd take on a girlfriend. He tried to be discreet, but Anna was obsessively jealous. She knew her husband well, and she'd constantly call him in hysterics to check on him. He never acknowledged what was going on, undoubtedly infuriating her even more.

Dog racing in Council Bluffs was a profitable and relatively easy enterprise for Syms and Lansky for three summers. Then, a new mayor, William Byers, took office. He deemed the track to be engaging in illegal gambling, and he shut them down. The men moved on. That was another typical pattern for Lansky. He'd run a business until he couldn't anymore and then move on to the next one.

Iowa had been an interesting sojourn for Lansky and solidified his contacts in the Midwest. In particular, he became friendly with Minneapolis gangster Davie Berman (whose daughter, Susan Berman, was later famously murdered by New York real estate scion Robert Durst).

Lansky was happy enough to move on. He had other businesses in the works. He fell in love with jukeboxes, specifically Wurlitzer jukeboxes.

The attraction for a man who was both mechanically inclined and artistically attuned was obvious. The machines themselves were beautiful. They were designed in an Art Nouveau style, in polished burr mahogany and framed with colorful neon bubble tubes and Bakelite. A mechanism inside the jukebox played vinyl records that could be chosen with a press of a button. Speakers placed behind a large grill ensured sound quality. That kind of workmanship meant they weren't cheap. Each one sold for $1,806, or nearly $30,000 today.

He saw the Wurlitzer jukebox as the perfect way to showcase the performers he featured in his clubs. By now, he was running or partnering in clubs in Saratoga, Florida, Cincinnati, and New Orleans. Costello was his partner in Saratoga and New Orleans, and Alo in Florida.

The jukebox business, however, wasn't that simple. Typically, there were middlemen who placed the jukeboxes and clubs on their route. They would supply the jukeboxes with records and repair them in return for 50 to 70 percent of the take. It was an all-cash business. As such, it was very appealing to entrepreneurs wanting to avoid taxes, especially mobsters. Turf wars often broke out over routes. Violence wasn't uncommon.

Lansky formed his own distributorship with two former Wurlitzer agents, Edward Smith and Bill Bye. He called it Emby—E for Edward, M for Meyer, and By for Bye. He decided to throw a party to celebrate the launch of the company and invited his children. There was a huge buffet and a long line of people going through it, filling their plates. One of the people in the line was Frank Sinatra.

Emby had exclusive rights to sell the Wurlitzers in New York and specific spots on the East Coast. Lansky wanted nothing to do with the middlemen. They were an unnecessary cost. He decided to operate his own routes. His experience on the streets obviously gave him an edge.

"There was violence," Milton J. Hammergren, a Wurlitzer vice president later testified to Congress. "Such as blowing out the windows of the store or blowing up an automobile or something of that nature. Or, beat a fellow up."

Asked by then-committee Counsel Robert F. Kennedy if there were killings, he replied, "Yes, there was."

The violence of the business didn't bother Lansky, but it did bother the Wurlitzer company. Eventually, they asked Lansky to sell out. He did, at a profit.

He turned his attention to television. Lansky was exceptionally astute in forecasting business trends. He foresaw the day when every bar and nightclub would want a television set. He already had a network from the jukebox business, so it made sense. There was, however, one significant difference from the jukebox business: The television sets didn't generate any revenue stream. Worse, the particular television set he invested in was a terrible product. It kept breaking down. Within two years, Lansky's television business went bust.

It was one of his few failed business ventures. Of course, it was one of his few legitimate business ventures.

His clubs were still going strong. His Arrowhead Inn in Saratoga was especially popular, attracting, radio, stage, and movie stars by the dozens.

One up-and-coming star at the time, Cuban-born singer and musician Desi Arnaz, wrote of fond memories of the Arrowhead in his memoir. He worked for famed bandleader Xavier Cugat at the Arrowhead, "one of the finest gambling casinos in New York State at the time."

One night, a guest asked that Arnaz sing a Cuban ballad, "Quiéreme Mucho," which he did. Afterward, the guest sent the headwaiter over to ask if he would sit with him. Arnaz balked because Cugat's rules were strict. Members of the band were not supposed to mingle with the customers.

The headwaiter assured him it would be fine because, "It's Mr. Crosby."

It turned out to be Bing Crosby, a singer and actor at the peak of his fame. Arnaz, who was just starting out in the business, was

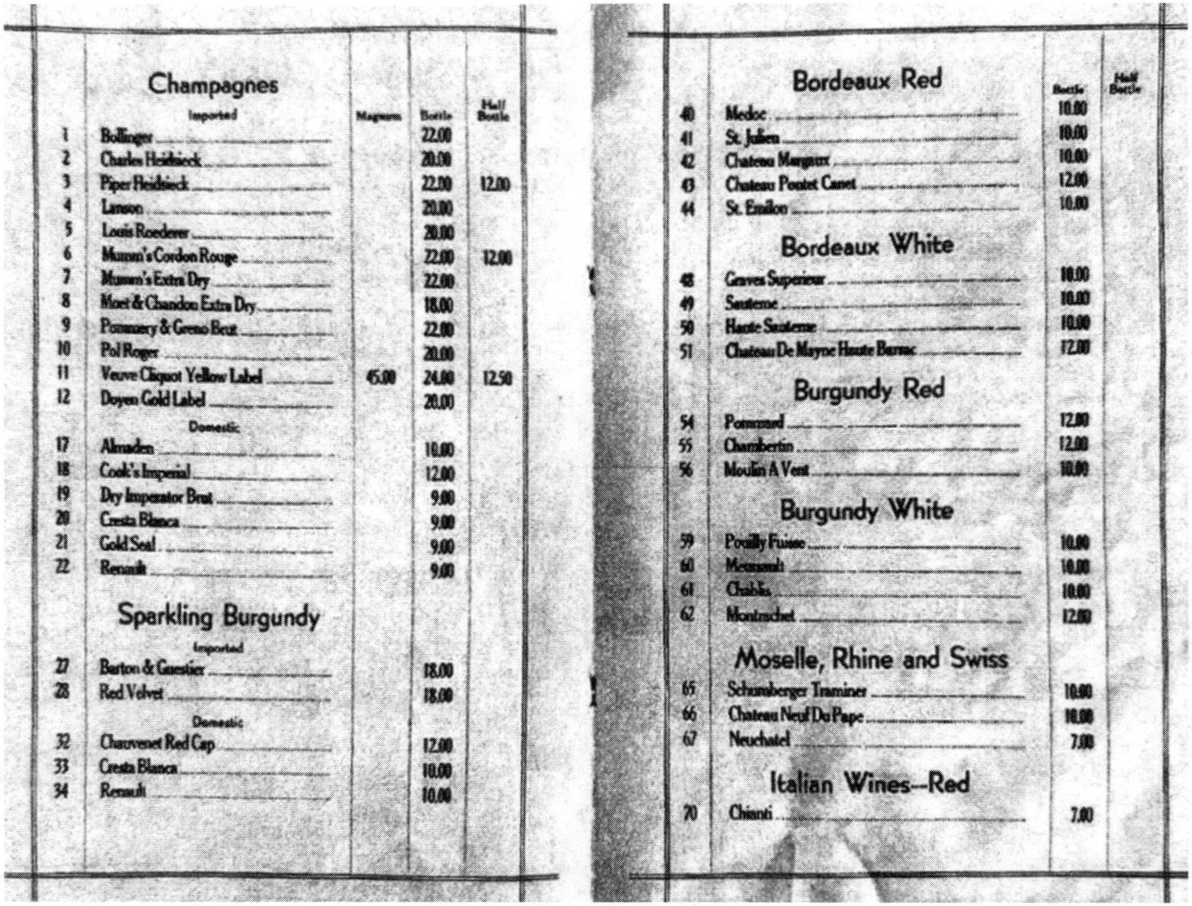

Champagnes

	Imported	Magnum	Bottle	Half Bottle
1	Bollinger		22.00	
2	Charles Heidsieck		20.00	
3	Piper Heidsieck		22.00	12.00
4	Lanson		20.00	
5	Louis Roederer		20.00	
6	Mumm's Cordon Rouge		22.00	12.00
7	Mumm's Extra Dry		22.00	
8	Moet & Chandon Extra Dry		18.00	
9	Pommery & Greno Brut		22.00	
10	Pol Roger		20.00	
11	Veuve Cliquot Yellow Label	45.00	24.00	12.50
12	Doyen Gold Label		20.00	
	Domestic			
17	Almaden		10.00	
18	Cook's Imperial		12.00	
19	Dry Imperator Brut		9.00	
20	Cresta Blanca		9.00	
21	Gold Seal		9.00	
22	Renault		9.00	

Sparkling Burgundy

	Imported	Bottle
27	Barton & Guestier	18.00
28	Red Velvet	18.00
	Domestic	
32	Chauvenet Red Cap	12.00
33	Cresta Blanca	10.00
34	Renault	10.00

Bordeaux Red

		Bottle	Half Bottle
40	Medoc	10.00	
41	St. Julien	10.00	
42	Chateau Margaux	10.00	
43	Chateau Pontet Canet	12.00	
44	St. Emilon	10.00	

Bordeaux White

		Bottle
48	Graves Superieur	10.00
49	Sauterne	10.00
50	Haute Sauterne	10.00
51	Chateau De Mayne Haute Barsac	12.00

Burgundy Red

		Bottle
54	Pommard	12.00
55	Chambertin	12.00
56	Moulin A Vent	10.00

Burgundy White

		Bottle
59	Pouilly Fuisse	10.00
60	Meursault	10.00
61	Chablis	10.00
62	Montrachet	12.00

Moselle, Rhine and Swiss

		Bottle
65	Schumberger Traminer	10.00
66	Chateau Neuf Du Pape	10.00
67	Neuchatel	7.00

Italian Wines--Red

		Bottle
70	Chianti	7.00

The Arrowhead Inn wine list. *Saratoga Room, Saratoga Public Library.*

bowled over. They started talking. Crosby, it turned out, loved Cuban music. He bought Arnaz a bottle of rum—Cuban Bacardi, of course—and asked him how much Cugat was paying him.

"Thirty a week," Arnaz said.

"That cheap crook," he said. "Come on, let's talk to him."

Cugat greeted Crosby, who, despite his affable on-screen image, could be tough and coarse to people around him. Crosby quickly dispensed with any polite small talk. "Listen you cheap Spaniard, what do you mean paying this fine Cuban singer thirty a week?"

"He's just starting, Bingo," Cugat replied.

"Never mind the Bingo stuff. Give him a raise. One of these days you are going to be asking him for a job," Crosby said.

Cugat, not one to miss an opportunity, said, "Okay, okay, how about singing a song with the band, Bing?"

"Will you give him a raise?" Crosby replied.

"Of course," Cugat said.

Crosby sang with the band, and the crowd went wild. It was the kind of thing that happened at Lansky's clubs all the time.

(Arnaz, by the way, got the raise. It was five dollars a week, and all he had to do was walk Cugat's dogs until they finished their business.)

The point of the entertainers was to draw in the crowds to the casino—the real moneymaker—and they did. The floor of the Arrowhead casino was separated by a walkway from the entertainment area. It had five roulette tables, five card tables, craps tables, birdcages, and a wheel of fortune. The birdcage was for chuck-a-luck, a game played with three dice inside a container shaped like a birdcage.

Lansky paid his Saratoga employees well, and they liked and respected him. Unlike other bosses, he stayed in the background and communicated his directives quietly. He knew that with the money he was making there, the last thing he needed to do was attract attention. They all knew who he was, of course.

The Arrowhead Inn matchbox. *Saratoga Room, Saratoga Public Library.*

Life was prosperous for Lansky, and his family was back in New York from Boston. They were settling into what was for them a comfortable rhythm. Then a cataclysmic event changed life for all Americans.

On December 7, 1941, the Imperial Japanese Naval Air Force launched a surprise attack on a US naval base in Honolulu. More

(continued)

than 350 Japanese aircraft dive-bombed six American ships in the harbor. They sank four of them and badly damaged the other two. More than 2,400 American servicemen died in the attack.

Up until that day, the United States had remained neutral in the conflict that was raging across Europe because of Hitler. Within hours of the attack, President Franklin D. Roosevelt declared war on Japan.

Everyday Americans felt the impact almost immediately. Europeans were accustomed to rolling blackouts that were designed to protect citizens and the military from enemy attack. US officials, even in vulnerable coastal cities like New York City, were initially reluctant to impose blackouts. The problem, however, was that the brilliant skyline of New York enabled enemies to see the silhouettes of American ships in the harbors. US ships were being sunk along the Atlantic Coast. The government declared it a "grave national emergency." New York and New Jersey had no choice but to impose the blackouts.

On February 9, 1942, just two months after Pearl Harbor, the French luxury liner, the SS *Normandie*, caught fire and capsized in New York Harbor. The US government had been converting it to a troop transport ship. The fire started when a spark from a welding torch set fire to life jackets and the ship's woodwork. The black smoke from the fire billowed all over the city. It was an ominous spectacle.

Not long afterward, Lansky drove his daughter, Sandra, down to see the wreck and explained the significance of the ship to her. Lansky avidly followed the news. He knew it was important to track politics and Wall Street to watch for potential impacts on his business, but he was also an American history buff. He knew the sinking of the *Normandie* was a critical moment in history.

He did not know at the time, however, the role he would play in the aftermath of that particular historic event.

Although the sinking of the *Normandie* was attributed to an accident of a welder's torch, US Naval Intelligence suspected something far more sinister. They worried that it was sabotage by Nazi sympathizers. They feared that enemy agents were working on the New York waterfront. They also knew that German U-boats loaded with spies were stealthily circling Long Island, just east of the city.

New York Harbor was the hub of US trade. More than 10,000 ships came in daily. The work of loading and unloading cargo, maintaining ships, and everything else required to keep freight moving was done by roughly 35,000 longshoremen. The work was harsh. It was not uncommon for men to lose fingers or arms. Nonetheless, it paid well and provided endless opportunities for larceny—catnip for organized crime.

Italians controlled the Brooklyn piers, and the Irish ran the West Side docks. The bosses exercised their control through the unions. Every day, union workers would line up, hoping to get an assignment that day. The guys who had the money paid a kickback to the hiring boss, thus ensuring a lucrative work assignment. The guys who wouldn't or couldn't pay a kickback either got a dangerous assignment nobody wanted or nothing at all.

The loyalties of many dockworkers were to their own little ethnic circles, not to the US government. Most of the Italians were immigrants and were deeply sympathetic to Italian dictator, Benito Mussolini, who was allied with Hitler. Some of them were rumrunners during Prohibition and had their own commercial fishing fleets in New York Harbor. US Intelligence suspected them of supplying fuel to enemy submarines.

Other workers were Nazi sympathizers and, in some cases, spies. US Naval Intelligence agents believed that they had spotted most, if not all, of the Nazi sympathizers. But they had far less information about the Italians.

The New York waterfront was an insular world. Dockworkers viewed outsiders with deep suspicion. It wasn't just because of their clannish loyalties. Everyone knew that the crime bosses running the docks would make sure that anyone who said a word or who was out of line would get a violent beating, or worse.

It was a terrifying predicament for the men at US Naval Intelligence. They reached out to New York District Attorney Frank Hogan, who enlisted his rackets bureau chief, Murray Gurfein, for help. As rackets chief, Gurfein knew organized crime and its players very well. He had, after all, assisted Dewey in prosecuting the Luciano prostitution case.

In March 1942, Gurfein reached out to a friend of Lansky's, Joseph "Socks" Lanza. Guys gave him the nickname because he was quick with a punch. He was a business agent for United

Seafood Workers at the Fulton Fish Market in Lower Manhattan. At the time, Lanza, a beefy and volatile man known for his penchant for violence, was under indictment for conspiracy and extortion. A lifelong criminal, he was not normally inclined to be helpful to law enforcement. Lanza's attorney pleaded with him to help. After he made it clear that his cooperation could help alleviate the legal penalties he was facing, Lanza saw the light and agreed to help.

Through his contacts in the fish market, he was able to place undercover agents on fishing boats and trucks—a significant victory for US Intelligence. He also set up a network of fishermen to watch for German submarines.

That was helpful, but far from enough. After a few weeks, it became clear that Lanza couldn't do much more. Lanza said he knew the solution to their problem—Luciano. He was the only man who was respected enough and who had the power and influence needed to get the waterfront workers to help in any significant way. Lanza was right, of course, but he also knew that access to Luciano would enhance his own reputation on the docks.

Lanza's suggestion posed a problem. Commander Charles Radcliffe Haffenden was running the operation. He had gone to great lengths to ensure the secrecy of their efforts. Instead of working out of a government office, he had set himself up in several suites at the Astoria Hotel in Times Square. It was not only comfortable and elegant, it was a much better cover for meetings with Lanza and his associates.

The need for secrecy was obvious for intelligence reasons, but there was another reason as well. If the American public knew that the US government was cooperating with the Mafia, it would be a public relations disaster. Anti-gangster fervor was still running high, and it would be hard to explain why upright American patriots were collaborating with criminals. There was a practical concern as well. Luciano was still serving his sentence at Dannemora. Getting to him would involve too many contacts in the prison system. The potential for a leak was high.

Haffenden decided to reach out to Luciano's lawyer, Polakoff. He knew he could trust his counsel. Polakoff was a successful criminal defense attorney who represented mobsters out of principle. Haffenden knew he was an honest man. Additionally, as a World War I veteran, Polakoff understood the stakes. Haffenden asked Gurfein to call him.

Polakoff demurred. He said he was no longer representing Luciano because the case was closed. Plus, he had an aversion to publicity and wanted to stay away from anything that might attract it.

"This is rather important," Gurfein replied. "I wish you'd come to see me."

Hearing the sense of urgency in his voice, Polakoff agreed to meet Gurfein. They talked. When he fully understood what Gurfein was asking, he told him there was only one person who could pull it off.

Meyer Lansky.

CHAPTER 7
Undercover Agents

POLAKOFF CALLED LANSKY in late April and asked him to come to his office. He didn't explain why he needed to meet him over the phone, and Lansky was savvy enough to not ask any questions. The two men understood each other well. Though they had each taken different paths in life, they respected one another. Each knew what the other could bring to the table.

When Lansky arrived at Polakoff's office on Fifth Avenue in Manhattan, Polakoff laid out what the government wanted.

Lansky's response was immediate: "I will be happy to help in any way I can."

Years later, Lansky told his family, "I was happy to handle the contract. I knew it was very necessary to watch the docks and what was going on with Italian fishermen."

They set up a breakfast meeting with Gurfein at the Longchamps Restaurant on 58th Street in Manhattan. It was an upscale restaurant that specialized in light French fare. Decorated with an Art Deco theme that appealed to upper-class customers, it had a men's grill that provided sufficient privacy for meetings such as this one. And it just so happened that Longchamps was one of a small chain of restaurants started by Lansky's old mentor, Arnold Rothstein.

It was just the three of them at the initial meeting. Haffenden had directed Gurfein to keep the circle as tight as possible to prevent leaks. A mobster and a prosecutor sitting down together to discuss business might have seemed unlikely, but wartime had united them in purpose. They got to the heart of the matter quickly.

"I understood the feelings of Italians," Lansky told his family years later. "It was really needed to convince Italians that their duty was first to help the US and that would be helping Italy when the war was over."

Lansky warned Gurfein that Mussolini was very popular with Italians. He said that US Naval Intelligence would have to be extremely careful about any moves they made.

Gurfein "wanted to know if we could trust Luciano," Lansky later testified. "I felt we could."

They kicked around what they should do to set up a meeting with Luciano. Polakoff said he didn't think he knew Luciano well enough to approach him with what they were asking. There was only one person who could make that approach—Lansky.

The men knew that they would have to meet him in prison because phones could not be trusted. Dannemora, however, was near the Canadian border, hours away from New York City. It was so far away that Luciano got few visitors in prison. The trip was just too long.

Polakoff was uneasy about the trip. It would take too much time away from his practice. And he had a more practical concern: The prison was in a small town, and strangers were immediately noticed. Gossip spread quickly.

Lansky proposed that Luciano be transferred to Great Meadow Prison, a maximum-security facility in Comstock, New York. Although it was more than 200 miles from New York City, it was a much more manageable trip.

On March 12, 1942—roughly two weeks after their meeting at Longchamps—authorities transferred Luciano to Great Meadow. As a cover, eight other inmates were transferred with him. As is typical in prison transfers, none of them were given any notice of the transfer, or told why. Luciano, like the other inmates, had no idea what was going on.

Three days later, the state's correction commissioner, John Lyons, sent a letter to Great Meadow's warden, Vernon Morhous, marked PERSONAL AND CONFIDENTIAL.

> *Dear Warden,*
>
> *This is to advise you that I have granted permission to Mr. Meyer Lansky to visit with Inmate Charles Luciano in your institution when accompanied by Mr. Polakoff, the inmate's attorney . . .*
>
> *You are authorized to waive the usual fingerprint requirements and to grant Mr. Lansky and Mr. Polakoff the opportunity of interviewing the inmate privately.*

Morhous was also instructed not to record the visits on the usual visitors' record.

For the government, this was moving at lightning speed. Time was of the essence.

In the first week of June 1942, Lansky and Polakoff boarded a train for Albany. They spent the night there and then paid a driver to take them another seventy miles to Great Meadow the next morning. Luciano, still completely unaware of what was going on, was taken to a room next to the warden's office. When he saw his old friends, Luciano was both stunned and delighted.

"What the hell are you fellows doing here?" he asked.

Lansky warmly greeted his old friend. He also had brought with him a special surprise for Luciano—a pastrami sandwich.

Lansky then explained the purpose of their visit. The US government needed Luciano to help enlist the services of all the Italians working the New York waterfront. If Luciano put out the word, there was no doubt that they would follow his orders and help the US effort.

Luciano, like Lansky, didn't hesitate. He said he would be glad to help.

He had one condition, however. He wanted his cooperation kept secret. There was a deportation order pending against him if he got released from prison. That meant he would no longer be under the protection of the US government.

"When I get out—nobody knows how this war will turn out—whatever I do, I want it kept quiet, private, so that when I get back to Italy, I'm not a marked man," he told them.

They assured him that his cooperation would be kept secret.

Polakoff had been right. Lansky was the only man Luciano could trust when his life was on the line. Without Lansky, there would be no cooperation from Luciano.

Haffenden was worried about German agents trained in sabotage techniques coming into New York. On June 13, 1942, his fears were realized.

On that day, four German saboteurs emerged from a submarine that landed on Amagansett Beach on eastern Long Island. Such landings were easy to make surreptitiously in the many bays and inlets of the island. The German agents quickly buried their equipment and uniforms. Despite that, a Coast Guard sentry, John Cullen, who was patrolling the area, spotted them. The leader of the group, George John Dasch, gave Cullen a $300 bribe to forget that he had ever seen him. Cullen accepted the money, and Dasch thought they were safe from capture. Cullen, however, was not easily paid off. He immediately reported the incident to headquarters.

A Coast Guard search patrol returned to the spot, but the men had already taken a train into New York City. Then they split up and agreed to meet two weeks later.

The Germans were well-funded. They had brought with them $83,000—more than $1.6 million today—to help them carry out their mission. But after their arrival, Dasch, a skittish and not entirely stable man, started having second thoughts.

The next night, Dasch called the FBI headquarters in New York City and said he would call the FBI office in Washington, DC, when he arrived there. He called that office on June 19 and said he wanted to speak to the same agent he had spoken to in New York City. He said he and the other men had been sent to the United States by Germany to commit "a wave of sabotage."

Agents scrambled to check out what he was saying. It turned out that the agent he has spoken to, D. F. McWhorter, had merely sent a memo about it to his supervisor. He had taken no other action.

Agents in Washington, DC, immediately took Dasch into custody and interrogated him over the next several days. He was difficult. Temperamental and high-handed, he tried to insist on dictating his own memorandum word for word. Nonetheless, they managed to extract his story.

His words were chilling. He said there was another submarine with four German saboteurs landing in Florida. Like the Long Island group, they had explosives and other sabotage material. They had a list of targets. They planned to bomb New York City bridges and tunnels and to poison the water supply. They communicated with invisible ink on a handkerchief. Dasch had a chemical to reveal what was written in the ink. Dasch was to meet up with his men in New York in one week and the Florida group a week later, on July 4.

Within days, the FBI rounded up all eight saboteurs. By June 27, FBI Director J. Edgar Hoover announced that the FBI had arrested eight German saboteurs.

For the US government, it was a much-needed public victory. But for Haffenden, Gurfein, and others in US Naval Intelligence, it was a warning shot. It underscored the urgency of their mission.

About two weeks later, Polakoff and Lansky made another visit to Great Meadow Prison. This time, they brought Lanza with them, so they could work out details of what needed to be done. As Polakoff sat off to the side and read the newspaper in an effort to stay out of their conversation, Luciano explained to Lanza "what to do and who to see." He also wanted him to make clear to everyone that Lansky spoke for him.

When he returned from the visit, Lansky told Haffenden that Luciano guaranteed that there would be no German submarines in the Port of New York. Even from prison, Luciano's word was law in New York harbors. But he needed Lansky as his trusted messenger.

As the operation continued, Haffenden and Lansky met regularly at the Astor Hotel. Haffenden would tell Lansky what he needed.

"I would seek the man that I thought could do best to fulfill his needs," Lansky later testified.

Haffenden told Lansky that he suspected there were spies in certain hotels. He wanted to place Naval Intelligence operatives there. Lansky said he would contact "certain people in the labor movement" and get it done. He also placed trusted waiters in restaurants and hotels. After years in the hospitality industry himself, he knew that waiters were valuable sources of information. They were always hearing things from restaurant patrons and other waiters. Lansky needed to know everything they heard.

At times, Lansky brought in certain trusted people to meet Haffenden. One was Johnny "Cockeye" Dunn. He knew the waterfront on the West Side better than anyone. After meeting with Haffenden, Dunn placed his men among the loaders on the waterfront. Anytime some guy got drunk in a bar and said something subversive, Dunn passed on the information. And when Haffenden wanted his agents to get union cards, Dunn got them.

More prison visits followed. In August 1942, at least five other men joined Lansky and Polakoff on their trip to Great Meadow, according to the prison record. There were Lanza, Costello, two men who gave false names, and Willie Moretti, Costello's cousin and owner of gambling operations in New Jersey and upstate New York.

By then, the discussions with Luciano might well have gone beyond just preventing sabotage of New York Harbor. Though they were committed to their patriotic duties, the opportunity to plan other activities under the cover of the US government was too perfect. Lansky had been telling his old friend for months that gambling was the future. He was determined to set up a nationwide gambling syndicate.

For the government, the operation was going well until there was an unexpected turn of events in November of that year. Lanza landed back in jail. Haffenden was worried. He turned to Lansky, who knew exactly what to do. He reached out to Joe Ryan, president of the International Longshoremen's Association, to ensure that their operation continued to run smoothly without Lanza.

Three months later, however, there was bad news. In their visit that month to Luciano, Polakoff had to explain to him that his bid to get his sentence shortened had failed. Luciano, quite understandably, couldn't understand why all his work on behalf of the US government wasn't rewarded. He was, after all, putting his own life at risk.

The news put the entire operation at risk. Without Luciano, there was no operation. Polakoff assured him that the judge had left open the possibility of clemency, but that seemed like a small crumb of consolation.

Once again, Lansky stepped in.

"I convinced Charlie, Frank [Costello], and many others that this was their country," he later told his family. "They owed a debt of gratitude. They thought I was right. After they heard from Charlie, that they follow what I put to them, we set the wheels in motion. I'm sure a lot was accomplished."

By May of 1943, the mission had expanded beyond protecting New York Harbor and placing undercover US agents in hotels and restaurants. Haffenden was working on plans for something else: a possible invasion of Italy.

He had huge maps of Italy on the walls of his suite. He needed to know if they were correct. He wanted pictures of every port and channel in Sicily. Once again, he turned to Lansky, who brought in Italians to look at the maps. Haffenden asked them if they could recognize their villages and for whatever details they could provide. They eagerly complied.

The idea of an invasion of Italy excited Luciano. He started telling Lansky how the Allies could invade Castellammare del Golfo on the tip of Sicily. A lot of residents of Castellammare del Golfo had immigrated to New York City, so they knew it well. It was not an easy target. The name literally translates to "Sea Fortress on the Gulf."

Luciano was so excited that he wanted to be part of the invasion force himself. He pressed Lansky to tell Haffenden that. Lansky did.

It wasn't just patriotism that motivated Luciano. He knew that before he could be part of any invasion force, he'd need a pardon first.

The news got worse for him in November of that year. His old antagonist, Thomas Dewey, was elected governor of New York. Prospects of a pardon seemed even dimmer.

Still, the operation had been extraordinarily successful in protecting US interests, all while being kept secret from the American public. As the war wound down, ending officially in September 1945, Lansky paid more attention to his businesses. He started working in earnest to set up a nationwide gambling network.

By then, Ben Siegel was already established in Los Angeles. The Syndicate had authorized him to organize the state of California for them and act as a front man for all their interests. Anyone who wanted to open a restaurant or nightclub business in town would have to see Siegel first and cut him in. There was one area Siegel was supposed to stay out of—motion pictures. The Syndicate already had that locked up. Things were running smoothly, and they didn't want any disruptions. But for a man like Siegel, who knew he was as handsome as any movie star and who liked to euphemistically call himself a "sportsman," staying away from motion pictures was impossible.

Besides, he had leverage. He had a friend, actor George Raft, whom he knew from their earliest days in New York City. Raft, though hardly a gangster himself, played gangsters in movies.

He knew how they walked and talked, and he liked hanging out with Siegel. For all of Siegel's ferocity on the street, he was a lot of fun. Through Raft, Siegel met and got to know many of the top people in show business. He also knew a lot about the "past associations" of movie studio heads. He had enough, in fact, to blackmail them.

Like so many other people who made the move to Hollywood, Siegel decided that he wanted to star in the movies. One day, he pulled Lansky aside and excitedly told him: "I'm going to do a screen test."

Lansky was aghast. He knew what their friends back east would think about that. He warned Siegel against it. "You can't do that, Ben," he said. "It's okay for Georgie, but not for you."

That didn't persuade Siegel. He got temporarily sidetracked, however, by an arrest in May 1944 for bookmaking. On paper, it was a fairly insignificant case, but it generated huge publicity because Raft was present during the raid. In the end, Siegel paid a $250 fine, and that was the end of it.

Lansky decided he needed to go to Los Angeles to see Siegel. Always on the lookout for new business opportunities, he proposed that they drive to Las Vegas, which was nothing more than raw desert at the time. He was always interested in buying raw land. He knew he wouldn't have to do anything to it and it would still go up in value. Over the years, when people asked him for financial advice, his first tip was always to buy raw land.

The trip did not go entirely as planned. The wires in Lansky's Cadillac literally melted. The heat and the dust got to him. He hated the place.

"There were times I thought I'd die in that desert," he recalled later.

But Nevada had something special that other states did not: Gambling was legal there.

That presented a tantalizing opportunity. Some guys—including some of Lansky's old friends from Minneapolis—jumped at it. Still, Lansky thought Las Vegas was too hot, too hard to get to, and generally unappealing. He invested in Siegel's El Cortez casino on East Fremont Street in Las Vegas, but little more. It turned out to be a wise investment. Siegel sold the El Cortez for a 27 percent profit. For all his bluster and vanity and show business aspirations, Siegel was very good at making money for his friends.

Lansky focused his energies instead on Hallandale, Florida. In the summer of 1945, he bought the Colonial Inn from showman Lou Walters (father of TV newscaster Barbara Walters). Hallandale, located in Broward County, was a haven just north of Miami for New Yorkers, including New York wise guys. For years, Broward was called the sixth borough of New York because there were so many New Yorkers there.

Even though gambling was illegal in Florida, Hallandale was a paradise for gamblers. There were banks set up to support the illegal gambling trade and an acquiescent sheriff who, for the right amount of money, happily looked the other way.

It was the job of the Hallandale city prosecutor, Joseph Varon, to collect the kickback money from the casinos and distribute it to the city commissioners. Although the kickbacks were entirely illegal, there was a codified system in place, with a fee for each table. Once, a commissioner complained that she had not gotten the correct payment, based on the fee-per-table bribe system. The bribes were so entrenched in the system that she saw nothing wrong with demanding the money she felt she was owed.

Varon knew better. He later lamented to his friends, "Some of those city commissioners were so stupid, they thought this was all legal."

(Varon was not the one who set up the payment system. That was arranged by his predecessor in the office, Stephen C. O'Connell, whose name is now on the College of Law at the University of Florida.)

As always when he opened a club, Lansky poured money into the Colonial Inn. He turned it into a plush nightclub with top-notch entertainment, like singer Carmen Miranda, who was known for her fruit-topped headpieces; comedian Joe E. Lewis, who was friendly with both Al Capone and Frank Sinatra; and, of course, bandleader Xavier Cugat. Costumes for the floor show alone cost upward of $40,000. Ads for the Colonial Inn featured a simple come-on that Lansky often highlighted in his other clubs: *30 Most Beautiful Girls*. While he never got into the business of prostitution because he genuinely abhorred it, Lansky knew very well what attracted men to his clubs.

In the years after the war, business was booming.

Then, on January 3, 1946, the news got even better. Governor Dewey, in one of his first official acts of the year, granted Polakoff's petition for clemency for Luciano. Although he felt bound to grant the petition for the Mob boss, Dewey made it very clear that while he was doing it, he didn't like it one bit.

In a terse statement, he said in part, "Upon entry of the United States into the war, Luciano's aid was sought by the armed forces in inducing others to provide information concerning possible enemy attack. It appears that he cooperated in such effort, though the actual value of the information procured is not clear."

Luciano, who did not have US citizenship, was deported to Italy. Dewey warned that if he dared to reenter the United States, he would be treated as an escaped convict. That meant he would incur additional penalties. Luciano would be required to serve the entirety of his maximum sentence without credit for good behavior.

It was hardly a ringing endorsement of Luciano's patriotism. But for Lansky, it was a great way to celebrate the new year. With Luciano out of prison, even more business would open up.

CHAPTER 8
Branching Out

News of Luciano's pardon spread quickly on the street. His friends wanted to celebrate his release. Lansky, however, had more practical concerns. On February 3, 1946, he, Costello, and Polakoff headed to a detention pen at Ellis Island, where Luciano had been transferred. They brought along with them a close friend of Luciano's, Michael Lascari. Their plan was to bring Luciano the clothes and personal possessions he needed for his departure.

They spent about twenty minutes with Luciano. He gave Lansky $2,500 in cash and asked him to turn it into traveler's checks. (Even though he was still in prison, Luciano's influence was such that he could get his hands on a large amount of cash.) He told them to let all the bosses know that he would be seeing them soon. It was a somewhat mystifying message, given that he was being deported to Italy. But Luciano needed his men to understand that he was back in business.

A few days later, Lansky and Lascari returned with the traveler's checks. It was a bittersweet moment because he was bidding his old friend farewell, but he knew Luciano meant exactly what he said.

The next day, prison authorities took Luciano to the SS *Laura Keene*, a converted ship scheduled to take a cargo of flour to Genoa, Italy. A cargo ship undoubtedly was more comfortable than a prison cell, but not to Costello, who visited Luciano on the ship. Costello showed up with a group of well-dressed men. They all had longshoremen's cards, which allowed them access to ships. Once he saw the food that the ship had to offer, Costello rejected it in disgust. He dispatched several men to shore to get lobster, spaghetti, and several bottles of wine from the Fulton Fish Market. Then they had a proper farewell party.

Lansky didn't join the party. It wasn't his style. Besides, he knew all too well that Luciano's departure from America would attract news reporters, and he didn't want the publicity. In fact, he left New York City for a few days just to make sure.

Las Vegas was consuming more of his time, but at a distance. As good as Siegel was at making money, he didn't share Lansky's aversion to publicity. On April 14, 1946, Walter Winchell, a syndicated newspaper columnist and radio host with a national following, dropped the equivalent of a news bombshell:

"According to the FBI, a prominent West Coast racketeer is endeavoring to muscle a prominent West Coast publisher out of his interest in a West Coast hotel."

Winchell was primarily a gossip columnist, but he had ties to both the underworld and law enforcement. He was a savvy operator, who knew the value of the information he was collecting. He sometimes engaged in a little trading, keeping certain gossip quiet in exchange for other scoops. His skill was such that when Winchell reported something, it very likely was solid information because it came from a good source.

In this case, the source was FBI Director J. Edgar Hoover. Hotel owner Billy Wilkerson had called Hoover in a panic after receiving a threatening phone call. He was sure that Siegel was the man behind the threat.

The FBI called Siegel in for questioning. He adamantly denied making any threats toward Wilkerson.

Wilkerson was a Las Vegas businessman. He owned the trade newspaper, *The Hollywood Reporter*, which he wielded like a weapon, while also running nightclubs. In early 1946, he embarked on building a massive hotel and casino, complete with a golf course, squash courts, horses, and a pool.

Unfortunately, Wilkerson was also a compulsive gambler. He lost money as fast as he made it. He needed a deep-pocketed investor. He turned to G. Harry Rothberg, a former bootlegger, who, with his brother, fronted for Lansky. A few months later, another investor turned up—none other than Siegel.

Siegel loved the idea of owning his own hotel and casino. The fact that someone else owned the project didn't matter at all to him. He immediately set about taking over, much to Wilkerson's consternation. Although he was no gangster, Wilkerson was a tough-minded businessman disinclined to walk away quietly. A clash between the two men was inevitable.

East Coast bosses noticed Winchell's scoop. They were not pleased. Lansky did what he could to temper their irritation. He knew he needed to deal with the situation in Las Vegas, but it was difficult from a distance.

At home, Anna informed Lansky of some personal news: Esther Siegel was divorcing Ben. Divorces were not common in the 1940s, particularly among traditional Jewish wives like Esther. She knew her husband was a philanderer, but she still loved him. She had tolerated his affairs, excusing them as flings. But when he met Virginia Hill, everything changed.

Hill had grown up poor. She was one of ten children born in Lipscomb, Alabama. Her father was said to be a drinker with a violent temper, who did little work and mostly cheated other people. By the time she was fifteen, Hill got out of there, eloping with a young man who had money. Within a few years, his appalled parents got the marriage annulled and gave her a sizable settlement.

That started a profitable pattern for Hill of getting her bills paid by wealthy older men. By the time she met Siegel, she had already been through several husbands and lovers, including Syndicate regular Joe Adonis. Like Siegel, she also aspired to be in movies. She had even gotten a screen test but failed miserably. She was much more talented at attracting lovers willing to buy her furs and jewelry.

Siegel's affair with Hill was more than a fling, and Esther knew it. She and Anna, still the best of friends, spoke constantly on the phone. She told her of her pain and of her plans to leave. She was granted a divorce in August 1946.

Lansky had little idea of what an impression that the Siegels' divorce had made on his wife.

For Lansky, the bright spot in his family life was his son Paul. He had returned from military school transformed. He started attending the elite Horace Mann School. Like his father, he liked discipline and organization. He was highly intelligent, too. Lansky loved his other children, but Buddy would always be a worry because of his disability and Sandra was a girl, highly strung like her mother. Paul was the one most like him. He was the one who could do great things.

Lansky liked challenging himself with tough sports, like boxing. When his sons were young, he took them to a big championship fight held at Yankee Stadium.

"When the first middleweight (160#) was defended in 1940, it was Tony Zale (champ) vs. Rocky Graziano (contender and popular wartime boxer)," Paul later recalled to his own son. "Buddy and I were so close to the ring we could reach up and touch it (2nd row, press seats). Al Jolson and his pretty daughter were behind us and offered us hot dogs. Later, I found out the girl was his wife!"

He continued, "Graziano hit Zale with many, many roundhouse rights for the first five rounds. I couldn't bear to watch the beating. In the sixth round, Zale landed a punch to solar plexus, and Rocky didn't get up. What a surprise!"

By the time Paul was fourteen, he was a huge boxing fan. As a treat one day, Lansky took his son to meet famed boxer Jack Dempsey, who had a restaurant on Broadway in New York. Paul was awestruck.

"His hand was as big as a bear's paw," he later recalled.

Other middleweight fighters he saw included Jake LaMotta, Georgie Abrams, Sugar Ray Robinson, and Marcel Cerdan.

Lansky himself boxed at George Brown's Gym in New York City. Brown was a well-known boxer and trainer and a good friend of famed writer Ernest Hemingway. Although Hemingway hated New York City, he would go there to meet his publisher on business. While there, he'd take a break to box with Brown. Hemingway loved the primal nature of boxing. He also absolutely hated losing at anything.

Lansky liked to take Paul to Brown's gym. One day, they saw Brown sparring with Hemingway in the ring. All of a sudden, Brown kicked Hemingway in the groin.

Stunned, Lansky asked Brown, "Why'd you do that?"

Brown replied, "If I didn't kick him in the groin, he would have kicked me."

Hemingway and Brown remained friends throughout their lives. Brown was fiercely loyal to the writer, even through his mental illness later in life. They lived by a certain code that they understood. Lansky understood it, too.

As loyal as Lansky was to Luciano, Siegel had always been his closest friend. He trusted him and protected him. He decided to turn his attention back to Las Vegas. Unbeknownst to him, so did the FBI.

On August 20, 1946, he and Siegel were speaking. Siegel asked him if "that guy" could send a car full of beer. Lansky asked him what it was for. Although Siegel obviously had been careful not to name names in the conversation, the FBI agent listening in took note.

Nine days later, a man "involved in construction" got a phone call from someone whose voice he didn't recognize. The caller identified himself as "your cousin from San Francisco" and told him to meet him at the intersection of Wilshire Boulevard and Eighth Street. The man agreed to meet him but had one of his employees follow him in another car in case anything untoward happened.

When he arrived at the designated spot, the man he was meeting turned out to be Siegel. He motioned for him to get into his car, but Siegel refused. He wanted to walk and talk.

Siegel told him that he knew the FBI was investigating him and was sure that his Las Vegas telephones were tapped. He complained that he was being shaken down daily and persecuted by the government. He told the man that he had invested every penny he had in the hotel-casino project, the Flamingo. If it didn't succeed, he would be destroyed financially.

The FBI took down every word.

The story of the strange meeting stayed tucked away in FBI files for years. Lansky couldn't have known how much the FBI knew about their Las Vegas ventures, but he was wary enough to shield his own involvement behind others. And although he was a master at juggling multiple business ventures at once, he couldn't be everywhere at the same time. Besides, he had even more pressing business. He was consumed with the idea of launching a casino in Cuba. In the fall of 1946, he went there to get the lay of the land.

Though things had been tense again between Lansky and his wife, Anna decided to join her husband in Cuba. Always a doting mother and aunt, she brought along her sixteen-year-old niece, Elaine. She and her younger sister, Ruth, often joined the Lanskys on trips to Miami, but this trip was an entirely new international adventure.

When they landed at the Cuban airport, Elaine was entranced by the Cuban dolls she saw for sale. She wanted to buy one for Ruth, but didn't have the money. Before she knew it, two bodyguards sent by Lansky picked them up and took them to a hotel. A little later, they took them to a house for dinner.

A man wearing an apron opened the door and greeted them warmly. Lansky wasn't there, but the man introduced himself as an "uncle." Other men were there, and they were all introduced as "uncles." Elaine was certainly old enough to know that these men were not really her uncles, but she didn't say anything.

They all sat down around a large table to eat. The man in the apron placed a huge bowl of spaghetti in front of Elaine. It was enough to feed the whole table. Elaine served herself and started to pass it around, but the uncle in the apron told her, "No, that's for you."

Elaine replied, "I can't eat that!"

The uncle in the apron decided to make it a challenge: "I'll give you a dollar if you eat the whole bowl."

Another uncle chimed in, "I'll give you another dollar."

Elaine made a quick calculation and figured that would be enough to buy her sister the doll at the airport. She ate the whole bowl.

After she got home from her trip, with the doll she bought for her sister, she glanced at the newspaper and was stunned to see a front-page photo of the uncle in the apron. It was Lucky Luciano.

She turned to her mother and said, "Mom, that's Uncle Charlie! I just saw him."

Her mother didn't say anything.

Elaine pressed her: "Mom, why didn't you tell me that was Lucky Luciano?"

Her mother replied, "You don't have to know everything."

Despite her mother's reticence, teenage Elaine knew something that US authorities did not: Luciano had slipped out of Italy into Cuba.

It had happened, of course, with Lansky's help. Near the end of October in 1946, Luciano arrived in Camaguey, Cuba. Lansky picked him up in a Jeep, a durable vehicle used in combat during the war to traverse rough territory. And as always, Lansky had worked out all the details. He had arranged for Cuba's interior minister, Alberto Pequeno, to grant Luciano an indefinite stay.

For Christmas week of that year, Lansky secured the top two floors at the Hotel Nacional in Havana for a meeting and reserved thirty-six suites for guests. The mezzanine was closed to uninvited guests to ensure privacy. This was to be an important meeting. All the top Syndicate bosses were to be there, including Vincent Mangano, Joseph Bonanno, Joseph Profaci, and Tommaso

Gagliano. They weren't the only Mob luminaries. Albert Anastasia and Vito Genovese attended as well, along with Lansky's close associates—Costello, Adonis, Moretti, and Michael Miranda. To have so many top mobsters there in one place was extraordinary, and they were there for one reason: Luciano.

With Lansky being Lansky, there had to be top entertainment as well. He flew in Frank Sinatra to perform there on Christmas. Sinatra arrived on a Pan Am flight with the Fischetti brothers, who were close to Al Capone, and then was whisked to the hotel. It was to be an event that was under the radar of US authorities. Cuba, after all, was another country.

Cuba did not lack for news reporters, however. A Cuban newspaper noted Luciano's arrival. That caught the US government's attention. Authorities assigned federal narcotics agents to surveil the meeting.

The meeting opened with a tribute to Luciano. Then, one by one, the racketeers walked up and handed Luciano envelopes of cash. By the end of it, he had $200,000, just what he needed to invest $150,000 in the Nacional—and pay off Cuban government officials—to turn it into a casino.

The meeting was successful. For Luciano, it was a triumphant return to business. And Sinatra, who performed on Christmas, was in his element. One evening, he enjoyed looking out on the city as he chatted with Luciano on the balcony of the Nacional.

An FBI agent snapped his photo. They already had taken one of his arrival in Cuba, as he descended down the steps of a Pan Am flight.

The photos were investigative gold. They were also great fodder for the tabloids. The FBI leaked a photo to the press. The resulting publicity was devastating to Sinatra. Being seen cavorting with a top mobster like Luciano was a crippling blow to Sinatra's career. Newspapers, the dominant media of the time, regularly published editorials railing against glamorizing mobsters. Even Sinatra's ardent fans couldn't abide seeing a celebrity like him with the Mafia's top boss.

Lansky was furious at what he saw as an invasion of privacy, but there was little he could do.

Normally, Siegel would have attended such an important gathering, but he was in Las Vegas, consumed by the Flamingo project. It opened on December 26. It was a disaster.

The timing around Christmas was terrible. Nobody wanted to leave home to gamble around the holiday. Siegel had planned to charter planes to fly stars in, but they didn't show. It seems that publisher William Randolph Hearst, who held sway over MGM because the studio produced his national news broadcast reels, had told them to stay away. Worse, the few people who did show up found themselves at an unfinished casino. The lobby was still draped in drop cloths. It was so bad that comic Jimmy Durante told Siegel, "Da place looks like a cemetery wid dice tables and slot machines."

Afterward, Siegel flew to New York to see his old friends, and they greeted him warmly. Behind his back, however, they groused about the Flamingo disaster, which was costing all of them money. They thought it was a stupid place to invest, and Siegel's difficulties reinforced their view.

Lansky was the only one in the meeting to take Siegel's side. "Let's really look into it," he urged them.

It was a tense time professionally for Lansky. At home, things were even worse. Anna was unhappy. On January 29, 1947, she filed for divorce. It was an unthinkable step, but she felt that she had been pushed beyond her limits. Always jealous and worried that her husband was having affairs (which he was), she suspected something more than a fling was going on. Her frequent talks with Esther, who divorced Ben because of his philandering, fueled her paranoia. Like Esther, she had confronted her husband about other women in the past, but he refused to talk about it, treating her as if she were crazy. She was, in fact, hysterical at times, but she wasn't wrong. She was *sure* there was something going on.

She often felt isolated and alone in her marriage. She was the one at home taking care of the children—Buddy, who was disabled and required nearly constant care, and Sandra, who was a spoiled, willful little girl. Paul, away at school, was a star student, and thus so independent that he didn't seem to need her.

Anna became depressed. She saw psychiatrists and other doctors every week, running up enormous bills and not finding an answer to her unhappiness. Lansky, always so self-disciplined and controlled, couldn't see the need for such expenses, especially when all those doctors' visits didn't make her feel any better. He told her he was going to stop paying them. He said he would send them to her father to pay. He was growing more irritated and angrier at her. They argued often.

In her divorce filing, she charged "extreme cruelty." At the divorce hearing, she testified, "He's out six nights a week, and on the seventh night, he's tired. He would think nothing of upbraiding me in the presence of the children. He never approved of anything I would say or do, whether intelligent or unintelligent. I'm sick of that stuff."

The final divorce decree, granted on February 14, 1947, gave Anna custody of the children, but allowed Lansky unhampered visits. He also got the right to select their schools and summer camps. He agreed to pay her alimony and her rent, but it was a fraction of his total income. As always, he had negotiated a pretty good deal for himself.

Anna was fed up. She had always loved her shopping and luxuries, but she didn't fight it. She just wanted out. She moved into a small apartment on Central Park South.

Lansky initially moved in with a good friend of his, William Morris agent George Wood. Not long afterward, he got an apartment in the New York neighborhood of Murray Hill, right across the street from the J. P. Morgan Library. In a move that startled his daughter, he hired an expensive interior decorator for the apartment. Anna had always been the one to handle the decor of his homes. While Lansky expected her to create a beautiful home for his family, it was never something that he spent any time on himself. It was entirely out of character for him, so much so that Sandra wondered if someone else in his life—another woman—wanted the apartment decorated to her taste.

Lansky said little about the divorce to anyone, not even his own family. He could, at least, take solace in the fact that his plans for Cuba were moving ahead. It was in Cuba, he knew, where he would make unlimited amounts of money with a casino, miles away from the prying eyes of the US government.

Then on February 22, 1947, there was more bad news. Luciano had been enjoying his life in Cuba. He could go anywhere as he pleased there, and the country had all the rum, women, and gambling he wanted to sate his every desire. He had resumed living the life he led before prison, only in Cuba. Unfortunately, Luciano didn't have the same modest temperament as his friend. He saw no point in keeping a low profile.

Luciano's activities caught the attention of an American newspaper columnist, Robert Ruark, who happened to see him in a restaurant in Havana while he was there on vacation. He knew he had a great scoop, and he wasted no time in reporting it. While some journalists might have been too afraid to out a major crime boss, Ruark was a hard-drinking tough guy in his own right. It offended him that a criminal he knew as a pimp and a drug dealer was out and about enjoying himself in the island paradise.

The news story embarrassed US Intelligence, who had believed up until that point that Luciano was safely away in Italy. The US Bureau of Narcotics notified the Cuban government that as long as Luciano was allowed to move around freely in Cuba, the US government would not release any narcotics for medical use. After all, they couldn't risk letting a drug dealer like Luciano get ahold of them.

Interior Minister Alfredo Pequeno called in his chief of the secret police, who arrested Luciano.

A month later, Luciano was placed on a freighter to Genoa, Italy. After the freighter arrived there, he was promptly jailed.

CHAPTER 9

Murder in Beverly Hills

PACIFIC TELEGRAM

June 21, 1947

From: Meyer Lansky
Miami Beach, Fla.

To: Sid Wyman
Flamingo Hotel
Hwy 91, Las Vegas, Nev.

Re: New Hotel Management

Sid,

Ben Siegel found dead in Beverly Hills . . . effective immediately change all locks in Casino Cage. No money transactions or markers over $1,000.00 until I arrive tomorrow evening. Business as usual with rest of staff.

No interviews with any News Bureaus!

Meyer

Ben Siegel, the handsome mobster from Brooklyn who had insinuated himself with the Hollywood elite in the 1940s, kept up a brisk schedule of meetings and calls on June 20, 1947. The

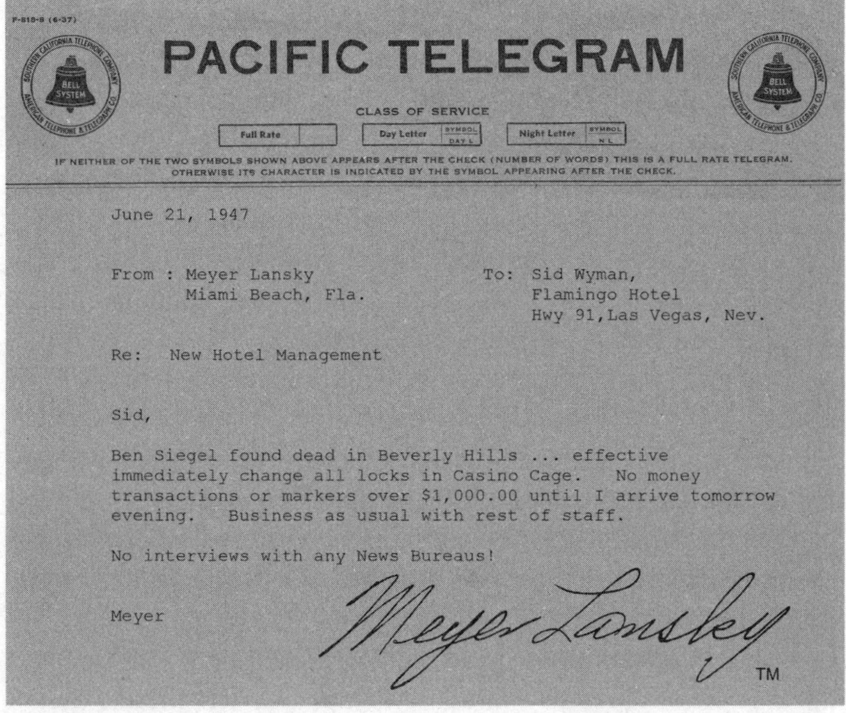

F-818-8 (6-37)

PACIFIC TELEGRAM

CLASS OF SERVICE

Full Rate | Day Letter DAY L | Night Letter NL

IF NEITHER OF THE TWO SYMBOLS SHOWN ABOVE APPEARS AFTER THE CHECK (NUMBER OF WORDS) THIS IS A FULL RATE TELEGRAM. OTHERWISE ITS CHARACTER IS INDICATED BY THE SYMBOL APPEARING AFTER THE CHECK.

June 21, 1947

From : Meyer Lansky
Miami Beach, Fla.

To: Sid Wyman,
Flamingo Hotel
Hwy 91, Las Vegas, Nev.

Re: New Hotel Management

Sid,

Ben Siegel found dead in Beverly Hills ... effective immediately change all locks in Casino Cage. No money transactions or markers over $1,000.00 until I arrive tomorrow evening. Business as usual with rest of staff.

No interviews with any News Bureaus!

Meyer

Meyer Lansky TM

Photo courtesy of Jerry Fox.

pileup of bills tied to the Flamingo hotel, Siegel's dream project in Las Vegas, caused his famous temper to flare in his lawyer's office. But he was still in a good mood after a session at Harry Drucker's hair salon—where he got a haircut, shave, and shoeshine. He had reason to feel confident. Just a few days earlier, he had met with Lansky, and everything was on track.

That Sunday night, Siegel went out to dinner with three others—Allen Smiley, Chick Hill, and Jerri Mason. Smiley, an associate who had been arrested with Siegel on a bookmaking charge in 1944, drove the group in his powder-blue Cadillac to Jack's, a new restaurant in Santa Monica. Chick Hill was Virginia Hill's brother, and Mason was Chick's girlfriend. They were staying at Hill's mansion at 810 North Linden Drive in Beverly Hills.

Missing from the quartet was Virginia. By all accounts, Siegel and Hill couldn't get enough of one another. But their coupling was a combustible one. A week earlier, she and Siegel had a blowout at the Flamingo. Hill saw Siegel talking to a cigarette girl and flew at her in a jealous rage, scratching her and pulling her hair. Siegel tried to pull her away. Hill screamed that he was a "murderer" and "gangster." Enraged, Siegel responded by hitting Hill in the face. She screamed that he broke her nose. He hit her again. She screamed that she would commit suicide.

Loud and violent arguments were nothing unusual for the tempestuous couple. This one, however, prompted Hill to declare that she was leaving. After doing just that, she called Siegel to say that she would come back if he apologized. He refused. She fled town, first heading to Los Angeles and then to Paris, where she had never traveled before. So it was that on the last night of her lover's life, Hill was out of town.

At Jack's restaurant, a valet handed Siegel a copy of the next morning's *Los Angeles Times* newspaper. After dinner, Siegel picked up a prescription at a local drugstore. Back at the Linden Drive mansion, he sat down on Hill's chintz sofa to read the paper. Smiley sat on an adjacent sofa near the windows. Chick Hill and Mason went upstairs. It was a lovely night. They didn't bother to pull the drapes closed.

Around 10:45 P.M., shots from a .30-caliber carbine blasted through the window. The first bullet ripped apart Siegel's head, propelling pieces of it across the room. The second one hit his chest. In quick succession, the gunman on the other side of the lattice outside the living room window fired seven more shots. In all, five hit Siegel. The gunman had been no more than fifteen feet away from his target.

It was sudden and swift. At first, Smiley thought it was firecrackers or some kind of gag. “Then I saw Ben slump on the davenport. His head was streaming with blood,” Smiley later testified.

“In less time than it takes to tell it, I dove to the floor and yelled to the people upstairs, ‘Lights out! Call a doctor! Call the police!’” Smiley said.

“They wanted to know what happened, and I yelled back, ‘Siegel’s been shot! Hurry up and get a doctor!’”

Then everything went quiet.

Within minutes, Los Angeles police arrived. As often happens in such situations, word spread instantaneously to the press. A syndicated columnist, Florabel Muir, arrived and walked through the crime scene. Perhaps it was the fact that murders were so rare in Beverly Hills that police were unprepared for the media attention. Or perhaps it was an artifact of a different time. In any case, no major police department would allow a journalist to walk through a crime scene like that today.

Word traveled even faster to Siegel’s gangland associates. An informant told the FBI days later that it had come as “a complete shock” to all of them. Their first call was to Siegel’s close friend and business associate, Meyer Lansky, but they couldn’t get through. The informant said he thought Lansky was “too smart” to talk on the phone because he suspected the FBI had bugged it.

The next day, on June 21, 1947, Siegel’s estranged wife and widow, Esther, called Lansky and bitterly complained that Siegel “did not have a single friend, only enemies” on the West Coast.

A gangland murder in the cosseted enclave of Beverly Hills was irresistible news. Reporters couldn’t get enough of it. Grisly crime scene photos—the kind that newspapers would never publish today—filled the pages of the daily newspapers. And theories on what was behind the brazen shooting abounded.

Police first suggested that it was revenge for the 1939 murder of Harry "Big Greenie" Greenberg in front of his Hollywood apartment. Greenberg had been a hired gun for the Syndicate, but the bosses were worried he would talk, primarily because he had been threatening to do just that. An order to hit him went out.

Though friends urged Siegel to stay out of it, he reportedly planned the murder right down to the very last detail, including the black sedan journalists called "the murder car." Police arrested Siegel in connection with the killing. But as often happened with such cases, a key witness unceremoniously died by falling out of a hotel window. Without a corroborating witness, authorities dropped the charges.

Another theory was that West Coast mobsters were angry that Siegel kept demanding a bigger take from their earnings to offset the mounting losses at the Flamingo. Police thought that a local guy—someone "with more guts than brains," according to a local investigator—shot Siegel to clear the way for his own ascension to the top of the West Coast gang.

The third and most prevalent theory—even today—was that East Coast mobsters, who had invested heavily in the Flamingo, had tired of the losses. Even worse, they were angered by the attention Siegel had been drawing to himself. Most mobsters preferred operating in the shadows. Siegel didn't. He couldn't help himself. He loved the limelight, and the limelight loved him.

Lansky had his own theory, which he discussed in an interview with the Salt Lake City office of the FBI after Siegel's murder. His theory was not reported in the press.

First of all, he asserted to the FBI agents that the Syndicate had nothing to do with Siegel's killing. He said he, Frank Costello, and Joe Adonis were surprised by the news. They received calls from all over the country but "were unable to answer."

The dry language of the FBI report continues:

> *Lansky said he and the others were not able to determine the identity of possible suspects. He stated that they were not contacted by Virginia Hill while Hill was in New York City before leaving for Paris and* [REDACTED] *that Hill may have told Adonis or Lansky about Siegel's attempts to defraud the Syndicate at the Flamingo Hotel in Las Vegas. Lansky believes the possibility exists that Hill's brothers may have killed Siegel.*

He told agents that "those hotheaded Southerners may have killed" Siegel because they were angry at how he treated Hill.

He said the Syndicate was conducting its own investigation into Siegel's death. He downplayed Siegel's role acting on behalf of the Syndicate in Las Vegas, but told agents that the "Syndicate is duty bound to try to solve killing itself to obtain revenge because of possibility of 'losing face,'" the FBI report says.

Lansky had been strikingly candid with FBI agents. He and Siegel were lifelong friends. More than once over the years, Lansky had stepped in to save Siegel. But above all, Lansky was a consummate businessman. He needed to protect the Syndicate and make sure the Flamingo stayed afloat. Hence the immediate telegram to Sid Wyman, one of the Flamingo's managers directing him to change all the locks in the casino cage, stop any transactions over $1,000, and bar any interviews with the press. Lansky would fly to Las Vegas the next day to take over the Flamingo.

Within ten days of Siegel's murder, however, the FBI got some stunning intelligence from an informant: Siegel "had made definite plans to kill" someone. The name is redacted in the FBI file.

The likely target of Siegel's rage was Billy Wilkerson. That decision very likely cost Siegel his life.

Meyer II, Lansky's grandson, remembers when he found out what was really behind Siegel's murder. It was 1972, when he was around fourteen. He and his mother were flying to Miami to visit Lansky for Christmas. (Even though Lansky felt strongly about his Jewish heritage, he always celebrated Christmas.) Meyer II saw a guy reading a book on the plane. He recognized it immediately because there had been a lot of publicity about it. It was *The Last Testament of Lucky Luciano*, billed as the famous mobster's posthumous autobiography.

Meyer II knew that his grandfather knew Lucky well. They had met as teenagers. Lucky and his gang tried to shake down Lansky one day as he walked home from school. His grandfather was not a big man, but he was tough. He fought back. That impressed Lucky. In fact, Luciano once said that Lansky was "the toughest guy, pound for pound, I ever met in my life."

They became lifelong friends. So, naturally, Lucky's book had to mention Lansky. And it did. It quoted Lucky as saying:

> *There was no doubt in Meyer's mind that Bugsy had skimmed the dough from his buildin' budget and that he was sure that Siegal was preparin' to skip as well as skim, in case the roof was gonna fall in on him. Everybody listened very carefully while Meyer explained it. When we got through, somebody asked, "What do you think we oughta do, Meyer?" Lansky said, "There's only one thing to do with a thief who steals from his friends. Benny's got to be hit."*

The problem is that the book was bogus. *The New York Times* reported that it had Luciano talking about events that happened after he died and attending meetings he couldn't have attended because he was in prison at the time of the meetings.

Meyer II didn't know any of that at the time. But his mother obviously had heard the story in the news, because when he pointed out the guy reading the book, she protectively pulled her son away. She didn't want him to know anything about it.

When they arrived in Miami, Meyer II immediately went to see his uncle Buddy, who lived at the Hawaiian Isle Hotel. He was his favorite uncle. He was always upbeat and funny and had great stories to tell. Despite having cerebral palsy, needing assistance to walk, and using a wheelchair occasionally, that really didn't dampen his zest for life. He was just fun to be around.

Some people underestimated him because of his disability, but there was nothing wrong with his mind. He was like an encyclopedia about life. He could talk about politics, sports, history. The fact that people underestimated him, though, gave him access to all sorts of information. Lansky's friends would never talk around twelve-year-old Meyer II, of course. But they spent a lot of time in Buddy's room, with him there, talking about everything.

So when Meyer II saw him, he asked him about Siegel's murder.

"I guarantee your grandfather had nothing to do with that," he said. "He was just as shocked as anyone else."

Then he went a step further: "I think the biggest suspect would be Billy Wilkerson."

Wilkerson was the Hollywood nightclub impresario who created the Sunset Strip. Handsome and often charming, he was a heavy drinker and gambler and lover of beautiful women—he married five times. Those qualities wouldn't have made him a particularly unusual character in Hollywood in the 1940s, but he had a singular influence because of his secret weapon, *The Hollywood Reporter*. It was the town's first entertainment trade daily.

Wilkerson started *The Hollywood Reporter* after the studios rejected a pet project of his, a movie called *Help Yourself.* Stung by the rejection, he decided to exact revenge through his own daily trade paper. He made sure to load it with juicy gossip—culled from digging through the studios' garbage—and his own caustic opinions. Studio bosses hated it. Wilkerson didn't care.

He had a simple creed: "Never forget a friend, never forgive an enemy."

Wilkerson knew the Mob guys in Hollywood well. The Mafia was often the only source of the high-quality alcohol he needed for his clubs. He counted Johnny Roselli, who started with the Chicago Outfit before moving to Hollywood and Las Vegas, as a friend. Siegel also patronized a high-end barbershop that he brought to Beverly Hills from New York.

By the fall of 1944, Wilkerson had accumulated gambling losses nearing $1 million. He decided he needed to own a casino to absorb his losses. It seemed like the perfect business for a gambler. In January 1945, he bought thirty-three acres outside Las Vegas. He planned to build a resort there. It would be called the Flamingo.

But by that fall, Wilkerson had given in to his demons once again and gambled away his ownership in the Flamingo. Investors approached his attorney, Gregson Bautzer. They wanted the land. Bautzer negotiated the deal. In exchange for the land and no further investment, Wilkerson would retain a one-third interest in whatever casino was built there. The deal also guaranteed that the rest of the investors would not be able to attach, sell, or otherwise diminish Wilkerson's holding.

Siegel was one of the investors.

Wilkerson wasn't entirely thrilled that Siegel was one of his new partners. He quickly realized, though, that Siegel could be useful. The United States had been at war. The war effort had made construction materials scarce. Siegel was good (with Lansky's help) at getting the black-market materials he needed to build the resort. Wilkerson had built, bought, and sold successful clubs over the years. He was used to being the boss. He treated Siegel like an errand boy. Siegel, understandably, didn't respond well to being patronized. Even though Siegel had no experience in building anything, he didn't see why that should stop him from doing what he wanted. Like Wilkerson, he was used to being the boss. A conflict was inevitable. He undermined Wilkerson's orders at every turn.

When a reporter, Westbrook Pegler, asked Siegel to describe his role in the construction of the Flamingo, Siegel barked, "This is my fucking hotel! My idea! Wilkerson has nothing to do with it! Do you understand? Nothing to do with it!"

Tensions festered until they reached a breaking point: The two men stopped speaking to one another. That didn't help the construction project. Costs were skyrocketing on the Flamingo, from

Meyer Lansky in the old country: Poland, 1903.

Meyer's mother, Yetta Sandler (Suchowljansky) Lansky, and father, Max (Suchowljansky) Lansky, New York City.

Paul Lansky's favorite portrait of his father, Miami, 1959.

Paul, Buddy, and Sandra's mother, Anna Citron Lansky, New York City, 1929.

Paul and Buddy Lansky beaching in Boston, 1934.

Meyer with sons Paul and Buddy near the American School in Havana, 1937.

Philadelphia's Dan Stromberg with Buddy and Paul Lansky at Roger's Corner, Madison Square Garden, New York City.

Teen Buddy, New York City.

Teen Paul "on the town" with Bob Annenberg, New York City.

Meyer Lansky, 1929.

The Beresford apartment building, Manhattan, home to Meyer Lansky's young family. *S. J. Peddie.*

Publicity photo for Meyer's Wurlitzer jukebox franchise ownership, New York City, 1940s.

Meyer at Owney Madden's Ranch, Hot Springs, Arkansas, 1934.

Paul Lansky at New York Military Academy, age 11, in 1943.

Cadet Paul Lansky, West Point, 1950.

George K., Paul Lansky, Don N., and Don A. at West Point, 1954.

Paul Lansky, 2nd LT, USAF, October 19, 1955.

Paul on a T-6, flight training school, 1955.

Meyer visiting his son Paul at flight training school in Bainbridge, Georgia, 1955.

Sandra, Paul, Meyer, and Buddy Lansky, Ballston Spa Hospital, 1953.

Paul visiting his brother Buddy in Sunny Isles Beach, Florida, 1955.

Rocky Marciano and George Brown, Paul's sparring coach, at George Brown's Gym, New York.

Jacob "Jack" Lansky with his brother Meyer.

Meyer Lansky with his grandson Meyer II, born August 1957.

Paul Lansky, his son Meyer II, and his wife Edna, Miami, Florida, 1959.

Meyer II in uniform, Brookline, Massachusetts, 1961.

Arnold Rothstein, "The Brain," Lansky and Luciano's mentor during Prohibition. He was murdered in 1928.

Charles "Lucky" Luciano, born Salvatore Lucania, who organized crime on a national level in 1931.

Benjamin "Bugsy" Siegel, Meyer's best friend, who would go on to develop the Flamingo hotel in 1946, putting Las Vegas on the map. *El Cortez/Bettmann/Getty Images.*

Frank Costello, "The Prime Minister" of the Mob, who succeeded Luciano as boss of the crime family before Vito Genovese took the top spot.

Billy Wilkerson, former developer of the Flamingo hotel and casino in Las Vegas before losing control of the property to Ben Siegel in 1946. *Wilkerson Archives.*

Chicago lineup, 1932: Paul Ricca, Salvatore Agoglia, Charlie Luciano, Meyer Lansky, John Senna, and Harry Brown.

Moe Dalitz, "Mr. Las Vegas," who straddled both sides of the law in developing Sin City, with Kentucky gambler Sam Tucker at the February 28, 1951 Kefauver hearing.

The Flamingo hotel in the 1950s, replete with live entertainment, the Chuck Wagon Midnight Buffet, and gambling tables. *LVCVA Archive.*

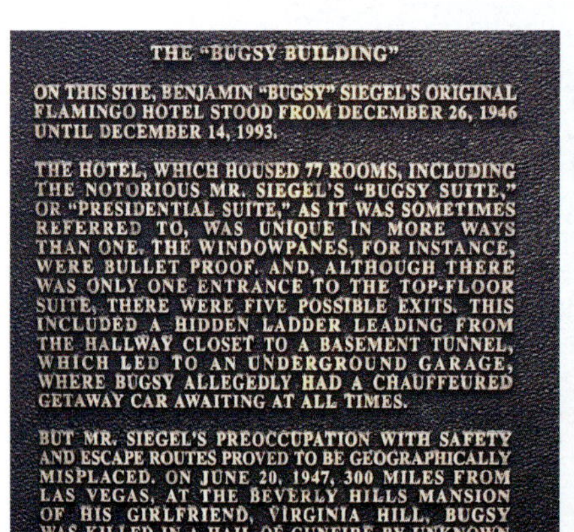

Ben Siegel's modern memorial in the Flamingo Wildlife Habitat, Las Vegas.

The Hotel Nacional de Cuba casino, through which Meyer Lansky expanded his international gambling empire, 1957. Watching the roulette game is Dino Cellini, and at the podium with his signature bow tie is Jack Lansky, casino boss. *Ralph Morse/The LIFE Picture Collection/ Shutterstock.*

Building site of the Havana Riviera, Malecon, Havana, Cuba, November 27, 1956.

Aerial of the Havana Riviera with Meyer Lansky's notes, March 19, 1957.

The man, the myth, the legend: Meyer Lansky, 1958.

Meyer catching a smoke break with his dog Bruiser, 1972.

Surveillance photo of Meyer walking Bruiser outside the Imperial House on Collins Avenue, Miami Beach, Florida, 1973. *FBI.*

The El Cortez Hotel & Casino, on its opening in 1941. *El Cortez/Special Collections and Archives, University Libraries, University of Nevada, Las Vegas.*

El Cortez today, Fremont Street, Las Vegas. *El Cortez/Chris Wessling, 2025.*

The Flamingo hotel as seen from the Strip in the 1950s. *LVCVA Archive.*

Among the Flamingo's guests in the 1950s were Zsa Zsa Gabor, Clint Eastwood, and Pearl Bailey. *LVCVA Archive.*

The Flamingo as seen from the Strip, October 2025.

Inside the Flamingo is Bugsy & Meyer's Steakhouse, which diners visit from all around the world.

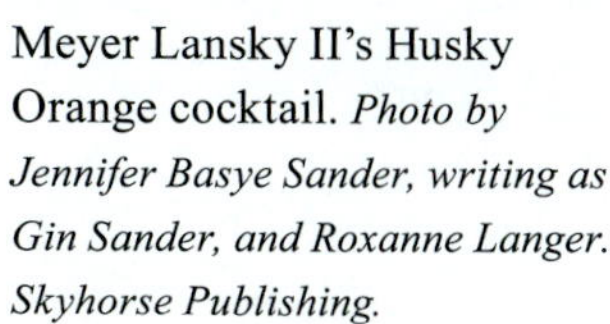
Meyer Lansky II's Husky Orange cocktail. *Photo by Jennifer Basye Sander, writing as Gin Sander, and Roxanne Langer. Skyhorse Publishing.*

The interior of Bugsy & Meyer's Steakhouse holds Meyer's Flamingo Room for diners, and The Count Room, a Mob-themed speakeasy, another mainstay of Flamingo Las Vegas.

$7 million to $12 million, Bautzer recalled in a previously unpublished 1977 interview. Even more perilous for Siegel, he had sold 150 percent of what he owned in the project.

"The boys were demanding their money back or evidence of their ownership. Siegel could give neither. He had a dilemma," Bautzer said.

Siegel called a meeting on December 26, 1946, at the Las Vegas office of one of his lawyers, Nevada Lieutenant Governor Clifford Jones. (Reports would later emerge that Jones had close, undisclosed financial ties to Siegel and other mobsters.) Siegel demanded that Wilkerson give or sell him his interest in the Flamingo or allow the issuance of additional stock, which would alleviate his financial straits. Wilkerson didn't care about Siegel's financial woes. He refused. He had an ironclad contract, and he was no pushover. Siegel went into a rage.

"Look, you will give me the thirty-three and a third and get paid for it, or I don't think any place you will live will be healthy for you!" he screamed.

Bautzer listened to the discussion in amazement, but he was also a tough-minded lawyer who didn't back down from anyone, not even a mobster with a penchant for violence. He immediately took charge. He told Wilkerson to leave the room. Wilkerson was only too happy to leave. He was terrified.

Bautzer told Siegel: "From this moment on, you had better put a couple of guys on Wilkerson and be certain he doesn't slip or get a scratch on his fingers or anything else to hurt him. I'm making an affidavit" to turn over to the authorities.

Siegel exploded. His lawyers calmed him down. He ultimately agreed to pay Wilkerson $2 million for his shares. But as with the loans he got from actors in Hollywood that he never repaid, he never paid Wilkerson.

That same month, reporter Victor Enyart was in Wilkerson's office when he saw him pick up a call from FBI Director J. Edgar Hoover. Wilkerson's faced turned ashen. He got off the phone and told Enyart that Hoover had just warned him his life might be in danger. The Syndicate was planning a complete takeover of the Flamingo.

Wilkerson decided not to take any chances. He fled to Europe.

So it was that both he and Virginia Hill were in Europe when Siegel was killed, a fact that was noted in newspaper reports at the time.

Uncle Buddy talked a lot to Costello, who often stopped by Lansky's apartment. He'd go there to meet with Lansky, but he often just hung around. It was a treat for Buddy, who reveled in Mob gossip. Buddy was engaging and fun, and people seemed comfortable confiding in him. Costello never carried a gun on him because he had been caught once as a kid with one and he didn't want the heat. There was too much to lose. He had strong ideas about how a gentleman should carry himself, getting rid of his Brooklyn accent, knowing how to run a business. Even though Costello had made his way as a feared Mob boss, he wanted the world to see him as a successful and legitimate businessman.

After Uncle Buddy's many conversations with Costello, he became convinced that the meeting about the stock shares led to Siegel's demise.

Wilkerson's son Willie, who extensively researched his father's life, agrees. He believes his father's friend, Johnny Roselli, was behind the hit. He thinks it's entirely possible that his father, a vengeful man, could have asked Roselli for help with Siegel.

Roselli liked Wilkerson. He had testified on his behalf. Roselli also wanted to go legitimate, and Wilkerson was his ticket to legitimacy. Roselli was behind bars at the time, but still might have issued the order, according to Willie Wilkerson.

That's an unlikely scenario, however, because civilians could never tell made guys like Roselli what to do. Meyer II doesn't think the Mob would have approved the hit. The Syndicate guys were happy that the Flamingo had started making money, so there would be no reason to kill Siegel.

Roselli had a lot of connections, though. He had ties to Los Angeles' corrupt mayor, Frank Shaw, and was his liaison to various gangs. He was also in cahoots with the Central Intelligence Agency because of their failed plot to overthrow Castro. Any one of his connections could have had a hand in it.

Regardless of who fired the fatal shots, there's no question in Meyer II's mind that Siegel's days were numbered after his fateful meeting with Wilkerson.

Meyer II just knew it wasn't true that Lansky okayed the hit because he knew his grandfather. He prized loyalty and his friends. And Ben had saved Meyer's life many times.

Ben's family knew, too. Just three years later, when Ben's daughter Millicent got married, who did she have walk her down the aisle? Lansky. Not only that, but he paid for their reception at the Waldorf Astoria Hotel.

He was happy to do it, and she was proud to have him at her side. Years later, she told people that, too.

"I would never have let Meyer walk me down the aisle if I thought he had anything to do with his death," she said.

The imposters and poseurs can say what they want. But if they want the truth, they need to listen to the people who know.

CHAPTER 10

An Anti-Gambling Fervor

LUCIANO'S ARREST AND deportation were setbacks, but Lansky was used to pivoting. He and Costello met in New Orleans with Silvestro "Silver Dollar Sam" Carollo, boss of the New Orleans crime family. They discussed setting up a national communications center there to transmit financial information for bookies. It would be a way for the gambling syndicate in New York to know instantly if there was heavy betting going on somewhere on a horse race or ball team. It was vital that kind of information be up to the minute for bookies.

With the clubs he owned in Florida, New Orleans, and Las Vegas, Lansky already had the pieces in place that he needed to feed a national communications network. The only problem, of course, was that gambling was still illegal in most of the country—not that Lansky ever viewed that as a serious problem.

Lansky was familiar enough with the anti-gambling rhetoric that was picking up steam across the country. He had heard politicians decry the terrible effect gambling had on families and its links to organized crime. He chafed against what he deemed the hypocrisy of those politicians.

"The same people who condemn gambling are the sinners who get the most out of it," he told his family in his later years.

He meant what he said. He knew, for example, that FBI Director Hoover was an avid gambler and often got tips on horses from Costello. Joseph McCarthy, the firebrand senator from Wisconsin, was another big gambler. Lansky also knew that at every place where he had a casino, the local politicians were more than happy to accept payoffs and to gamble themselves. It was just a cost of doing business. As long as that was kept quiet, everybody profited.

As compliant as local officials were, the anti-gambling fervor was catching on with the citizenry, with the help of scintillating exposés in national magazines. In early 1947, *Collier's* magazine ran an article about Costello, calling him "American's Number One Man of Mystery" and detailing his nationwide gambling enterprises. The Florida newspapers immediately picked up on the story, bemoaning the presence of "Northern mobsters," including Lansky, in Broward County. That kind of publicity, coupled with the shocking murder of Siegel in Los Angeles, only heightened fears of organized crime and its associated gambling operations.

In December 1947, an attorney who lived in Hollywood, Florida—in Broward County—spoke up at a meeting of city commissioners. He demanded that they do something about the illegal gambling in the city.

"Mr. Mayor, I want to know what you mean to do about the gambling," said the attorney, William Flacks.

"You all know the situation, and you know that the police chief has given no instruction to stop it. You know that every tavern, poolroom, and night spot runs gambling. It has got to come to a stop, and I ask for a motion that will stop it."

Flacks was not wrong. Gambling had been integral to the area's exponential growth. After the Florida Supreme Court legalized slot machines in 1935, they became ubiquitous in Broward County. Casinos quickly followed. Gambling provided an influx of cash and jobs. All of it was readily embraced by local farmers, who supplied food to the casinos; bankers, who extended loans; and local government officials, who happily acquiesced as long as they got payoffs. In particular, the local sheriff, who also received regular payments, conveniently ignored the gambling.

The problem was that illegal gambling tended to attract other crimes. As much as some citizens enjoyed the influx of money, others were greatly disturbed by the crimes that often popped up along with it—armed robberies, prostitution, and theft.

After Flacks finished speaking, a hush fell over the room. After all, these were the very city commissioners who were receiving regular kickbacks to allow the illegal gambling.

But one city commissioner, who had a finely attuned instinct for the winds of politics, stepped up and sponsored a motion to ban gambling. This put his fellow commissioners in a bind. They felt they had little choice but to quickly follow suit and approve the ban.

It was a stunning moment. They were voting to stop the cash flow to themselves. But it was also a testament to the strength of the public's anger over gambling.

The anti-gambling fervor was not confined to Hollywood, Florida. Less than two months later, there was action next door in Hallandale, where Lansky had his clubs.

On February 12, 1948, Florida Assistant State Attorney Dwight Rogers Jr. filed a civil nuisance action against the Colonial Inn. He had the backing of local civic leaders. That was enough to spur an order to local deputies to start gambling patrols—something that would put a serious crimp in the casinos' business. That was tantamount to throwing down a gauntlet. Everybody knew who was behind the casino operations, and they understood the potential for violence. Authorities deemed the situation dangerous enough to assign Rogers a bodyguard.

Bolstered by the local support, Rogers pushed ahead and subpoenaed the Colonial Inn's financial records. Lansky, naturally, was not inclined to turn them over. There was a court hearing.

At the hearing, Lansky's attorney, Joseph Varon, told Circuit Court Judge Otis Farrington, "Your Honor, we just don't have any of the subpoenaed records."

Farrington, who well understood both the law and human nature, considered this briefly and replied, "Well, we're going to recess for lunch; and if you and your client don't have the records back here after lunch, you and your client are going to be spending time at the Iron Bar Hotel."

Varon and Lansky walked out to his car, accompanied by Rogers's bodyguard, and got the records out of the trunk. They returned to court and turned over the records, thus avoiding an unpleasant stay in jail.

Rogers got an injunction. The Colonial could continue operating as a club, but without any casino. Lansky had been through this before. It didn't make sense to run the club without the casino, as it was the gambling that was the moneymaker. Always mindful of public relations, he invited the local press to come in and finish off the food and liquor before the whole place closed down. It made for some favorable press. But he and his partners had another reason for the invitation: They wanted to know who had spearheaded the anti-gambling campaign and even offered reporters money to tell them. They were hoping that they could give whoever it was a cut of the profits so that they could keep operating.

They never got the answer as to who was behind it. They decided to move on. Lansky still had his other clubs, Club Greenacres and La Boheme. Later in life, he wondered if there was something more than anti-gambling morality fueling the drive to shut down the Colonial Inn. He mused that perhaps there was a "conspiracy" to depress the local real estate and "steal the properties from the defunct owners."

Like Farrington, Lansky understood human nature.

Meanwhile, trouble was brewing in Saratoga Springs, where he still operated two casinos, the Arrowhead and Piping Rock. In July 1948, Mrs. Philip Weiss threatened to file suit in Saratoga County over the illegal gambling.

Unlike the officials in Iowa and Florida, her grievance had nothing to do with public morality. It was entirely personal. It began two years earlier when her husband stole horse race results by having his electrician connect his phone to a bookie's phone line. It might have been a momentarily slick move, and a profitable one at that, but it wasn't long before his competitors discovered it. Furious, they harassed him relentlessly. So did the local police. It was so bad that Weiss gave up his betting business. Hoping to move on, he opened a restaurant. That wasn't enough, however, to appease the people he had offended. One day, a police officer came in to the restaurant, pulled out a gun, and chased out sixty diners.

That was very bad for business.

It also infuriated Mrs. Weiss. Her husband had been trying to run a law-abiding business, only to be shut down by a corrupt cop. She could scarcely contain her indignation. She went to Albany, the capital of New York, to see the newly elected governor, Thomas Dewey—the very man who put away Luciano. He did, after all, have a reputation for crime fighting and rooting out corruption. She never got to see him, but that didn't stop her. She launched a letter-writing campaign to her congressmen and judges. Finally, she got a monthly publication called the *National Police Gazette* to print her story. It was an unusual place for her story, because the *Police Gazette* was at that time known mainly as a girlie magazine. Nonetheless, Mrs. Weiss got a platform for her complaint.

Complaints like the one from Mrs. Weiss were nothing new, and Lansky didn't see any need to stop what he was doing. He continued operating his clubs in Saratoga Springs. He needed the money flow. But he didn't foresee how Mrs. Weiss's grievance would affect him later.

At the time, he was finding himself increasingly distracted by both international and personal events.

In the mid-1940s, there was a movement to create a homeland for Jews in the Middle East. He was captivated by it. It stirred something very deep inside him. He hosted fundraisers in Florida, and they were highly successful. Far less publicly, he met with Israeli agents who had very specific needs: They wanted to buy American weapons and they also wanted to block Arab countries from doing the same thing. They were particularly concerned about a Pittsburgh arms dealer who was arranging weapons shipments for the Arabs through the New York waterfront.

Once again, Lansky was the man uniquely qualified for the mission. He tapped his waterfront contacts, and part of the Pittsburgh shipment mysteriously fell overboard.

It was vintage Lansky, and he relished the action. He was thrilled when the State of Israel was formally created, and recognized by President Harry Truman, in May 1948. He always followed current events because he needed to know how they could affect his various businesses. But he developed a particular fascination for the new nation of Israel and avidly followed events there.

On the personal front, a new woman was consuming his attention. Her name was Thelma Scheer Schwartz. She called herself Teddy. She was loud, used street lingo, and favored cheap-looking clothes. She had none of Anna's style and panache, or her ladylike manners. She seemed to be an unlikely match for Lansky, but it was clear that she had set her sights on him. Even FBI agents noted it in a memo. Teddy started working as a manicurist at the Embassy Hotel, which had never regularly employed a manicurist, but which happened to be the place where Lansky had his daily shaves and haircuts.

She told friends that they had met in Florida, but Sandra knew they had met far earlier. Teddy and her husband, Philip Schwartz, had lived in the same building as the Lanskys did when they were first married, 201 W. 85th Street. Teddy had seen the Lanskys around the building and sometimes asked Meyer for advice, according to Sandra. Teddy claimed later that she only vaguely remembered meeting Lansky in the building and that they didn't really connect until she was about to divorce her husband. Sandra never believed that. When she later thought about it, she recalled that her father had hired a decorator when he moved into an apartment during her parents' divorce. It was so unlike him to take a personal interest in such superficial things in his home. She was sure that another woman must have been behind it.

Whatever the truth was about when Teddy and Lansky met, their marriage was inevitable. Teddy epitomized the classic gangster's moll. She fully understood that her beloved's business activities were illegal, and she didn't care. She didn't want to know, and that was something Lansky prized about her. Unlike Anna, she didn't ask questions. She was fiercely loyal. In her eyes, Lansky could do no wrong. Unlike Anna, she looked up to him. In choosing Teddy—and Lansky had his choice of women—he was sloughing off any pretense, any hypocrisy. He wasn't trying to ascend to any higher stratum of society, because he was already there, whether or not the morality police liked it. In Teddy, he had someone who would always support and care for him.

Later, Teddy, trying to emphasize the supposedly accidental nature of their meeting, would say that she wasn't looking to get married when she met Lansky. His children, however, thought otherwise. When they looked at Teddy, they didn't see a supportive spouse. They saw a gold digger.

In any case, Teddy divorced Philip Schwartz in August 1948. Four months later, on December 16, she and Lansky flew to Cuba and quietly got married. They kept it so quiet that when Paul and Sandra came down to Cuba a few days later to celebrate Christmas with their father, they had no idea he had gotten married. He never said a word. It was only when nineteen-year-old Buddy came down to Cuba a week after his siblings that Lansky said something. He told Buddy about his marriage but swore him to secrecy. Sandra only learned about the marriage months later after she returned to New York and saw it in the newspapers.

Whether Lansky kept it a secret because Teddy was embarrassed by the obvious questions about when they met, or because he was secretive about a lot of things, is unclear. But it was hardly an auspicious start to their marriage.

Six months passed before Lansky and Teddy would take their honeymoon. On June 28, 1949, they set sail on the cruise ship *Italia* from Pier 54 on the Hudson River in New York. He reserved the Regal Suite, an elegant three-room suite on the Promenade Deck that ran the entire length of the ship. Before they arrived, he had it filled with flowers and champagne. The cruise didn't come cheap. It cost $2,600 one way, or about $35,000 today. It was the kind of luxury Teddy loved.

It was to be a five-week cruise to Europe, and it was the perfect way to start their honeymoon. At least that's what he told federal agents, who grilled him earlier in the day as to why he was taking the trip. Their interest wasn't mere harassment of a high-profile organized crime figure, though that was certainly part of their intent. They knew that steamer trunks on ships to and from Europe were a means of smuggling drugs. And since Luciano, now finally living in Italy for real, had a drug-dealing conviction, they were suspicious that Lansky might be a means of smuggling drugs.

It was a preposterous premise. Never in his career had Lansky been charged with any kind of drug dealing, and they knew it. He told the Bureau of Narcotics agents, "This is just a pleasure trip."

The federal agents, however, were not persuaded. Besides, they were on orders to pursue the investigation. They followed him to the ship and, as often happened, one of them tipped a reporter at *The New York Sun*. Jumping on the scoop, the reporter raced to Pier 54 just in time to see Lansky.

"I don't want any pictures made, please," he said. "This is just a pleasure trip."

Prepped by his federal source, the reporter asked Lansky if he planned to see his old friend, Luciano, on his trip.

Lansky slammed his cabin door in the reporter's face. It was a rare moment of losing his cool publicly, but it was a reflection of how offended he was by the suggestions that he might be smuggling drugs.

His efforts to avoid publicity failed miserably. The next day, *The New York Sun* ran a photo of Lansky on the front page. He was outed.

The reporter, Malcolm Johnson, spared no details: "Lansky and his wife, a slender, attractive brunette, whom he married last winter departed in an atmosphere of champagne and orchids, in the manner befitting Lansky's reputation as a powerful and wealthy underworld figure. The Regal Suite, which they occupied, is the most luxurious that the *Italia* affords."

Johnson went on to detail Lansky's sordid underworld connections, emphasizing his friendship with the recently departed Siegel.

The press coverage didn't stop there. Reporters, who were being fed a steady stream of tips by frustrated federal agents who wanted nothing more than to keep the heat on Lansky, kept up the news stories after he and Teddy landed in Rome.

"Reports here indicate that Lansky, traveling in the luxury befitting his reputation as a powerful and wealthy Mob figure, is considerably peeved over the cool reception he's getting on his 'vacation' tour of Europe. He has complained bitterly that the American authorities are putting the whammy on his trip and he wants to come home," read a quote in one news wire story.

Authorities had hoped to prevent Lansky from landing but couldn't because his passport and visa were in order. They were determined to keep up the pressure, however, through surveillance and frequent leaks to the press.

"The theory here is that Lansky came to Italy to organize something big with Luciano," the story read.

On that point, they were not wrong. Despite his protestations to the press, Lansky did, indeed, plan to visit Luciano. They met in the Sicilian village of Taormina. As always, they had a great deal to discuss. Lansky was still intent on building a casino on Cuba.

Still, for all his focus on business, Europe held him in its thrall. On July 19, 1949, he wrote to Paul:

> *Paul, I can write pages about Rome, but this is all the paper I have. They are very short of paper here. I will describe it all to you when I see you, it is simply something beyond anyone's imagination. The Vatican leaves you breathless. I would venture to say if it was built today it would cost $50,000,000,000.*

The trip to Europe opened Lansky's eyes to a new way of seeing the world. To be sure, he had spent his early years in Europe, but he had never traveled beyond his shtetl there. His early years had been spent in the kind of poverty that he just wanted to forget. Traveling to some of the most beautiful places in Europe activated his imagination and the urge he had to create something magnificent. He knew how to make money, but he wanted to do something more than that.

Lansky's letter to his son reflected the slight shift in their relationship. While he would always advise and correct Paul, as he thought a father should, he would confide in Paul in a way he couldn't with his other children. Paul understood him. He was the child who was most like him.

Buddy understood his father just as well, but Lansky worried that his disabled son would always need someone to care for him. Sandra, meanwhile, reveled in her role as the spoiled youngest child. She spent her time shopping, riding horses, and hooking up with men. Meyer understood Paul's disgust with his sister, but throughout his life, he tried to help his daughter.

All three children knew that Lansky's remarriage would devastate Anna. As angry and bitter as she felt about her ex-husband, she had never dreamed that he would remarry. When the story broke, Buddy took a cab to all the newsstands and bought up all the newspapers so his mother wouldn't find out.

But it was inevitable that Anna would find out, and she was, indeed, crushed by the news. In the months after her divorce, her mental health had deteriorated even further. Once always so elegant and refined, she traipsed around her apartment in a housedress with unkempt hair. Her behavior was becoming increasingly erratic. She was talking to herself, making little sense. Where she once had loved her salon visits and shopping sprees, she stayed home alone. She had been the one who was warm and social, but now she cut herself off from people altogether.

Her family visited her often and supported her financially. Lansky regularly sent his brother, Jake, over with cash to pay his alimony. Whenever Jake handed her an envelope with cash, she would react with disgust, tossing it in a drawer untouched. She retreated from the world. Her strange behavior and obvious decline deeply upset her children, but they didn't think they could do much about it.

Lansky's European trip had been something of a respite, despite the pressure from the federal agents. He couldn't ignore, however, the anti-gambling rhetoric in the States. He knew it was bad. One of the things that had kept him alive over the years was his ability to spot threats. Despite his initial decision to ignore Mrs. Weiss's complaints, the publicity she generated started to make waves.

Saratoga Springs was going to be a problem.

CHAPTER 11
Kefauver's Crusade

JUST FIFTEEN MINUTES before midnight on November 18, 1949, Lincoln Fitzgerald walked out of his palatial home in Reno, Nevada, to open the garage door and pull out his car. It was his nightly ritual. He and his wife, Mata, would then leave for his casino, the swanky Nevada Club.

As he pulled up the garage door, his body silhouetted against the light from the garage, a gunman crept out from the bushes beside his house and shot him with a .12-gauge shotgun. The blast tore a three-inch hole in his side and severed his spine. The gunman fired another shot, barely missing his head, before fleeing into the night.

Mata, who was inside their home, heard the commotion and came running outside. She found her husband bleeding out on the ground. She called police. Emergency responders rushed him to the hospital.

Doctors gave him blood transfusions to keep him alive, but they didn't think he'd make it. Police posted guards at his hospital room. When they asked him who shot him, Fitzgerald refused to say. Since nothing was stolen, police theorized that the motive was revenge. Fitzgerald had moved to his exclusive neighborhood in Reno after years of running casinos in Detroit. Authorities thought some Detroit mobster might have taken revenge for bad blood there.

Authorities couldn't help but note the similarities between Fitzgerald's ambush and the one that killed Siegel. The attempted murder was yet another gangland shooting linked to gambling. It made national headlines for days. Fitzgerald, who was fifty-seven, survived, but just barely. He didn't leave the hospital until the following April. He returned home a changed man, paranoid and reclusive and walking with a limp.

One Florida newspaper noted that Fitzgerald had moved to Reno after having been "eased out" of the Colonial Inn in Broward County by a syndicate group led by Lansky. The story didn't specify what that meant, but the implication of violence was clear.

The anti-gambling fervor, stoked by a steady stream of headlines about gangland shootings and politicians corrupted by bribes, reached a fever pitch across the country. It was an ideal climate for ambitious politicians wanting to make a name for themselves. Fighting for the reform of a pernicious evil is the best kind of politics. Estes Kefauver, a senator from Tennessee, understood that very well.

Born into a political family—his father was mayor of his hometown of Madisonville—Kefauver grew up to become a lawyer. He ran for Congress and won. After serving five terms in the US House of Representatives, voters sent him to the US Senate. He was, by all accounts, his own man. He was unafraid to take unpopular stances if he believed they were right. He wasn't, however, particularly popular among his colleagues. He affected a morally superior air. They found his condescension insulting.

But, like any seasoned politician, he knew a good cause when he saw one. In 1950, he headed a US Senate Committee investigating organized crime. In May of that year, he launched the committee's first hearings, not in New York, Detroit, or Chicago, but in Miami, Florida. That was, of course, where Lansky spent much of his time. Additionally, local authorities had already done a good deal of investigating there. It was already fertile ground for a crusading senator. And it would make for good press.

The Kefauver Committee found corruption everywhere in Miami, from restaurants to cigar stands. It also found that the gambling syndicate's political connections went all the way up to Florida's governor, Fuller Warren. Investigators turned up evidence that organized crime figures had contributed to his campaign. Furious that the committee looked into his campaign finances, Warren refused to cooperate with them. He accused Kefauver of being "an ambition-crazed Caesar who is trying desperately and futilely" to be a presidential candidate.

On June 19, 1950, barely three weeks after the first hearing in Miami, *LIFE* magazine, a national publication, published an in-depth report on gambling, the "nation's biggest racket." It included photos of the "tycoons of gambling," including Lansky and Costello, among others. It also took pains to point out the societal costs of gambling, particularly on the poor—"why the little fellow always loses." It included a flattering photo of Kefauver and his allies.

It was great publicity for Kefauver. It was terrible publicity for Lansky and only augured what was to come.

Warren wasn't wrong about Kefauver's ambitions, but his protestations were not enough to derail the committee. The allegations against Warren ultimately ended his political career. He wasn't the only casualty of the committee. Broward County Sheriff Walter Clark tried to avoid answering the committee's questions but wound up admitting that most of his income came from a company that oversaw gambling. By July of that year, he was out of office. More witnesses testified, especially about the Colonial Inn, which was described as the largest and most profitable casino in Broward. By August, Lansky and his brother, Jake, were indicted for violating Florida's anti-gambling laws. The case was trumpeted as a victory in the press, but it ultimately amounted to very little. The Lanskys resolved the case a month later by paying a $2,000 fine.

Kefauver was picking up steam. Miami was the first of fourteen cities where the committee planned to hold hearings. They stopped in New Orleans, Kansas City, Detroit, Chicago, New York, and Las Vegas. Interestingly, the committee did not stop in any cities in Kefauver's home state of Tennessee, even though there was plenty of gambling there. No good politician goes after his own base of support.

What made these hearings so newsworthy and effective was that they were televised. Lansky had been right about the potential of television, even if his attempt at launching a business with them failed. Most homes in the United States didn't have one in 1950, but they quickly became increasingly popular. As word spread about the Kefauver hearings, more Americans tuned in.

By October, the committee moved to Manhattan. That provided a priceless opportunity for some political grandstanding. Senator Charles Tobey, a Republican from New Hampshire and a staunch Kefauver ally, attacked Governor Dewey, who, like Kefauver, harbored presidential ambitions. Tobey, who like Kefauver grew up in a religious home, could summon up righteous outrage like no other.

"Taking Saratoga as Exhibit A," Tobey declared. "What is the reason the governor and the state don't come down like a ton of bricks?"

Saratoga, of course, was another place where Lansky had been running successful clubs.

On October 11, the inevitable happened. The committee subpoenaed Lansky to testify. The last thing he wanted to do was get involved with that circus. He ultimately did testify, but he did it in a way that was very different from the other witnesses. He did not appear before any television cameras.

That's because he didn't go in there unprepared. He researched Kefauver. He knew that he gambled heavily. According to Sandra, he and Polakoff met with Kefauver privately and showed him all the gambling IOUs he had accumulated. Whether or not her claim about the IOUs was true, Lansky and his lawyer managed to persuade the sanctimonious senator to allow him to testify privately—a major victory.

Lansky's testimony was unrevealing, at best. He admitted associating with Frank Costello, Joe Adonis, Frank Erickson, and Charles Fischetti. He admitted traveling to Italy in 1949 but did not say whether he contacted Luciano. And he was "evasive" about his Florida interests, the FBI noted.

Kefauver, for his part, tried to strike back at Lansky publicly by telling reporters that he was the "big wheel" in a $26-million interstate gambling empire. He said Lansky ran fifty clubs and would be cited with contempt.

It was a big charge and made a splash in the headlines. But Kefauver never cited Lansky with contempt.

Years later, Lansky noted the irony of his dealings with people like Kefauver: "The elite always looked upon gambling as an evil. Only when they [the elite] used it as a pleasure or for personal gains was it legitimate and not sinful."

Lansky clearly had made an impression on Kefauver. On November 20, 1950, the senator gave a speech to the Economic Club of Detroit. He detailed Lansky's various business interests, linked him to Costello and Luciano, and said, "He's a very smart operator—a man of a good deal of cunning and intelligence."

In January 1951, the committee convened in New Orleans. A local TV station got permission to televise the hearing. That ignited an immediate and overwhelming public reaction. The courthouse holding the hearing couldn't accommodate the crowds, and letters poured into the TV station. From then on, more and more Americans tuned in to the hearings. They were riveted both by the fiery indignation of the senators and the titillating details of the underworld.

In March 1951, the committee returned to New York for a hearing at the Foley Courthouse in Manhattan. Public interest was so intense that it would be broadcast by three national networks. By then, Kefauver was a national celebrity. This hearing was to be the apex of the committee's work. It was only appropriate that they call before them an underworld star—Costello. An interim report of the committee had already labeled him America's "Number One crime boss."

Costello, having learned from Lansky's experience, negotiated his own deal. After first meeting privately with the senators, he agreed to appear before the committee publicly only if his face didn't appear on television. Committee members reluctantly agreed. Costello showed up in a powder-blue suit and was immaculately groomed, as usual. Much to the irritation of his questioners, however, he refused to answer questions about his net worth.

Tobey summoned up his characteristic indignation and opened up a tough line of questioning about Costello's naturalization to become a US citizen. "Did you ever offer yourself to the war services of your country?" he asked Costello.

"No," Costello replied in a raspy voice that sounded very much like a gangster to viewers, but that he said was due to a throat infection.

"Bearing in mind all that you have gained and received in wealth . . . what have you ever done for your country as a good citizen?" Tobey demanded.

"I don't know what you claim, what you mean," Costello replied, sounding a little shaky.

"Well . . . you must have some things that you've done that speak to your credit as an American citizen. If so, what are they?" Tobey demanded.

Flummoxed for a moment, Costello came up with a response: "I paid my tax."

Spectators roared with laughter.

It was absolutely humiliating for Costello. Here this expensively dressed mobster, who had more money and power than most Americans could even dream of, appeared obviously nervous and shaken, especially as the camera focused on his dancing fingers. It made for a lasting impression and likely hastened his subsequent fall from power. And despite his assertion that he paid his tax, he was prosecuted for tax evasion after the hearings.

Years later, Lansky defended his old friend: "Instead of being looked upon as a savior for all he did for them with no financial gain to himself, he suddenly became a gangster and whatnot. The old saying what did you do for me lately. They then twisted the whole purpose of his mission and he was made the scapegoat."

Lansky went on to complain about the politicians who broke with Costello and claimed their fear of the underworld as an excuse. Lansky knew they had no reason to fear him: "Show me one incident where a politician was physically harmed through Frank's doings, but they sure harmed him and never hesitated to take a loan from him. Frank was too easygoing for all the alligator-skin politicians."

Throughout his life, Lansky scorned what he saw as the hypocrisy of politicians. He dealt with them only when he had to. Costello, by contrast, loved the world of politics, and thought he could hold his own in it. Lansky was not so sure. He was convinced that the politicians Costello thought were his friends would betray him.

Lansky wound up testifying privately before the Kefauver Committee three times. Although he avoided the public humiliation suffered by Costello, he could not dodge the consequences of the committee's investigation. Aside from having to close his profitable clubs, he lost something he treasured: his privacy. Millions of Americans had watched the hearings. Lansky could no longer move around easily in relative anonymity. It was so bad that he stopped indulging in a favorite pastime of taking Sandra to Broadway musicals. The audience would stare at them. It was just too uncomfortable. Worse, reporters showed up at the family's apartment, trying to get his children to comment.

If Costello's testimony had amused viewers, it absolutely could not compare with the testimony of Siegel's old flame, Virginia Hill. Although she had never made it as an actress, she knew how to make an entrance. She showed up in a $5,000 mink stole, gloves, and a wide-brimmed hat. Once she was seated, she complained about all the photographers' flashbulbs.

"Make them quit doing that," she told the committee in a slight Southern twang. "I'll throw something at them in a minute. I hate those things."

The committee members told the photographers to finish up and then began to press Hill on where she got her money. Hill explained that men, including Siegel, gave her gifts. "The only time I ever got anything from them [gangsters] was going out and having fun and maybe a few presents."

She continued, "For years, I've been going to Mexico. I went with fellas down there, and like a lot of girls, they started giving me things, bought me everything."

She seemed utterly at ease batting away the committee members' questions. Told that IRS agents believed that she carried cash for gangsters, she shot back, "That is not true, and if they told that, that is a lie. The only cash I've ever carried is what belongs to me."

She was appealingly blunt and direct. As she answered questions about Charles Fischetti, a Chicago mobster and cousin of Al Capone, she pursed her lips in distaste. She made it clear that she didn't talk to him.

That piqued her questioner's curiosity, so he asked, "You don't like him?"

Without hesitating, she replied, "No."

Laughter rippled through the room. The audience loved her.

Her public appearance before the committee, however, did not compare with the private session beforehand. Tobey wanted to know why certain men kept giving her money over the years, even though she had been married four times and had numerous high-profile lovers, like Siegel. Hill tried to deflect his questions, but he wouldn't give up. Finally, she got fed up.

"You really want to know why?" she asked.

"Yes, I really want to know why," Tobey replied.

"Then I'll tell you why. I'm the best cocksucker in America," she said.

That best summed up Virginia Hill—bold and unapologetic about her choices in life. But her tough talk masked an underlying pain. Years later, in 1966, she committed suicide in Austria at the age of forty-nine.

The cavalcade of news stories and newsreels about the hearings seemed unending. New York City Mayor William O'Dwyer, also a former prosecutor, appeared voluntarily and often sparred with his inquisitors. But he spared no words when it came to naming the six men who ran the East Coast crime syndicate: Ben Siegel, Frank Costello, Joe Adonis, Albert Anastasia, Abner Zwillman, and Meyer Lansky.

That prompted front-page stories across the country about the "Rulers of the Underworld." Accompanying the stories were large photos of each man. It was like a lineup.

After fifteen months of hearings, Kefauver took his own victory lap. He crowed, "We have a cleaner America as a result."

To critics who accused him of grandstanding, he replied, "We didn't expose anyone who didn't deserve to be exposed."

The hearings had been bad for business. Lansky was bleeding money. He tried to regroup by opening up a new resort in a part of Florida he thought had real potential: the Florida Keys. He filed the paperwork for Plantation Yacht Harbor in Key Largo with Mike Spinella, who had recently been deported to Italy. Seymour Eisen, who was Lansky's bookkeeper in Saratoga, was listed as vice president.

Journalist Hank Messick opined that Lansky opened the place to provide a hideout for gangsters avoiding subpoenas from the Kefauver Committee. In fact, the Kefauver probe was winding down when Lansky bought the resort. His purchase was a legitimate one, fully declared. The real reason he bought it was that he hoped it would provide financial security and stability for Buddy. His oldest son enjoyed women and gambling too much. Lansky sent him to the Plantation in the hopes of straightening out his life. In a postcard later to Paul, he called it "one of your brother's enterprises."

In April 1951, he got a bit of good news. Congressman Arthur G. Klein, a friend of Costello's through Tammany Hall, had selected Paul as one of his appointees for West Point. It was a prestigious appointment. Paul immediately wrote him a thank-you note. Klein responded by writing that he was the only one of his forty appointees to do that.

Their correspondence continued over the years, and Klein seemed genuinely impressed by Paul, writing:

You really are a most unusual boy. Most of the boys that I have appointed to either the Military or Naval academies have forgotten all about me after they have sent that first letter of thanks, which I believe is somewhat mandatory. It is a credit to your family and to your upbringing that you go to the trouble to write now and then . . .

While it was true that Klein and Costello were on friendly terms, that connection wasn't what got Paul into West Point. He had been determined to get the prestigious appointment on his own merits, and he did. After attending the Horace Mann School, Paul spent a year at the Sullivan School, a prep school in Washington, DC, that specialized in placing grads on service academies like West Point. Unlike his brother and sister, who did not graduate from high school, he graduated with top grades and good references. His acceptance into West Point was a dream come true.

As thrilling as it was for the Lansky family, it caused a stir in political circles when it became known. One congressman griped that the son of a notorious mobster used political connections to get into the distinguished military academy. Lansky was furious. He called Kefauver and demanded an apology.

He got one. Kefauver, the man who had doggedly pursued Lansky for the better part of fifteen months, wrote a letter to Klein's office, in which he said in part:

The fact that Arthur appointed Lansky's son to West Point came out in executive testimony in New York, but I felt, as you do, that a boy like this should be given a break if he is entitled to it. Everything I heard about the boy was good and I didn't release the testimony to the press. I thought it very unfortunate that Dick Moser brought up the questions and if I had been there, I would have interrupted before it came out. I am very, very sorry and I think it affected vey adversely our . . . Committee hearings. Chaps like this who have had a poor opportunity should, of course, be given every break and I know that is what Arthur was trying to do. The Lansky boy has justified the confidence which was placed in him.

It was a small but meaningful victory for Lansky after months of setbacks thanks in large part to the Kefauver Committee hearings. Kefauver, buoyed by the intense public interest and his personal acclaim (*TIME* magazine made him Man of the Year), tried to extend the committee hearings. He had limited success. His congressional colleagues clearly felt he had hogged the spotlight long enough. Finally, the hearings wound down.

That did not mean, however, that there would be any letup in the scrutiny on Lansky and his friends. The committee's attacks on Dewey had infuriated the New York governor. After all, he was the reform-minded prosecutor who had gone after the biggest boss of them all—Lucky Luciano—and had done so at grave personal risk. Dewey could not let the political attacks on him go answered.

In June 1951, he quietly convened a Grand Jury of an Extraordinary and Special Trial Term of the Supreme Court in Ballston Spa, New York, next door to Saratoga Springs.

Its mission was to investigate organized crime in Saratoga Springs. It was, indeed, extraordinary.

CHAPTER 12

Saratoga Implodes

In 1951, Saratoga Springs was a small town, with a little more than 15,000 residents. To be sure, some of those residents—like the Whitneys, the Vanderbilts, and the Guggenheims—were spectacularly well-heeled. Money was the town lubricant. Saratoga Springs residents liked their horses, their mineral springs, and their gambling. It was everywhere. It wasn't just in the lake house casinos; it was in barbershops, newsstands, and bars. Everybody knew the gambling was illegal, but no one was inclined to put a stop to it. There was just too much money to be had for everyone.

Dewey's special grand jury was not so inclined. There was, according to prosecutor Paul W. Williams, a conspiracy so vast and overriding in Saratoga that it was clear that "the forces of organized crime [are] allied with and protected by persons holding high public office and wielding political power."

More than $250,000—or more than $4 million today—was paid each year in "tribute" to politicians. Virtually everyone was on the take, from bankers to casino workers to sheriff's deputies.

Williams approached the case in a classic prosecutorial fashion: He started at the bottom and moved his way up. He described his method as moving up the rungs of a ladder. First, there were members of the public, "who constitute the lowest rung of the ladder." Then, investigators moved on to the second rung—"crap dealers, stick men, box men, ladder men, black board men, and other gambling personnel." The third rung consisted of gamblers. At the top rung were the prosecutor's prize: public officials.

The idea was to get the people in the lower rung to turn on people in the next-highest rung, and they did.

Over the course of forty-four months, or nearly four years from June 1951 until January 1955, the twenty-three grand jurors took testimony from 810 witnesses. Old friends testified against one another. Sheriffs resigned under pressure. Both Republican and Democratic party leaders found themselves charged with crimes. Witnesses went missing. One man committed suicide. It was gut-wrenching for many Saratogians. They literally turned on one another to save themselves.

Unlike the Kefauver investigation, the Dewey grand jury wasn't a traveling road show. As such, it didn't generate the steady flow of nationwide headlines and TV newsreels that the Kefauver Committee did. But in the end, it arguably had a greater impact in terms of actual cases that were made. The grand jury laid out the collusion among mobsters, law enforcement, and the Saratoga political machine. By the time it concluded, it had indicted forty-nine people. Of those, forty-one were convicted of crimes.

Given how widespread the tentacles of corruption were in Saratoga Springs, Dewey couldn't be sure he could trust any local judge to oversee the case. He appointed Judge Leo Hagerty. As Erie County District Attorney, Hagerty had prosecuted a Mob underboss three times. The man finally left town and moved to Ohio, remarking that he'd stay away from New York as long as Hagerty was district attorney. That was just about the best job reference Hagerty could have gotten in Dewey's eyes. He needed someone who would not be intimidated.

Lansky watched the Dewey grand jury developments warily. He knew that his Saratoga clubs were the next law enforcement target, but he was still reeling from the damage the Kefauver Committee had done to his clubs in Florida. After closing the Colonial Inn, he also had to shut down his Greenacres and La Boheme clubs in Hallandale. He needed to drum up new business.

In October 1951, Lansky had dinner with Willie Moretti, by now a Genovese family underboss. Moretti, dapper and garrulous, was also Sinatra's godfather. When Sinatra was a young singer and wanted to get out of his contract with bandleader Tommy Dorsey, it was Moretti who facilitated it. He didn't waste time with wordy negotiations. He got to the point. He shoved a gun down Dorsey's throat. Dorsey released Sinatra from the contract.

Moretti had made a splash when he testified before the Kefauver Committee. Instead of taking the Fifth, as many of the other mobsters did, Moretti parried the senators' questions with jokes and occasional tidbits of information. His wisecracks prompted laughter in the audience, and he loved it. Apparently, Moretti was a ham.

Lansky and Moretti met at Dinty Moore's, one of Lansky's favorite restaurants in the heart of the Broadway theater district in Manhattan. It was a glamorous place, with gold-plated faucets in the restrooms. It attracted a celebrity clientele, though the owners took care to treat them with discretion. Sandra Lansky loved the place, and her father often brought her with him to meetings there. He brought her along for this one.

That particular evening, Moretti was in the mood to reminisce. He recalled the Atlantic City convention, where Lansky and Luciano had effectively organized warring gangsters into the National Crime Syndicate. Moretti turned to Sandra, who was all of fourteen years old, and joked, "He took your beautiful mother on her honeymoon with Dutch Schultz. Is that any way to treat a lady?"

Pleased with himself, he turned back to Lansky and said, "Meyer, Meyer, where is the romance?"

Lansky, clearly uncomfortable, didn't see the humor in the joke. He, like many of his friends, had seen Moretti's performance at the Kefauver hearings. "Willie, you talk too much," he snapped. Then he asked for the check. He and Sandra left.

The next day, while Sandra was in school, she noticed a janitor reading the newspaper. She happened to glance at the headline. It stopped her in her tracks.

"Dead! Mob Boss Exterminated in N.J." Right below the headline there was a photo of a man on the tile floor of a bar with a pool of blood around his head. It was Moretti. Sandra ran to the bathroom and threw up.

As was typical in the Lansky household, they never talked about it.

Moretti was rumored to have syphilis, and there were concerns among those close to him about his mental state. Clearly, though, Lansky had been right. Moretti talked too much.

By the following March, Lansky finally caught a break. Cuban strongman Fulgencio Batista, his old friend, returned to power in his country. He asked Lansky to serve as his gambling advisor. He wanted him to add "a touch of class" to Cuba's casinos.

Lansky was all in. After the Kefauver hearings that wreaked disaster on his businesses and his friends, he was fed up with politicians and the US government. It wasn't just their full-throated moralizing that drove him crazy, it was the fact that those very same politicians enjoyed gambling themselves and often expected deep discounts to boot. He knew he'd very likely see some of those same politicians enjoying themselves in Cuba, but at least he wouldn't have to worry about the US government prosecuting him there.

On that last point, Lansky was wrong.

In June 1952, FBI Director Hoover sent a request to the FBI's legal attaché at the US Embassy in Havana. He wanted as much information as possible on Lansky's activities in Cuba. Agents had, in fact, been keeping an eye on Lansky when he was in Cuba. The attaché complied with his request.

Still, despite the prying eyes of the FBI, Cuba was promising. Unfortunately, the Dewey grand jury was heating up, and Lansky found his attentions increasingly pulled there. On August 6, 1952, Costello appeared before the grand jury in Ballston Spa in the heart of Saratoga County, New York. So did his dentist, Dr. Charles Singer, who had been listed as president of the Arrowhead Club from 1936 to 1946. Costello said little and left almost immediately after he appeared, but it was enough to spur newspaper headlines and photos.

It was exactly the kind of attention Lansky didn't want. Under New York law, grand juries are supposed to operate in secret. With this one, however, leaks kept finding their way to the newspapers.

A couple weeks after Costello's appearance, newspapers reported that it had expanded its investigation to the Piping Rock, Lansky's other club with Costello. By September 3, Frank S. Hathorn, the Saratoga County sheriff who had resigned under pressure the previous year, testified before the grand jury about both the Arrowhead and Piping Rock. His testimony was important, as he was the first one to link Lansky to illegal activities. He testified that Lansky and the other casino owners paid local lawmen to deliver cash to the bank.

As he followed the Saratoga news, Lansky knew exactly where this was headed. He discussed developments with Polakoff and decided to also hire a local Saratoga Springs attorney, Eugene Lynch.

The grand jury indicted Lansky on September 10, 1952. He was charged with twenty-one counts of conspiracy, gambling, and forgery. The forgery charge resulted from the allegation that he obtained two forged signatures in order to get a summer liquor licenses for the Arrowhead. Lansky, of course, was the most prominent of all the defendants. His name was always listed first in the court documents. Although the charges against him were relatively minor, the presence of his name added cachet and importance to the investigation. His name alone elevated it from an investigation into small-town corruption to something much bigger—national organized crime. Newspapers across the country carried the story.

New York State Police arrested Lansky that same day. Accompanied by Polakoff, he pled not guilty and posted $10,000 bail. News photographers had been tipped to be there to capture the moment, and they did. The next day, Page 1 photos ran of Lansky, dressed in an expensive gray-green suit, and Polakoff, looking every inch the prosperous attorney that he was, walking out of the courthouse.

Lansky, in trying to minimize the publicity, turned himself in quietly. Unfortunately, the same was not true of his codefendants. Five of his six codefendants failed to show. That prompted a nationwide alert for the men and, of course, more headlines.

The details of the indictment came out in the press. Indictments are typically terse documents, listing criminal charges and a few basic facts. This one, however, ran fifty-two pages. Indicted with Lansky were Joseph "Doc" Stacher, Herman Weiner, George Brown, Charles Maloney, John "Okay" Coakley, and James "Piggy" Lynch. The main reason for the length of the indictment was the detailed narrative that prosecutors planned to use to make their case. A few gambling charges weren't enough to enrage the citizenry. They needed to lay out what they considered to be the conspiracy.

The indictment explained how the clubs operated. The restaurants and entertainment were part of the conspiracy: "The restaurant should be operated on a lavish and extravagant scale and provide food of choice quality and of greatest delicacy, should entertain its guests with performances by stage and screen celebrities of national reputation and with widely popular dance orchestras."

The restaurant and entertainment with it were operated for one reason only: "solely to attract clientele to the casino, but it should be pretended and represented that the ownership and operation of the restaurant were separate from the ownership and operation of the casino."

Using good food and high-end entertainers to attract customers was hardly a crime; in fact, it was a pretty good business model. But in the indictment, it was a conspiracy. Worse, in the case of the Arrowhead, it alleged that the club's owners established an account in a phony name in a local bank and created a dummy corporation "to provide a cloak of respectability."

Williams alleged that Republican leader James A. Leary controlled Saratoga National Bank, which "departed from regular and ordinary bank practices to . . . a startling degree."

Beginning Monday, August 4, 1947

The Newly Decorated **Arrowhead Inn** Saratoga's Smartest Rendezvous

Presents

A George Hale Production

STARRING

Carmen Miranda

Maurice and Maryea

Maureen Cannon

Myros

Nina Novak

The Harry Conover Cover Girls

Leo Reisman and His Orchestra

Frank Marti and His Latin-American Orchestra

ARROWHEAD WILL CONTINUE TO PRESENT THE LEADING STARS OF RADIO, STAGE AND SCREEN

ARROWHEAD IS AIR-CONDITIONED

RESERVATIONS SARATOGA 3000 "BONARDI"

Carmen Miranda, one of the Arrowhead Inn's high-end entertainers, provided Lansky's operations with "a cloak of respectability." *Saratoga Room, Saratoga Public Library.*

The problem, however, was that Leary's name wasn't on any bank paperwork. The person holding the controlling shares of stock was Herbert C. Stone. That was odd because the bank employees apparently had no idea who Stone was: "Upon being questioned as to who Stone was, the personnel of the bank stated frankly that they had never met or seen Stone, had no idea who he was and for years believed him to be a nominee for the defendant Leary."

Grand jurors wanted to question Stone, who did, in fact, exist. He was a bespectacled, nervous-looking man with a receding chin. They couldn't question him because he fled. So did Arrowhead cashier George Brown. And Patrick J. Grennan, described as a "bagman," or a guy who distributed the illegal cash to politicians. And Arrowhead steward Henry Stieglitz. And Lansky's old friend, lawyer Louis Weiner.

Stacher, who was holed up in Las Vegas, fought New York's efforts to extradite him. He disappeared before one hearing, prompting authorities to launch an extensive and highly publicized search for him.

It was a circus, and the drumbeat of publicity was only making it worse for Lansky. In December 1952, US Attorney General James P. McGranery announced that he would move to cancel Lansky's naturalization. He said that he had concealed a criminal record when he became naturalized, thus nullifying his application. That was, in fact, true, because Lansky had not mentioned his youthful criminal record on his naturalization application. But it was also true that Lansky hadn't been convicted of any crimes since he had applied for naturalization thirty years earlier.

McGranery's announcement might have seemed like a stretch because the offense was so trivial compared to all the other crimes Lansky had been accused of, but it was the one that had the potential to do the most damage. Of all the law enforcement actions against him over the years, that one truly worried Lansky. He considered himself a patriot. He had, after all, helped the nation prevent sabotage of its harbors during World War II. Deportation would mean the end of his career—and his life—as he knew it.

Once again, he turned to his trusted attorney, Polakoff, for help. He filed motions to fight it. In January 1953, FBI agents interviewed him at Polakoff's Fifth Avenue office. Lansky, according to the FBI agents' notes afterward, refused to answer many questions. He did say, however, that "he never did anything illegal except maybe a little gambling, if one wanted to call that illegal."

While speaking to the agents, he couldn't help a little strategic bragging about Paul. He told them that he was a West Point cadet and that if he had not gotten into West Point, he had wanted to be an FBI agent.

If his bragging about Paul scored any points with the agents, it wasn't reflected in the memo they wrote afterward. The meeting ended inconclusively.

By the spring, Lansky had made his mind up about the Saratoga case. Polakoff had gotten the most serious forgery charges against him dismissed, so he was only facing misdemeanor charges. Polakoff was certain they would prevail at trial, but Lansky dreaded the publicity circus that would result. Even if he won acquittal, the damage from the publicity would far outweigh any win.

On May 2, 1953, Lansky appeared before Judge Hagerty in court. He was, as usual, well-dressed, but appeared "bored" to reporters. Asked his occupation, Lansky said he was an "unemployed tool and die maker." He agreed to plead guilty to five misdemeanor charges of conspiracy and common gambling. He just wanted the case to end.

What the reporters interpreted as boredom on Lansky's part was actually something very different. He was seriously ill. As usual, he didn't complain, but it would catch up to him later.

At the bench, Judge Hagerty appeared stern. What was left in the case against Lansky wasn't much, but Hagerty wasn't persuaded that it was minor, given all the problems he believed were associated with illegal gambling. As he prepared to sentence him, he told Lansky, "The court is not inclined to sympathy in your case."

Hagerty sentenced him to forty days in jail and a $2,500 fine. Lansky entered the Saratoga jail (which has since been torn down) with just two books under his arm—a Bible and a dictionary.

Lansky's first problem in jail was one that inmates complain about all the time—the food. He found it absolutely inedible. As usual, he came up with a solution. Through his Saratoga attorney, Lynch, he found an elegant rooming house on North Broadway owned by Mrs. Elizabeth Winde. Lansky paid for a woman to stay there. The woman was not Teddy, as she was staying in New York City with Sandra. The woman, whom Lynch's family assumed to be Lansky's girlfriend, brought meals freshly prepared by Mrs. Winde's cook to the jail for Lansky every day.

Gerard King, another convicted gambler, resided in the cell next to Lansky's. King liked to portray himself as a law-abiding citizen who had dabbled in a little gambling, but that wasn't entirely true. He ran Newman's Lake House, which was a profitable casino and club that also had plenty of associated illegal activity.

Like many other defendants, when the police came looking for him, King went on the run. His brother put on Gerard's coat and hat, grabbed a cigar, and took off in his Cadillac. When the police finally caught up with him, they were surprised and infuriated at the bait and switch. They decided to search King's mansion in Ballston Spa. They looked high and low but didn't find what they were looking for. They missed the huge bag of cash hidden in the grand piano. The episode became a favorite family story.

Ultimately, police caught up with King, and he landed in jail. He and Lansky were the only inmates in the jail, so they basically had the run of the place. Lansky, according to King, was an exercise fanatic. He was also a gentleman, generously sharing his rooming house meals with King. When he wasn't exercising or reading, he'd play games of arithmetic with King. He'd have King write down a column of figures and add them up in his head in seconds. Occasionally, King challenged him and told him he was wrong. Lansky would urge him to check. He did. Lansky was never wrong.

While in jail, Lansky stuck to regular routine. At 10:00 P.M., several nights a week, he would use the jail pay phone to call Buddy, who knew to be ready with *The New York Times* financial pages. Then they would go over the daily stock quotes together. Lansky liked airline and steel stocks.

In life, it's human nature to stay away from people in trouble, as if it were some kind of contagious infection. Lansky's son Paul did just the opposite. Rather than be embarrassed by his father's jail term, he remained steadfastly loyal. He assured his father that he believed in him. Touched by his son's support, he wrote him in May 1953:

Paul you are all that a Father hopes to have in a child. Your deep love and devotion you have shown me since I'm here made a deep impression in me. Also your humane and charitable deeds toward others make me proud of you. With your miserly time you get for yourself in the city, yet you always found time to visit the crippled children . . . Humane deeds are more important that heroic deeds.

The two had always been close, but Paul's loyalty when he needed it most cemented their bond.

By July, Lansky was hospitalized for a kidney infection. He was seriously ill with diabetes and kidney disease.

Though seriously ill, he told King that he was less worried about that than he was about the prospect of deportation. Despite McGranery's high-profile announcement, formal charges hadn't been filed yet. He knew, however, that they were coming.

Whether it was his debilitating illness or the fact that he was stuck in jail and unable to conduct much business, Lansky mused at times about his own mortality. He told King that it was his dream to be buried in Israel.

Lansky got out of jail early. Afterward, he stopped by Lynch's house. When he saw Lynch's nine-year-old son, he reached into his pocket and tossed a bunch of coins at him, saying, "Here you go, kid."

That was Lansky, always throwing money at people.

Years later, a story circulated around Saratoga Springs about Lansky's final drive to the airport out of town. He purportedly threw a wad of cash over the seat at the driver and promised him one favor. The story had just the right amount of gangster cachet and a touch of mystery.

Sadly, that story isn't true. But it was a measure of Lansky's impact on Saratoga that residents are still telling stories about him today.

CHAPTER 13
"Reformers" Join the Fight

AFTER A THOROUGHLY unpleasant time in Saratoga, Lansky was happy to get out of there. He went back to Florida, which felt like a refuge. He loved living near the ocean, far away from the harsh New York winters. It was easy to conduct business there, particularly as he started to line up plans for Cuba. He was proud of his Florida clubs. They had a certain cachet. Respectable people, like Joseph Kennedy and Secretary of Defense James V. Forrestal, had been regular customers.

Many Floridians loved him as much as he loved Florida (even if they didn't always admit it publicly). He'd pay good prices for the lettuce and beef he needed for restaurants. He made sure to hire locals. He always donated to local causes, and he did so generously. He wanted people who worked with him to prosper, because he believed that would bring everyone up.

But after the Kefauver hearings, the stage was set for more reformers to claim a piece of the spotlight. There is nothing more intoxicating to a politician than to lead the charge for reform. It's particularly appealing when the target of reform has already sustained a few attacks. Although Lansky served only a couple of months in jail in Saratoga, the nationwide publicity greatly damaged him. Reformers smelled blood.

In May 1953, it was the Miami Crime Commission's turn. It had provided key evidence to the Kefauver Committee, but its contributions were eclipsed by the senators' turns as interrogators during the televised hearings. Some of the investigators justifiably felt that Kefauver had stolen their thunder. Commission Director Daniel P. Sullivan decided to make a speech to the Crime Commission of Greater Miami. The subject of his speech was none other than Lansky. He decried him as one of the top racketeers in the country.

But he didn't stop there. He railed against "a trend toward an increase in nightclubs featuring filthy shows and pervert hangouts featuring so-called female mimics. These places had become public gathering for perverts and sexual degenerates and a magnet drawing to this area of degenerates from all parts of the country."

Just how Sullivan had become familiar with such lurid details of the clubs was unclear. But the injection of moral fervor into the war against the Mob was irresistible. Authorities stepped up their attacks on Lansky and his friends.

By August 1953, the US Immigration and Naturalization Service ordered Lansky's friend Joe Adonis deported. By September, the Internal Revenue Service filed a $248,791.51 tax lien on Lansky's Plantation Yacht Club in Key Largo, Florida, the place where he had installed Buddy in an effort to straighten out his life. And in December, officials working on the denaturalization proceedings against Lansky turned up the pressure.

He submitted to questions from Assistant US Attorney Robert W. Sweet at Polakoff's office. He kept his answers brief. As always, he was polite. The stakes were impossibly high, and he knew it.

It seemed as if everything he touched was being called into question. In January 1954, even one of his proudest achievements—helping the US government fight sabotage of New York Harbor at the dawn of World War II—was called into question. After a US government report revealed the role of mobsters like Lansky and Luciano in covertly protecting the nation's harbors, a political firestorm erupted. Anti-corruption crusaders railed at getting in bed with mobsters, especially for the war effort. The revelation was so controversial that New York Senator Herbert H. Lehman, who had been governor from 1939 to 1942, had to publicly deny that he ever gave mobsters permission to visit Luciano while he was in prison.

Perhaps it was fitting, then, that the Piping Rock, Lansky's highly successful club in Saratoga, burned down in August 1954. The club was uninsured. Investigators determined that the fire was caused by arson. No one was arrested, but stories circulated around town that a "Mob guy" nicknamed "Harry the Torch" set the fire.

Preoccupied with his collapsing businesses and the onslaught from government officials, Lansky paid little attention to his family. Anna had always been the one to care for the children, but after the divorce, her mental illness had only worsened. Teddy took on the role of stepmother, but she was miserable at it. The children despised her, and although she tried to pretend otherwise, she didn't like them much either.

In Lansky's view, Buddy and Paul were sons and were okay on their own. Buddy might have been disabled, but he was smart and charming and had no problem ingratiating himself with people. Sandra was the one he worried about the most. He often importuned Paul to keep an eye on her and to encourage her to try harder in school. As much as Paul wanted to please his father, he felt little affection for Sandra. Paul saw his sister as a spoiled child obsessed with material things.

On that point, he was right. For years, Sandra had been given whatever expensive toy she wanted whenever she wanted it. Since her parents' divorce, she had been largely unsupervised, and she took full advantage of that. As a teenager, Sandra often sneaked out to clubs. Without Anna to keep an eye on her, she ran wild. With the money and freedom to do whatever she wanted, Sandra thought she was much more worldly than she really was. But thanks to who she was, she was quietly protected by her father's underworld friends.

When she was sixteen years old, she met a dashing older man, Marvin Rapoport, at a horse show at Madison Square Garden. He was handsome and charming and seemed thoroughly smitten with her. Anna, roused from the seclusion of her apartment, didn't like him. They had met years earlier, when Sandra was a little girl. Now years later, Anna was suspicious of Rapoport's motives.

Sandra, however, was convinced that this was true love. Before long, Rapoport proposed, and she said yes. Buddy, who had always been closer to Sandra than Paul was, tried to talk her out of it because she was so young, but he didn't make any headway. She was adamant. Given the choice of being stuck in an apartment with a stepmother she despised or married life with a glamorous man who seemed to adore her, she knew what she wanted. She wanted Marvin.

Lansky hated the idea. He wanted her to finish high school before even thinking of marriage. He sat Sandra down, and they had a serious talk. By the end of it, he was sure that they had an understanding: She could get married after finishing high school.

Sandra, however, emerged from their talk with a completely different understanding. She crowed to Buddy that her father had given her permission to get married immediately.

Before the misunderstanding could turn into a familial battle, Rapoport's family intervened. His mother was worried about her darling son and wanted nothing more than to see him get married. He was flamboyant and far too interested in feminine pursuits. He loved picking out Sandra's dresses and supervising her hair appointments. His mother lobbied for her son and Sandra to get married immediately. She was convinced that a marriage would straighten out her son and be good for Sandra as well.

Lansky gave in. He really didn't know what to do with Sandra anymore. At the very least, there would be someone to take care of his daughter. Other family members were not so sure, however.

Lansky talked daily to his brother-in-law, Julie Citron. Often, Citron's wife, Ruthie, answered the phone. Whenever Lansky called, she'd turn to her husband and say, "Julie, Jesus Christ is on the phone."

Lansky always laughed.

When news of the impending nuptials got around the family, Ruthie was aghast. She said to Lansky, "You're letting your daughter marry a fag?"

Lansky just shrugged and replied, "Ruthie, what do you expect me to do?"

Lansky, a man authorities called one of the most powerful and feared mobsters in the country, felt so powerless in dealing with his family that he threw up his hands and allowed his spoiled teenage daughter to marry a man he knew was wrong for her.

The two married and rushed off to an expensive European honeymoon, paid for, of course, by Lansky. As much as Sandra loved shopping, Rapoport loved it even more. Before long, he was paying more attention to his expensive purchases than he was to Sandra. She quickly became disenchanted with her husband but didn't feel she could tell anyone because she had been so insistent on getting married. The last thing she wanted to do was admit she had been wrong.

Paul was the one bright spot in the family for Lansky. He was inordinately proud of Paul's admission to West Point. He visited him there twice a month. Like Paul, he loved the discipline and order of the stately campus located about fifty miles north of New York City in West Point, New York. Anna did not go on these visits. Whether it was her illness or Paul's resentment at what he viewed as her showiness, the estrangement between Paul and his mother never fully healed.

Not surprisingly, Paul excelled at West Point. Unlike his siblings, he never tried to get by on his last name, not that it would have helped him there. If anything, he was determined to work harder in order to prove that he had done it on his own. His father was thrilled. As Commencement Day approached, Lansky made preparations to attend the ceremony with his family.

There was a complication, however.

For the commencement speech, West Point brass reached out to no less than President Dwight Eisenhower, a West Point graduate himself. Eisenhower was wildly popular, and his West Point connection made him the perfect choice for the speech that year. Eisenhower's political operatives, however, did not want the president anywhere near an event that would be attended by a notorious mobster. They adamantly opposed the idea.

There were discussions. In the end, Eisenhower declined to give the commencement speech at West Point that year. He agreed to give it the following year.

On the eve of Paul's commencement, the cadets' commandant went to Paul's room. That was an extraordinarily rare occurrence. He turned to Paul and said, "Cadet Lansky, you were one of us when you started four years ago, and you will be one of us when you graduate."

It was a show of support to a young man who had done everything he could to earn it. Paul never forgot it.

Although Paul rarely spoke to friends about his father, it was clear to them that there was a deep bond between the two of them. Lansky came to the graduation ceremony with Sandra and Teddy. It was a weeklong celebration with military pomp and pageantry, and Lansky loved it. Again, Anna did not come.

Afterward, Paul gave his father his graduation ring. Lansky treasured the gift.

Immediately after graduating, Paul commissioned with the US Air Force. He attended fixed-wing training in Georgia and Texas and got his wings.

Paul's success was a much-needed boost for Lansky. The pressure from authorities wasn't letting up. His businesses in Florida were already in a shambles. Now they were turning their attention to Las Vegas. FBI agents made it clear that they were looking into his interests in the Thunderbird and Sands Hotels in Las Vegas.

Lansky's Las Vegas properties were of particular interest to the FBI director. Hoover's own gambling was usually confined to bets on horse races—aided by inside tips from Costello—and there's little evidence that he gambled in Las Vegas. But Las Vegas had something other investigations did not—the involvement of a high-ranking elected official. Hoover kept copious investigative files on elected officials of all stripes at all levels of government. He did not release them publicly but made sure the targets became aware of them. Sometimes, it was an oblique comment directly to the person. Other times, it was through a well-timed leak of sensitive information to a prominent columnist like Walter Winchell. Hoover understood very well how to wield his power strategically to ensure that he stayed in the job he loved.

The elected official in question was Nevada Lieutenant Governor Cliff Jones. FBI agents in Las Vegas reported to Hoover that Lansky and his brother, Jake, were not the only ones with a piece of both the Thunderbird and Sands. Jones had a piece, too. Later, he would also get a piece of casinos in Cuba.

As much as Hoover might have wanted to keep that information to himself for his own purposes, word leaked to journalists at the *Las Vegas Sun*. They dug in. In October 1954, the newspaper published a series of investigative articles about corruption in the gaming industry. Given the risk of retaliatory violence in a wide-open city like Las Vegas, it was a courageous move. The stories quoted liberally from surreptitiously taped conversations—including one in which Jones claimed to have "a fix" in with another Las Vegas newspaper. Whatever protection he thought that afforded him was not enough. The effect of the series was devastating. Jones's political career ended. He resigned as a national committeeman.

The Nevada State Tax Commission had to take action. In October 1954, it opened a yearlong audit into the Lansky brothers' stake in the Thunderbird.

The irony for Lansky was that he hated Las Vegas. He couldn't stand the desert heat. Jake lived and worked there, but Lansky stayed away. He managed from a distance. He made sure that the casinos stayed on budget. He ensured quality control by giving a commission to the dealers at the end of each shift. If things ran well and honestly, they got the commission.

He also managed the skim. The basic skim involved taking cash out of the counting room every night before the count was completed. If the cash wasn't counted, it couldn't be taxed as income. It was the easiest way to pay off interested parties.

The slot machines required a system of their own. According to the FBI, an insider would deliberately misread the coin-weighing devices to give a lower count. Afterward, he would transfer the excess coins to a floor box, where the coins would be exchanged for bills. Then the cash would be removed from the casino.

Cash, however, can be bulky. And as the Las Vegas casinos became more successful, that basic skim wasn't practical, because there was too much money coming in. That's why they started the system of comping people. Investors who had hidden interests in casinos much preferred coming in person and being comped. They would get free rooms, meals, drinks, and private entertainment. They gambled on credit up to the amount of their share in the casino. It didn't cost them a thing. At the end of the junket, they would cash in their chips and leave. It was free money.

If an investor didn't want to gamble himself, he might organize a little junket of his own to Las Vegas. That way, he could impress his fellow travelers with his largesse. The gamblers in his group would, in turn, pay their debts directly to him. Their IOUs were never entered into the books. There was no count, no paper trail. Again, free money.

Sometimes, to attract a big-name entertainer, they had to throw in a free gambling credit. Or they might give a really big-name entertainer, like Sinatra, points in a casino.

There were infinite permutations of the skim. It was a complicated system, one that required a mind like a calculator to track. Lansky had that, and his friends knew it. They also knew that he wouldn't cheat them. He always made sure to spread plenty of money around. Lansky's friend, Doc Stacher, later told Israeli journalists that about 20 percent of the casino profit was skimmed and not taxed.

Authorities were fascinated by the skim. By the end of the audit, they were convinced that Lansky had illegally skimmed millions of dollars. The Nevada Gaming Commission determined that he had a hidden interest in the Thunderbird Hotel through his brother. That was enough for them to put Lansky's name on a list of eleven notorious mobsters who were not allowed to have a gambling license in Nevada. The mere presence of any of those men anywhere near a casino could mean revocation of a license.

It was an ominous development. Jimmy Alo turned to Lansky and said, "We gotta get out."

They did.

That didn't mean he was gone from Las Vegas. He still had many friends there. After Paul visited the city with a friend in July 1955, he received a letter from Lansky's old friend, Dalitz, telling him: "The purpose of this letter is to tell you that the facilities of the DESERT INN are available to you and your friends at all times, and that should you get a vacation or a spell of leave, we earnestly request you to be our guest."

He also mentioned Paul's father: "I spoke to your Dad on the phone the other day, and informed him that you had visited us. I am about to fly to Havana on Monday, so that I can meet him Tuesday."

Dalitz was planning to invest in Lansky's next venture in Cuba. Batista was back in power, and the potential for making big money was there. As Lansky later told a friend, "I couldn't get that little island out of my mind."

The denaturalization proceedings were still hanging over his head, but Lansky got a bit of good news about them in April 1955. The US Supreme Court ruled favorably for Costello in his deportation case. That meant it would be much harder to pursue the case against Lansky. The US Attorney's Office in the Southern District recommended that the denaturalization proceedings against him be dismissed.

That wasn't the end of the case, however. It would not be formally dismissed for several more years. But the US Attorney's recommendation all but ensured that Lansky was no longer in danger of being deported.

That was a setback for the government, but law enforcement didn't give up. FBI agents started investigating Lansky's ties to the garment industry in New York. They noted that Vito Genovese, a feared mobster who would rise to run the Genovese crime family—his namesake—oversaw "the Italian element" of the garment industry. Lansky oversaw the Jews. He and Genovese decided which vendors dealt with which manufacturers, ensuring they got a cut in the process.

The garment industry was a highly insular world, with ethnic ties that rivaled those on the New York waterfront. Agents were never able to penetrate it enough to make a case. Lansky's friends in the garment business were loyal, and he stayed friends with them throughout his life.

After the break in the denaturalization case, Lansky set about tying up loose ends. He paid off his tax liens. Then he set his sights on Cuba.

Things would be entirely different on the island nation. It was one thing to manage someone else's operation, which he had done again and again.

This time, he wanted to build his own place from the ground up.

CHAPTER 14

The Triumphant Return to Cuba

IN THE MID-1950s, Havana was an international destination for people who wanted a good time. Its Caribbean climate and culture, smooth rum, and beautiful and accommodating women made it irresistible to tourists. Airline travel was coming into its own, and Cuba was just a quick plane ride away from Miami. Batista knew that Cuba was poised to cash in on foreign money, but to do it, he needed to clean up the gambling. For that, he needed Lansky.

He asked him to come back.

Cuban casinos were notoriously corrupt. They were full of loaded dice, rigged roulette wheels, and shady dealers skilled at cajoling suckers into losing money. Many gamblers just didn't see the point of spending their money there. For Batista, that was disastrous. There was just too much money to be made if things were run properly. He named Lansky the country's "gambling reform" advisor.

It was an astute move. Lansky, of course, made sure that Batista was well-compensated with suitcases of cash. But for Batista, it was more than the cash. He might have been corrupt, but he also cared deeply about Cuba. He was convinced that an influx of foreign investment would provide jobs to Cubans and lift many out of poverty. The only way to ensure that was to persuade foreigners that they wouldn't be cheated.

Lansky and Batista understood each other. Money eased their communication, of course, but it was more than that. Each man had a vision, and each one knew that the other man was essential to his vision. Batista wanted to bring Cuba into the modern age. Lansky wanted to build his own hotel.

Lansky immediately got to work on cleaning up the casinos. He paid to have his dealers specially trained so that they could handle everything from craps to roulette, a particular Cuban favorite. Inside the casinos, he placed a few trusted dealers on ladders to watch for any cheating. He paid them commissions so that they made more money if they ran a clean game. He also banned Cuban prostitutes from the casinos because he knew Cuban men did not want foreigners abusing their women.

He knew it was critical to instill a sense of pride in his employees. He insisted on a dress code. Dealers had to wear tuxedoes. Just as he had in his earlier casinos, he required male customers to wear a jacket and tie and women to wear cocktail dresses or more formal wear. He knew it would create a classy atmosphere. People would be more inclined to spend money if they dressed like money.

Luis Castaneda started working there when he was nineteen years old. His educated parents—his mother was a teacher and his father was an engineer—were disappointed in his career choice. But he was drawn by the good pay and the glamour. Tall, slim, and handsome, he fit in perfectly. Castaneda was also bilingual—a special asset. He worked at the Hotel Nacional and became so adept at dealing 21 that crowds gathered just to watch him.

Lansky liked him. They often chatted in the Nacional's cafeteria, where Lansky read the English-language *Havana Post* every morning. He called the *Post* his Bible because it had the stock tables, which he followed assiduously. Then Lansky would stroll through the casino checking operations. Castaneda was well aware of his boss's reputation, but he found him to be down-to-earth and a gentleman. They often bantered with one another.

One night, the dealers were bored because there weren't many guests. To amuse themselves, they staged races in the casino. When their manager discovered what they were doing, he angrily berated them. Lansky walked by and simply smirked. As intolerant as he was of cheating, he didn't mind his guys having a little fun.

"He was good to people he could trust," Castaneda said.

And as he had in other places where he ran casinos, Lansky donated money to charities. He built two Jewish schools in Havana. Word spread quickly that he was a soft touch for Jewish causes and charities benefiting children.

As always, Lansky's brother, Jack, and their friends joined him at the Nacional. Some were partners, like Santo Trafficante Jr. Lansky liked Trafficante. He was low-key and well-read. He knew how to keep things quiet. Jack was skilled at running the day-to-day operation, and Lansky was skilled at making sure the investors got their piece.

Anyone wanting to open a casino did what everyone else did to get permission—they went to Lansky. "He handled all the okays for Batista," recalled casino operator Tex McCrary.

Before long, it caught on that any Mafia-connected casino was likely to run honest games. Gamblers showed up in droves.

That did not make everyone happy. One night, a US Embassy official entered the casino and asked about Lansky. He asked Castaneda if he knew him. Castaneda said he did, but offered nothing else. The official had similar conversations with the other employees. He got nowhere. They were loyal. It wasn't just the good pay. Lansky treated them with respect.

FBI records confirm that the US Embassy's legal attaché regularly sent information about Lansky but couldn't establish that he was committing any crimes. For Lansky, being in Cuba was a great relief. He loved the climate, the people, and the distance from the United States. He knew that US authorities were watching him, but it was a far different kind of pressure than he experienced in the States.

Batista, at Lansky's suggestion, pushed through a new hotel law in 1955 to encourage hotel construction. The law granted tax exemptions to new hotels and similar tourist establishments. It allowed any new hotel with a more than $1 million investment and a nightclub to apply for a casino license without any background checks. The law also allowed for government loans to projects the government deemed worthy. Lansky used the law—and government funds—to open casinos and funnel money to Batista's family.

It was the perfect setup. He wanted his business concerns kept quiet, and he didn't want his people investigated. Lansky finally could realize his dream of building his own hotel. By the spring of 1956, he started work on the Hotel Riviera. It would be his personal masterpiece, unlike anything else ever built in Havana.

He hired Irving Feldman as his builder. Feldman had overseen a number of large hotel projects in Miami. Lansky gave him a simple directive: nothing but the best. Lansky weighed in on every design decision.

They set the building on the beach, but at an angle, for greater visual impact. Visitors approaching the hotel immediately knew they were arriving somewhere different. It was sleek and modern, but with nods to Cuban heritage with touches like the turquoise mosaics.

For the interior design, Lansky chose Albert Parvin, who had supplied furnishings to Las Vegas hotels and casinos. Lansky then hired his architects, Philip Johnson, who had helped design the Seagram Building in New York, and a Cuban architect, Manuel Jose Carreral. As always, he knew to hire locals. Carrera introduced him to sculptor Florencio Gelabert, who was known for his modernist sculptures evoking Cuban marine life. Gelabert found Lansky to be reserved and kind.

During this time, Lansky frequently wrote to Paul about the challenges of construction. He was eager to impart some wisdom to his son, and Paul, an engineer, was eager to receive it. One important piece of advice: "You never want to build something when you don't own the land underneath it."

It was clear that he was hoping to bring Paul into his business. In February 1956, he told Paul about a deal he was putting together for another hotel:

> *I will get stock for my efforts in putting the deal together. This should be a lucrative deal for me. The land has been purchased, this morning, I met with the architect. His height is 4′11′ . . . (He is dean of Harvard architectural school. Just think of all the brains in so little a body.)*

Although he never evinced any embarrassment about his own short stature, he simply couldn't resist poking fun at a man even shorter than him.

He then moved on to what he called "our personal problems." He and Sandra had been arguing over money:

> *Sandra has written me a letter of apology and she and Marvin are returning Monday. I have teed off on them pretty good and I'm not through yet, the rest will come Tuesday. I let him know that I don't intend to buy a son-in-law, either he comes down to his size or let him go his own way.*

Although Paul was one of the few people he could confide in about his worries for his family, he much preferred talking about business. On March 7, 1956, he wrote about planning for the Riviera:

> *Johnson will be our architect, he is very well thought of at present he is doing the Seagram building on Park Ave. 40 stories $3.5 million complete cost. He loves our* [site] *and expects to make it the most beautiful hotel today.*

Architects are dreamers. They may make something most beautiful but at what price glory. We want something and make money for us not a monument. We know how to protect ourselves against that matter.

He continued: "Are you following up on your correspondent course in accountancy? I wish you would also practice Spanish if you intend to enter in our business. This is not a bad place to live."

He was writing to Paul from the St. Moritz Hotel, where he usually stayed while in New York. The St. Moritz had a European charm Lansky loved and was designed by the same architect, Emery Roth, who designed the Beresford, the apartment building he had settled in with his young family. It was a place where people of note, like Lansky, could stay and have their privacy ensured.

Given the setting, it's not surprising that Lansky's thoughts turned to his family. He was worried about Anna. He wrote Paul:

I hope I didn't alarm you about your Mother. She isn't worse mentally, it is just her lack of vitamins that caused this condition but if she goes on the same way she will detiorate [sp] *to a danger point. I spoke to the Doctor yesterday and I have to talk to him again today, we will decide today whether to call on you or not. You will hear from me as soon as I get something definite.*

Buddy should be the one to carry the ball in this matter but he is useless all he is good for is his big love.

"His big love" was Buddy's girlfriend. He had met Annette, a hostess at the Rascal House Restaurant in North Miami Beach. She was twenty-six years old, twice divorced, and had a young son. She figured that she and Buddy could take care of each other. Lansky was ambivalent about her. At times, he called her "a good girl." Other times, he thought she was a gold digger.

Still, he was mainly worried about his ex-wife. A few days later, he again wrote to Paul: "I'm trying hard to find a doctor who would be patient enough to convince her to take her treatments willingly, whether I'm successful remains to be seen."

He updated Paul on his travel plans and then added: "Business is good for Buddy and Marvin. For materialistic people that is all that is necessary. How are things with you? That is more important to me than anything else."

For a man famed for making money, he was offended by materialism. A week later, he wrote that he was still trying to do his best for Anna:

> *Speaking of your Mother, I will do my best but unfortunately, we can't get the proper cooperation from Sandra or your Brother. With him I'm discusted* [sp]. *You would think eve* [sp] *if she was a well person he would show more interest to see her. But all he can see is his love* [his girlfriend]. *He just watches the clock and runs like a baby waits for its milk. Sandra visits her often enough but lacks the ability to cope with this kind of condition. I'm trying hard to get her to go to a tutoring and learn something. It would do her a lot of good. Anyhow we will keep trying. We must have faith and patience. You can write both of them and shame them diplomatically.*

Lansky never spoke of her diagnosis. Family members knew that some doctors suggested schizophrenia. What was obvious to all of them was that she had long periods of crippling depression. The warm, lively woman who doted on her children would stay alone in her darkened apartment for weeks.

Lansky felt helpless to do much about it, and Sandra, the one he hoped would help her mother, was of little use:

> *Your sister left me last nite in a huff. She received her money in the Bank which amounts to about $2,400. She has a good buy on a horse for $1,400, but she can't afford to keep the horse. If I would give her $200 a month she*

can keep the horse. Well I let her have it in no uncertain words.

I have been begging her to go to nite school that she wouldn't do. I would pay for schooling but no horses. I really don't no what goes through that mind of hers, but I know nothing solid.

Sandra was always demanding money from her father. She never had enough.

Meanwhile, Lansky watched the Cuban political developments warily. He wrote Paul: "Havana had a radical flareup Sunday. I hope that doesn't affect business."

He assured Paul he was pressing ahead. Lansky traveled constantly between Cuba and New York for business. When he was in New York, he often held business meetings at the St. Moritz.

What he didn't know was that, as discreet as the hotel's owners were, the FBI had made inroads in its intelligence gathering. A "reliable source," unnamed in the FBI file, provided information about a meeting held at the hotel on May 18, 1956.

No less than thirty-five top racketeers, including Lansky, convened there. They were there to discuss Costello. The men had determined that his "usefulness as the head of the Eastern syndicate was at the end." For the time being, they decided to replace him with Lansky's trusted friend, Vincent Alo. That was an indicator of Lansky's prominence in the Mob. Everyone knew that when Alo served to pass on Lansky's orders, his word was good.

By the end of May, Lansky was back in Cuba and looking forward to breaking ground on the hotel. He wrote Paul:

I expect to get very busy here as soon as our mortgage goes through and we will not put a shovel in the ground until we get a mortgage. The only way to start a business is to have all the money on hand, not to seek it later. We should have a mortgage in a couple of weeks and then you will see one of the most beautiful constructed hotels not only in Cuba but the World.

A few weeks later, he updated his progress: "I am here to get all my privileges that I'm entitled from the signed and when we are signed we are ready to break ground. This will be a beautiful place."

In July 1956, he marveled at the significance of air-conditioning:

Air conditioning has really become a must. When you look back you wonder how the people in the tropics lived without it. Without air conditioning you didn't have thousands of visitors South and the Southerners didn't have the stamina for work that they have today. Miami and Havana are enjoying the biggest summer season in all history.

A week later, he wrote to Paul:

The weather here is hot but not bad if the bugs are not out. But, thank God for air conditioning. I'm leaving for New York Sunday and will be back here Friday. How long I will stay south I don't know yet. I hope to have the answer after our meeting in New York. This meeting will tell us whether we break ground soon or we will delay matters. The cost of building has grown so high for first class hotels that it frightens you to start building unless you get a 60% mortgage and that is hard.

In letter after letter, it was obvious how close father and son were and the pride Lansky felt about Paul's accomplishments: "It must be a great satisfaction to you to be able to conquer your challenge . . . I really envy your adventurous trips. By nature, I'm a wanderer and Alaska is one of the places I will visit before long. But first comes the business without the money you can't go very far."

Paul confided in his father about his new lady friend. Lansky wrote back in August 1956 that he and Teddy were planning a trip to see him because he and his architect needed to be in Las Vegas the following month: "If your lady friend isn't busy working, we will be happy entertaining her for you. I may spoil her a bit you know I'm an artist at that job."

Paul worried about the financial strain on his father and offered him money. Lansky thanked him, but demurred: "We are all well and not in need of anything material. All we want is good health. The rest is selfish."

By September 1956, he had more family news for Paul: Sandra and Marvin were divorcing. "Sandra is far from being all at fault here. He is far more at fault than she is," he wrote.

What he did not say was the reason for the divorce. Marvin left Sandra for a man.

A little later, he wrote Paul with more details:

> *I hope Sandra's trouble didn't shock you although it is sad. Paul, Sandra has her faults and she still has time to correct them. Her happiness depends on her own conduct and what she does with her time. I hope to get her a job in Saks.*
>
> *Marvin is definitely mixed up, he needs a doctor. I had him pegged a long time ago that he was a cutie pie. I hope that his lust for wealth doesn't crush him. Anyhow we will not let him get away with anything.*

By December, he was back to updating Paul about the Riviera:

> *The hotel is progressing very well, exceptionally fast for Cuba. We hope to have the roof on May 15 . . . After the building comes the staff. The beauty of the hotel is one*

selling point, but service is very important once you get the people in and I'm a stickler for service. I know what it takes to give service and I will have the most modern equipment you can buy to assist in giving good service . . . My aim is to go after small conventions. That is a very desirable business from a spending standpoint.

That was Lansky, always thinking business. Months later, he wrote:

A hotel of this size should be on the boards for at least one year. This means that you would have a picture of everything before you put a shovel in the ground but you will find investors aren't interested when you tell them about the great length of time so you do the next best thing.

He was far less confident about Sandra:

Sandra is really a problem . . . I'm trying to do my best to help her and I will keep trying until I see no hope. I made things very plain to her that she will be the only looser if she doesn't correct herself.

By now, Paul had married. His wife, Edna Shook, was an intelligent and beautiful blonde who had modeled in New York City. Lansky attended the wedding in Tacoma. Edna liked her new father-in-law. He had a certain presence that impressed her. But as was typical in the secretive Lansky clan, Paul told her only that his father was a successful businessman. Lansky gave them $2,200—or close to $24,000 today—as a wedding gift.

After Lansky returned to Cuba, he wrote Paul that he very much wanted to establish close ties with Edna. He asked Paul to send his wife's birthday date: "Events like that, if we remember them, will bring us closer to her. The distance keeps us strangers that is why I'm happier to telephone when your [sp] not there because I want her to know that I don't just call for you."

Before long, Lansky received thrilling news: His first grandson was born on August 4, 1957. Paul was equally thrilled. He decided to name his son Meyer Lansky II.

Lansky hated the idea. He thought it would be a terrible burden on the boy. But nobody could change Paul's mind. He wanted to honor his father. The name stayed, and Lansky accepted it.

Lansky wrote him: "Family's [sp] really make you conscious of your financial status. They lift and force your ambition to make good, and that is good for you."

Sandra continued to worry him, and he asked Paul to reach out to her:

> *I spoke to Sandra today. She is well and so is Gary but she is terribly mixed up and needs our help. She is lonesome from lack of work. She has to do something. I'm trying to be as patient as my nerves will permit me, I realize you can't put ultimatums on these problems. I may interest her to come down to Florida to us at least she will be closer to part of the family. She really needs guidance. I wish you do write her to give her some security. She feels that she is not wanted because of her conduct.*

Back in Cuba that fall, Lansky made sure to funnel money to the Mafia bosses back in the States. His generosity typically kept even the greediest guys satisfied. It wasn't enough, however, for Albert Anastasia, the feared and brutal leader of Murder, Inc. Anastasia heard the stories of all the cash coming from Cuba. He began to fume that he wasn't getting what he was due.

Anastasia traveled to Havana with one goal in mind: a bigger share of the profits for himself. His demands alarmed Lansky. He knew Anastasia would never be satisfied. Lansky had a remarkable ability to juggle the demands of many people, but Anastasia was the kind of man who not only killed people, but relished doing it. For several days, Lansky was not himself. He was edgy and distracted, according to his driver.

Anastasia returned to New York and met with Trafficante. The two men shook hands. Anastasia walked out satisfied that they had a deal.

He was wrong.

CHAPTER 15
Underworld Reckoning

ALMOST A YEAR after the Mob conclave at the St. Moritz, Frank Costello returned home to his apartment on Central Park West after a dinner with friends. A large man jumped out of a black Cadillac. He followed him into his building and shot him in the head. As Costello crumpled onto a leather couch in the apartment lobby, the man ran off into the darkness.

Costello survived. The bullet had only grazed him. When police questioned him, he professed ignorance. He hadn't seen anything. He hadn't heard anything. Police eventually arrested Vincent "Chin" Gigante, a Genovese protégé. Costello, however, refused to testify against him. The case died.

Not long after the shooting, Costello stepped aside. Genovese took over the crime family Luciano once helmed.

Such was the politics of the underworld. Lansky had been in on the high-level meeting that decided Costello's fate. He seemed to have similar inside information on Albert Anastasia. Santo Trafficante Jr., after his meeting with Anastasia, told Lansky about their meeting. Lansky listened. Then he told him to fly to Florida.

"Won't that tip off Albert?" Trafficante said.

"Don't worry about Albert," Lansky replied.

Lansky flew to New York for a few days, then went to Florida and back to Cuba. The quick trip wasn't unusual. He was constantly traveling. Trafficante also came up to New York for a few days.

Just weeks after his trip to Cuba, Anastasia walked into the barbershop at the Park Sheraton Hotel on Seventh Avenue and 57th Street in New York on the morning of October 25, 1957. Anastasia sat down, closed his eyes, and said, "Haircut." The barber put towels on his face. Suddenly, two men with scarves covering their faces entered.

"Keep your mouth shut if you don't want your head blown off," one of the men told the barber.

He did what he was told.

They fired five shots into their target. Anastasia lurched forward. He tried to grab his attackers, but he was confused by the images in the mirror. He collapsed, dead on the floor.

As so often happened in gangland killings, Anastasia's bodyguard had conveniently stepped away—a clear indicator to police that the hit had been approved. The Park Sheraton was the very hotel where Lansky's mentor, Arnold Rothstein, had staggered after he was shot twenty-nine years earlier.

The audacious murder prompted front-page stories, replete with photos of the blood-soaked corpse, across the country. Police got a tip about Trafficante's meeting with Anastasia. Even more interesting, Trafficante had checked into the Park Sheraton just two hours before the shooting. Then he disappeared. Police couldn't come up with anything implicating him. No one was charged.

Lansky was not in New York at the time of the shooting. That didn't stop law enforcement from keeping an eye on him. An FBI Airtel noted that a week after the shooting, Lansky changed his residence to Miami. In Cuba, agents snapped a photo of him and Teddy with another couple at the Hotel Riviera and sent it back to the main FBI office in New York.

Then, on November 14, 1957, a seemingly mundane event blew up. It happened in Apalachin, a small town about 150 miles northwest of New York City. A New York State trooper, Edgar Croswell, was investigating a bad check at a local motel when he noticed a young man booking a number of rooms there. He knew the young man was the son of Joseph Barbara, a wealthy beer distributor who had a criminal record and history of bootlegging.

Croswell was a dogged investigator. He followed up. He and another trooper drove to Barbara's estate and saw more than a dozen cars with out-of-state license plates. When a local food supplier told him about the huge food order he had gotten from Barbara, Croswell knew something was up. He alerted authorities, and they set up a barricade.

What Croswell had discovered was a national summit of organized crime. When the mobsters realized that police were on to them, many of them—out of shape and wearing expensive shoes—bolted out the back into the woods, slipping and sliding in the mud. Some got away; others did not. The Mob conclave prompted big headlines and embarrassing descriptions of the fat city slickers.

It made for fun news stories, but it was a huge embarrassment to FBI Director Hoover, who for years had publicly insisted there was no such thing as organized crime.

Mobsters are as sensitive as anyone to bad publicity, and the finger-pointing started. They suspected a leak. Genovese had pushed for the meeting after the Anastasia murder and had arrived at the summit with one of his closest associates, Russell Bufalino, the boss of the Pittston, Pennsylvania family. The intention was to crown Vito as the boss of all bosses, and also hand off Anastasia's rudderless family to Carlo Gambino, renaming the borgata after him.

Some Genovese allies thought Lansky had a motive to leak because they believed he detested him. It was Genovese who had tipped authorities to Luciano's presence in Cuba, leading to his deportation. And it was Genovese who stirred up resentment about the division of money in Cuba. Lansky's old friend, Doc Stacher, believed Lansky had tipped off authorities about the summit in order to humiliate Genovese.

Lansky never would have tipped off law enforcement. He did, however, avoid going to Apalachin. He had attended every major Mob meeting in the United States in the past century but did not go to this one. Where others saw a conspiracy, he merely saw work. He was determined to finish the Riviera by the deadline he had set for himself. He mentioned it to Paul over and over. Besides, he had made a bet with Conrad Hilton, who was also building a hotel in Havana, that he'd beat him.

Lansky won the bet.

The months of planning yielded dazzling results. The expansive lobby had marble tables inlaid with gold. Each piece of furniture was placed for maximum aesthetic effect, such as the midnight blue settee placed against a pale gray marble wall. Floor-to-ceiling windows offered expansive harbor views. At the center of the lobby stood a bronze statue created by Gelabert of two elongated figures dancing. It was called *Ritmo Cubano*, or "Cuban Rhythm." Outside, there was another Gelabert sculpture of *La Sirena y El Pez*, or "The Mermaid and the Fish." By the pool, there was a spectacular three-tiered diving board.

The hotel was the first in Havana to have central air-conditioning, cooling twenty-one floors. The casino had gold-plated slot machines, and the kitchen had a top chef. There was a spa and salon and shopping. The total investment was $18 million, with half paid by the Cuban government. Even though it was Lansky's hotel, down to the custom-designed cocktail picks designed by Gelabert, he was listed as kitchen director. The casino license was in the name of Eddie Levinson, a Lansky friend and bookmaker who had invested in various Las Vegas casinos.

The Riviera opened on December 10, 1957. Lansky told Paul that he spent $120,000, or $1.3 million today, buying ads for it in major publications throughout the United States, Canada, and Latin America. Ginger Rogers headlined opening night. The show was broadcast on live television, with Steve Allen hosting. Lansky wasn't impressed by Rogers's performance, but the crowd loved her. He also hosted a private party for VIPs. Batista stopped by. So did a famous Cuban banker, Julio Lobo y Olavarria.

A few weeks later, on January 18, 1958, Steve Allen hosted his Sunday night prime-time show from the Hotel Riviera. Lansky flew in a roster of luminaries: Steve Lawrence, Don Knotts, Xavier Cugat, Edgar Bergen, Mamie Van Doren, and Rosemary Clooney.

The Hotel Riviera was a place where you could stay for days and get every need met. And that was exactly what Lansky wanted. He was determined to give his customers every reason to stay and gamble. They did.

It was the glittering culmination of years of work, but he didn't have the chance to savor it. After his months of intense focus on the Riviera, his health gave out again. He was hospitalized in New York. Afterward, he flew to Tacoma to spend Christmas with Paul. It was a welcome respite, but brief. On January 4, 1958, a violent storm shattered the windows of the Havana Riviera and flooded the lobby. He needed to return to Cuba.

Then he had to fly back to New York on more hotel business. This trip, however, would be anything but routine. On February 3, 1958, FBI Director Hoover sent out a memo to all offices with a directive:

"The fact that Lansky currently is out of your territory should not deter you from conducting a continuous, assiduous and imaginative investigation into his background and activities."

When Lansky flew into Idlewild Airport (now known as JFK Airport) in New York on February 11, undercover detectives were waiting. They didn't grab him immediately. They followed him for three hours to see where he went, convinced it would yield clues about Anastasia's killing. But Lansky's stops were anything but revealing. He stopped at a Hoffritz for Cutlery store and A. Sulka and Co., a shirtmaker and haberdasher—simple errands of a busy businessman.

Police grabbed him as he got out of a cab at 54th and Broadway about 10:30 P.M. They took him to the W. 54th St. station. There, he was questioned for three hours by Inspector Frederick Lussen.

"Police believe that Anastasia was murdered because he was attempting to muscle in on the flourishing Havana casinos. Lansky is the kingpin of the Cuban gambling industry . . ." the *New York Post* reported.

Once again, Lansky disappointed the police. After he was done, Lussen told reporters, "Lansky was no help at all."

However, mindful of Hoover's admonition to be "imaginative" in their investigation, authorities booked him for vagrancy, even though he had a $1,085 roll in his pocket and owned a home in Hollywood, Florida.

Their justification? "Lansky listed himself as a gambler. That isn't recognized as a worthwhile trade in this state," police told reporters.

Lansky emerged from the police station well after 1:30 A.M. He was greeted by a gaggle of reporters and photographers who had been alerted by police. He paused briefly and said only that he was in New York for medical treatment. But after one reporter suggested that Lansky didn't move in the highest social circles, Polakoff pulled him away and called the reporters "a miserable bunch of rats."

The news accounts that followed noted that Lansky wasn't dressed in his usual meticulous style. The *Post* theorized he was in disguise because he was wearing a "cheap-looking grey suit, a battered hat and a plain white shirt."

A judge later dismissed the vagrancy charge. He noted that while being a gambler was a distasteful occupation, it was not enough to charge him.

Lansky had become accustomed to law enforcement's predilection for leaking things to the press. He shook it off. Nearly two weeks later, however, he received disturbing news.

Batista, bowing to US pressure, officially barred him from Cuba as "an undesirable alien." When a reporter asked Lansky if the news surprised him, he said, only, "There are lots of things in the world that surprise me."

That same month, the thirst for any scrap of information about Lansky became evident when an FBI agent noted that he was wearing built-up heels in his shoes.

With everything going on, Lansky still worried about Sandra. He urged Paul to keep in touch with her:

I think she is changing for the better a bit. Marvin has been very nice to her during this period and it may be a good sign. Me keeping a personal contact with him may help things, for Garys sake it would be best for both of them. Paul I don't blame you for being angry with Sandra but search your soul and see if you were right in the manner you approached it. I expected to have a joyable Christmas dinner with my good child and bad child, but it is still mine can you understand that.

You should have better knowledge of diplomacy and more patience; let us use as much patience with our own as we do with strange people. She is still your sister and I know you want to be proud of your sister, I too want to be proud of my daughter but we can't help her and make her good by just forgetting her. No matter how bad our own are they are still our own. You can do more for her by keeping contact with her than by taking the easy way and saying I don't care to bother with her any more. You don't give up that easy.

His health problems flared up again. He decided to manage his business affairs from Florida, where he could get some rest. In March 1958, he wrote Paul:

The political condition of Cuba is critical and we hope that some compromise be made soon before it gets to serious. So far we have been lucky that nothing to serious has happened round Havana to affect business to seriously. But from now on in, we can expect anything. All we can hope for now is quiet for the month of March and then let things happen and get it over with.

Then, on March 10, 1958, there was more bad publicity. *LIFE* magazine published an exposé: "Mobsters Move in on Troubled Havana."

It was accompanied by a full-page photo spread. One of the prominent photos included in the spread was none other than one of Lansky.

LIFE magazine was the dominant weekly magazine of the era. With well-written articles accompanied by full-page photos, it had more than thirteen million subscribers. It was one thing to be the subject of New York tabloids, which was bad enough, but *LIFE* magazine reached an entirely different and broader national audience.

Edna's cousin subscribed to the magazine. When she saw it, she immediately called Edna. "You've gotta see this, Edna!" she exclaimed and brought over the magazine.

When Edna picked it up, she was astonished to see her father-in-law—the man she thought was simply a successful hotelier—listed as "No. 1 gambler and organizer of the Havana boom."

She asked Paul about it. He dismissed her: "Don't buy those things!"

Paul was reverting back to a tried-and-true Lansky family habit: Just ignore it and don't talk about it. They didn't. But Edna no longer had any illusions about her father-in-law.

In April 1958, the Nevada Gaming Commission issued a critical ruling: It barred anyone who operated a casino in Las Vegas from also operating in Cuba. The message was clear. Cuba was viewed as overrun by mobsters, and they didn't want them in Las Vegas—even though Vegas wouldn't even be in existence if it hadn't been for the foresight of people like Lansky and Siegel.

The ruling didn't upset Lansky. He had already decided that Las Vegas wasn't for him. But Dalitz decided to cash out of Cuba and operate solely in Las Vegas. Dalitz had started out in Detroit and then moved his bootlegging operation to Cleveland. He had relished Prohibition days when he could outrun federal agents with speedboats and outwit them with secret compartments, but he wanted to go legitimate. He wanted to remake himself into a civic leader in Las Vegas. In later years, he did just that.

Lansky bought him out, but it ended their friendship. Lansky was typically pragmatic about business deals, but there was something about the Dalitz deal that left him soured. He moved on. He decided to go all in with his Cuban casinos.

That month, he wrote Paul:

> *When the political problems settle in Cuba, the Riviera will be worth 20 million dollars* [or $220 million today]. *For two years I have been begging the tourist commission and the labor organizations to consider open ports for Havana tourists, they are now convinced what a great asset it will be to compete with the tourist business that goes South. If that ever comes through and I have good reason to believe that they will have to put it through, business will jump 20 fold here . . .*
>
> *As soon as things settle in Cuba, I will fly to visit you. I'm afraid to leave now with the condition as it is. It is really bad and most people get very panicky in a time like this, I don't. You take the good with the bad and always look to the future. It will be good.*

By June, the FBI reported that doctors had ordered Lansky to take a month of bed rest in Florida because of severe ulcers and anemia.

In fact, he went back to Cuba. The FBI discovered this after persuading an airline ticketing agent to provide agents with any information on Lansky's airline reservations.

Gossip columnist Dororthy Kilgallen picked up the news and reported an item in the *New York Journal-American*:

"Witnesses to Meyer Lansky's return to Havana say it was nothing less than triumphal, with high-ranking members of the police force embracing him as if he were a brother. To quote one observer: 'The way they greeted him, you'd think he'd captured Castro.' "

The mood in Cuba had turned. Unemployment was high, and corruption was rife. Many Cubans, struggling to support their families, resented the money outsiders were siphoning off the island. In an effort to quell protest, Batista's army killed dissenters. A bloody scene began to unfold on Cuban streets. Young men's bodies turned up on roadsides, obvious victims of Batista's army.

Cuban mothers marched in the streets, exhorting Batista and his army to stop murdering their sons. Meanwhile, Fidel Castro was hiding out in the mountains with his band of revolutionaries. Castro's specific plans for Cuba were vague, but he was already a hero among Cuban youth for leading an attack on an army barracks in Santiago de Cuba on July 26, 1953. The revolt failed, but the revolutionaries' courage inspired the hopes and dreams of their countrymen.

Among the ruling elite, few people took Castro seriously. They had a good thing going on, and they firmly believed Batista's superior military would rule the day. For a time, they were right.

But the situation was deteriorating. Demonstrations at universities had caused them to be closed for nearly eighteen months. Trade unions were starting to break away from supporting Batista. Respected citizens started to hedge their bets by secretly funneling money and support to the rebels.

Lansky decided he needed his own security force. He asked Paul to round up seventeen West Point cadets who spoke Spanish and said he'd fly them down to Cuba. Paul tried but couldn't find many cadets who spoke Spanish (and he never discerned why his father had asked for exactly seventeen cadets).

Years later, Paul admitted to being devastated that he couldn't help his father. "I failed," he lamented.

Lansky still traveled back and forth to New York, so much so that the FBI's Miami office set up steady surveillance there. Agents wanted to place a source in the Tuscany Hotel, where Lansky was staying, but ultimately deemed it impractical.

Every time he was back in Cuba, Lansky kept up his faithful correspondence with Paul:

Here it is 6 A.M. and I'm awake. You would think I have to be up to work. I do have to catch up on a lot of paperwork. Early morning is a good time to do it.

It was good to talk to you and Edna. I am happy to hear that you are all well, also that you are doing well in your school work. Before long it will be behind you.

If only the Indians in Cuba would settle down and make peace, everything would be well with me.

I'm feeling well and everyone else is well. I'm sending you $100.

Lansky almost always included money in his letters to Paul, even though his son never asked for it. And he delighted in shipping food to him, especially around the holidays. That Thanksgiving, he sent Paul's family a turkey and $100. As a man who was experienced choosing cooking staffs and sophisticated menus, he also couldn't help dispensing a little cooking advice for Paul's wife:

"I don't know how Edna makes her dressing? It is good to put liver in your dressing best of all is chicken giblets. She may also find her Turkey tastier if she bases it with a chicken consommé."

And although his son was an accomplished military man and engineer, Lansky couldn't help chiding him ever so slightly: "I received your interesting letter. If it was a little more I would find it more interesting also if I may be critical of the paper you use."

Nonetheless, his pride in his son was evident: "But all in all you show great ambition."

And he delighted in his grandson:

"I know how happy you feel about Meyer II taking his first step. It brings back memories to me. I don't think there is a week difference between you and your son starting to walk. You will enjoy him more and more until he gets bratty (not like you I hope)."

As always, he worried about Paul's relationship with Sandra. In September 1958, he wrote his son:

Paul, have you ever considered forgiving Sandra? To err is human; to forgive is divine. I don't think you are showing good wisdom in this matter. Remember, whatever is said and done, she was the one who was and is with Mother all the time. I know you wish Sandra well. We can't help her [by] *just saying the hell with her. I'm sure you can find a spot in your heart for her. It isn't fitting for you to act like you are acting. You will accomplish more by being in touch with her.*

By late November, he returned to Florida for more medical treatment. He couldn't stay long, however, because he needed to get back to Havana for the Hotel Riviera's New Year's Eve party. It was to be a grand event. Hundreds of people had already reserved their spots.

On the day of the party, however, the hotel suddenly starting getting cancellations—200 of them. Lansky was so sick, he couldn't attend to it. He had to spend the night in his room. That didn't stop Teddy from enjoying herself. While he was in bed, Teddy danced the night away in the nearly empty ballroom.

It was a bad omen of what was to come.

CHAPTER 16
Cuba Collapses

IT WASN'T LONG before the reason for the 200 canceled reservations at the Hotel Riviera's New Year's Eve celebration became evident. Castro's rebel underground in Havana had ordered Cubans not to celebrate the holiday at the casinos. Instead, many went to friends' homes for quiet parties. News of rebel victories and civilians joining the rebels was spreading. The New Year's revelers didn't know what to expect, but nobody wanted to be on the losing side.

Neither did Batista. As much as his government-controlled mouthpieces were declaring that he had been victorious against the rebels, he finally was starting to understand that wasn't the case. The insurgents were winning skirmishes across the country. His own soldiers were refusing to fight. In early December 1958, he sent his children's passports to the US Embassy to secure visas.

On December 29, a three-day pitched battle in Santa Clara in central Cuba left mass casualties. Batista soldiers were defeated and demoralized. Seeing that the situation was dire and not wanting to be on the losing side, rival generals started planning a coup. Batista, always careful to be on the lookout for enemies, became aware of the plotting against him. He dispatched one of his generals to negotiate with Castro. The rebel leader would have none of it.

Eyeing his increasingly limited options, Batista turned to the United States to begin discussions about asylum for himself and his family in Florida. Again, he was rebuffed. Anti-Batista sentiment had been building in the United States. By the end of the month, the US ambassador demanded that he resign immediately.

Batista shared none of this with Lansky.

As Cubans ushered in the new year shortly after midnight, Batista quietly gathered his family and closest supporters around him. He broke the news that they would have to flee the country. They filled suitcases with money and their belongings and drove to an air force base. They took off at 2:40 A.M. for the Dominican Republic, where Dictator Rafael Trujillo offered them asylum.

By dawn, Cubans were waking up to a new day in Cuba. There was no television news broadcast, because the country's largest TV station canceled regular programming and played Beethoven's Ninth Symphony instead. That wasn't enough to stop the news from getting out, because Cubans had their own informal and highly reliable network among themselves. Within hours, Cubans knew that Batista had fled and that the rebels were victorious. They surged through the streets to greet the conquering heroes. Emotions were high. They were both jubilant and seeking revenge after years of murderous oppression.

In Havana, the crowds looked to destroy anything connected to Batista. The first thing they smashed were the hated parking meters, which only rich Cubans able to buy cars could afford. Then they went after the slot machines. In the smaller casinos not run by Lansky, they had been adjusted to pay out less to the players so that Batista and his cronies could take more for themselves. Then they looted some of the homes of former government officials.

Lansky's casinos weren't the crowds' first target, but he knew it was just a matter of time—and not much of it. He immediately moved to secure his properties. He sent orders to stash the money in vaults. He and his driver, Armando Jaime Casiellas, scooped up millions of dollars to hide.

Trafficante was worried. Lansky, amazingly calm in the crisis, advised him, "The best thing to do now is pull back, to be absolutely invisible. Close the casinos, and fast."

Rebel troops began to arrive in Havana. They rushed into the casinos, destroying roulette wheels and craps tables. Cubans celebrating the rebel victory fired pistols in the air, and violence erupted. But within hours, the rebel troops managed to restore a sense of order to the city. No Americans were injured or killed. One prominent American, Ernest Hemingway, who lived on a farm on the outskirts of Havana, was delighted with Castro's victory. Batista had invited Hemingway to meet him several times, but he always refused. His sympathies were with the rebels, according to his grandson, Patrick.

Even though Lansky ran three casinos in Havana, and casinos were seen as symbols of the regime's corruption, he was not harmed.

He wasn't ready to leave yet. He decided to run the Hotel Riviera himself, with Teddy's assistance. They did everything from cooking to housekeeping. A few loyal employees stayed behind to help, but most fled. Lansky, who was still ill, hobbled down to his kitchen at the Riviera to give out free food to the guests. Teddy mopped the floors. Over the next few days, Lansky worked feverishly with the US Embassy to get his guests who wanted to leave out of the country. His brother Jack's two daughters had been visiting for the holiday, and he chartered a boat to get them out of Cuba and back home safely to Miami.

Paul had turned down all of his father's past invitations to join him in Cuba, but he wasn't about to abandon him in a crisis. He flew down to Havana to help his father. So did Sandra. When she arrived at the airport, her uncle Jack picked her up. He knew Paul was there to help his father, but he was justifiably suspicious of Sandra's motives.

He told her, "Your father is broke. Your father is dying. You're getting nothing."

She was offended and hurt, but her uncle wasn't wrong. Her entire relationship with her father revolved around his money.

American newspapers picked up on the story of the Cuban Revolution. The tone of the stories was often breathless and even sympathetic toward Castro's rebels. False rumors about Lansky were flying out of the country, and the newspapers gleefully reported them. One reported that Lansky had fled Cuba with actor George Raft, who worked as a greeter at El Casino De Capri in Havana. Another reported that Lansky was back in the United States and that the FBI was looking for him there. Lansky typically ignored the lies that were spread about him, but after he got a call from a Miami Beach newspaper columnist asking him about the FBI looking for him in the States, he decided he needed to do something.

On January 4, 1959, Lansky called the legal attaché at the US Embassy. He wanted to make it clear that he was not running away from Cuba. He said he was staying at the Havana Riviera, even though he was very sick and should be in the hospital. He called the embassy because he wanted to establish it as a matter of record that he was still in Havana.

That same day, he gave an interview to the *Las Vegas Sun* newspaper. He scoffed at reports that he and his brother had returned to the United States. And in spite of the chaos in the streets, he expressed confidence that a new government would emerge from Castro's liberation and that it would permit American gamblers to operate.

"No doubt they'll soon be around to talk with me," he told the *Sun* reporter.

It was an amazing display of grit and determination. After years of planning, he had finally achieved his dream of building his own hotel and casino, only to see it collapse literally overnight. He was loath to let it—and the millions in income it generated—go. He had to make sure his investors understood that. Lansky, always so averse to publicity, decided that he needed it now.

By January 7, he flew from Cuba to Miami—not because he was abandoning Cuba, but because his health had deteriorated so badly that he needed to see his American doctors. FBI agents detained him in Miami. They weren't there to arrest him. They wanted to know everything he knew about Cuba. For all the times that authorities had arrested him for spurious reasons as an excuse to convict him of something, this time, they wanted his help.

He readily gave them his assessment of the situation. He told them the larger casinos had not been damaged, but the smaller ones had.

Two weeks later, after another stint in the hospital, Lansky returned to Cuba. He wasn't ready to give up. He opened the casinos to tourists only. He knew that it would be suicidal to allow Cubans to gamble there because of the anger over the Batista regime's corruption. Besides, many of the rich Cubans who might have been his customers had already fled the country. He was gambling that the new regime would want the money brought into the country by rich Americans. The problem was tourists stayed away. Vacationing in a country overtaken by rebel fighters was not particularly appealing.

Castro finally emerged from the mountains and held a press conference on January 22, 1959. He flew in 200 newspapermen as guests of the revolutionary government. He held his press conference in none other than the Copa Cabaret of the Havana Riviera. He may have picked Lansky's hotel because it was one of the few functioning hotels left, but it is also true that Castro understood American politics very well. Lansky might be useful to him at some point.

Around the same time, a group of 300 mothers whose sons were killed by Batista forces met with the press at the Riviera. They demanded justice. They wanted revenge. They told reporters that they supported summary executions of the Batista soldiers who were still in Cuba. They got their wish. The revolutionary Cuban government held its first court martial of people it deemed "war criminals" in Havana's Sports City Stadium before 18,000 people. The spectacle whipped the crowd into a bloodthirsty frenzy.

It was a perilous time. Lansky was scrambling to keep the Riviera afloat, but on February 1, 1959, he suffered an attack of pericarditis, an inflammation of the membrane that encloses the heart. He was hospitalized again in Florida. Large amounts of fluid formed around his heart, and he suffered a major heart attack while at the hospital. They placed him in an oxygen tent. He hovered near death. An anxious Teddy stayed by his side. Family members worried it might be the end.

On February 11, 1959, the *New York Herald Tribune* reported that the McClellan Senate Rackets Committee wanted to interview Lansky but couldn't find him. The implication was that he was on the run and in hiding. Authorities obviously hadn't bothered to check Florida hospitals.

As Lansky was trying to battle back from his heart attack, he got more terrible news on February 26, 1959. His old friend, Abner "Longy" Zwillman, committed suicide by hanging himself in the basement of his New Jersey mansion. They had been friendly since his days of running operations for his mentor Arnold Rothstein. They also had vacationed together with their families at the Jersey Shore. Like Lansky, Zwillman grew up poor and was the son of Jewish immigrant parents. He got his start smuggling whiskey and later branched out into illegal gambling. Unlike Lansky, he had added prostitution to his rackets and tried to insinuate himself into the movie business. He even dated actress Jean Harlow, duly impressing his mobster friends.

Zwillman's death came less than two weeks after the FBI arrested several of his associates for bribing jurors in his tax evasion trial, which had ended in a hung jury three years earlier. The McClellan Committee had also subpoenaed him. Because his body had some unusual bruises, some people suspected that Vito Genovese—fearing that he would spill his guts—had ordered a hit on him. Another rumor—which Lansky vehemently denied—flew around that Lansky had ordered his death. Nonetheless, Zwillman's death was ruled a suicide.

It was yet another loss in a life where a friend or loved one could be killed at any moment. As always, Lansky said nothing about it to his family. He was pragmatic in life and in death.

Somehow, Lansky managed to rally physically and was released from the hospital.

In April 1959, he updated Paul on his health with his characteristic irony: "This is a good morning and long last I'm leaving the hospital [ten weeks] . . . Thank your mother-in-law for her prayers, the Mormons, my rabbis were here and they prayed for me. I, myself, didn't say a prayer but just seeked a good doctor and good scientific medicine."

Three weeks later, he struck an even more optimistic tone: "Day after day I'm feeling stronger and should be in good shape in June."

He was still preoccupied with Cuba. He wrote Paul:

> *Did you read anything about Castro in the papers? Have you seen him on television? We built up a Frankenstein and now we are left with a bear by the tail. Our press really have a way to make trouble for our country. I hope he doesn't cause our country great troubles in the Caribbean area. Why we invited this communist to visit our country? I don't grasp.*

He returned to Cuba, but the political situation there was worsening. He decided he had to leave, and this time, he brought along his mistress, Carmen. With Teddy often in Florida while he stayed back in Cuba to manage things, it was relatively easy to hide his dalliance. He always believed he was a good husband, but he, like his mobster friends, often had a woman on the side. Now, worried about Carmen's safety, he wanted to get her out of the country.

Things got even worse. On May 6, 1959, the Cuban Judicial Police arrested Lansky's brother, Jack, along with Dino Cellini, the Riviera's floor boss, on charges of international narcotics trafficking. US Bureau of Narcotics Commissioner Henry Anslinger had demanded their arrest. Castro, eager to cultivate good relations with the US government in the hopes of getting foreign aid, went along with Anslinger's demand.

Trafficante happened to be sitting in the Riviera when they were arrested. Upon hearing that Cuban authorities were looking for him as well, he sneaked out the back and went into hiding.

Of all the people loyal to Lansky, Jack was the closest. They spoke constantly and trusted each other implicitly. Unlike his brother, Jack had managed to stay out of the spotlight. Cellini was a longtime, valued Lansky employee. The arrests of both men came as a shock to Lansky. What he did not know was that Cellini's brother, Gottfredo, who worked as the evening manager at the Riviera, had been an FBI informant for the last two years.

Unlike others arrested by Castro's men, Jack and Cellini managed to avoid jail. They were held under house arrest at the Havana Riviera.

Tensions spiraled after Castro issued a warning in a pirated radio broadcast: "I'm not only aware of gangsters in Cuba, I'm inclined to execute them."

Lansky wasn't the only one with a sense of foreboding about Castro. In May, he confided in Paul:

> *The FBI has asked my doctor if I'm well enough to talk to if able they would like to discuss the Havana situation. They feel I can be helpful. I warned the authorities when it first happened now they are awakened. This is a communist regime so sure as God made apples. Whatever I can do to help the government I sure will. I could see it coming before it happened. From dictators we go to communism and vice versa.*

For Lansky to freely offer his insights to the same agency that hounded him relentlessly was striking. Throughout his life, he had an extraordinary ability to compartmentalize various aspects of his life. More importantly, his fervent patriotism trumped any anger and resentment he felt toward the "hypocrites" in law enforcement. And as always, he had hope for a better future.

Lansky was still recuperating from his hospital stay when he agreed to an interview with FBI agents at his lawyer Joe Varon's office in Hollywood, Florida. Agents thought Lansky appeared pale and drawn, and he moved as if he were in a lot of pain. He told them that his doctor said he could only be on his feet three or four hours a day. He agreed to meet with them, he said, because, "regardless of the public opinion of his personal life, he feels strongly about the security of the United States," the FBI report says.

Agents were impressed by his "excellent grasp of political science, current and past, and his ability to express himself."

Lansky told them that the situation in Cuba made the country ripe for Communist factions to entrench themselves in the government, and he saw Communism as a serious threat to US democracy. "He advised he had heard many rumors that there are Communists in high places in the Cuban government and that soon the entire government will be Communistic," the agents wrote.

As evidence of his contention, he made an astute observation: He wondered where the rebels got the money to wage an expensive war against Batista and suggested that the money had come from Communists.

As he was speaking to the FBI agents, he knew the information he was providing them could put him at risk. "I had to be very careful with whom I talked," he said years later. "The American police force spent their time and men watching me, instead of the Commies."

As he often did in meetings with officials, Lansky disarmed them with his honesty about his own situation. He admitted that he would sustain heavy losses unless the situation changed in Cuba and that that possibility influenced his decision to talk to the FBI. But he stressed that he wanted them to be aware of what was happening in the Cuban government before it developed into a threat to US national security. He knew, because of his years in Cuba, that he was uniquely positioned to provide the US government with critical insights. For the FBI agents, the tenor of the interview was striking. It certainly wasn't anything like their interviews with other mobsters.

The FBI files don't reflect whether they discussed what Lansky was doing behind the scenes to get his brother and Cellini released from house arrest. (A rumor circulated that he placed a $1-million bounty on Castro's head and then later withdrew it.) Eight days after that FBI interview, the Cuban government freed them. Interior Minister Luis Orlando Rodriguez told *The New York Times* that he got word from the US Embassy that neither Jack Lansky nor Cellini were wanted by US authorities and that they should be released.

Years later, Lansky mused about the Cuban political situation to Zali de Toledo, who became his mistress in his later years. "They [the rebels] gained a lot of sympathy from the peasants. They also wormed their way into *The New York Times* editorial staff."

His observation about *The New York Times* was apt. The paper's coverage of Castro was rapturous. Their correspondent, Herbert Matthews, clearly had been dazzled by Castro's charisma and cause.

At the same time, Lansky told de Toledo, the United States was completely ignorant of what was happening on the ground in Cuba because it had completely failed in gathering intelligence.

"The Embassy was made up of mostly good drinkers," Lansky recalled. "All they mingled with was the upper strata, never went to the rural areas to see how the real masses lived."

Although that might have seemed ironic coming from a man who catered to the wealthy, he never lost sight of his roots or his deep sense of connection to the poor.

The summer after Batista fled, Cuban police arrested and jailed Trafficante. While in jail, like most well-heeled mobsters, he lived comfortably. He bribed guards to bring in meals from the outside every day. But the threat to his life was very real. The Cuban command spoke about executing him, and that talk made its way to Trafficante. He knew he had to get out. His attorney, Frank Ragano, won his release by paying a $1-million bribe to the firing squad. Trafficante escaped to Florida before top government officials found out about it. For the rest of his life, Trafficante, profoundly bitter about his losses, worked with the anti-Castro émigrés to dethrone Castro.

Lansky was a realist. He knew when to accept defeat. When he sat down with the FBI agents in Varon's office, he told them he didn't anticipate returning to Cuba.

He bought a house at 612 Hibiscus Drive in Hallandale, Florida. It wasn't ostentatious, but it seemed secure. It was located in a private, exclusive community, and there was only one road into the development, FBI agents noted. That was important because it made the home more difficult to surveil. Moreover, Lansky, with his typically adroit understanding of the levers of government, persuaded local police to place a substation there. That meant that anyone entering or leaving the subdivision would be checked. His neighbors surely loved the extra security. Lansky's motive was a little different. He was trying to impede pesky surveillance.

The purchase was a significant step for Lansky because previously, he had always rented places when he stayed in Florida. The Hibiscus Drive house was his first permanent home there. The purchase signaled the end of the Cuban chapter of his life.

Castro's takeover cost Lansky $9 million, or more than ten times that in today's dollars. He paid back all of his investors, but that meant there was very little left for him. He never talked about it with his family, saying only, "I crapped out."

When asked about his money by reporters, he would make a wisecrack that he was going to the poorhouse. The reporters thought it was a joke, but it wasn't. It was clear to his family that he was mad at himself.

He would spend the rest of his life trying to recoup that loss. For that, he looked toward London, the Bahamas, and Las Vegas again.

CHAPTER 17
Doubling Down Elsewhere

LANSKY HAD SURVIVED a revolution. Overcoming the maladies ravaging his body was a much tougher fight. By June 1959, he was back in the hospital and revealed a rare moment of self-pity to Paul:

> *When I can get around I want a vacation away from my family and friends. I just feel like moping and gazing. I'm terribly tired of people I know and family. All the same chatter everybody loves you but no one does anything to help you.*

Paul was the only person in whom he could confide like that. The people in his life, especially his family, always had their hand out for more money. Paul was the one person who never asked him for anything. Paul was the only one who worried about his father's financial situation and tried to give him money.

By Christmas of that year, Lansky rebounded emotionally and embraced his role as the family patriarch. He was back to worrying about Sandra: "If Sandra is feeling better I will spend the weekend with her. She is having woman's trouble and a great bit of mind trouble to get attention and sympathy. You and me will never suffer from that illness, but unfortunately many do."

Before long, Paul shared some news that lifted Lansky's spirits. On January 6, 1960, he delightedly wrote his son:

Dear Capt. Paul,

Congratulations and how does it feel to be called captain? Seriously talking Paul do you have the necessary uniforms (are they in good shape). If not I want you to have them. It's important for you to have the cloths, fit properly and look new.

Paul had been promoted to captain in the Air Force. Lansky couldn't have been prouder. Paul's wife, Edna, thought the relationship of father and son was distant because they seemed stiff around one another. There were none of the affectionate hugs and kisses she experienced in her family. But, in fact, Lansky and his son had a deep bond. They understood one another.

The following month, Lansky wrote Paul again:

The judge was most proud to hear from you. He was so elated that he sent the letter to me with a friend of ours and warned him to be sure to return it. It is the little thoughtful things that man is judged by. I know you are fully aware of it. I also want to mention that the letter was neat. I apologize for being critical.

Even though Lansky's own spelling and punctuation were far from perfect, he had a habit of correcting Paul's letters. He did the same thing to his grandson when they started corresponding.

He loved books by and about great leaders. It made sense, since he certainly had met many of them. He continued in his letter to Paul:

Mr. Rosenberg has sent me a set of World War II books by [Churchill] *also a record of his most important speeches.*

At this moment the television is showing the President's [Eisenhower] *trip. He is a real Soldier, trying his best for his Country in a troublesome world. I wish him success.*

Lansky was sounding like a retiree in Florida. That was undoubtedly what he would have liked people to believe. FBI Director Hoover, however, believed otherwise. He sent a directive to the Miami FBI office chiding them for failing to penetrate "the upper echelon hoodlum and racketeering figures." He went on:

> *You now have residing in your territory one of the very most important individuals in the national crime picture in the person of Meyer Lansky. Information developed in Bureau investigations over a period of many years indicates strongly that Lansky is a very important individual in a segment of the criminal element. In pursing investigations in your Criminal Intelligence Program, you should not overlook the possibility of employing extraordinary investigative techniques with reference to Lansky. Because of the loss of the lucrative Cuban gambling situation, Lansky is presently in a position of having to make decisions as to his future course of action. This may be a propitious time for close coverage of Lansky.*

Hoover wanted action. It was clear he would not let go. He demanded a report back within three weeks.

He was right about Lansky's losses in Cuba. He needed to make money. Despite his tenuous health, he was determined to line up new business.

His first stop was the Bahamas. It made perfect sense. Much like Cuba, it was an island—a string of islands, in fact—just fifty miles east of the tip of Florida in the Caribbean. For tourists, the white-sand beaches and calypso of its Afro-Caribbean culture were potent lures. For savvy businessmen, the banks where you could deposit money without creating a traceable paper trail were the ideal tax haven.

Best of all for Lansky, it was a British colony. That was important because in 1960, Great Britain legalized some forms of gambling. That paved the way for licensed casinos in the

Bahamas. Lansky avidly followed current events. He understood well how changes in the law could influence his business choices. By now, gambling in the Bahamas seemed like a good bet.

He approached Bahamian Finance Minister Sir Stafford Sands with a proposition: He and his investors would pay Sands $2 million in exchange for a permit to operate casinos.

Sands was definitely the right man to approach. His position in the Bahamian government made him the point man in promoting tourism on the islands. He also had extravagant tastes. He loved expensive lounging jackets and elaborate paperweights, and he couldn't resist a grand gesture. If he was having dinner for four people, he'd order caviar for 100 people. He loved making an impression.

Legal papers were filed to incorporate a new company in the Bahamas—Bahamas Amusements Ltd. Such incorporation papers were filed all the time and typically generated little interest. What made these papers noteworthy were the shareholders and the timing. The shares were divided between Louis Chesler, an old friend of Lansky's from Canada who sold him on the idea of gambling in the Bahamas, and Georgette Groves, wife of American financier Wallace Groves, who had been convicted of fraud. The lawyer handling the paperwork was none other than Sands.

The following month, the Grand Bahamas Executive Council granted a special exemption to Bahamas Amusements Ltd. At least four members of the Executive Council had lucrative "consulting" agreements with the newly incorporated company. So did two other top Bahamian politicians, including the premier's son.

It was a very profitable arrangement for the involved government officials. It also followed a tried-and-true Lansky playbook: Spread the cash around to the political players who can influence key policy decisions that make you money.

Lansky later said coyly that he had "no knowledge" of Sands. The minister, however, said otherwise when he testified before a Royal Commission investigating gambling in the Bahamas several years later. He testified that Lansky had offered him $2 million. The commission found he had accepted the bribe. Sands resigned in disgrace as interior minister in 1967. His resignation wasn't a total defeat, however. He was able to leave the Bahamas with the fortune he had amassed.

Chesler, too, confirmed Lansky's involvement. He said he had sought his advice on casinos. After all, it wasn't easy setting up an operation of this type, especially in another country. He considered Lansky "the dean of gambling" and asked for a meeting with him. They met at Miami's Fontainebleau Hotel, a favorite Florida hotel of Lansky's, where he also had an ownership interest (along with the Singapore and Eden Roc). Chesler showed him a list of prospective casino employees. Lansky looked over the list, making suggestions. He also agreed to bring in his old friend George Sadlow to help him get started.

Sadlow was the ideal choice. He had worked with Lansky and his brother both in Havana and Las Vegas. He brought in Cellini, the valued casino employee Lansky had helped spring from Cuban detention. Sadlow and Cellini became two of the only employees trusted with the nightly count at the casino at the Lucayan Beach Hotel in Grand Bahama.

Lansky later insisted that it wasn't his operation. "I wasn't ever involved in gambling in the Bahamas. They did seek advice from me and I answered what was asked to the best of my knowledge."

In a sense, he was being truthful. He wasn't running the casino. He likely got some compensation for his advice, though not on the scale of what he would have gotten for actually running the casino. For him, it was merely a business meeting.

Gambling in the Bahamas generated all sorts of investigative reports in newspapers in the 1960s. American officials were genuinely worried that the Bahamas were becoming an "outpost for U.S. gangsters." The stories usually placed Lansky in the middle of it all. The mere mention of his name gave the stories a certain cachet. As much as he hated publicity, he was gaining a worldwide reputation.

The irony was that he wasn't physically up to the punishing day-to-day work of managing a casino. His health was just too fragile. That didn't stop him from trying to set up new business, however.

After the debacle in Cuba, Lansky had no illusions about gambling as a business: "I am for it when it is in a moderate form and the poor are not affected financially. When the purpose of gambling is for economic reasons, that it will bring prosperity to an area, true, but only for a short time. In a few years, it will dry up the residents in the area, especially the poor. The outside ownership will walk away with the money," he said later.

"I'm for it if it will serve the purpose of entertainment and the money rolls back to the area. Controlled limits of loss; ownership belongs to the area. Profits are taxed to the hilt."

He had the sophisticated understanding of the economics of gambling that few people had. Ironically, the publicity he deplored had helped make him the go-to person for advice on setting up casino gambling.

He turned his attention to London. Vincent "Jimmy Blue Eyes" Alo set up the investors for the Colony Club, a casino in the affluent Mayfair section of London. Cellini worked there and, as they had in Havana, set up a school for dealers (though they called them croupiers in England). Another old friend, George Raft, acted as greeter there. A handsome and well-known actor who also knew his way around the streets, he was perfect for the part. He greeted guests, signed autographs, and danced with the women. It became, according to mobster Vinny Teresa, "the place to be" in London. It was also known for being an honest operation.

That sounded very much like a Lansky-run club. In fact, he had only a small stake in it. His connection, though, proved to be an important conduit for the highly profitable junkets. As Teresa explained:

> *When you wanted to run junkets to the Colony Club, the man you made arrangements through was either Lansky*

> *or his right arm, Dino Cellini. They'd give you the clearance and make sure you got a piece of the profits. If you were a Mob representative running a junket to the club, they kicked back 15 percent of all the money lost by the people you brought. That could result in some very serious money being made because this was a class operation, on a par with some of the best casinos in Las Vegas. The Colony was good for at least three to four million bucks a week in action.*

Teresa was a lieutenant in the Patriarca crime family of Boston. Known as "Fat Vinny" because he tipped the scales at more than 300 pounds, he was a good earner for the Mafia. He loved running gambling junkets because of the money he made and the parties that went along with them. In a tried-and-true Mafia tradition, he later became an informant against the Mob, and would even publish an early tell-all in 1973, aptly titled *My Life in the Mafia*. That fact would directly affect Lansky in the coming decade.

As much as Lansky hated the desert heat of Las Vegas, he felt pulled back into it when Albert Parvin, the old friend who had overseen the interior design of the Hotel Riviera, wanted his help. Parvin, along with partners Raft and singer Tony Martin, wanted to sell the Flamingo hotel. Lansky knew someone who was interested—Morris Lansburgh. He set up the deal and got a $200,000 finder's fee on a $10.5-million sale. Lansky's name didn't show up in any sale paperwork, but he did report the fee on his taxes. Given the breadth of Lansky's far-flung business activities, it was a relatively small deal for him. But it would come back to haunt him years later.

In the 1960s, Vegas was the epicenter of cool. It was the decade of the Rat Pack. The moniker came from actress Lauren Bacall, then married to actor Humphrey Bogart. One morning, she saw the group—Frank Sinatra, Dean Martin, Joey Bishop, Sammy Davis Jr., and Peter Lawford—after a night of heavy drinking. They were seriously hungover. She said they "looked like a goddamned rat pack."

They loved it. The name stuck.

Sinatra was the undisputed leader of the pack. At the time, he was the biggest star in the country, although his personal life made as many headlines as his professional life. He had an affinity for wise guys, having grown up with them in Hoboken, New Jersey. He had gotten his start singing at the old carpet joints. He knew all the scams and the skim well. As part of his payment, he got points in the casino. That made him very wealthy.

Sinatra and his buddies would spend their evenings singing, joking, and riffing. It didn't feel scripted, because it wasn't. People in the audience felt as if they were part of a very cool, private party. Everybody wanted to be there.

Those were, for many people, the halcyon days of Las Vegas. The Mob paid entertainers well but didn't charge the public a lot because they knew that good entertainment would attract high rollers (a lesson learned from Lansky). One night, songwriter Artie Schroeck wanted to see Sinatra. He snagged a front-row seat by slipping the maître d' a silver dollar and buying a couple of drinks. It cost him all of $5 to see his idol.

Patrons had to be dressed. Absolutely no shorts and T-shirts. Casino operators wanted to create an elegant experience—another Lansky rule. Everyone felt safe because Las Vegas was considered an open city. No one would be killed in turf wars there.

It was loose and comfortable for everyone. Singer Frankie Valli marveled that one night after a show, Lansky (or one of Lansky's minions, he's not sure) pressed $5,000 into his pocket as a thank-you. That was Lansky, always throwing money at people.

Sam Giancana, boss of the Chicago Outfit, loved hanging out with Sinatra and his pals. He would fly to Chicago to collect his skim. Sometimes, he'd take his daughter, Antoinette, with him. She loved the glamour. As a child, she met Lansky, but she didn't really know him. Her father did, however, and talked about him often.

"It was always Meyer this, Meyer that," she recalled. He was the guy who made everybody money.

Lansky had stakes in several casinos. They provided a relatively steady income, but he still worried about money. He supported two of his children, his parents, other family members, and an occasional mistress. Just as important, his standing in the underworld derived from that fact that he was able to make guys money. It was getting harder and harder to make a big score.

Sandra was especially demanding. She always needed more money. Once she separated from Rapoport, she would go out all night and sleep all day. Lansky made sure his friends at the nightclubs kept her safe. She thought she was leading a glamorous life because she slept with celebrities like Dean Martin. But it left her no time to tend her infant son, Gary. She'd leave him in the care of a nanny. Paul and Edna visited her in New York once, and Paul was furious at what he saw. He was hardly a moralist, but he was appalled at her inattention toward her son.

Buddy, by now married to Annette, was very different from his sister. Despite his disability, he had no problem working. His problem was gambling. Like most inveterate gamblers, he got himself into deep debt. Because he got into debt to some serious people, Lansky covered them. Buddy told his father that the reason he gambled so heavily was because he wanted to buy nice things for his wife. Lansky blew up. He demanded that he divorce Annette. He had once thought of her as a "great girl" but came to believe she was only interested in his money. Buddy acquiesced.

When they divorced, she didn't demand any alimony. Lansky had been dead wrong about her.

In January 1962, Lansky lost his old friend, Charles Luciano. The Mob boss died in the unlikeliest of ways for a mobster—natural causes. He had gone to the airport in Naples, Italy, to meet a filmmaker who wanted to make a movie about his life. After the meeting, he collapsed of a heart attack and died. He was sixty-five years old.

Since his deportation to Italy, Luciano's influence over the American Mafia had diminished, but not disappeared. His word still carried weight. He was a good ally to have, but more than that, he and Lansky were friends.

The following May, Lansky suffered another heart attack. He decided to recuperate at the Volney Hotel, located on East 74th Street in New York, because it was close to the hospital where he was being treated. One night, he was listening to a television news talk show hosted by David Susskind, a well-known TV interviewer. After one of the panelists said organized crime was second in size only to government, Lansky turned to Teddy and said, "We're bigger than U.S. Steel."

What he didn't know was that someone was listening. FBI agents heard the remark. They had placed a microphone in Lansky's room. They were set up in the room next door. There was no warrant, no court order. The wiretap was entirely illegal, but that happened quite a bit at the time.

Lansky's comment became public five years later, when *LIFE* magazine reported it. A little later, it was immortalized when the movie, *The Godfather Part II*, came out in 1974 and Hyman Roth, the character reputedly based on Lansky, said to Michael Corleone, "Michael! We're bigger than U.S. Steel!"

Lansky would wince whenever he heard that remark repeated. He hated being associated with it. His observation wasn't wrong, however. The Mafia had insinuated itself into virtually every aspect of American life, and the FBI was doing what it could to beat it back.

While New York FBI agents were listening in on Lansky at the Volney Hotel, Miami FBI agents were trying to place a bug in his Hallandale home. They knew he would be in New York for several weeks and that this was their chance, but they were having trouble circumventing the burglar alarm Lansky had installed.

"Residence in Hallandale, Fla, remains unoccupied and attempts at establishing HCS but technical problems are formidable," one Airtel from Miami to the director said.

Just how FBI agents knew so much about Lansky's personal travel schedule or how they knew to bug that particular room in Volney Hotel wasn't spelled out in FBI files. Instead, the files are replete with oblique language and redactions. Deep in the files, however, there is one reference to the source that is not blacked out. The memo refers to the source as a "she."

Sandra Lansky was an FBI informant.

CHAPTER 18

Hoover Homes in on Lansky

THE COLLAPSE OF her marriage flattened Sandra Lansky. She started popping prescription pills. She shopped constantly. She continued going out to nightclubs, looking for a new man. It was an expensive lifestyle. Despite her father's efforts to get her a decent job, she didn't work. When she did manage to get a job, it didn't last long. She simply couldn't summon the effort to work. Lansky, a dutiful father, paid her living expenses, but he set limits. They were high limits, but limits, nonetheless.

She needed money. The FBI pays confidential informants.

Sandra later explained her cooperation with the FBI in her memoir, *Daughter of the King*, saying that she had been tricked into feeding them information by a dashing older friend she thought was in love with her. In her telling of the story, however, she left out the part about how she provided extensive information about her father's activities over a long period of time. She told agents about where he traveled and when. She explained who his friends were. She listened in on his phone calls.

For their part, the FBI agents thought she was deeply angry at her father. She told them that he had her mother committed so he could marry another woman, Teddy.

Whether she was right or wrong about Lansky's motives for divorcing her mother, Sandra's undercover work for the FBI was a stunning betrayal. As frustrated as he was with Sandra's dissolute lifestyle, Lansky adored his daughter. Throughout his life, he did everything he could to help her. He even importuned Paul—whom he knew couldn't stand Sandra—to try to step in and help.

Sandra was just one of the people who visited Lansky during his three-week stay at the Volney. While there, he had a constant stream of visitors and telephone calls. Although he was supposed to be getting some much needed rest, he was busy conducting business.

And FBI agents heard all of it.

While his crack about U.S. Steel got a lot of attention, it was the comments he made in unguarded moments to his friends and business associates that were the most revealing.

One morning, he was feeling expansive. He bragged about reading three books at a time: a history book, a grammar book, and a book about French quotations. He said those were the things you need with no education. He went on to expound on various subjects, "and his listeners expressed awe at his knowledge," the FBI files note.

Although Lansky wasn't a man who often felt sorry for himself, it was clear that his health problems and the vicissitudes of age were taking a toll. He complained that the necessity of making a living was "taking a lot out of him" and remarked how lucky people are who "fall into it."

He then explained to some unnamed associates, whose names are redacted in FBI files, the intricacies of hotel soap contracts. It sounded very much like a routine business discussion, but Hoover immediately seized upon it. He directed agents to find out everything they could about hotel soap contracts in Las Vegas. (Nothing ever came of that investigation.)

On another day, he spoke with two men about federal law enforcement:

Unidentified man: "I kept telling them I have nothing to see ya about. This time I'm not going to even answer the question if I know ya or don't know ya."

Second unidentified man: “Get your lawyer. That’s what they’re for. You shouldn’t talk to them.”

First unidentified man: “I wanted to know what he wanted to know.”

Lansky weighed in: “It’s better not to talk to them than to be inquisitive. They’ve got to get tired sometime.”

He was clearly hoping that he would outlast the federal investigators.

Later, one man boasted, “The feds, they don’t bother me.”

Lansky replied, “Well, I get bothered by them to the extent I know what I’d like to do and I know what I can’t do.”

At one point, he turned philosophical:

“You gotta treat the good with the bad, that’s life. Some of us never learn it. Some people never learn to be good. One quarter of us is good. Three-quarters is bad. That’s a tough fight, three against one,” he said, snickering.

Lansky clearly thought he was among the one-quarter who were good, or, as he would put it, “unhypocritical.”

An avid student of human nature, he then made an observation about people in law enforcement that some would consider prophetic:

“They’re nothing but racketeers, every one of them. After five years, they get out, get on a big corporation payroll . . . It’s a new Mafia. The investigators are going to get investigated. It’s just a matter of time.”

One day, a tailor came to visit him at the Volney. While Lansky tended to whisper or change the conversation whenever Teddy entered the room, he felt freer to talk when it was just guys in the room. Someone brought up Attorney General Robert Kennedy. Lansky made it clear that he had no use for Kennedy:

“Let me tell you something. Anybody that hasn’t lived hasn’t the right to tell anyone else anything. He’s a young boy, thirty-seven years old. He hasn’t lived yet, and he wants to tell others how to live. He’s an arrogant punk.”

Meyer II beside a portrait of his grandfather in The Count Room speakeasy at Flamingo Las Vegas, September 2025.

The Hotel Nacional de Cuba in the 21st century.

The Hotel Habana Riviera—formerly the Havana Riviera—Cuba, 2015. Castro outlawed gambling in 1959, so the hotel has no casino today. *Courtesy of Randy Wells.*

Meyer Lansky's promotional brochure, "Havana in the Grand Manner," produced in 1956.

Meyer II promoting the Havana Crossing Collection at Stanley Furniture, High Point, North Carolina, October 2016.

Meyer II with Randy Wells, the creator of the Havana Crossing Collection, Park Hill Showroom, Las Vegas Market, 2023.

Meyer II visiting the Seward Park Library in Manhattan's Lower East Side in 2015, where his grandfather studied from 1911 onward.

Meyer II standing in the infamous Lower East Side doorway, through which Joe Masseria fled from assassins, to promote AMC's *The Making of the Mob: New York, 2015.*

Meyer II with his wife Dani Porter-Lansky, opening night of Bugsy & Meyer's Steakhouse, Flamingo Las Vegas, July 2, 2020. *Courtesy of Erik Kabik Photography.*

Meyer II with his sister Myra, Meyer Lansky's only granddaughter, 2021.

Meyer II stands proudly with the historic Flamingo wall display in the Oscar Goodman Room at The Mob Museum, Las Vegas, 2022.

The Lanskys' merchandise in The Mob Museum's gift shop, 2018. (A big thank-you to Event Network.)

Bona fide bobbleheads. Manufactured by the National Bobblehead Hall of Fame.

Heidi and Joe Marino of Vegas Mob Weddings, with whom Meyer II officiates ceremonies, Flamingo Las Vegas, 2022.

Meyer II when he was known as Bryan Mason, Tacoma, Washington, 1975.

Meyer II's headshot, 1982.

Meyer II on *The Real Godfathers,* A&E, 1996.

Meyer II and Johnny Fratto on *Deadliest Warrior's* "Jesse James vs. Al Capone" episode, Spike TV, May 3, 2010.

Meyer II signing copies of Robert Lacey's *Little Man* (1991), and the *Meyer* (2019) graphic novel by Jonathan Lang, the latter at CrimeCon 2022, Paris Las Vegas.

CBS Photo Archive/ Getty Images.

TriStar Pictures/ RGR Collection/ Alamy Stock Photo.

Photo 12/Alamy Stock Photo.

Meyer Lansky in film and TV: Lee Strasberg (as the fictional Hyman Roth) in *The Godfather Part II* (1974), Ben Kingsley in *Bugsy* (1991), and Anatol Yusef in *Boardwalk Empire* (2010–14).

Meyer II at the lake house of the former Henry Kaiser estate, West Shore Lake Tahoe, where *The Godfather Part II* was filmed in 1973 and (spoiler) Fredo Corleone was killed. No Hail Marys were said this time.

Meyer Lansky's donor window at the first synagogue of Miami Beach, now the Jewish Museum of Florida-FIU, 2013.

Meyer II, Antoinette Giancana, actor Lou Martini Jr., the real Tony Montana, Frank Cullotta, and Henry Hill at the Las Vegas Film Festival, 2011.

Meyer II interviewing for the third season of *Mobbed Up* at CrimeCon 2022, Paris Las Vegas.

Antoinette Giancana, daughter of Chicago Outfit boss Sam Giancana, with Meyer II at the American Library Association Annual Conference, Chicago, 2014.

Meyer II on stage with Emmy Award-winning CSI Atlanta and Cold Case Investigative Research Institute Founder and Director Sheryl McCollum at CrimeCon 2022, Paris Las Vegas.

Meyer II and Dani with Henry Hill in 2011 at the M Resort Spa Casino, and in 2012 at the now-closed Mob Bar in Las Vegas. RIP to a good friend. *Courtesy of Lisa Caserta.*

Meyer II with Suzanne Dalitz, daughter of early Las Vegas businessman and philanthropist Moe Dalitz, in February 2012.

Phil Genovese, grandson of Vito Genovese, with Meyer II at the premiere of AMC's *The Making of the Mob: New York, 2015.*

Meyer II with Alan Parsons of the Alan Parsons Project, Bugsy & Meyer's Steakhouse, Flamingo Las Vegas, 2024.

Danny Zelisko, Lisa Parsons, Dani Porter-Lansky, Tabitha Parsons, Meyer II, and Alan Parsons enjoy some quality time over some quality soups and steaks, 2024.

Jimmie "J.J." Walker of *Good Times* fame with Meyer II, Las Vegas, 2019. Dyn-o-mite! *Courtesy of Cliff Lawrence.*

Ernest Hemingway's grandson Patrick Hemingway with Meyer II, Seattle, Washington, 2024.

Meyer II with Frank Cullotta, Tony Spilotro's Chicago Outfit and Hole in the Wall Gang associate, The Mob Museum, Las Vegas, 2019.

Meyer Lansky's grave, Mount Nebo Memorial Gardens, Miami, Florida.

Meyer II paying his respects to Lucky Luciano at St. James Cemetery, Queens, New York, 2015. *Courtesy of Phil Genovese.*

Later, the conversation drifted into another man and his mistress. A friend of Lansky's said the man never took his girlfriend out in public. "She gets anything she wants except going out publicly," he said.

Lansky responded in a way that likely reflected his rationalization of how he handled his own dalliances: "That's okay. He loves his wife, he loves his family, and he doesn't want to embarrass them."

A few days later, he expressed his frustration at the constant investigations into his activities:

> *Teddy was having trouble with the help. Every maid I got was contacted by the FBI, and they were quitting. So I decided I better call these [obscenity]. So they said we'd like to see you at your house. There was a knock on the door and they said, 'May we come in?' I said, 'We'll sit in your car.' They said, 'It's a little too hot . . .' I said, 'What the [obscenity] do you know of me?' Sure, I was a gambler. My doors were as wide open as the Fountainbleau Hotel. But it didn't take in a poor unfortunate class of people that couldn't afford it. Nobody was forced to gamble or to come there. Your [obscenity] reformers that came there and ate my food and your newspapermen and many big officials, they didn't pay the [obscenity] check. If it was so [obscenity] terrible, why didn't they pay their [obscenity] check?*

By early June 1962, Lansky was starting to feel stronger. He talked about his plan to go to the museum to buy a photograph of Aristotle contemplating a bust of Homer. He loved the ancient philosophers. Although he never finished high school, he believed that reading works by Socrates and Aristotle was the mark of a well-educated man.

And, as often happened, the conversation drifted to the Kennedys, whose large Catholic family was beginning to dominate US politics. One man compared Catholics to Communists, opining that he didn't know which was worse.

Lansky replied, "We've always had Catholics as congressmen and other top levels in government. There's only forty million of them, but they're well-organized and they're all educated. That left us in a spot."

By June 8, 1962, FBI agents were in a panic. They knew that Lansky would be wrapping up his stay at the Volney soon, and they still didn't have a bug in his house. Three days later, the FBI's New York office sent an urgent teletype to the director, informing him that Lansky and his wife checked out of the hotel. They decided not to follow him to the airport in order not to jeopardize their informant.

The informant had to be someone close enough to Lansky to be traveling with him.

The news of Lansky's return to Florida set off a scramble in the Miami office of the FBI. They had had three weeks of an empty house to install a bug, but they had failed to do it. Now that the Lanskys were coming back home, there was no time to lose. They had to get a bug installed in the house. Hoover demanded it.

Agents raced to the house at 612 Hibiscus Drive in Hallandale the next day. After getting inside, they determined the best place to put it was in Lansky's study around his desk. Listening devices in the 1960s were not as small and discreet as they would become in later years, but they found a way to hide it. They got it done by 1:00 P.M. and got out.

Just three hours later, Lansky and Teddy arrived home.

So began more than eighteen months of the bug demanded by Hoover in Lansky's home. It had not been authorized by any court, since the laws didn't require it at the time. Only Hoover could authorize it, and he regularly did that. His obsession with Lansky was such that he insisted that agents send him daily summaries of his activities.

Lansky seemed unaware of any listening devices in his home for a long time, but years of self-imposed discipline had created a habit of caution. He rarely mentioned names, occasionally referring to "that guy" or "the old man." And he never discussed sensitive business.

Still, the installation of a listening device in the home of a man considered to be one of the top hoodlums in the country was a coup for the FBI. Even better, at the same time that the Lanskys returned home, their informant furnished them with something that was literally good as gold to them: a list of all the names and telephone numbers contained in Lansky's address book. It is impossible to overstate how valuable that was to agents. They would now be able to track connections that they even didn't know existed previously. It was literally a road map.

Lansky was much too careful with his personal information to allow some random person to get access to it. To be able to copy all the names and telephone numbers in Lansky's address book required someone very close to him who understood they were valuable.

Informants' names are redacted in the FBI files, but it's likely that Sandra was the one who provided agents the address book. She was one of the few people close enough to him to get access to it and to have the time to copy it for them.

At the time, Sandra and her father were often at odds. He was upset by her late-night partying and her failures as a mother. The only way he could think of dealing with it was to either throw money at her or abruptly withhold it.

Teddy did what she could to discourage him from giving Sandra money. When she and Lansky were first married, she tried to establish a relationship with Sandra, knowing how much her father loved her. But over time, as she watched Lansky fall ill time and time again, she became concerned about their financial situation. Money was not coming in the way it used to. And every time he gave his daughter money, Sandra, rather than using it on learning a marketable skill, spent it on parties or closets full of clothing she never wore. It grated on Teddy. Unlike her stepdaughter, she was a careful shopper with a taste for cheap things. She even sold her used clothing out of their garage to raise extra cash.

Lansky sometimes listened to her, but other times, he'd shut down the conversation. FBI agents overheard their bickering over Sandra. She was a source of constant tension. And yet, he had no idea of the extent of her betrayal of him.

Right after the Lanskys returned home to Florida, FBI agents followed him to a favorite haunt, Junior's Restaurant in Miami Beach. They noticed what had been worrying Teddy:

"Subject appeared to have deteriorated greatly in health and appearance since last observed by Miami agents in April of 1962."

Over the summer months, FBI records show that a source was giving them information about Lansky's activities—a "meet" with an associate at the Miami airport, a planned trip to Europe, a "New York hoodlum" he planned to meet. They didn't have the details of the meetings, but being able to know where he was going saved FBI agents critical time. Despite the inside track they had been given, they didn't unearth anything criminal.

That fall, Lansky and Teddy took a seven-week tour of Europe, with a stop in Tel Aviv. When they returned to Miami, agents searched their baggage but found nothing. When they sent in their daily summary, they couldn't hide their disappointment:

"It was evident that they expected a thorough search and took pains not to have anything of an informative or incriminating nature in their possession."

Lansky knew he'd be searched when he flew home to Miami. He also knew that FBI agents were surveilling him. They made no secret of it, and that was by design. They wanted him to know that he was unwelcome in their city.

Lansky tried to maintain an equanimity about the surveillance. He once saw an FBI agent watching him at the Windrift Hotel in Miami. Lansky approached him. He jovially mentioned his recent trip to Europe, but he slipped in a small complaint about an interruption engineered by the FBI. The agency had notified Interpol that Lansky would be traveling to Europe, and Interpol tracked him down.

"The Interpol couldn't find [REDACTED], but they could find a poor little Hebe like me," he said.

The fact that Lansky could retain his composure and even joke with agents set him apart from other mobsters facing the same pressures. Sam Giancana, for example, would become abusive and obscene when contacted by FBI agents. Lansky was always polite.

While in Florida, he had a routine. He'd leave home around 10:00 A.M. and head for the Singapore Hotel, of which he was part owner, in North Miami Beach. He'd hold meetings and would pause for lunch at a table that had been reserved for him. Then he might play cards. Alo often joined him there. By 3:30 P.M., he'd head home. He never held business meetings at home, which was a source of frustration for the FBI, whose agents were listening in.

Most days, he had a driver, either Phil "The Stick" Kovolick or sometimes Bobby Blanche, two old friends from his days in Brooklyn. Kovolick was of Russian-Jewish descent, and Blanche was Italian. An informant told the FBI about a conversation he had with Blanche when he asked Blanche why he, being Italian, worked for the Jewish Mob:

"Blanche stated that he had been with the Jewish Mob for many years and that he found them to be more trustworthy and generous people to work with than the Italians."

Then in November 1962, the FBI reactivated "a highly confidential source" who had previously provided valuable information on how the skim worked in Las Vegas. The source told them that Lansky and his wife were engaged in a "bitter dispute" over Sandra. That source's name is redacted in FBI files.

That Christmas Eve, Lansky was back up in New York and meeting with Anna's psychiatrist, who also saw Sandra. When Sandra arrived for the 9:00 A.M. appointment, her father was already there waiting for her. The doctor turned to her and delivered what had to be a disastrous news. He told her that she was mentally incompetent. If she didn't agree to do what he told her to do, he'd have her confined to a mental institution. He told her that she'd have to come to weekly appointments with him if she wanted to stay out of a mental hospital.

The doctor's ultimatum blindsided Sandra. Whether she suspected her father of telling the psychiatrist what to do with her is unclear, but it is clear that her relationship with her father had fractured.

Lansky returned to Florida, and the daily surveillance by law enforcement resumed. FBI agents were frustrated by the lack of usable information. They were getting bolder.

In May 1963, Lansky was eating at Junior's Restaurant on Collins Avenue in Miami Beach. An agent stopped by his table and asked if he was going to be in town for a while because another agent wanted to talk to him. Lansky said yes.

"Lansky asked why the FBI was still following him around and he was told that the FBI likes to know what people like him are doing and where they are spending their time," the report reads.

People like him. The message was clear.

That fall, Lansky got involved with some oil interests in Michigan and Ohio. An informant alerted the FBI, and teletypes went out to Detroit and Cleveland. While he was in Gaylord, Michigan, agents followed him on to the main highway. Most of the time, Lansky or his driver slowed down, allowing agents to catch up. This time was different. Lansky's car took off at speeds up to eighty-five miles per hour, and then it shot off the main highway.

Disappointed agents sent a teletype to the director explaining the situation and adding, "Neither he nor the car has been seen since."

It had to be a satisfying moment for Lansky. He could still outrun the cops.

Despite his fragile health, he was constantly on the move. Agents tried again to follow him when he was in Massachusetts in October:

> *NYO* [New York Office] *advised today subject, Miami top hood driving a 1963 white Impala bearing Florida License*

> *10297 traveling from Massachusetts area. Last observed vicinity of Tapanzee Bridge NY Thruway. Above car carrying two white males picked up in Newark on Garden State Parkway at Rout 22, Union, NJ at approximately 4:15 today . . . NYO advised bureau instructions to follow subject to ascertain activity, contacts and keep bureau advised. Armed and considered dangerous.*

Meanwhile, Paul was assigned to do a second tour in Vietnam. Lansky followed the war closely. If he was worried about Paul's safety, he didn't say it outright. He wrote him:

> *I read about the base being attacked I don't know if it is the one you are at? I do read lots about Saigons internal trouble. How does this bastard expect to fight the Communist when he can't straighten his own house out.*

Paul had asked about hotel operation. Lansky responded with characteristic modesty: "It is to much to write about but when you get home if you are interested I will tell you the little I know and get you the structure in book form."

He concluded by telling Paul how much he loved his pool and golf, adding a wry note: "All the comforts do make you soft but I'm willing to stay soft from now on."

In October 1963, a tsunami hit organized crime. It came in the form of Joe Valachi, a low-level Mafia soldier in the Genovese family. A deeply angry and paranoid man, he had killed a man in prison who he thought had been sent by Mob boss Vito Genovese to kill him. The problem was that Valachi killed the wrong man. Terrified that he would be sentenced to death for killing the man, he agreed to become a rat. He met with investigators from all over the country. More dramatically, he agreed to testify before the US Senate's McClellan Committee investigating organized crime.

He described the history and rituals of the Mafia in gory detail. It was the first time any made member of the Mafia had publicly violated the Mob's code of silence, or *omertà*. The hearings were televised. A nation watched them, transfixed. Attorney General Kennedy lauded it as a major breakthrough in his war against organized crime.

Kennedy alleged, among other things, that Lansky had shared interests in Las Vegas and Cuba with Vito Genovese. In fact, he said that wherever Lansky operated, Genovese did, too. It was enough for Hoover to double down on efforts to get him. He ordered more surveillance.

Then, on December 3, 1963, FBI agents listening in on the Lansky household heard something disturbing. It was around 9:45 A.M. Someone visiting Lansky seemed to be "tampering with objects" next to the bug. No one was speaking. It was apparent that someone suspected that a listening device had been planted in Lansky's study. In a panic, agents shut off the device. An hour later, they reactivated it.

For hours, they didn't hear much. Then at 9:30 P.M., someone again seemed to be looking at and under objects near the bug. Again, agents didn't hear anyone speaking.

The next day, they heard several people come in and look for the bug. For the third time, no one spoke while they searched Lansky's study.

On December 5, 1963, agents removed the bug. They had been made.

CHAPTER 19

A Deepening Father-Son Bond

THE FBI MAY have removed the bug from Lansky's Hallandale home, but that didn't put an end to the surveillance. Even though agents in Miami complained that they never saw anything of much use when following him, Hoover insisted that they continue sending daily summaries to him. Miami was the lead office because Lansky had a home there. Miami agents had to coordinate with agents throughout the country constantly. Anytime he went out of town—which he did all the time—urgent teletypes went out from Miami to FBI offices in other cities.

That included Tacoma, Washington. That was where Paul lived with his family.

At his wife's urging, Paul decided to resign his Air Force commission so that he could take an engineering job at Boeing in Seattle. Edna was tired of moving the family from base to base and thought that a civilian job would settle things down. Besides, she was becoming interested in real estate and wanted to pursue that.

Lansky visited Paul and his family several times a year. They loved his visits. He always made it like Christmas. He would bring gifts and take the family out to dinner. Once, he noticed that Edna didn't have a watch. He quietly gave her a very expensive one on his next visit.

Paul, unlike his father, was tightfisted with money. He considered dinners out an extravagance. It might have been his way of rejecting what he viewed as the excesses of his mother and sister, or perhaps it was simply his way of exerting control. He didn't stop his father from giving his family presents, because he knew it brought his father pleasure, but he rejected extravagant gifts for himself. When he graduated from the University of Michigan with a master's degree, Lansky offered to buy him a car. Paul flatly rejected it.

Paul was determined to make it on his own. "You make your own way in this world," he told his son, Meyer II.

Lansky, for his part, understood his son's desire for independence, as it mirrored his own. Unlike his relationship with his daughter, he knew how to deal with Paul. In one letter discussing an upcoming visit, he wrote:

"You make the plans for my visit with you as you would like to have it, but here is what I would suggest. You and Edna hardly go out. I suggest you get a babysitter ready and plan what entertainment you wish and I will entertain you."

He often told Paul that he never wanted to be an imposition on the family, so when he visited, he stayed at the Winthrop Hotel. He'd come over in the afternoon and then take the family to the Winthrop for dinner. Meyer II loved it.

It always felt like an occasion when Lansky visited—because he made sure it was. Even as a young child, Meyer II knew there was something different about his grandfather. He had a commanding presence and was incredibly observant. He wasn't like other grandfathers in that he dressed meticulously. Meyer II remembered laughing to himself when Lansky showed up in Levi's one day to go with Paul to inspect a tree farm Paul was interested in buying. The jeans were so out of character with his city slicker grandfather's style.

Whenever Lansky visited, Paul would pick him up at the airport. Every time, the FBI agents were there, watching and making it obvious that they were watching. It made Paul uneasy. He was, after all, a West Point graduate. He took his oath to his country seriously. He loved his father deeply but hated seeing the agents at the airport every time he picked him up.

They didn't limit themselves to Lansky's visits, however. At Boeing, Paul helped administer the Air Force contracts. As usual, he did well at the job and got along with his colleagues, including office-mate Bill Foley. One day, a coworker pulled him aside and told him something unsettling: FBI agents were questioning workers at Boeing about him.

It was both humiliating and infuriating for Paul. Like his father, he viewed these intrusions as pure harassment, which they were. But unlike his sister, he never once wavered in his love and loyalty for his father.

They never talked about it, but Lansky never brought Teddy along on these visits. None of his children could stand her. They saw her as crude and moneygrubbing. While Paul thought of his mother as hypocritical, he appreciated her taste and class. Teddy was the complete opposite of his mother.

When Lansky returned to Florida, he kept up a steady stream of letters to Paul. In June 1965, he wrote how happy he was to get a photo of Paul and Edna's new baby, Myra, and then of his upcoming plans:

"I expect to leave home for business for a week or ten days. It is growing hot here and after a while it gets on your nerves. Aside of that everything is well."

In nearly every letter, he enclosed \$50 or \$100, which would be worth ten times that today. He always urged his son to go out and have some fun, or to buy a gift for his family. Often, Lansky mentioned that he was sending Paul salami, a family favorite.

Although Paul was an adult with a family of his own, his father couldn't help but dispense advice in another letter:

"As for you, you should make a change, you are entitled to earn much more than you are earning. Don't procrastinate if you are going to make a change do it soon."

He also gave him specific instructions for a gift for Meyer II's upcoming birthday:

"You buy $100 bond and the rest you get him a gift from me. If it is alright with you and his mother to get him a stingray put the balance to it and buy him a stingray. I will return the money to you when I get back."

Though Meyer II was just a child, he knew his grandfather was special. Once, while the family was living in Boston, the family went to a fancy restaurant. Lansky and his parents were dining with friends of Frank Sinatra. Meyer II accidentally knocked over a champagne bucket. The waiter and restaurant manager ran over. He expected a reprimand. Instead, Sinatra's friends waved them away, saying, "Don't worry, he's Meyer Lansky's grandson."

Lansky never hesitated about introducing his friends and business associates to his family. When Meyer II was just seven years old, he met "Trigger Mike" Coppola, a former bootlegger who reportedly murdered his own wife to prevent her from testifying against him. By the time Meyer II met him, Coppola was gravely ill and in Boston to get medical treatment. Meyer II didn't learn anything about Coppola's history until years later.

Lansky felt enormously proud of Paul but worried about his lack of business savvy. In October 1965, he wrote him:

"Paul, I'm sorry to say you are selling your ability too cheap. I was hoping that by how you should be earning at least $12,000 a year. We will speak about your economic future at great length when I see you."

As Meyer II grew, his athletic abilities became evident. He loved playing any kind of sport, and this delighted Lansky—not just because he loved sports, but he thought it might be a lucrative career path for his grandson. He wrote to Paul:

"I will find great pleasure watching Meyer start his base-ball [sp] career . . . Sports carreers [sp] are very compensating today."

Lansky, despite his constant health battles, loved competing in sports. He'd swim with his grandson, and he loved power walking.

In late 1965 and early 1966, an investigative journalist, Hank Messick, published a series of articles about Lansky in the *Miami Herald.* The stories proclaimed that organized crime had taken root in South Florida, in large part through Lansky's career and connections. The stories described Lansky's past and associations, but there was one particular detail that stood out:

"Lansky today is a very rich man—his wealth is estimated at $300 million. Much of it is believed to be in numbered accounts at the International Credit Bank of Switzerland."

The statement doesn't say who estimated Lansky's worth or how it was known that Lansky had any money in Swiss banks. But Director Hoover knew the value of cultivating journalists to get stories out. By the mid-1960s, he had to be frustrated that his agents' constant surveillance was turning up nothing usable. Passing on information to favored journalists was—and is—a time-honored tradition of law enforcement. It steps up the pressure on the target.

The number, worth $771 million today, was entirely false. He had lost everything in Cuba. Lansky was making enough to live fairly comfortably, but he spent what he earned. He liked his creature comforts, but he also wanted to erase the memory of his impoverished childhood. Years later, he said of his youth, "It was difficult. It's not something I can even explain. That's why you need an education."

At least one person, however, thought the story of Lansky's $300-million-dollar fortune was true and saw a business opportunity—Richard Nixon's brother. He reached out to Lansky to suggest buying land in Washington and Oregon. Lansky demurred. But the $300-million figure would haunt him for years.

It wasn't entirely impossible to believe that Lansky had hidden money in Swiss bank accounts. He and Teddy had, after all, taken several European trips, including stops in Switzerland, and he had used an intermediary to deposit some funds in a Swiss bank. The advantage was apparently nothing more than avoiding paying taxes on it, but the total wasn't anywhere near the number cited in the Messick stories.

The articles infuriated Lansky. Around that time, Meyer II noticed something among his friends. Every time his grandfather came to visit, his friends' fathers would stop by the house. His family never talked about Lansky's fame or exploits, but other families in Tacoma clearly did. It was beginning to dawn on Meyer II that his grandfather wasn't like other grandfathers.

One day, Meyer II heard on the radio that his grandfather had visited John Connally, who was then the governor of Texas. The next time he saw his grandfather, Meyer II said, "Hey, I heard your name on the radio."

Lansky just smiled and said, "You did?" Nothing more. That was Lansky. He'd never reveal any more than he had to. But Meyer II saw a look in his eye. It was as if he saw that his grandson was figuring something out.

Tacoma was an easy and comfortable place to grow up. Paul's family lived in a leafy, affluent, and very safe neighborhood. Meyer II always walked to school. One day, when he was eleven years old, he was walking to school and noticed a white van with no windows parked on the side of the road. Two men were dressed in jumpsuits, the kind worn by city workers. They were standing at the back of the van, as if they were about to unload equipment. But Meyer II saw that there was nothing to unload. He immediately knew something was wrong.

Then two men stopped him. One of them asked him, "Are you Meyer Lansky?"

Paul had warned his son over and over never to talk to strangers—a common parental warning, but one taken very seriously in the Lansky household. Meyer II took off. He knew a shortcut under a bridge and through a ravine. The two men couldn't catch him.

He ran to his school. An administrator called his parents. When they heard what happened, they knew immediately the danger their family was in. The menace of Mafia violence was very real in the 1960s. The threat from people trying to cash in on Lansky's supposed fortune was also very real. Edna took the children to Ann Arbor, Michigan, where Paul had gotten his master's degree. They took care not to stay in their old house. Instead, they stayed in the home of a nanny who had worked for the family when they lived there.

When they returned to Tacoma, two FBI agents were stationed at Meyer II's elementary school. One of his classmates walked up to an agent and said, "Are you Meyer's bodyguard?"

They may have been posted there ostensibly to ensure the boy's safety, but it was also an easy way to continue their surveillance of the family.

Lansky was beside himself when he heard the news. He knew that it very likely wasn't one of his Mob associates behind the kidnapping attempt. It was too clumsy and amateurish. Besides, they'd have no reason to hurt his family. He was the guy who made them money.

He was sure it wasn't that. He was convinced, however, that Messick's stories about his supposed $300-million fortune were the reason.

Years later, he still bristled at that: "It should not have been hard to draw a rough estimate to know it was an exaggerated lie," he said, adding, "Honest reporting is very important in our society. Unfortunately, a few exaggerated liars create much doubt for the many."

In October 1966, as Paul's family was preparing to visit, Lansky wrote him, not about a phantom fortune, but about the mundane household costs he wanted to pick up for his family:

"Here is what I suggest about shopping. Edna and the children may need some clothes now, so why wait. Do you have some cash to lay out until I see you; if not, I will mail it to you. Let Edna and the children buy what is most necessary for themselves now and will fill in later."

He loved dispensing advice to Paul, who eagerly sought it in business matters:

> *I'm happy to hear that you are all in good health, health is the most important all other things will take care of themselves.*
>
> *In answer to your real estate—get rid of your old buildings all it will do for you is good practice of learning how to be a janitor. Don't worry about the work you haven't shouldered, you should have never bought them. But, you can make that under the trials of experience and there will be nothing lost.*

And he added a melancholy note: "I don't look forward to a happy future. The beast in man is growing stronger and the educated beast isn't less beastly, but, much trickier."

Lansky didn't say it, but he had a sense that authorities were zeroing in on him. The reference to "educated beast" could have been a reference to his bête noire—Attorney General Robert F. Kennedy, who had not slackened in his crusade against organized crime.

That fall, Paul's family visited New York. As usual, Lansky had planned all sorts of fun for them. He took them to grand New York tourist attractions. Although he wasn't an effusive grandfather, he was always, in Meyer II's view, interesting. It was never boring to be around him.

Edna took Meyer II to see his grandmother, Anna. Edna called ahead of time to let her know that they were coming. They knocked on her apartment door. She opened it, looked at them, yelled, "Go away!" and shut the door in their faces. She hadn't recognized them.

They tried again. This time, when she came to the door, she recognized them. But she seemed disoriented, asking him, "How's school?" She let them in, but they didn't stay long. Her deterioration was depressing to everyone in the family, but they didn't know what else they could do.

On June 5, 1967, Israel launched an air strike against Egypt, beginning what later famously became known as the Six-Day War. Lansky watched the news apprehensively. He wrote to Paul:

> *Since Monday I have been glued to television and radio. I wonder if the Israelis were losing, whether Russia would have been so persisting in a cease fire. Where were these Russians who claim to speak for all the people when the Arabs were threatening little Israel to push them into the sea.*
>
> *It got me sick to see the beast in man when the Egyptian and all other Arabs were being incited in hate and false patriotism how beastly they looked; and this goes for all people when they act like sheep.*

Although he was a world away in Florida at the time, events in the Middle East clearly felt very personal to him, as he wrote Paul in a rare confession:

"I don't know what I'm going to do, if I had peace of mind around home I would stay put right here. I guess that is asking to [sic] much even at 65."

The following spring, just two days after Robert Kennedy announced his plans to run for US President, Lansky wrote Paul:

"I never had any doubts about that weasel [RFK] trying to seek the Presidency. My vote will go to anyone but him."

Like his brother, Kennedy was assassinated, in 1968. Richard Nixon went on to win the presidency. Within a few months of taking office, Nixon proposed yet another campaign against organized crime. On one level, it was the kind of political bluster Lansky was adept at ignoring. The problem was, there was a real war against organized crime, and him specifically, closer to home. A grand jury was convened to investigate allegations that he was skimming millions of dollars from Las Vegas casinos.

After Lansky appeared before the grand jury, a reporter asked him for comment. As usual, he kept his feelings under control:

"I don't want to take the drama out of your stories, so I don't think I'll say anything," he said, walking away, smiling.

He was polite to the reporter, but he was raging inside. He complained to Paul:

"I'm not busy at all. I can't do business. I have been so loused up by newspaper and political vultures and this makes it impossible for me to get any credit for business."

In August 1969, Internal Revenue Service agents raided the Flamingo in Las Vegas. They seized credit accounts and other records. The FBI agents noted that Bernard Sigelbaum, who ran junkets to the Flamingo, was caught on a bug saying, "Meyer wants a breakdown."

Lansky decided he needed to do something about his own safety. He sold his house in Hallandale and moved to a beachfront apartment with tighter security. He told a reporter that he moved because he was worried that some "young Turks" might try to kidnap him. Although he didn't say it, he was still brooding over the attempted kidnapping of his grandson.

Back in Tacoma, some of Meyer II's friends asked him to join their group, the Aphid Blues Band. He had a speaker system and a drum set, so he was, of course, a perfect addition.

One day, they were practicing in the basement, when Paul came down and said, "Hey, would you like to play for his sister's birthday party on Saturday?"

The band, all twelve- and thirteen-year-olds, were thrilled. "Great, a gig!" they whooped.

Mike Dupile, one of the bandmates, noticed a short guy to his left who was flanked by two very large men. Meyer II said, "Guys, meet my grandfather."

Lansky enthusiastically encouraged the young band: "You boys sound great. Keep it up, and I'll have you playing in Vegas."

Then he handed each of them a $50 bill. They were even more thrilled.

Dupile went home for dinner and excitedly told his parents about it. His father, who worked as the chief accountant for the city of Tacoma, asked, "What's Meyer's last name?"

"Lansky," Dupile replied.

Dupile's father pushed his chair back, walked around the dinner table, stuck his finger in his son's face, and screamed, "He's public enemy number one! You can't go back there!"

Dupile, shocked and speechless, had no idea what he was talking about, but he was absolutely terrified of disobeying him.

He never went back to his friend Meyer's house, and that was the end of the band.

CHAPTER 20
Lansky Flees to Israel

AS LANSKY CAST about for new business and perhaps a new place to live, he watched Israeli politics with apprehension. Without warning, Israel launched airstrikes against Egypt in June 1967. The surprise attack caught Egyptian forces off guard. After some half-hearted resistance, Egypt and its Arab allies agreed to a ceasefire within days. The war was infamously dubbed the Six-Day War. It was a resounding victory for Israel and allowed it to occupy large swaths of new territory on the Gaza Strip and West Bank. Despite the fact that his beloved Israel had scored a decisive victory, the war left Lansky deeply troubled.

He wrote Paul some worried missives. He was right to feel anxious about the anger of the Arab people. The Six-Day War and Israel's seizure of land would have lasting political consequences, and Lansky knew it.

In his letters to Paul, he turned to his own situation. He complained about how all the publicity about him had hurt his business. It worried him. He had been dreaming of retiring to Israel, but the political situation seemed too unstable.

The following March, he turned his attention to US politics. Bobby Kennedy had made a name for himself as a fearless crime fighter. Young and boyishly handsome with a brood of bumptious children, he was a new kind of politician. He mixed easily with Hollywood celebrities. He appealed to the idealists of the 1960s. He cared about the people, not himself.

Lansky knew better.

Lansky needed a break. Worn down by the bad publicity and his poor health, he decided to vacation with Teddy in Acapulco. It was supposed to be a relaxing getaway, but they had some unexpected company: The FBI followed them there. In fact, the FBI assiduously tracked Lansky's movements all over the country.

Lansky and Teddy flew back home to Miami on March 4, 1970. Upon their return, US Customs agents searched their baggage. Lansky had a vial of Donnatal, a medication used to ease stomach cramping, in a gold pill case Teddy had bought him. The Customs agents found the pills and asked him about them. He said he took them for his stomach ulcers, but he couldn't produce a prescription. In fact, his pharmacist had given him the pills for the trip. The agents let Lansky go home but kept the pills for testing.

What should have been an uneventful return home became anything but that. The US Customs agents immediately alerted the FBI's Miami office, which sent an urgent teletype to Hoover—an extraordinary amount of effort for a vial of ulcer pills.

Within a week, the lab determined that the pills were exactly what he said they were—Donnatal, a mild stomach medication. They were exempt under federal laws. In other words, there was no federal crime.

That didn't stop the FBI, however. If authorities couldn't charge him federally, perhaps they could do it under state laws. They advised Florida state authorities, "who will attempt to prosecute the subject under proper Fla. statute," according to an urgent teletype to Hoover.

For years, the US government had suspected Lansky of smuggling drugs from Cuba and Mexico. They never found any evidence of that, but that didn't dissuade them from believing it. Hoover, in particular, had not given up on proving that, even though anyone who knew Lansky knew that he would never do that. He hated the dirty business of illegal drugs, no matter how much money could be made from it.

Three weeks after US Customs Agents searched Lansky's baggage, agents from the Florida Department of Law Enforcement showed up at his house. They had confirmed that he had filled prescriptions for Donnatal at the local pharmacy but determined that there wasn't a prescription for this particular bottle of Donnatal. They arrested him for having drugs without a prescription. They charged him with a felony violation of the state's barbiturate statute. The potential penalty was up to two years in prison and a $1,000 fine.

For a bottle of stomach ulcer medication.

The Florida cops didn't come on their own. They came with a cadre of reporters, photographers, and television crews. That ensured, of course, that the story of Lansky's arrest would be published in newspapers and on TV stations across the country.

It was a minor offense, if at all. Lansky had nothing in his luggage to suggest that he was a big-time drug dealer, which he wasn't. It was also Good Friday, he later recalled. That meant that he wouldn't be able to find a judge to set bail because none would be working on Good Friday, so he'd have to spend the weekend in jail. It was a setup, and he knew it.

"Lansky has been extremely irritable," the FBI file noted.

That observation was noteworthy because Lansky was always polite with government agents. At times, he even joked with them. He was keenly aware always that he needed to appear in control. A flash of irritation around law enforcement was highly unusual for him. It was also understandable. He was tired, anxious about his future, and furious about the phony publicity.

From the FBI's perspective, the arrest was a huge success. A teletype to Hoover noted, "Extensive favorable newspaper publicity extended by subject's arrest."

In one of those stories, a *Miami Herald* reporter couldn't resist making a little fun of Lansky:

"Meyer Lansky, rated by police as one of the most powerful men in organized crime, was arrested and jailed Friday and charged with not having a prescription to soothe his nervous stomach."

The publicity ginned up by the authorities grated on him. They had long ago abandoned any pretext of neutrally enforcing the laws. They were doing everything they could to pressure him. They saw a man who kept getting away with his criminal activities and was making millions while doing it. No amount of surveillance and wiretaps ever seemed to catch him. It was embarrassing.

The title of an article about Lansky in *The Atlantic Monthly* in July 1970 summed up their feelings: "The Little Man Who Laughs at the Law."

Lansky saw it very differently. He told his friends and family that he was retiring. To be sure, he was still trying to line up business to earn money to support his family, but he was not interested or able to work on the level he had before. He insisted that the reason authorities couldn't find the crimes they were looking for was because he wasn't committing them.

After his arrest and jailing, when he was able to make a call, Lansky called his lawyer, who called his doctor. He got a statement from the doctor saying that Lansky would be taking Donnatal tablets for the rest of his life for his chronic condition.

They got a court hearing. His lawyer, Varon, argued that Florida law enforcement had no authority over US Customs and thus couldn't charge his client. The judge agreed. He dismissed the charge. The prosecutor was so angry at the judge's decision that he stormed out before he finished his statement.

Afterward, a reporter asked Lansky, "Do you have an ulcer?"

"Three of them," he replied matter-of-factly, pointing to his stomach. "I've had them for twelve years."

It was a feeble denouement to the whole episode. For all the teletypes and news articles proclaiming him to be a crime kingpin, authorities had actually believed that a bottle of Donnatal would be his undoing.

Nine days later, Lansky wrote Paul to send him money for his granddaughter Myra's birthday. But he didn't say much more, only, "I'm just not in the mood for writing."

Lansky was depressed. He knew his health was failing. Mentally, he felt under siege by the constant stream of headlines and intense government pressure. He never admitted weakness. He had always been in charge and able to manage any situation. But his life in the United States was becoming unmanageable.

He knew, too, that a federal grand jury was investigating his involvement in a massive multimillion-dollar skimming operation in Las Vegas. A federal grand jury investigation is a serious business, spanning months or even years. Grand jury proceedings are secret, but that doesn't stop witnesses from talking to one another. Day after day, word leaked out about witnesses testifying.

Then in May 1970, FBI agents reached out to Lansky about a matter of grave importance. They had received information from their Seattle office and needed to talk to Lansky about it. As much as the FBI wanted to arrest Lansky for a crime, they were also obligated under FBI policy to notify him if he or his family were in danger. Although the specifics are deleted in the file, it's clear that they were discussing the kidnapping attempt on his grandson.

Lansky already knew about it. He confirmed to them that there had been an attempt to kidnap Meyer II. He told the agents that he was grateful that they were concerned. He said it might have been because of his "notoriety" in the press, or because some younger members of "a certain Italian group" might envy him. He acknowledged that there were "nuts around" and then made an almost wistful observation: "He also stated that many of his old Italian friends are no longer living and he does not know the younger element well."

He added, "When I walk the streets, I never know when I may get it."

He agreed to notify the FBI if there were any more threats.

It was an extraordinary conversation between Lansky and the men who had been part of Hoover's yearslong crusade against him. It was also a rare acknowledgment from Lansky that he didn't have the kind of protection he enjoyed in the past, thanks to his close friendship with Luciano. His old friend was long gone, and the up-and-comers in the street life cared nothing about the past.

Shortly after that long conversation with the FBI agents, Lansky started thinking about making a major change. At the time, several of his friends from his old Bugs and Meyer Mob days were looking toward Israel. One of them, Doc Stacher, had already moved there after the United States issued a deportation order against him. In 1950, Israel passed the Law of Return, which allows all non-Israeli Jews and converts to relocate to the country and acquire Israeli citizenship. The goal of the law was to foster the growth of a Jewish state.

Lansky decided to move to Israel. He would apply for citizenship. Although he was never a particularly observant Jew, he was a Jew in his bones. He had long thought of Israel as a spiritual home. In the 1940s, he had enthusiastically raised money for and arranged arms shipments to Haganah, the Zionist paramilitary group formed to defend Israel.

When he visited the country for the first time in 1962, it had felt, in a way, like a homecoming. It was a reminder of his family roots. He didn't have to worry about a "young Turk," as he put it to the FBI agents, killing him there. So, in his mind, it only made sense for him to spend his final years there.

Israeli authorities weren't so sure. Although Law of Return offered refuge to people with Jewish mothers, like Lansky, there was a clause exempting people wanted on criminal charges. There was also the matter of Israel's most important ally—the United States—and its investigations into Lansky. Israel could not afford to alienate the United States. Israeli officials immediately dispatched a state attorney to the US to find out whatever he could. He returned to Israel with two suitcases full of committee and police reports.

Although he tried to keep his plan of moving to Israel quiet, Lansky's arrival immediately made news there. On January 25, 1971, the Israeli newspaper *Haaretz* reported on his application for citizenship. He protested to the reporter, “I don’t want to make money here. I want to live here.”

That same week, he wrote to Edna, because he hadn’t heard from Paul: “I haven’t heard from my son in a long time. I wrote to him a couple of days after I spoke to him. Some of the mail is going lost so I wish he mentions whether he received my letter or not. Whenever you write make mention of my preceding mail so that we may have a check on it.”

Lansky didn’t know it, but US authorities had arranged to have the US Consular Section of the US Embassy in Tel Aviv intercept his mail.

In his letter to Edna, he told her a little bit about his new life in Israel:

> *As for my life it is a little dull. I’m not* [used] *to being this inactive, but I will get to doing something. Teddy has been ill most of the time. It isn’t any easy change for all people. It isn’t easy for Americans to adapt themselves to a foreign land and custom. She doesn’t complain but I know she misses her home.*

Two weeks later, he wrote Paul, telling him how happy he was to hear from him. He told him he had applied for citizenship and would keep him apprised. He complained that he had “a little too much time on hand.”

That was not what US authorities thought. By March, news stories were circulating that a massive underworld summit was being planned in Israel. Acting on orders from Interpol, Israel barred three Jewish mobsters from entering the country. Others who were reportedly planning to attend just stayed home. The so-called summit never came off.

That same month, the US Department of Justice formed Task Force Eighteen to investigate all of Lansky’s activities. The FBI, which loves to give its investigations flashy names, dubbed the probe “Operation Financier.”

"It is the intention of the department to exert every effort to effect prosecution of Lansky and/or his subordinates," the teletype to Hoover read.

On March 4, 1971, Israeli agents served him with a subpoena to testify before the grand jury in Florida on March 10. Lansky didn't show. His lawyer, E. David Rosen, claimed he wasn't well enough to travel. Authorities gave him a second, later date. Again, Lansky didn't show. He was found to be in contempt.

When he next wrote Paul on March 21, he didn't give him any indication that he was in any kind of legal jeopardy.

First, he apologized for not answering Paul's previous letters immediately: "I'm slow to get in the mood of writing so forgive me. I do carry on a wide correspondence."

He waxed philosophical:

Paul, 20 yrs. is a long time when you look ahead but when you look back it is a short time. You have now reached the middle of your life. I'm reaching the end. I hope that when you reach my age it will be a better world for both your children and all people. This world will never live in peace if it isn't worthwhile living for all of us.

And, as he often did with Paul, he talked politics:

Israel has to stand firm for secured borders, the time hasn't reached where a small nation can depend on the U.N. for security. Also she can't depend on outside help all the time; people soon forget politics changes who knows what mood the people and politics of our own country will be in 10 yrs. from now . . . if Russia becomes the dominating force here, Western Europe would become a pawn in Russian's hand. Oil the bloodlife of W. Europe. I wonder how many Europeans really see this danger.

Where Paul's wife saw a stiff formality between father and son, discussing world affairs was their way of drawing closer. At home, Paul read everything he could to better understand the situation in Israel and the Middle East. He tried to find a way that he could help his father. Lansky was too proud to ask for anyone's help, but Paul had a feeling he would need his. He wanted to be prepared.

Then, on March 25, 1971, authorities indicted Lansky in Florida. They charged him with contempt for refusing to testify in the case about the skimming of funds from Las Vegas casinos. Worse, from his point of view, four of his friends were indicted on charges of skimming from the Flamingo. The four defendants in the case were Morris Lansburgh, president of Associated Resort Hotels; Samuel Cohen, a millionaire with interests in Miami hotels and real estate; Samuel Belkin, a former Flamingo employee; and Jerry W. Gordon, another former Flamingo employee.

It wasn't much of a case. There was only one piece of evidence tying Lansky to the Flamingo. It was a $200,000 finder's fee that he claimed in his income taxes after he facilitated his old friend Albert Parvin's sale of the hotel for $10.6 million to Landsburgh, Cohen, and Daniel Lifter a decade earlier.

Legally, it wasn't a hard case to fight. He might have a convincing defense, but the immediate legal peril for Lansky was that the indictment could cause the United States to revoke his passport. If that happened, he could be expelled from Israel. He understood that the real fight would play out in the back rooms of politics. Behind the scenes, he reached out to influential people in the Israeli government for support.

One of those influential people was Louis H. Boyar, a multimillionaire romantically linked to Israeli Prime Minister Golda Meir. He was also a prominent Democratic fundraiser based in Los Angeles. He interceded with the Israeli government to get Lansky's visa extended. Months later, when a *Los Angeles Times* reporter asked him about it, he said he didn't know Lansky. Boyar contended that he did it purely on principle. He believed that every Jew wishing to enter Israel should be allowed to do so.

Boyar wasn't alone. There were others who thought Lansky was being unfairly pilloried and that he should be allowed to stay. For now, he could stay in Israel, but he knew his situation was tenuous.

Then Lansky received unsettling news: His old friend, Phil "The Stick" Kovolick disappeared. Kovolick was called "The Stick" because he was their driver in Bugs and Meyer Mob during the Prohibition years. He had helped Lansky run the Colonial Inn in Hallandale and had remained one of Lansky's most trusted and longtime friends. When Paul's family visited Florida, Kovolick was the one who Lansky trusted to babysit little Meyer II when the adults went out to dinner. The two of them played cards—Go Fish and Old Maid—or he'd watch Meyer II at the pool.

Three weeks after his disappearance, Kovolick's body was found sealed in a steel drum at the bottom of a rock pit in Hallandale. Police charged John Alvin Baxter with first-degree murder. Baxter was convicted and later sentenced to life imprisonment. The motives for underworld murders are often murky, but Kovolick had been under investigation for illegal gambling, corruption, and bribery. Someone likely was worried that Kovolick would cooperate with authorities.

When Lansky next wrote Paul, he didn't mention Phil's untimely demise. He explained that he was behind in his letters because of his move to the Accadia Hotel in Herzliya for the summer. He thought the weather there would be more pleasant. He congratulated Paul on his knowledge of Israel and then mentioned that his sister, Esta, had just visited:

"Esta was of the opinion that I was pining away here. I thought my sister knew better than that. I was mistaken. I can have a very wide social life here if I wish it but I keep it very limited."

As dismissive as he was of his sister's observation, Lansky was, in effect, a prisoner of his own notoriety. Doc Stacher had introduced him to some friends in Israel, but they were not in the same league as his old friends in the States. He missed watching the TV news—in Israel, it was all in Hebrew, which he didn't speak. At least the weather was agreeable. He had to hold tight.

As he often did in his letters to Paul, he urged him to stay in touch with Sandra and Buddy. He fervently wanted his children to be close, but they weren't. They were leading very individual lives, very much apart from one another. But that didn't stop Lansky from hoping. He told Paul that he was happy that Paul had recently seen his sister:

"I'm sure you found a change from the last time you saw her. I hope from now on that you keep close to one another."

Paul was an obedient son. He knew how important it was to his father, but he couldn't abide Sandra. They would never be close. She was vain, materialistic, and a burden to his father. Buddy was different. Despite his disability, Buddy was eager to work and embraced life. Buddy was, in Paul's view, "pure love."

In trying to unite his children, Lansky seemed to be trying to tie up loose ends. He was hoping that a home in Israel would be his last stop. He knew that US authorities were determined to convict him of something, but he thought he just might outrun the charges and he could spend his remaining years in Israel. After all, Doc Stacher had been allowed to stay there after his conviction on tax charges.

His hopes were dashed, however, on May 18, 1971. That's when the United States notified its embassy in Tel Aviv that the government was revoking Lansky's passport.

The fight was on.

CHAPTER 21

"Battling for My Rights"

LANSKY WAS TRYING to live quietly in Israel. He needed some rest, but it was also on his lawyer's advice. He figured that keeping a low profile would improve his chances of securing Israeli citizenship. Still a gambler, he thought it gave him the best odds.

He was probably right. That is, until the newspapers weighed in on his case. In June 1971, there was an onslaught of articles in the States. *The New York Times* reported that the US Justice Department's special strike force was investigating seventy men connected to Lansky. Then, Jimmy Hoffa, the imprisoned teamster boss, was called before a grand jury probing whether Lansky's associates gave money to union officials for low-interest loans from the union's pension funds.

In Israel, Jewish newspapers pounced. One paper, *Haaretz*, reported that Lansky had organized crime ties and also had a financial interest in the Dan Hotels, where he had been staying. Another paper, *Yedioth Ahronoth*, called Lansky a gangster. Reporters from Miami were jumping in with their own stories.

The stories pushed him into a level of infamy that was impossible to tamp down. He complained about the heat in Israel, in more ways than one, in a June 17, 1971, letter to Paul:

"Here it is beastly hot and will remain hot until the end of October. For me it is hot in more ways than the weather the publicity is always growing worst. Any means to make money and these are the people that want to mold a better human being."

He went on to comment on another huge international story, *The New York Times*' decision to publish the *Pentagon Papers*:

"Of what I read I don't like what went on in secret with our Congress being aware of it but I don't think that the Times should have printed secret papers without consulting the Pentagon or the State Department, this is to serious a matter for them to be the judge alone."

Lansky, in his heart of hearts, was a conservative. He was not one to applaud broadsides against the government. For all his anger at the law enforcement pursuit of him, he believed deeply in American democracy.

By July, Lansky decided to pursue a legal remedy more aggressively in Israel. He wrote a letter, which he had hand-delivered to the Consul General of the US Embassy in Tel Aviv:

"In reply to your letter of May 18, 1971, I hereby notify you that I desire a hearing, in accordance with the passport regulations, to establish the basis for said revocation. Sincerely, Meyer Lansky."

Then he sued *Yedioth Ahronoth* for 1 million Israel pounds for calling him a gangster.

And in a move that went against everything he had ever hewed to in the past, he gave his first-ever interview. He chose a sympathetic Israeli journalist Uri Dan, who essentially reported Lansky's argument for why he should be allowed to stay in the country. Basically, Lansky argued that he was merely an old Jew who had made good among the Gentiles but was not forgiven for his Jewishness.

On July 12, 1971, he wrote to Paul about it:

"My birthday was very quiet except for the press. I don't know what they printed in the States, here, they carried my interview much verbatim. I'm satisfied with the result. I also started building a case against one of the papers. I was forced into it."

As he often did in his letters, he asked about his grandchildren and Edna:

"How is Edna feeling? Is she watching her weight? It is very important for her to keep her weight down."

He added, "My health is good. Teddy could be better but my problem of staying here is big. I have good hope that it will all work out."

Just two days later, he seemed a little less optimistic in a letter to Paul:

"I'm battling for my rights."

More bad publicity ensued. Vincent "Fat Vinny" Teresa, a low-level Mob associate of the New England Mafia, testified before a televised Senate subcommittee investigating organized crime. He was a loan shark and organized gambling junkets. His nickname was apt. As he testified before the McClellan Committee, his double chin literally spilled over his shirt.

Asked about organized crime, Teresa opined, "It starts with gambling. Without gambling, they got nothing."

He said he was testifying because he was worried about getting killed because his protector, New England Mob boss Raymond Patriarca, was in prison. Asked if he could turn to someone else in the organization, he said, to laughter, "Nah, you can't trust 'em. They're a bunch of shady characters."

That prompted laughter in the hearing room, but Teresa was right. It was in sharp contrast to Lansky, who had operated for years without a protector. He could do that because he was a moneymaker and one of the few trustworthy people in a world of perfidy.

Teresa's testimony continued. At one point, he injected a bit of drama sure to get attention by pointing a finger: "Meyer Lansky is the biggest man in the casino gambling business."

Reporters ate it up and dutifully reported his testimony. By then, there was little Lansky could do to counter the bad press. In his next letter to Paul, he didn't even mention the Teresa testimony. He opened up his letter by talking about a far more anodyne subject—the weather:

What I would give for [60°F] *and rain we will have it late Nov. not before. After a while this hot sun really makes you sluggish what was it like when we didn't have air conditioning anywhere at least today if you don't have it home you have it somewhere. I have no kicks it is the land of Jews.*

Like yourself, I have forgotten nearly all the sports, I don't watch television because it is mostly all in Hebrew . . . If I ever get settled here I will have a television set, then I will be able to see the English programs.

A little later in the same letter, he grew contemplative:

"How is it possible in this animal world for one nation to live in peace without being armed to the teeth. I often wonder how long can the hot tempers of leaders we may get in different countries can we keep peace. Just let us hope that wiser men are born in the future."

Lansky didn't know it, but that same month *Haaretz* reporters met with the fifty-man investigative team assembled by the Justice Department strike force. They wanted every bit of information they could gather. They needed to justify revoking Lansky's passport, which they did days later. Then the FBI raised the stakes of the investigation by changing its moniker from "Operation Financier" to "Operation Fugitive Financier."

Haaretz then ran a front-page story asserting that Lansky and Doc Stacher tried to buy documents that reporter Yigal Laviv had gotten from the Ministry of Justice. Laviv said the offer was made through an intermediary.

Again, Lansky kept quiet. In his next letter to Paul, he said nothing more about the bad publicity. Instead, he chided Paul gently about his appearance:

"I received your letters with the pictures all looked great except you with that brush over your lip when will I receive a picture of you—natural face."

Possibly aware that authorities might be reading his letters, he touched only lightly on his quest for citizenship:

"We are enjoying the retirement like two old people do in retirement. The days will remain hot for Sept. but much shorter nites are beautiful. Me and my dog have our daily exercises he may have his citizenship much before me."

On that point, he was prescient. He didn't know it, but none other than Israeli Prime Minister Golda Meir told his advocates in the government that she wanted absolutely no Mafia in Israel.

On September 10, 1971, Lansky made an extraordinary appearance on Israeli TV to plead his case for citizenship. Asked by the interviewer if he was worth $300 million, he smiled and said, "Three hundred million? I wish I had *a million* dollars."

His voice was deep and strong. Even though he was under siege in the press and in the courts, he appeared absolutely in command.

He complained about being harassed. "I was singled out for some reason. They needed an image," he said.

"They accused me of making a president. Now I don't know Mr. Nixon any more than what I read in the newspapers," he declared.

He blamed the news media for his problems. "I didn't know as I was growing older it was going to get worse."

It was an astute, if not sardonic, observation. The pressure from authorities had only intensified as he was trying to retire and get out of the business, as presumably less of a threat.

Finally, the interviewer asked him what he knew about organized crime. On this point, Lansky gave a legalistic answer that was almost laughable: "I have no knowledge of it."

Despite the implausibility of his last answer, Lansky felt good about the interview. He seemed convinced that he could sway public opinion in Israel through the sheer force of his personality. He was sure, too, that the law was on his side. On October 14, 1971, he wrote to Paul:

"Nothing new with me the same old battle, it will take a few months before we get to court. I'm sure we have a good chance to win. If not I will be in a battle again, but I will not die worrying. What will be will be."

He couldn't resist another comment on the mustache he hated on Paul:

"It would be a good idea to grow the beard maybe it would cover up the brush, also may keep you warm in the winter. I often wonder what makes you tick."

In late October that year, there was more bad news. The US Justice Department, under Attorney General John Mitchell, issued a superseding indictment against Lansky. It charged him with skimming $36 million from the Flamingo hotel from 1960 to 1967. Because the indictment was handed up by a grand jury in Nevada, a lawyer for Lansky reached out to Las Vegas Mob lawyer Oscar Goodman to be Lansky's local counsel.

Goodman—a flamboyant Vegas figure who would later serve as the defense attorney for Tony Spilotro, the doomed Chicago Outfit mobster turned Vegas skimmer—was thrilled by the call. He received "a handsome retainer" and immediately started seeking delays because of Lansky's poor health. The judge, persuaded that Lansky's medical condition was real and serious, ultimately dismissed the case.

For Lansky, it was a legal victory. For Goodman, it was a windfall. Even though Goodman never met Lansky while representing him, his phone started ringing off the hook.

"This time my client was the biggest name in the criminal underworld. You can't buy that kind of advertising," he wrote in his memoir, *Being Oscar.*

In Israel, Lansky was in a holding pattern. On November 1, 1971, he wrote to Paul:

"At present, I can't tell you much about myself. I'm waiting for my day in court."

That day came two weeks later. An Israeli court issued a temporary injunction barring Lansky's expulsion. Lansky's case became an international *cause célèbre.*

Again, when writing to Paul, he avoided the details of his legal case. Instead, he focused on a favorite subject of his—food. Although he was a notoriously picky eater and maintained a disciplined regimen to stay slim, he thought of himself as something of an expert on food:

I envy you when you write about food in San Francisco. Our good is good but I miss the cold water fishes, we do have a lobster and good shrimps, but no clams or oysters. I also miss my smoked fishes all else is O.K., except steaks and roast beef this country lacks the grazing ground for large cattle. Television I miss too we get a movie in English a few times a week. I'm not much for movies at present we have a series every week on Churchills war years which I enjoy. There is other movies in French but the words are in Hebrew. I also miss the news daily on television.

And, as he often did, he weighed in on US politics. He told Paul he was disgusted by President Nixon's court appointments:

It only proves they haven't any consideration for the people only to perpetuate their wealth and power. If the Democrats come up with a good candidate the Congress will be against him, it will be some time before we get an intelligent Congress to stand with the President for matters that will bring back our respect in the World also what is best for our Country not looking for favors to trade with the President.

By December, Lansky was writing Paul about the lack of Christmas decoration, something he seemed to think was odd in a country of Jews:

We hardly know it is Christmas you don't see Santa Clause [sp] *or any windows dressed up for the occasion, you do see it in Jerusalem, more so in Bethlehem. Hanukah* [sp] *ended this week it is really a sight to see here. The influx of Christians at Christmas is tremendous. There isn't a room to be had in all of Israel. Jerusalem and Bethlehem you can't breathe.*

As low-key as he was trying to be, the publicity wouldn't stop. In January 1972, Jack Anderson, a nationally syndicated columnist with tremendous influence, published a column calling Israel a "Sanctuary for Racketeers." He listed the mobsters fleeing to Israel: Meyer Lansky, Harry Stromberg, Joe Stacher, Morris Schmertzler, Al Mones, Hyman Segal, Frank Ritter, and Claude Lipsky. He also noted that US dollars had been traced from US banks to Israeli banks—a suggestion that some Israeli officials might have been paid off.

The story stung, but Lansky was preoccupied with his court case. A *Jerusalem Post* article laid out the evidence against him. The Kefauver hearings came back to haunt him:

> *After hearing over 500 witnesses, including Lansky and top-ranking gangsters, the committee concluded that gambling enterprises formed the hard-rock core of organized crime in U.S. cities and that the gangs operating the gambling enterprises "are the survivors of the murderous underworld wars of the Prohibition era." One witness, Barney Rudinski, who was employed as a "debt collector" by the gambling clubs, informed the committee that he had never killed anyone without an o.k. from above and that at least until 1941 killings had to be cleared in New York with Lansky.*

The Rudinski testimony was improbable, at best. While Lansky certainly had enormous influence over underworld operations, he never had the final say on who was to be killed.

On March 22, 1972, the day of his hearing before the Israel High Court of Justice finally arrived. The US Justice Department delivered two suitcases full of evidence to the court. In fact, the prosecutor in the case, Gavriel Bach, met personally with Attorney General Mitchell in Washington, DC. Mitchell took pains to say that the United States didn't want to interfere in the case. But in a political sleight of hand typical in Washington, DC, he was willing to quietly provide information on Lansky's criminal background.

The most damaging evidence in the case was of an underworld summit that Lansky was supposed to have attended in Israel. In reality, though, it amounted to nothing because authorities stopped it after tips from Interpol and British police.

When the trial opened, a brisk traffic of sightseers poured in. Ironically, they had little interest in the facts of the case. They were there for one reason. As described by a reporter from *The Jerusalem Post*, they sat down for a bit, "gazed raptly at Mr. Lansky, and left again, their noisy movements visibly annoying the bench."

Lansky wrote Paul about the trial. First, he apologized for not immediately answering his son's letter from just a few days earlier:

> *I have been very busy preparing for the trial. The D.A. is through. We had one day and we will have another day after the holiday and then wait for the decision . . . It will be a few months before the decision will come down. Until then more time waisted in uncertainty. Don't worry what will be will be.*

As preoccupied as he was with his trial, he made a point of praising his son's values:

> *Paul, I admire you for your attitude of loyalty to your work and country. I wonder if the people giving a half job instead of a full job realize that they are paying it themselves. The more it costs to run the country the more taxes we have to pay. That is the problem with the world of people—one half wants to live off the other half. Your attitude is the proper attitude stick to it.*

He was genuinely proud of his son, and their bond had deepened in recent years. He also knew, however, that there might be another audience reading his letters.

Lansky would have to wait six months for a decision.

Meanwhile, in June 1972, the United States indicted him again on charges of tax evasion connected to gambling junkets to London. Mobster Teresa claimed to have firsthand knowledge of the junkets.

By September, Lansky's battle for citizenship came to an abrupt denouement. The Supreme Court of Israel ruled that Lansky would have to leave Israel. He walked out of the courtroom and glumly told the reporters waiting there, "A Jew has a slim chance in this world."

He wrote Paul that the decision was "most disappointing" and then quoted French philosopher Cardinal Richelieu: "Let the most honest man write a few lines and I will ruin him for life."

He promised Paul that it wasn't over: "Don't worry. I'm not giving up."

Horrified, Paul wanted to make a last-ditch argument to the Israeli government about everything his father had done for Israel. He wrote a letter to Israeli Interior Minister Yosef Burg, who was supportive of Lansky, and asked that it be published in Israel:

"Simply put, Dr. Burg, Israel was in in dire need. You asked for help. You got the help—and some of the help came from people like my Dad."

He went on: "Did Israel not accept assistance from people like my Dad about whom unfavorable comments had been made? When did they not accept such assistance?"

Paul's fierce defense of his father gratified Lansky. He wrote him:

"Your letter is very well put. We will decide at a later date whether to use it for the press or just to show it to him. It is a really strong letter . . . Don't worry I'm not giving up. I'm not in the habit of giving in easily."

Lansky's display of bravado notwithstanding, it was over. He had to leave. Five days before his deportation deadline, on November 5, 1972, he boarded a plane bound for Geneva. Teddy stayed behind to pack up their things.

He made a point of leaving around Election Day, reasoning that the national news of a presidential election in the States would eclipse the news of his travel. But even that wasn't enough to crowd him out of the headlines. As usual, Lansky made international news. Back home in Tacoma, Meyer II walked into the family's TV room and saw his father watching the news. A map appeared on the screen as broadcaster Walter Cronkite announced the news of his grandfather's departure from Israel.

What ensued after his first flight from Israel was dizzying, as Lansky hopscotched across the globe while being chased by authorities. This came even after he offered any country that would take him $1 million and an additional substantial investment in the country.

The FBI notified the legal attaché in Bern, who informed them that Lansky had left Geneva and was headed to Brazil. At midnight, Lansky boarded a Swiss Air flight en route to Rio de Janeiro. He landed there November 6. Brazil rejected him. Again, it was on the nightly news.

He then boarded a plane to Paraguay. He had some reason to be confident that Paraguay would accept him because he had sent $50,000 to an honorary counsel there. But when he landed in La Paz, Paraguay, he looked out the window and saw the honorary counsel flanked by two men. They solemnly told Lansky that he could not get off the plane. The reason, they explained, was that they had to bar anyone arrested for drugs.

The only time Lansky was ever arrested on any drug charge was when he was arrested in Miami for having ulcer medication.

Lansky then headed to Buenos Aires, Argentina; Lima, Peru; and finally Panama. Each country rejected him. The FBI sent out a teletype labeling him a fugitive.

He had no choice but to continue on to Miami. The FBI sent out an alert to ensure that he would not be turned away in Miami. The agency also helpfully alerted the press.

He landed in Miami at 6:10 A.M. on November 7, 1972. FBI Agent Kenneth Whittaker arrested Lansky for failing to answer the summons to appear before a grand jury in Miami. He took him to a detention cell at the US Marshal's headquarters. After posting a $250,000 bond, Lansky emerged wearing a rumpled blue suit and white shirt open at the collar. A judge ordered him to surrender his passport and restricted him to Broward and Dade Counties in Florida.

Reporters had raced to the courthouse. Exhausted and dispirited, Lansky told them, "That's life. At my age, it's too late to worry. What will be will be."

Again, it was on the nightly news.

FBI functionaries were triumphant. "Extensive press coverage afforded at the airport," said one teletype.

Back in Tacoma, Meyer II watched the news in disbelief. Three days later, he watched more disconcerting news.

Teddy had followed her husband and landed in Miami, only to be greeted by a gaggle of reporters. She was angry and looking for a fight. She screamed at them to stop harassing her.

A female TV reporter taunted her: "Mrs. Lansky, you're supposed to be seventy and sharp. You don't look seventy and sharp!"

Teddy spit in her face.

CHAPTER 22
A Difficult Homecoming

LANSKY RETURNED HOME to a different United States. The war in Vietnam had deeply divided the country. Tens of thousands of young Americans—Lansky scorned them as hippies—protested being drafted to a war on the other side of the world that they didn't understand and didn't want to fight. One day, Meyer II was riding with him in a car when Lansky spotted long-haired teenagers on the side of the road. All of sudden, he rolled down his window and spat out, "Get a haircut!"

He just couldn't abide what he viewed as a lack of patriotism on the part of the nation's young people. Meanwhile, his own son, Paul, would serve two tours in Vietnam without hesitation. That was the kind of patriotism Lansky applauded.

As the nation's divisive politics played out, the fissures in Paul and Edna's marriage were surfacing as well. One day, Meyer II was playing in the rafters of the family's garage and found some tapes up there.

Puzzled, he called out to his mother: "Hey, Mom, look at these!"

Paul walked into the garage and snapped, "Hey, get down from there!"

But it was too late. Meyer II had accidentally discovered something that could not be ignored. Years earlier, Edna had discovered that Paul had been cheating on her. Furious and in tears, she called her father-in-law. Lansky flew in from Florida to tell his son in no uncertain terms to shape up. And Paul did. As much as he had carved out his own life separate from his father and his siblings, he still deeply respected his father and yearned for his approval.

But the tapes. Edna pressed her husband. Confronted with the evidence, he had no choice but to tell her the truth. Paul had connected a tape recorder to the family's home telephone system. Every day he would switch out the tapes and listen to them. Ever since the confrontation with his father over his cheating, he had been systematically bugging his wife. The irony was that he had been doing this at a time when they feared their home was being bugged by the FBI.

The revelation stunned Edna. She thought back on her telephone conversations with her mother. Over and over, she had confided her feelings about her fraught marriage to her. She complained that Paul was always away working, and when he was home, he was locked away in his study. She complained that he constantly scrutinized her expenses. She complained that he rarely engaged with the children. And yet, every night, Paul would come home and cheerfully ask about dinner.

In some ways, it was a betrayal greater than another woman.

For Edna, it was over. She decided to leave. She felt so hurt and angry. She didn't want the last name of Lansky anymore, the one that had been such a source of pride for her husband. She decided to strike back.

She changed her last name to Mason. She had never liked her first name anyway, so she changed that, too, to Malana. She would become Malana Mason, a much more glamorous-sounding name that fit so well into a West Coast sensibility.

Changing her last name meant that she would change her children's last name as well. Her son's name was a problem. The name Meyer Lansky evoked such strong reactions. To truly shed the past and start a new life, he needed to change his first and last names.

She broached it with her son. At first, he was not sure what to do. But she pushed. "Why do you want it? It's never done anything for you anyway."

Meyer II liked his name and the reaction it got, but he didn't feel much of an emotional connection to his father. Paul was never home, and when he was, he was busy. The children's world revolved around their mother. As they were leaving in the car, Meyer II saw a street sign called "Bryant." That was it. He would become Bryan Mason.

There was no discussion of how the name change might affect him emotionally.

As was typical in the Lansky family, Paul kept his separation a secret from his father.

Paul knew that his father's own divorce had deeply pained him. And even though Lansky and Anna had not lived together for years, he faithfully sent her money and talked to doctors about her care. He often confided to Paul his worries about her. He urged his son to visit her. After all, he often said, she was his children's mother.

But there was more to it than Paul's understanding of his father's pain. Paul had succeeded where his brother and sister had not. Lansky loved being a grandfather to his son's children. To his mind, his son had achieved the perfect American family.

Paul simply couldn't bear taking that away from his father.

Yet, for all his insistence that his son hew to good old-fashioned family values, Lansky did not practice what he preached. And like his son, he had an extraordinary ability to compartmentalize.

When Lansky left Israel, Teddy stayed behind for a few days to pack up the apartment. Another woman in Lansky's life stayed behind temporarily in Israel as well—his mistress, Zali de Toledo.

They had met at Jerusalem's Dan Hotel. Lansky often ate with friends and hangers-on in the hotel lobby. De Toledo, a young, comely divorcee who was intrigued by the rich American tourists frequenting the hotel, worked there as a waitress.

One day, the hotel's owner, knowing of de Toledo's interest in the Americans, decided to introduce her to one. He brought her over to Lansky's table and made the introduction. He smiled, and she smiled. Later, she described it as being hit by a "thunderbolt."

Lansky disengaged from the men around him and approached de Toledo with a proposition: "I can't get ham and eggs in this hotel," he said. "How about if you buy the eggs and I buy the ham, and you cook them for me?"

It was hardly the smoothest of come-ons, but it did honestly reflect his feelings about the food in Israel. He complained about it to Paul all the time.

De Toledo was a little nonplussed, but managed to blurt out: "Sure, I'll cook you the eggs."

The next morning, she heard a knock on the door. Still in her nightgown, she opened it. There was Lansky, holding a bag. "I got the eggs, too," he said with a grin.

De Toledo threw her arms around him, and their affair began. She was more than forty years younger and several inches taller than Lansky, but she was sure she was in love.

Because Teddy often traveled from Israel to the States to handle matters at home, de Toledo and Lansky often had extended periods of time together. They settled into their own form of domesticity. Lansky would come over every morning for breakfast. Then they would part ways and each go about their day.

De Toledo even met Teddy, who clearly didn't see her as a threat. They became friendly. Teddy seemed to think she could impart her years of hard-won wisdom to the young woman.

One day, de Toledo was playing with their dog, Bruiser—a number of accounts spell the dog's name as "Bruzzer," but Lansky spelled it as "Bruiser" in his letters—and kissed him on the mouth. Teddy decided it was the time to give her some important counsel:

"My dear, you never kiss a man or a dog on the mouth," she said. "You never know where their mouths have been before."

De Toledo took her comment as a kind, not crude, remark.

Women constantly threw themselves at Lansky. It was obvious to de Toledo that they had read stories about his so-called $300-million fortune. Although she rarely asked for money, he was always very generous. He paid for her dental surgery, bought her jewelry, and rented her an apartment. One particularly sentimental gift he gave her was the gold key Virginia Hill had made for Ben Siegel to get into her mansion. It was inscribed, "Always in my heart."

She felt they had a deeper connection that went beyond money. She was right. Their relationship did not end when he left Israel.

For the time being in Miami, however, he had to deal with the pressing legal issues facing him at home. Although he didn't have a $300-million fortune, he had enough money to live comfortably. It was clear, however, that, given his failing health, the money would not be flowing as it had before. The legal bills mounted. Teddy was worried. She decided to do something about it. Without telling her husband, she started reaching out to his old friends for help.

One was Moe Dalitz, his old partner in the Cuban casinos. After Dalitz left Cuba, he put down roots in Las Vegas. The city was a place where a gangster could become a city father. Dalitz did just that, becoming a successful hotel and casino developer. For the first time in his life, he was legitimate.

Teddy called him. He didn't answer. She called again and again. Still, he didn't answer. Finally, she reached out to a friend who worked with Dalitz. That summer, Dalitz's sixteen-year-old daughter, Suzanne, had come to live with her father and work in his hotel. His father's friend approached her.

"Your father won't meet with Teddy Lansky," he told her. "She really wants to talk with you."

Suzanne couldn't imagine why Teddy Lansky would want to have lunch with her, but she agreed. They met at the famed Stardust Casino. It was big and impressive. Going there felt like an occasion.

Suzanne knew little about her father's business affairs, but she knew it was problematic enough to spur her parents' divorce when she was just six years old. Teddy appeared. She seemed desperate, even weird, to Suzanne. She made clear that she wanted something from Suzanne's father. Over and over, she insisted that Dalitz owed Lansky.

That Teddy could harangue a sixteen-year-old about her father's finances was astonishing in itself and unsettling to the teenager. Afterward, Suzanne told her father about the encounter. He stiffened. With Nevada's strict gaming licensing requirements, he wanted nothing to do with anyone with a criminal taint. One whiff of a connection to a guy like Lansky could cost Dalitz his gambling license. Dalitz also knew that Lansky was under constant surveillance by the FBI.

He told Suzanne that he didn't owe Lansky anything.

Teddy returned home empty-handed.

Whether Lansky ever found out about the luncheon is unknown.

Meanwhile, Lansky was sorting out his business affairs in Miami. His brother, Jack, lived in an apartment in Hollywood, Florida. Lansky often visited him there. Jack was one of the few people whose counsel Lansky trusted implicitly. He had become a seasoned casino operator and businessman and had managed to keep a far lower profile than his older brother. They talked constantly.

Often, they would take their conversations outside, walking along Surf Road and the beach in pants and shirts. With everybody else in swimsuits and shorts, they made for an incongruous sight. One day, a neighbor who was also an aspiring journalist, asked the men why they did that.

Lansky's response was simple: "They can't hear us."

The brothers had reason to be cautious. A Bell South telephone repair van was always parked outside the apartment complex. Everybody living there knew there were no problems with the phones.

By February 1973, Lansky's legal situation worsened. A federal grand jury convicted him of contempt because he didn't leave Israel to answer grand jury questions two years earlier. The ramifications were serious. He could wind up in federal prison, where he would likely die because his health was so fragile.

Prosecutor Dougald McMillan had persuaded the grand jury that Lansky had been healthy enough to travel from Israel. In reality, however, he was suffering. He underwent open heart surgery in March.

It was a long recovery. In May, he wrote Paul:

"I'm making good recovery. It is 2 months since I smoke a cigarette how about you cutting down to a half pack day."

As he often did, he enclosed $50 and asked about Edna and the children.

He still did not know that Paul and Edna had separated.

That same month, a federal judge sentenced him to one year and a day in prison. Lansky's lawyer argued that he was seriously ill. He said he had quit smoking, cold turkey, after having a five-pack-a-day habit for years. But he needed more heart surgery. The judge agreed to delay his trial for tax evasion, but only for a couple of months.

In July, Lansky appeared in court to plead not guilty. The key witness against him was Vincent Teresa.

He was testifying in exchange for a reduction of his sentence for a conviction of securities theft. A practiced witness, he had already testified in nineteen previous Mob trials.

Teresa considered himself a swashbuckler and bon vivant. In the courtroom, however, he struck a different pose. To mask his identity, he wore a false beard and mustache. To keep him safe, court officers surrounded him. That alone made an impression on onlookers.

Teresa testified that he had traveled twice to Miami to make in-person payments to Lansky. He said he gave him a total of $90,000 in $100 bills.

Teddy countered with testimony that they had been staying at the Sheraton Plaza in Boston during one of Teresa's trips, and she had the hotel bill to prove it.

Confronted with that fact on cross-examination by Lansky's lawyer, Teresa said Lansky must have had a double.

Teresa might have thought that was a plausible answer, but the jury didn't. After a seven-day trial, the jury acquitted Lansky.

Although his testimony failed to convict Lansky, Teresa bragged about it later to journalist Thomas Renner: "The federal government tells me I'm the first one they've been able to find willing to say he paid Lansky money from casino profits."

He went on to explain how it worked:

"Now, Lansky didn't come to me and say: 'Vinnie Teresa, I want you to do this.' It doesn't work that way. He can't give orders to any Mob guy unless he has an okay from that guy's boss, and to do that, he has to go through Jimmy Blue Eyes . . . If he tried to call me direct and bypass them, he would be in a lot of trouble. Lansky's too smart to do that . . .

"He can sit with the Mob bosses because he makes them so much money. But if he got out of line, if he defied them, they'd wipe him out in a second."

The court victory buoyed Lansky's spirits. He wrote to an old friend, Joseph Sheiner, a member of the Israeli Security Agency who had supported his bid for Israeli citizenship:

"It was a great victory for me. Whatever else happens now does not matter."

He filed an appeal of the contempt conviction and tried to focus on his health. Physically, Lansky was diminished. Anyone could see it. Paul, always worried about his father's health, went to Florida in August to visit him. That was when he finally told him about his divorce. It was the kind of thing he felt he had to say in person, not in a letter and not over the phone. As much as Lansky wanted his son to have a stable marriage and family, he always sided with his son. In all the letters to Paul that followed over the years, he never again mentioned Edna.

On August 10, 1973, he wrote Paul: "Your visit was an inspiration for me. Everyone enjoyed your company here."

He also indulged in a little political commentary: "Watergate was laid to rest for a while and in comes Agnew. What do you think of that? I love the way they cry about the unfairness of being tried in the press but they do the very thing they dislike. Let's get the dirty laundry out and wash it clean."

As someone who felt he had been pilloried in the press, it had to be satisfying to see it happen to politicians like Nixon and Spiro Agnew for a change.

Edna and the children moved to Ontario, California, for a year. Meyer II loved being away from the rainy Tacoma winters. Although the final divorce decree gave Paul visitation, Meyer II didn't see his father much. Paul was always away. He did try to explain the divorce to his son, in his own way. He said only, "These things happen."

Meanwhile, where Teddy saw a man nearing the end of his life and income-producing potential, Lansky's notoriety only continued to grow. The movie *The Godfather* had come out in 1972. Based on the best-selling novel by Mario Puzo, it was an epic tale of a Mafia family in New York. It became one of the highest-grossing movies of all time.

Puzo co-wrote the screenplay. He always insisted that he didn't personally know any mobsters, but the story had an authenticity that turned even real mobsters into fans. The movie was so popular that producers demanded a sequel. *The Godfather Part II* was released in 1974.

It was the sequel that cemented Lansky in the public imagination. One of the main characters in the movie was a Jewish mobster and investor named Hyman Roth. The details of his fictional early life closely mirrored Lansky's real life. Like Lansky, Roth started out as a car mechanic. Born Hyman Suchowsky, he shortened his name to Roth, as Lansky did. Asked who he admired most, Roth cited Arnold Rothstein, Lansky's mentor. Roth even worked with the Corleone family during Prohibition.

In the movie, Roth is an older mobster in poor health living in Miami—again, not unlike Lansky. He brings Michael Corleone into an extremely profitable gambling business in Cuba under Batista's government. In one iconic scene, mobsters gather on a balcony to celebrate Roth's birthday. A waiter brings out a cake decorated with a map of Cuba. Roth cuts it and makes sure that each mobster gets a piece—just as Lansky made sure his buddies each got a piece of the profits from Cuba.

There is also a nod to his murdered friend, Moe Greene—the Vegas mogul who was shot through the eye in the first film, the "Moe Greene special" clearly a Bugsy Siegel homage—when bemoaning his fate to Al Pacino's Michael Corleone:

> *There was this kid that I grew up with. He was a couple years younger than me, and sort of looked up to me, you know. We did our first work together, worked our way out of the street. Things were good and we made the most of it.*
>
> *During Prohibition, we ran molasses up to Canada and made a fortune—your father, too. I guess as much as anyone, I loved him and trusted him. Later on, he had an idea to make a city out of a desert stopover for GIs on the way to the West Coast.*
>
> *That kid's name was Moe Greene, and the city he invented was Las Vegas. This was a great man—a man with vision and guts—and there isn't even a plaque or a signpost or a statue of him in that town.*
>
> *Someone put a bullet through his eye. No one knows who gave the order.*
>
> *When I heard about it I wasn't angry. I knew Moe. I knew he was headstrong, and talking loud, and saying stupid things.*
>
> *So when he turned up dead, I let it go, and said to myself: This is the business we've chosen. I never asked who gave the go-ahead because it had nothing to do with business.*

Not surprisingly, Lansky loved the performance of the actor Lee Strasberg, who portrayed Roth. He called him up and complimented him: "Hey, you did a good job."

Strasberg politely thanked him, but was shaken. He had never been called by a mobster before.

As amused as Lansky was by Strasberg's portrayal of him, he played down his fame to his family. He always believed that the less they knew, the better for them. After the divorce, he had no contact with Edna, but he maintained close ties to his grandchildren, particularly Meyer II, now known as Bryan Mason.

Meyer II, for his part, was enthralled by his grandfather. Although he didn't know much about Lansky's business activities, he loved the way he could take command of a room simply by entering. He knew that Lansky wasn't like other grandfathers. Over the years, he had heard snippets on the news, and he couldn't miss the reaction of people when they heard the Lansky name. He wanted to know more.

After his parents' divorce, he asked them if he could visit Lansky in Florida during his summer breaks. They readily agreed. Lansky loved his visits and never gave him a hard time about his name change. He'd pick him up at the airport—always waiting in the background, never making a show of himself—and have all sorts of activities planned. Hymie "Cummerbuns" Krumholtz drove them around, and Lansky occasionally jumped out to use a pay phone.

They often went to the Singapore Hotel, a favorite hangout of his grandfather's. Lansky's friends were always there, and they ribbed him mercilessly. A favorite joke directed at Lansky was, "Oh, he's a lot taller than you!" Lansky always joined in the laughter. He loved the camaraderie.

One day, Hymie started talking about watches. Meyer II wasn't sure, but he seemed to be talking about stolen watches. Lansky snapped. "Don't ever say anything about the watches I gave you, Hymie! If I give you something, don't ever say anything!"

Meyer II said nothing, but thought to himself, *Oh my God! They're still doing stuff in their seventies!*

Another Lansky buddy was Albert "Tick-Tock" Tannenbaum, a notorious Mob hit man. He and Lansky were an unlikely alliance because they were not in business together. Moreover, Tannenbaum had turned stool pigeon years earlier when authorities pressured him to testify about a Mob hit they suspected had been led by Siegel. It's likely that Lansky kept him around as a bodyguard. With dark eyes and an angular face, his brooding demeanor often rattled people. When Meyer II met him, a chill ran down his spine. He could just feel the menace. He kept his distance.

Meyer II usually shared a room at the Hawaiian Isle Hotel with his uncle Buddy. They had fun together. Buddy had a zest for life and always knew the juiciest gossip. Lansky tried to impose some order on the two, always making sure Meyer II hung up his clothes properly. But he also always gave him $300 in running-around money.

Sometimes he'd ask Meyer II what he wanted to do with his life. His grandson wanted to be a bartender. He loved the idea of working in the hospitality industry. It just felt like he belonged there. He was pretty sure his grandfather wouldn't approve, so he told him he wanted to be a carpenter or builder.

"Nothing wrong with that," Lansky replied.

When he finally summoned up the courage to tell him what he really wanted to do, Lansky, who was certainly familiar with the difficulties of making a living in the hospitality industry, gave him a long look and said, "Read a few good books. Write a few letters. What more do you want out of life?"

Lansky could be inscrutable. Meyer II desperately wanted to know more about his grandfather's life, but he knew not to ask direct questions. There seemed to be an unwritten rule about that. Lansky noticed that his grandson was quiet around him. One day, while he was visiting, Lansky turned to him and said, "Is there something you want to ask me?"

"You know Frank Sinatra, don't you?" Meyer II ventured, knowing that he was asking about a part of his grandfather's life that he probably didn't want to share with him.

"Meyer, don't believe everything you read," he responded.

Meyer II laughed, but also knew not to press the issue. Like his grandfather, he could read the cues. He saw the look on his grandfather's face. It was as if he were thinking, *Oh, he's figuring it out about me.*

CHAPTER 23
Troubles Close to Home

US AUTHORITIES WERE determined to convict Lansky in court, and he was just as determined to fight back. By the end of the summer of 1974, he could exult over two more court victories. His appeal of his contempt conviction succeeded, and a Nevada judge ruled that he was too ill to travel to Las Vegas for the skimming case against him. He hoped that with those victories, his life would quiet down a bit.

It didn't.

A new book, *The Last Testament of Lucky Luciano* by Martin A. Gosch and Richard Hammer, came out. It was such a sensation that it earned $1 million even before its publication date. Readers delighted in its details. The life story of one of the most famous mobsters of all time, written in his own words, was irresistible. Reviewers culled out stories that had never been told before and pondered their significance. It was, in short, a huge hit.

The only problem was that it wasn't true.

The New York Times published an article that raised real questions about its authenticity. The book was purportedly based on taped conversations Gosch had with Luciano before he died, but there were no tapes and the notes had supposedly been destroyed. The article noted that the book had Luciano discussing events that occurred after he died in 1962. It had him at meetings that he could never have attended because he was in jail at the time. There were also errors about the Mafia.

Moses Polakoff, the lawyer who represented both Luciano and Lansky, was personally involved in some of the events described in the book. He told the *Times*, "Not 5 percent of the accounts bear any resemblance to reality."

The *Times* exposé did little to quell the fascination with the book. Because Luciano and Lansky had been so close, Lansky's name naturally came up.

In answer to a journalist's question, Lansky wrote in reply:

"Answering a malicious Liar like Gosch serves no purpose. I don't know whether he really knew C. L. [Charles Luciano]. I'm positive he would never reveal or speak of personal matters to him."

Most troubling to Lansky was the allegation that he, Lansky, had had a hand in Siegel's murder.

"If I knew C. L., I know Gosch/Hammer quotes are ridiculous. If it was in my power to see Benny alive, he would live as long as Matusala [Methuselah, the Biblical patriarch who lived 969 years]. This was a terrible shock to me."

He and Siegel had had a deep bond. Even after Siegel's death, Lansky had remained closed to his widow and children. Describing his friendships with mobsters, he said:

"I was more human about it. I believe in live and let live. I gained through my friendship with certain [men], the least I could do is compensate by being honest to them. He, Mr. Gosch, was just out for one thing like all the rest of them. Just the almighty dollar."

He went on to tell the journalist:

"Honest reporting is very important in our society. Unfortunately, a few exaggerated liars create much trouble for the many."

It was maddening to him. By nature, Lansky was an optimist. He trusted in his own ability to turn things to his advantage. But by mid-1975, he felt worn down. What he saw as hypocrisy grated on him. The constant pressure from law enforcement was exhausting. He wrote to a friend, Fred Weisgal, a civil rights attorney and official in the Israeli Ministry of Justice:

"I'm much discusted with life here. Every other week, I'm handed a subpoena."

Authorities had failed to convict him of any crimes, so they started issuing him grand jury subpocnas about *other* people's crimes. One was the murder of Johnny Roselli, a mobster from the Chicago Outfit who rose to power in Hollywood and Las Vegas in the 1940s and 1950s. In 1975, Roselli had testified before several grand juries and was subpoenaed by the Senate's Church Intelligence Committee hearings. He testified in secret about the CIA-coordinated Mafia plots against Castro in Cuba and his belief that Castro might have retaliated against JFK. His testimony exposes a CIA connection to organized crime and the withholding of critical information from the Warren Commission.

In early 1976, Roselli was called back for more testimony. The newly formed House Select Committee on Assassinations (HSCA) was gearing up to reinvestigate JFK's murder. Roselli was expected to be a key witness, potentially linking the assassination to CIA-Mafia operations. Both Mob bosses and potentially some individuals within the government feared what he might reveal under oath. On July 28, 1976, Roselli disappeared from Miami. On August 9, his body was found stuffed in a steel drum floating near Dumfoundling Bay, Florida.

Lansky was not involved in Roselli's murder. Despite the authorities' efforts to link him to the crime—and generate more headlines—he had no information for the grand jury.

One bright spot in his life was his grandson Meyer II's annual visits. He loved Meyer II's natural athleticism and his youthful enthusiasm. He constantly quizzed Meyer II on current events. As forbidding as Lansky could seem to others, he delighted in Meyer II. He wrote Paul to tell him that he missed his grandson when he wasn't around.

Paul knew how worried his father was about Anna and Paul's brother and sister. Paul tried to step up and help his family the way his father wanted. Despite his strained relationship with his mother, he still visited her in New York when he could.

Lansky was grateful. He knew it wasn't something Paul wanted to do but that he was doing it for his father. In December 1975, he wrote Paul:

"It is really kind of you to spend Christmas with your Mother. I don't know what your desires are for New Years. If you wish to come to Florida you are always welcome as my guest."

Their bond was strong, and Lansky loved seeing Paul, but he was feeling the urge to move again. He was increasingly fed up with his legal fights in the United States. He began reaching out to Israeli friends to see if he could return there. He knew it would be a tough fight. In March 1976, he wrote to de Toledo:

> *I do feel pessimistic about being allowed to enter. I'm being patient for it for two reasons: utmost is you, second, a condemnation by me could be harmful to us Jews. You don't just live to revenge your feelings, you must always feel for others. That is what it is all about.*
>
> *If only it was possible to separate the country, the people, from the cowardly politicians who allowed me to travel when they willfully and knowingly knew in their hearts they were lying to me! Yet I have to be careful how I speak because I never wanted to cause any disturbance to the country.*

He might have been tempered in his letter to de Toledo, but he wasn't giving up. He decided to gather his family around him for the Christmas holiday. Paul was unable to join them. Lansky wrote him that they would toast him at dinner. He then expressed his frustration with Sandra's husband, Vince Lombardo, a low-level mobster, for whom he had absolutely no regard:

> *Today I will have to listen to simpleton and his story's. He has his last chance: either he learns how not* [to] *lie and keep his mouth shut or eat alone. If he can't discipline*

himself he will be out with us. I will control the time limit that I want to spend with him. My most important reason for going is Gary. He is a good boy. I'm terribly sorry about the children especially Meyer who asked if he could visit with us. I hope you got through to him that he is always welcome.

Lansky did try to refer to his grandson by his new name, but at times he slipped and used his given name.

Sandra was still the problem child, and there was little Lansky felt he could do about it.

By the late 1970s, Lansky was in his seventies. He knew time was short. He wrote Paul:

"You say time is moving fast but don't push it, it moves fast on its own."

Paul was one of the few people with whom he could discuss his interest in history and current events. In particular, he was fascinated with great men. Part of it was because he knew and did business with well-known politicians and celebrities most Americans only read about. But he also understood intuitively how certain men had shaped history. He told his son what he thought of various generals—Douglas MacArthur, Dwight Eisenhower, and George Marshall. He liked Marshall the best because, although he didn't say it, Marshall reminded Lansky of himself:

"[Marshall] had things done constructively in a modest manner; MacArthur a capable intelligent man but too arrogant his errors was caused by his arrogance; Eisenhower a kindly modest man was corrupt by Wall St. and the Bankers."

He cited a quote that underscored the importance of reading up on current events:

"If anyone believes that a nation can be both ignorant and free, they believe what never was done and never can be."

In another letter to Paul, he warned that history was fast-changing and was even prescient:

"Russia has to be watched carefully. Not to repeat the same error as we did with Cuba."

Paul seemed to be getting on with his life, and Lansky was pleased. He wanted nothing more than for his middle son to be happy. In February 1977, he wrote him:

"I'm happy to hear that you are having a good social life and enjoy the cooking you do. As long as you enjoy your own cooking you can do without a wife. Having a maid is much better."

And, as he often did, he touched on the national news of the day:

"In today's world you can't be without an intelligence organization I don't approve all that the CIA did but Congress and past Presidents were much at fault."

Lansky always followed current events because he was interested, but also because knowledge of current events helped him plot his next moves. After Menachem Begin's surprising election victory in Israel in May 1977, he reached out to *Jerusalem Post* journalist David Landau.

He asked him excitedly, "What do you think David? Do you think I can come back now? I'm sure Begin would appreciate what I did for him in 1948."

Landau had to explain to Lansky that it really wasn't up to Begin. The new Israeli prime minister had to rule through a governing coalition, meaning that he would have to cut deals with opposing sides just to run the government. There was no way he could bring Lansky back by fiat.

"It was a rather sad conversation," Landau recalled.

Nonetheless, Lansky felt sure he would prevail. He called de Toledo in Israel and told her, "Honey, I'm coming!"

As much as she loved her relationship with him, she tried to discourage him. She knew that the publicity over his coming to Israel would be ruinous to both of them.

But Lansky was not one who was easily deterred. He continued reaching out to Israeli friends for counsel. Then, in late June, disaster struck. It involved Lansky's forty-eight-year-old stepson, Richard Schwartz.

Schwartz had been drinking at the restaurant he owned, The Inside, in the exclusive resort community of Bay Harbor Island, Florida. After wrapping up his night there, he decided to go over to another restaurant, The Forge, to continue drinking. He came across Craig Teriaca, a professional golfer who was also drinking heavily, at the bar.

It's unclear exactly what happened next. The two men exchanged words. Police never determined what sparked their argument, but it may have had something to do with a ten-dollar bill on the bar. Whatever the reason, Schwartz pulled out a pistol. He shot Teriaca twice in the chest, mortally wounding him.

The killing was bad enough, but Teriaca was the son of a bookmaker, Vincent Teriaca. He reputedly had ties to the Genovese crime family. And he wanted revenge.

Headlines popped up the next day, all leading with "Lansky's stepson." It was inevitable, but irritating to Lansky. He didn't like his stepson and tried to have little to do with him. Schwartz was a bigmouth, always throwing around the Lansky name. He would go to the garage where Lansky parked his car, say he was Lansky's son, snap his fingers, and demand the car. Lansky himself would never treat a parking attendant in such an imperious manner. Schwartz's behavior embarrassed him.

As much as Schwartz liked to drop his stepfather's name, the connection wasn't enough to get him out of this particular jam. Police arrested him and charged him with aggravated assault. Teriaca died twelve hours after the shooting. Authorities upgraded the charge to second-degree murder. Schwartz posted a $5,500 bond and was released.

Miami police, however, didn't know about his release. Florida's state attorney immediately revoked his bond, and detectives went out looking for him. They found him at his daughter's home and rearrested him there. Teddy wanted to post bond for him, but Lansky refused. He was afraid something bad would happen once Schwartz got out of jail.

Lansky knew Teddy was suffering, but he handled it with his habitual emotional distance. He wrote de Toledo:

"My status is much the same personally. I am very well. My wife's condition is terrible. I don't know what may happen with her. She is really torturing herself. She is losing confidence and ambition in life. This is a true tragedy."

Teriaca's funeral set off a "donnybrook," according to news reporters who attended. Befitting his underworld connections, about twenty burly mourners stood sentry to prevent any uninvited guests. When they saw television newsmen show up outside St. Joseph's Roman Catholic Church in Miami Beach, they attacked. A couple of newsmen were seriously injured.

More headlines followed. Lansky hated the publicity, but he was more worried about his stepson's safety. He didn't like him, but he didn't want to see him killed. He knew, however, that there would be consequences for Teriaca's murder.

Less than a week after the shooting, he wrote to de Toledo:

"Matters in my wife's family slowed my writing. Her son himself in serious trouble at a bar while drunk. It is not going to affect my life, but it is making a real wreck of her."

Teddy was beside herself. She doted on her son. She hated the idea of him sitting in the Dade County Jail. In August, Schwartz was released on his own recognizance. Teddy was thrilled.

Lansky was not. He dreaded what he knew would happen.

Schwartz's own lawyer warned him that he would be better off staying in jail. He had gotten a tip from a former client that his life was in danger. Schwartz, who seemed to think he was invincible because of his family connections, replied, "I'll be careful."

He wasn't careful enough, however.

On the morning of October 12, 1977, Schwartz drove up to the service entrance of his restaurant. He had resumed running the venue. Before he could even get out of his car, he was hit by a single shotgun blast to the chest through the driver's side window. A Bay Harbor Island policeman heard the shot and ran to the scene, but he was too late. Schwartz was dead.

A crime scene photo of Schwartz's body, covered with a bloody sheet and sprawled beside his car, appeared in the local newspapers. One investigator said the powder burns on his body indicated the shotgun had been less than six inches away from him.

Teddy, of course, was devastated. Lansky did what he could to comfort his wife.

Police concluded that Schwartz's death was revenge for Teriaca's killing. They worried that his killing would set off a gangland war in South Florida. Again, newspaper headlines linked the Lansky name to a potential gang war. The prospect of gang warfare was absolutely titillating.

But there was no gang war. High-level mobsters, who would have had to sanction such a war, didn't care about the death of Richard Schwartz. In their world, he was nobody.

No one was ever arrested in the murder. Years later, a journalist said that a Miami cocaine dealer said that he and a hit man hired by a Cuban drug kingpin had killed Schwartz.

After his stepson's murder, Lansky wanted more than ever to return to Israel. In November 1977, he wrote Prime Minister Begin about the possibility of returning:

Mr. Begin,

I have a very keen desire to live in Israel, but unfortunately, I am verboten. To begin with, when I spent time in Israel, I fell more in love with the country than I was before. My one wish is to be able to spend the rest of my life—which, I presume, can't be too long, as I am 75 years old.

I have, unfortunately, become a product of the media. Much of this has been exaggerated, as only the press can do. They, as you must know, can make or break. On the other hand, I do not profess to being a Saint, but I have never been 99% of the way I was built up. As you may know, charges in the U.S. were built up against me, but the courts threw all that out. So how much harm can an elderly, sick do to Israel, as has been used as a pretext against me?

It may please you to know I carry a pretty good reputation among many important Jews. I can enter, as I have, any other country without criticism, except the place of my heritage.

I would appreciate it if you would consider my case and help me enter the one country I truly desire to be in.

It was a remarkably heartfelt letter. It also revealed how Lansky saw himself in the world. He was used to dealing with politicians of all stripes. He felt completely at ease with world leaders. He regarded some of them as his friends. He saw nothing wrong with making a personal plea to a newly elected prime minister. He felt confident that Begin would at least read his letter and consider his argument.

Begin never answered.

In January 1978, Israel rejected Lansky again.

"I don't care what people think about me," he told a Miami reporter, "just the people who have dealt with me."

The reporter noted Lansky's poor health and wrote that he had purchased two gravesites in the Mount of Olives Cemetery in Jerusalem.

It was a bitter blow, but he refused to reveal publicly how deeply hurt he felt. He was more candid when he wrote de Toledo:

"I'm hurt, but I wouldn't give them the satisfaction of letting those bastards affect me. I'm not going to forget it. I just want to make sure that what I have in mind will not be used as a propaganda against Israel by Arabs. The press could make a holiday with it."

Yet his bitterness was evident in his sarcasm:

I don't know if I told you that I intend to raise a beard, join the religious party, then solicit the aged, [go] to an old age home and rob them, then go to a synagogue on Saturday and ask for forgiveness.

Forgiveness granted, and they start over on Sunday. Don't you love this life of hypocrisy? As Lincoln said, "You can fool some of the people some of the time, but you can't fool all of the people all of the time."

He was down, but it wasn't over. He tried again through the Israeli courts. By August 1980, the Interior Ministry finally agreed to give Lansky a tourist visa—but only if he agreed to post a bond of $100,000 and agree to stay no more than thirty days.

After so many attempts to get permission to enter Israel, it was a significant victory. But Lansky, the dealmaker who thought that money could make any problem go away, felt deeply insulted. He couldn't believe that Israeli authorities had the temerity to set any conditions on his return to the country.

He refused the deal.

CHAPTER 24

Final Days

LANSKY FELT DEEPLY hurt by the insulting Israeli deal. He had always fought back, but this time, it cut more deeply. He still kept his emotions tightly in check, but now it were as if his body were revealing his inner turmoil. His health, which had been precarious for at least a decade, deteriorated. One day, he was out with friends when he started coughing up blood. He was immediately admitted to the hospital, and doctors found a tumor on his lung. They had to cut out half his lung to remove it.

His doctor refused to comment on the rumors, but the diagnosis was obvious. He had cancer.

In the 1980s, a diagnosis of cancer was the equivalent of a death sentence, and he knew it. He said little about it even to those closest to him. His letters to Paul slowed.

He settled into a quiet retirement. He and Teddy still lived in their comfortable, but not extravagant, condo at the Imperial House in Miami Beach. He'd walk Bruiser—by now blind—along Collins Avenue and nod to neighbors. It seemed as if he went everywhere with Bruiser. People regarded it as an incongruous sight—a powerful and feared mobster patiently walking a tiny, disabled dog.

Barry Neuman ran a car repair business and often worked on Lansky's navy blue Mercedes. (By now, Lansky had finally abandoned his Chevrolets and indulged in a Mercedes.) Lansky usually waited for his car with Bruiser. One day, the repairs were going to take longer than expected, so Neuman offered to drive Lansky home. He gratefully accepted his offer.

On the ride home, he decided to repay the favor with a little advice for Neuman: "Buy raw land for cash and forget about it. It will make you money. I don't care how much trouble you're in, if you throw enough cash at it, it will go away. If you ever have to kill anyone, do it yourself."

Neuman was pretty sure the last bit of advice wasn't a joke, though he didn't know Lansky well enough to be certain. He never forgot it.

Even in retirement, Lansky knew how to make a lasting impression.

He was no longer healthy enough to play tennis with his buddies, but he ate breakfast with them regularly. They'd rib each other endlessly. Then they'd get serious and play gin rummy, which, of course, is a betting game. The stakes were never high. It was always a matter of a few dollars. That didn't matter, though. They'd argue furiously over a few dollars, laughing uproariously the entire time.

In 1981, there was a television event that Lansky and his buddies decided warranted a party. It was a miniseries called *The Gangster Chronicles*. It was a crime drama, purportedly based on facts, about Luciano, Siegel, and Lansky. Actor Michael Nouri played Luciano, and Brian Benben played Lansky's character. Because Lansky was still alive—unlike Luciano and Siegel—the TV producers changed the name of Lansky's character to Michael Lasker to avoid any legal complications. Dead men can't sue for libel or slander; living ones can.

Lansky, his brother, Jack, and their friends and their wives gathered together to watch the series. They laughed and hooted throughout the show, delighting in the actors' portrayals, even if they weren't always quite right. As accustomed as he was to being at the center of national news, it was something else to see his own life portrayed on TV.

Siegel, not surprisingly, was depicted as a violent psychopath. One guest objected to the portrayal. He said he thought someone should sue the television company.

"What are you going to sue them for?" Lansky asked, laughing heartily. "In real life, he was even worse!"

The TV series was a rare bright spot after years of legal battles and health crises. Lansky relished his time with his old friends, and the feeling was mutual.

Another bright spot came when Paul announced his plans to remarry. Lansky was delighted. Although he never saw a problem with having a mistress on the side, he always thought marriage was a stabilizing force in one's life.

Even though Paul mostly had little use for his sister, Sandra, when she offered to host the ceremony at her condo in Miami Beach, he gladly accepted. He knew that would make it much easier for Buddy, his father, and his father's friends to attend.

Paul's friend from Boeing, Dick L'Heureux, happened to be in Miami to speak at an engineering conference around the same time. Paul invited him over for the afternoon before the wedding ceremony, which was to take place that evening.

L'Heureux was happy to catch up. While he was there, two men, whose names he remembered as Sal and Guido, showed up. They didn't make much small talk. As Sal bent over the kitchen sink, his jacket flew open. L'Heureux caught a glimpse of a large gun on his hip. Shocked, L'Heureux reeled back. Paul quickly walked over and explained that the man was just a private detective. Because of who his father was, security was necessary.

L'Heureux said nothing, but scoffed inwardly. *That man is no more a private detective than I'm a man on the moon*, he thought to himself.

Sal and Guido left. Then it dawned on L'Heureux: They had been checking the house for bugs.

A little later, Paul told L'Heureux, "My dad's coming over, and I'd like you to meet him."

L'Heureux looked out the window and saw Lansky pulling up to park, putting two wheels on the right berm (parking clearly was not his strong suit).

"Paul," he said, "is it okay if I pahk here?" L'Heureux was struck by his still distinctive New York accent.

Paul introduced them, and they shook hands. Lansky made an impression on the younger man. Though he was small in stature, his grip was strong.

Lansky family members and friends started to trickle in. Men in suits showed up, often asking Lansky for a private conversation. They would walk over to the vestibule and chat for a few minutes. Some left afterward, while others stayed. To L'Heureux, it seemed like unusual behavior for a wedding, but nobody else seemed to think so.

One man who apparently had recently had facial surgery took the back of L'Heureux's hand and placed it against his jaw.

"You see that?" he told L'Heureux in a distinctive gravelly voice. "I'm one tough sonuvabitch, I was in the hospital this morning. When Meyer Lansky's son is getting married, there's ain't no way I'm not coming."

The man was Harry Stromberg. Hailing from Philadelphia, Stromberg had gotten to know Lansky during Prohibition through Rothstein. He later became heavily involved in rackets like prostitution and labor racketeering.

A little later, L'Heureux went over to talk to his girlfriend, Claudette, who was sitting next to a woman. As he bent over to talk to her, the woman turned to her and said, "Is this man bothering you?"

She quickly reassured her that he was not. The incident became a standing joke between the two, who later married.

The ceremony was brief. Miami's head warlock presided over it. Nobody in attendance seemed to think that was the least bit odd either.

At the wedding, it was obvious that Buddy's physical condition had worsened. His cerebral palsy had advanced to the state where he could no longer even feed himself. Uncle Jules Citron, who had been the uncle who tenderly cared for Buddy as a child, discreetly asked family members what kind of financial arrangements they had made for Buddy's care after his father's death. Everybody knew that Buddy had gambled away the money he had and that Sandra spent whatever she got. Paul was the only Lansky child who had made something of himself. Citron approached him and asked him if he would help Buddy financially.

Paul, always so tightfisted with his money, refused. As much as he loved Buddy, he just couldn't see why he should bail him out. His decision drove a rift between the two brothers that never healed.

Not long after Paul's wedding, Buddy went into the hospital for another painful spinal surgery. Doctors had assured him that the surgery would reverse his decline. It involved attaching a metal halo to his head and spine, an onerous and uncomfortable contraption. This time, it actually worked. When it was removed, Buddy could eat and talk far better than he could before.

Despite the improvement, he was by now a quadriplegic. After years of living independently and joyfully, he needed twenty-four-hour-a-day medical care.

Reluctantly, he approached his father about paying for a full-time aide. Lansky—like Paul—was dubious. He thought Buddy wanted money to pay off his gambling debts. He told Buddy to check out the price of an aide. When Buddy came back to him with what he had learned, Lansky snapped, "Where am I going to get that sort of money from?"

His response was profoundly uncharacteristic for him. Lansky had never stinted in paying for Buddy's medical bills in the past. His plaintive question was a reflection of his stark, new reality: He had enough money to live out his limited time on earth, but his free-spending days were over. Despite all the Mob pundits who claimed to know that Lansky had stashed away $300 million, the truth was that he had not.

He lost most of his fortune when Batista's regime in Cuba collapsed, and he had spent years trying to come back from that. Legal and medical bills sapped his savings, and he still couldn't refuse when the right charity asked him for help. When it came to his own son, however, it was more complicated. He couldn't tamp down his fury over Buddy's gambling losses. Guys who lost at gambling were suckers. He hated the idea that his own son was a sucker.

It was apparent to everyone in the family that something needed to be done to ensure his care. Lansky, always so meticulous and careful to plan ahead when it came to business, put nothing in writing. Instead, he talked to his brother, Jack, and urged him to take care of it. It made sense because Jack had reaped the benefits of Lansky's business ventures over the years. Jack, ever loyal, promised him he would. That would have to do for the time being.

Lansky never complained about his financial situation, but he made it clear that he didn't have the money he used to have. When de Toledo asked him whether he was planning any trips, he wrote her:

"Europe is out. The style I like to travel in is beyond my means."

Meanwhile, he still wanted to visit Israel one last time. He wrote to de Toledo, saying:

"I miss the country because of my deep feeling for the people . . . I planted a rose there and I would like to be with it and caress it all the time."

By January 1981, his evanescing fortunes clearly weighed on him. In another letter, he conceded that he had some worries about Buddy's health:

"If only I had you now. Don't fear to get old. Grow old gracefully and loveable [sic]. I'm having a hard time with illness in the family. It may be serious. I will let you know more definite."

By the end of the year, he admitted to his younger lover that he was experiencing the travails of old age:

At this moment, I'm in the hospital, but all is well. I will be checking out tomorrow morning. I wasn't in the best health when I last spoke to you, this was my reason to take all kinds of tests to get rid of some aches. What more can I say? Things are not what they used to be. Age is taking over. When you look around at the patients, I can't complain. What I do wish is that life doesn't rob me . . . Senility. I see lots of my friends hitting the age. I'm far from it now. I do suffer from forgetfulness, I also lack the spirit to want to get around.

But it was not to be.

By the summer of 1982, he knew he wouldn't be traveling anywhere anymore. He wrote his friend, Fred Weisgal, to tell him it was too late for him. He had been thinking about taking another cruise to Alaska—a place he and Paul had always talked about—but was stopped by some bad news. His cancer was back and had spread.

He had to undergo debilitating radiation. He said it burned his throat. Walking and even breathing were difficult. Teddy cared for him the best she could, but she was an emotional wreck.

By the end of the December 1982, she gave up. She took him to Mount Sinai Hospital. It was clear that it was the end. Doctors tried to make him comfortable, but they could do little more than that. Paul and his aunt Esther flew in. Sandra was there at the hospital. Lansky begged Sandra to make sure Buddy was taken care of. She promised him that she would.

Two prominent Miami rabbis arrived at the hospital. They had an offer for the family: They would take Lansky to the Mount of Olives in Israel so he could die and be buried there. They had a private plane standing by ready to take him.

Paul rejected them: "You didn't want him in life; you're not getting him in death!"

It's unclear just how the rabbis knew of the gravity of Lansky's condition. Paul certainly didn't tell them. Family members believe it might have been Teddy, who likely didn't want to pay for a funeral.

A short while later, Lansky died. It was January 15, 1983. He was eighty years old.

The funeral, as befitting Jewish law, was held within twenty-four hours at the Panciera Funeral Home in Hollywood, Florida. Nondescript white vans and Broward County police cars ringed the property. It seemed as if half the Broward County police department had cameras trained on the place.

Even though law enforcement treated it like a Mob funeral—taking down license plates of everyone who drove in—Lansky's funeral lacked the typical accoutrements of one. There were no garish floral arrangements or flamboyant displays of grief. As in life, Lansky left this world in a quiet, understated way. Friends and family members flocked to the funeral home, but they did it discreetly.

They held the wake at Sonken's, a restaurant regarded as *the* Mob hangout of South Florida. It was a place where the maître d' wore a tuxedo and entertainers like Sammy Davis Jr. and Frank Sinatra mingled with the mobsters. It was a favorite of Lansky's and the perfect place for his wake.

At the time, Meyer II was working as a bartender at the Red Lion Inn in Seattle, Washington. He was twenty-six, working the late shift at the bar and attending community college classes during the day. He and his grandfather had stayed in touch over the years, but he hadn't seen him lately. He learned the news of his grandfather's death from a TV news broadcast.

He knew immediately that he had to fly to Miami. He told his boss that he had to leave for his grandfather's funeral. His boss was confused. He knew Meyer II as Bryan Mason. He had no idea he had any connection to the notorious mobster. Like his grandfather, Meyer II always kept quiet about his connections.

He arrived too late to attend the funeral. He went to Lansky's condo. Teddy was sitting shiva, the Jewish tradition in which mourners visit the family's home over a period of seven days to offer condolences. It was crowded. All sorts of people were coming and going. Meyer II saw two men whispering to Jimmy Blue Eyes, whom he knew as his grandfather's business partner. Curious, he approached a young guy nearby and asked, "Who are they?"

The man replied, "I don't know. I never ask."

Meyer II wasn't sure, but he thought one of the men talking to Alo looked an awful lot like Sonny Franzese, the murderous underboss of the Colombo crime family.

As was typical of a Lansky family gathering, nothing about it was typical. Family members warned Meyer II: "Don't talk to anyone. The FBI is watching everything."

He didn't see his aunt Sandra, who apparently was angry at Teddy and refused to show. As he was trying to absorb everything, her husband, Vince Lombardo, walked by. "Where's my dad?" Meyer II asked.

"Your dad just left to get back to Kathleen in Korea," Lombardo replied.

"His wife?" Meyer II asked.

He didn't know that his own father had gotten remarried.

Throughout it all, the TV was on. A news broadcast came on with video of Lansky and news of his death. Teddy turned to Meyer II and said, "In case you don't know, that's your grandfather."

That was so typical of Teddy. She had to be cutting and sarcastic. She obviously knew that Paul's divorce had resulted in Meyer II having far less contact with his grandfather than he had wanted, but she didn't care.

Meyer II returned to Seattle after a few days. News had spread throughout the community of who he really was, and it caught him off guard. A pretty blonde hostess at the Red Lion, who had never given him the time of day in the past, sashayed up to him and said, "Hi, how are you?"

Everybody thought he was going to inherit millions.

It was confusing and uncomfortable for Meyer II. People he barely knew started hitting him up for money. His bosses treated him differently. He didn't know how to handle it, and he didn't know how to grieve the grandfather he had so admired.

Teddy didn't help matters. The entire Lansky family viewed her as a gold digger, and she didn't prove them wrong. Instead of giving out some mementos to family members, she kept everything—even Paul's West Point ring, which he had given his father. While Teddy always claimed that she never asked her husband about his business, she tracked their financial situation carefully. She knew that he didn't have millions of dollars to leave her. She scraped and grasped at whatever she could.

Lansky's will made his brother, Jack, the owner of all his assets on paper. He trusted Jack more than anyone and knew that he would do what he could to take care of his family. But he didn't account for the ravages of time. Jack's own health was bad. He suffered from glaucoma and other ailments. After his brother's death, he seemed to lose his bearings. He wasn't the confident and competent business manager anymore. A part of him died with his brother.

Shortly after Lansky's death, Jack and Jimmy Blue Eyes visited Buddy at the rehabilitation center where he was now living. It was a home for indigents. He assumed he was only there temporarily. He fully expected to move back to the Hawaiian Isle Hotel, where he had lived happily for years. The men explained to him that they were doing everything they could for him, but that he would have to cover his own expenses with his Social Security check. They also made clear to him that he was not going anywhere. There was no money to cover it.

But Jimmy Blue Eyes did follow through with a commitment to his friend. He raised nearly $300,000—nearly a million dollars in today's money. It was a remarkable outpouring of generosity by Lansky's friends. That kind of generosity was hardly typical of mobsters, but it reflected their esteem and genuine fondness for Lansky.

The money was to be divided equally among Teddy, Buddy, and Sandra. Jimmy Blue Eyes figured Paul didn't need the money because he had been successful on his own. He gave Buddy's share to Sandra because of her promise that she would take care of her brother.

Sandra may have made that promise, but like many of her promises, she didn't keep it. When Buddy asked her for the money to pay the facility bills, she simply lied to him and said she'd do it. And then she didn't.

Buddy, desperate to get his bills paid, thought that some publicity might help. He spoke to a *Miami Herald* reporter. He didn't out his sister, but said, "Where did the money go? That's what everybody wants to know."

Teddy visited Buddy. She brought him chicken soup in mayonnaise jars, but nothing more.

"I never asked my stepmother for help," Buddy told the reporter. "I felt if she wanted to do something, she would offer. It's not like she doesn't know the circumstances."

When Jimmy Blue Eyes found out about Buddy's bills not being paid, he asked Sandra about the money.

Her response: "I blew it."

Buddy, the child Lansky worried about the most, got none of it. The Lansky family had never been particularly cohesive, but Sandra's betrayal of Buddy united them. They were furious and stopped speaking to her. Even Teddy was offended, though mainly by the fact that Sandra—and not she—had gotten most of the money for herself.

Buddy was humiliated by his situation, but accepted it. "Money breeds contempt. You can pick your friends, but you can't pick your relatives," he said.

Eight months after Lansky's death, his brother, Jack, died. It was perhaps fitting that the two brothers, so close in life, died not far apart in time. Jack left all his assets to his widow and children. That infuriated Teddy. She figured that it was her money because, in her view, Jack wouldn't have had any of it but for her late husband. Not surprisingly, Jack's family didn't see it that same way. They did, however, feel more of an obligation to Buddy than she ever did. They covered his expenses at the home.

Buddy died shortly before Christmas in 1989.

By then, Meyer II was thinking more about his future. For that, he needed to understand his past. His father retired to Gardnerville, Nevada, right outside Carson City. Meyer II decided to go live with him and his new wife. He dreamed of opening his own bar and thought this could be the time.

Before long, he moved to Las Vegas.

He could do something else as well. He decided to change his name back to his birth name—Meyer Lansky.

It was, he thought, a way of honoring his grandfather.

EPILOGUE

THE FAMILY INFIGHTING that followed Lansky's death was nothing compared to the battle that erupted nearly six years later. This time, two different families were involved—the Genovese and Gambino crime families. The fight was over something Lansky had never encountered while he was alive—a Hollywood movie about his life.

It made perfect sense to produce a movie about his life. Lansky rose from hardscrabble origins to the pinnacle of power and money. He hobnobbed with world leaders, celebrities, and some of the toughest mobsters in American history. He negotiated lasting Mob deals that shaped the course of the Mafia for decades. And he created the modern-day casino.

Given the company he kept, it was perhaps not surprising that a high-stakes dispute broke out over the proposed movie.

As word about the Lansky movie circulated, the Genovese family stepped in to ensure that a favorite actor of theirs—James Caan, a Jewish kid from Queens who relished hanging out with wise guys—portray Lansky. Caan had a starring role as the don's oldest son, Sonny, in *The Godfather*. Mobsters loved the movie. They loved it so much that detectives who surveilled mobsters noticed that many of them started to affect the mannerisms of the actors in the movie.

Casting Caan in the movie would ensure that the Genovese family would get a cut. The man behind the Genovese extortion attempt was none other than Jimmy Blue Eyes himself, Vincent Alo, according to the FBI.

Caan was a perfectly reasonable choice for Lansky, except for one thing. A Hollywood studio executive, Eugene Giaquinto, was backing a rival Lansky movie. Giaquinto had his own Mob ties. At the end of 1988, MCA Inc. suspended him for allegedly funneling money from the company's employee benefit plan to the Bufalino crime family of Pittston, Pennsylvania.

He also bragged about his ties to John Gotti, then the leader of New York's Gambino crime family, according to the FBI. Giaquinto referred to Gotti as "G" on phone conversations. The FBI knew that because agents were listening in.

Giaquinto's friendship with Gotti was critical because when he heard about the Genovese movie, he was overheard saying on the phone that "if they want war," he could make one phone call and have planeloads of mobsters flying in to Hollywood.

Meanwhile, Caan was seen discussing his own deal for a Lansky movie at a Beverly Hills restaurant called La Dolce Vita with members of the Los Angeles Mafia family. He had acquired the rights for the movie from Teddy.

Central to the whole drama was a man named Martin Bacow. He was scriptwriter and producer and was close to Teamsters Union President Jackie Presser. Bacow said he knew Lansky personally and that he had his blessing on his script. The movie would include a startling new revelation: Lansky allegedly helped fix the 1960 presidential election of John F. Kennedy.

Bacow explained the conflict to the *Los Angeles Times*: "What they tried to do was become my partner. They wanted to put Jimmy Caan in the movie," he said.

"Their thing was to try to stop it and get a piece of the action because they're estimating the picture to do $100 million. When you're talking about $100 million, that's a lot of money, even if you say it real fast," he said.

In fact, Lansky never gave the project his blessing. Nor is there any evidence that he tried to fix the 1960 presidential election.

The Lansky movie project went south after the FBI started snooping around. No one was more upset than Bacow. "All the studios are scared to even talk to me now," he complained.

A few years later, a biography of FBI Director Hoover prompted an hour-long *Frontline* piece called, "The Secret File on J. Edgar Hoover." It opened with examples of Hoover's predilection for the high life, thanks to the generosity of Lansky and Costello. It also featured an interview with a "Lansky underling" who talked about Hoover's penchant for betting on horses.

"If Hoover won, he got paid, and if he didn't win, they would just forget it," the man said.

Even in death, TV producers were using Lansky's name as a hook.

Numerous actors of note went on to portray Meyer Lansky in film.

In 1990, Mark Rydell depicted him as the Mafia-affiliated owner of many of Cuba's casinos in Sydney Pollack's *Havana*.

In 1991 alone, two movies featured him as a character: *Mobsters*, in which he was played by Patrick Dempsey, and *Bugsy*, where Ben Kingsley delivered a no-nonsense, commanding performance. Both films, being Hollywood productions, dramatized and glamorized what really happened, of course.

Bugsy, in particular, perpetuated the 1975 myth from *The Last Testament of Lucky Luciano* that Lansky's hand was forced by the Mafia Commission, and that he ultimately sanctioned the hit on his friend Ben Siegel for the overinflated cost of the Flamingo's construction from the initially projected $1 million to an eventual $6 million. It also invented Virginia Hill's fictionalized theft of $2 million from the casino's funds that led to her jilted lover's untimely demise. Entertaining cinema fare, indeed, but it cemented the decades-long narrative in the public imagination that unfortunately sustained more fiction than history.

Robert Lacey's *Little Man* biography was also published in 1991 (it was a big year for Meyer Lansky), which contains interviews with Meyer II. While that was an informative, researched, and respected account, only now, a quarter of the way through the 21st century, can the younger Meyer speak with the benefit of hindsight to fully delineate the legacy his grandfather left behind—and from the inside as the Lansky heir, at that.

The elder Lansky was also featured in *The Untouchables* revival series, which ran from 1993 to 1994, this time with Marc Grapey filling the role.

In 1999, a movie finally was made about Lansky's life. It was a TV movie, titled simply *Lansky*, starring Richard Dreyfuss.

That same year, Oscar Goodman, who had represented Lansky in a small part of the skimming case against him, was elected mayor of Las Vegas. Newspapers never failed to cite his claim to fame—he represented Lansky. He and his wife, Carolyn Goodman, served as consecutive mayors, extending their political dynasty to a quarter-century until 2024, keeping the Mob—and Lansky—alive in the public discourse and city life. Vegas never forgot its roots, or its branding.

In 2005, Dustin Hoffman portrayed Lansky in *The Lost City*.

From 2010 to 2014, Anatol Yusef went on to embody a young Meyer Lansky over the full course of *Boardwalk Empire*'s five-year run, in which he, Luciano, and Siegel ultimately emerge as the series' victors, establishing the National Crime Syndicate at the end of Prohibition, which financed all their future enterprises, lawful or otherwise.

In 2014, Lansky's daughter, Sandra, released a memoir, *Daughter of the King*, though this publication centered more on her personal recollections, thoughts, and feelings regarding her father than on an accurate and objective insider's account of Meyer Lansky's life and legacy.

By now a legendary historical figure, Lansky appeared as a major figure in the eight-episode 2015 AMC docuseries *The Making of the Mob: New York*, played by Ian Bell. Meyer II was featured in the series as a reliable speaker and expert on the topic, alongside notable historians, authors, actors, and political figures such as Oscar Goodman, Rudy Giuliani, Gay Talese, Frankie Valli, *Sopranos* veterans Frank Vincent and Vincent Pastore, and others.

Featured in too many books to count, Meyer Lansky has become a lasting staple of pop culture, joining the pantheon of American legends, be they Carnegies, Kennedys, or Sinatras. He's even been immortalized in music, from songs by artists such as Sagol 59, the "Israeli godfather of hip-hop," to American rappers including Jay-Z and Wu-Tang Clan's affiliate Myalansky of the Wu-Syndicate.

Lansky was featured yet again in a 2018 film, *Speed Kills*, played by James Remar.

In Las Vegas, Bugsy & Meyer's Steakhouse—an upscale restaurant equipped with a speakeasy called The Count Room—opened in the Flamingo in July 2020, further cementing the Lansky legacy in the public's eye via one of the nation's oldest casinos, the very one he helped develop in his burgeoning gambling empire. Meyer II donated various family heirlooms and photographs to the restaurant, including images of him and his grandfather, which are on display as of this writing. Tourists, hotel guests, and celebrities from all over the world have been known to frequent the steakhouse, including Alan Parsons, whom Meyer II dined with.

Then in 2021, Hollywood produced the first full-fledged biopic on the big screen, again titled *Lansky*, starring Harvey Keitel in the titular role. He delivered a sobering, accurate performance, and spoke just like the real Meyer did, according to Meyer II.

Two years later, in 2023, Sandra Lansky passed away.

A year later, in 2024, Lansky's son Paul also passed.

Since then, Paul's son, Meyer II, decided to keep the Lansky legacy alive for posterity. He received a New York publisher's notice and told his grandfather's story in this very book, *The Lansky Legacy*. (In a sense, the New York-Vegas connection has come full circle.) His goal is to pass on the torch for the next generation, setting the record straight for years to come.

To think, a little Jewish boy playing craps—rolling the dice in the streets of New York, realizing it was better to *be* the house and control the odds—went on to launch a worldwide gambling empire, from traditional casinos to online gambling and even high-end resorts and hotels that value luxury, service, and presentation. He reinvented more than one industry, and showed the world how to do it *right.*

Over the years, so-called friends and family members have tried to cash in on the Lansky name. Meyer II marvels at the number of people he's never met who claim to have been close friends of his grandfather. Some have had a flimsy connection to Lansky. Others have been outright fraudsters.

Lansky would have been offended by the cash grab made in his name. As successful as he was in making money, he really didn't care that much about it. He liked the power it gave him, whether it was the leverage in making a deal or giving a hand to someone less fortunate. But he never measured himself in terms of how much money he made.

There was something more lasting in the phenomenon that was Meyer Lansky, even after his death. In life, he was never a showman, never one to seek attention. It seemed as if the more he tried to dodge the reporters and cameras, the bigger he became.

He always worried about his family. As splintered as they were, they made their own way in life—for better or worse. The children and grandchildren of mobsters have a perspective on life that few other people can understand because they haven't lived it. It's difficult to explain.

And yet, for Meyer II, there's an immense feeling of pride as well, in who his grandfather was and what he accomplished. He was a singular historical figure who transformed organized crime and the business of gambling and helped finance the development of one of the biggest tourist and entertainment meccas in the world in the form of Las Vegas. Who knows what Cuba would be today had Castro not seized power?

And even though he worked with criminals on a daily basis, Lansky managed to earn a reputation as an honest man who dealt fairly with his business partners. He was a financier of passion projects and dreams that shaped the world we now live in, one way or another.

As for the people who would scoff at that characterization, it's likely that Meyer Lansky would shrug off their criticism.

He never did worry about what people thought of him.

POSTSCRIPT
Vegas Today

THE STATE OF NEVADA did two things in the 1930s that changed the course of Las Vegas history: It legalized gambling and it lowered the residency requirement for dissolving marriages, enabling so-called "quickie" divorces.

For astute businessmen in the Mob, those were the makings of a perfect playground. They wanted in.

Las Vegas was an open city, meaning that enterprising mobsters were not bound by turf rules. Anyone could operate there.

In the early 1940s, Las Vegas was a hot, dusty, cowboy town, with a few gambling roadhouses along Highway 91 and a couple of Western-style hotels with casinos such as the El Rancho Vegas and the Hotel Last Frontier. After investing in El Cortez and selling it at a profit, the opening of the upscale and sophisticated Flamingo resort in 1946—helmed by Bugsy Siegel and backed by Meyer Lansky and the Mob—changed all that.

The Flamingo followed a casino model pioneered by Lansky and heartily endorsed by fellow mobsters because it made them buckets of money: Keep it classy, bring in top-tier entertainment, the best chefs, and experienced managers, and do everything you can to keep the gamblers gambling.

That ushered in the era of the Rat Pack—Frank Sinatra, Dean Martin, Sammy Davis Jr., Peter Lawford, and Joey Bishop. Their performances were usually unscripted and fueled by booze. They just seemed like a group of guys having fun, and the audiences loved it.

The entertainers acquired their nickname after actress Lauren Bacall saw them nursing hangovers after a long, boozy night. She took one look at them and said they "looked like a goddamned rat pack."

They loved it, so it stuck. They coined a slogan: "Never rat on a rat."

The Rat Pack brought glamour, cool, and sheer fun to Las Vegas, and you didn't have to be a high roller to enjoy it. You could see a Sinatra show if you bought a couple of drinks and slipped the maître d' a silver dollar. Or you could hang out with Martin, an experienced card dealer, because he often felt like dealing cards himself at the Stardust.

Sinatra was the undisputed leader of the pack. He was, after all, the biggest star in the country from the late 1950s through the early 1960s. He initially decamped at the Desert Inn between Desert Inn Road and Sunset Avenue on the Strip.

Then the Mob brought in Jack Entratter, the assistant manager of the Copacabana in New York, to manage the Sands Hotel and Casino. Entratter knew exactly how to cater to his clientele, particularly the stars. He was accommodating and always discreet, and he made sure his staff operated the same way. Before long, the Rat Pack made the Sands—run by Lansky's pal, Doc Stacher—their headquarters.

They weren't the only top entertainers in Vegas. Anybody who was somebody performed there. Even the elusive actress Marlene Dietrich, famous for her reclusiveness, performed at the Sahara—after she secured a paycheck of $35,000 a week in 1953. It was a lot of money, but the Mob knew she was worth it. She was the kind of attraction who could bring in the gamblers.

Entertainment wasn't limited to the headliners. There were sideshows, opening acts, and the ubiquitous showgirls, whose sparkling and suggestive costumes were inspired by Parisian cabaret shows like the Folies Bergère. If it wasn't one show, it was another—anything to keep you at the gambling tables.

Prostitution and drug use happened, to be sure, but the Mob discouraged both because they inhibited gambling.

By the mid-1960s, under pressure from federal authorities, the older mobsters started cashing in and selling out. It was a slow process, as they were reluctant to give up their cash cow.

In 1971, the Chicago Outfit sent Anthony "Tony the Ant" Spilotro to Las Vegas, ostensibly to manage the gift shop at the Circus Circus Hotel & Casino. In reality, he was there to oversee the skimming operation, wherein Mob employees would take cash off the top of the daily receipts and pass the money up the line to their Mob bosses. It was a way to evade taxes, of course, and was an essential source of revenue for the Mafia.

Frank "Lefty" Rosenthal, a Jewish bookmaker for the Outfit turned casino mogul, ran the Stardust, Fremont, Hacienda, and Marina, while Tony the Ant did the skimming. It was a tenuous business relationship at best, with Rosenthal being a Mob associate who was technically subordinate to Spilotro, a made man, though their hierarchy was often fractious and disputed in Sin City, where rules and territory went out the window.

Spilotro, an experienced burglar and thief, was also supposed to manage burglaries in Vegas. A lot of money was coming into the city in the form of high rollers and entertainers with expensive tastes, and it only made sense that the Mob bosses wanted their cut. Spilotro pulled together a motley group of middle-aged guys to rob places like high-end jewelry stores. Their signature method of breaking in was to blast or drill a hole in the establishment's wall. Thus, they got the name: "The Hole in the Wall Gang."

It was successful until it wasn't. Spilotro had an unsettling knack for grabbing the spotlight (so much so that he was depicted by Joe Pesci in the 1995 movie *Casino*, with Robert De Niro portraying Rosenthal, though their names were changed to Nicky Santoro and Sam "Ace" Rothstein). Worse, one of his confederates, Frank

Cullotta, decided to rat. That was all too much for the Chicago Outfit. In June 1986, Tony and his brother Michael were found dead and buried in an Indiana cornfield.

When Meyer Lansky II was in his early twenties with his family, his mother suggested that he go to Caesars Palace. He was interested in working in the hospitality industry. So, he dutifully went to the casino, walked upstairs, and knocked on the door of Harry Wald, who ran Caesars. No one answered, so he went downstairs and sat at the bar.

Before long, two burly security guards approached him and said, "We need to talk to you."

They took him to a room and told him he could not—ever—knock on Wald's door. Meyer II immediately explained who he was and why he was there, but they were unmoved. They patted him down and even made him take off his boots. They also made clear that they were related to the Fischettis, feared enforcers from the Chicago Outfit. Meyer II knew exactly who they were, and it frightened him.

That wasn't enough to deter him from pursuing a career in the hospitality industry, however. He wound up getting a job in a casino cage, where he learned how to deal chips (called "checks" at the casino) and how to deal with customers. Because he was counting money, he was on camera at all times. He learned how to make sure that the camera saw what he saw. There was no room for cheating.

In the 1980s, casinos were still fun. There was a thrill when a customer hit it on a coin-drop slot machine. You could hear the rattle of the coins dropping into the trough at the bottom and the whoop of the winner. It was exciting. The manager would immediately get a photo of the jackpot winner next to the winnings. A cocktail waitress would be right there offering a free drink.

If a man won big, the manager might invite the wife over to the salon for a complimentary spa treatment. He would definitely comp them for dinner and maybe even their room. The idea was to *keep the gambler there*. They knew that the longer the gambler stayed and played, the more likely it was that the house would get its money back.

Everybody was treated like a high roller—not just the high rollers. The manager would know the husband's name, as well as the wife's. They made the effort to keep it personalized. An average guy could feel like a big deal. Everyone had the same chance at winning.

It wasn't just the customers who got personalized treatment. Employees did, too. Up until the 1980s and early 1990s, there was still a family feeling among casino employees. In the early days, when Moe Dalitz heard that the mother of one of his employees had been hospitalized, he paid her hospital bill.

There were volleyball games and staff birthday parties. It wasn't surprising to see an entertainment headliner like Kenny Loggins hop onto the table of celebrating employees (after the plates and wineglasses had been removed) and sing "Footloose" to the crowd from there. There were even all-expenses-paid ski trips to Squaw Valley, California, for the staff. It was like summer camp, only all year round.

The bosses knew that happy employees were more likely to keep their customers happy—and gambling.

The push to keep people gambling wasn't limited to customers. The bosses encouraged staff to cash their paychecks at the casino so they would stay and gamble. Salaried employees received preloaded debit cards, which they could use at the casino health club, tanning beds, or a great restaurant meal. It was effortless, and it was fun, and the money kept rolling in.

Those days are gone. The coin-drop machines have been replaced with slots that spit out a printout if you win. The volleyball games and the staff parties are no longer. All the original hotels, except for Circus Circus, have been blown up and replaced with bigger edifices and corporate-run mega casinos.

The Hacienda is now Mandalay Bay; the Marina, absorbed into MGM Grand; the Sands, replaced by The Venetian and The Palazzo; the Stardust, now Resorts World; the Desert Inn became the

Wynn and Encore; and El Rancho eventually gave way to the newest hotel as of this writing, the Fontainebleau, which shares the name of the Miami Beach casino in which the elder Meyer Lansky once had business interests. A beautiful construction, but the interior resembles more a museum of modern art than a traditional hotel families would once drive up to in the middle of the desert in a 1950s Oldsmobile.

Throw in Caesars, Harrah's, Park MGM, The Cosmopolitan, and Planet Hollywood for good measure, and the Strip—while undeniably glamorous and visually attractive—now looks far different from its original landscape. Hotels like Paris, The Orleans, and New York-New York take visitors to different times and places all over the world.

You can sit in the luxurious Eiffel Tower Restaurant while watching the synchronized Bellagio fountains spewing their magic to mesmerized passersby in the thick of Las Vegas Boulevard. Not to mention the Las Vegas Monorail, a convenient way for tourists to travel the Strip while sparing their sore feet, and the Convention Center, which now occupies the site where the Riviera once stood.

Many of the old casino signs can be seen in the Neon Museum, a graveyard that honors the Old World in the usual tourist fashion. Even the Tropicana and Mirage recently joined the ranks of the fallen to make way for a Major League Baseball stadium and a guitar-shaped Hard Rock casino, respectively.

As Meyer II would say with a hint of nostalgia when watching the numerous hotel demolitions over the years: "Out with the old, in with the new."

Corporate America is always thinking bigger, though not necessarily "better." Out-of-state investors, shareholders, and hedge funds certainly enjoy the prospects of more immediate, short-term gains rather than the logistics of balancing the needs of visitors and locals in one of the world's most frequented tourist meccas.

Off-Strip casinos like Red Rock and Durango have capitalized on the frequently trafficked outer limits of the growing city, which constantly undergoes construction and expansion in all directions, a widening metropolis surrounded by desert rock and man-made lakes. Golf courses are aplenty and ubiquitous, even on Lake Las Vegas, a Tuscany-styled resort area not far east of the Strip. There, amid some of the finest views in the world, is a waterside Roaring Twenties-themed venue called simply The Speakeasy.

One is hard-pressed to imagine this being a possibility without Lansky's century-long influence from Prohibition to the conception, financing, and development of Las Vegas itself. Were it not for him, the entire city and its flourishing outskirts may have just remained another uneventful stopover town on the way to California. In a world without Lansky and Siegel, the only planes flying in and out of Vegas may have been to and from Nellis Air Force Base.

And thanks to Lake Mead and the Hoover Dam, Nevada can supply water and power to the growing populace, even if the grid may be strained at times with record heats and expanding populations. (How much infrastructure the city can sustain as it carves its outward path, especially in upscale residential regions like Henderson and Summerlin, remains to be seen.)

Just north of the Strip, Fremont Street pays homage to the days of old with its flashing incandescent bulbs and bargain rib dinners, a relic forever frozen in time, though its cheaper prices continue to draw in a crowd, with people flying in from all over the world. There they can bet at the largest sportsbook in the world at more modern hotels like Circa, or dine at El Cortez, which sports the Siegel's 1941 restaurant, where diners can sit under a mural of Bugsy Siegel and order the Meyer Lansky Burger.

Visitors—and locals—can even be married in the many wedding chapels at the top of the Strip by an Elvis impersonator, or at the Flamingo, by Meyer Lansky II and Vegas Mob Weddings.

Speakeasies like the 1923 Prohibition Bar at The Venetian and Mandalay Bay—as well as The Bootlegger Bistro south of the Strip, Capo's Restaurant & Speakeasy, and The Count Room at the Flamingo's very own Bugsy & Meyer's Steakhouse, among others—provide a convincing glimpse into the entertainment of yesteryear, transporting patrons back in time to the days of rum-running and underground liquor service that scream not only the Mob, but Meyer Lansky himself. They have his influence and business model written all over them. His blueprints were timeless.

Las Vegas is also known for the world-renowned talent it draws in. It has hosted numerous residencies and live acts who were Sin City staples and regulars over the decades, from the animal-based magicians Siegfried & Roy to singers Wayne Newton and Lady Gaga, illusionist David Copperfield, musical acts Blue Man Group and Cirque du Soleil, and countless other top-tier performers—with "The King" himself, Elvis Presley, topping the list. *Viva Las Vegas!*

Countless movies and series have been set and filmed in Sin City, for better or worse, including *The Hangover*, *Leaving Las Vegas*, *Fear and Loathing in Las Vegas*, the 2012 *Vegas* TV show, and of course, the 1995 cult classic *Showgirls*—though the Stardust survived the movie by eleven years, so it certainly wasn't the movie that brought it down. Martin Scorsese's *Casino* was also released in 1995, depicting the Stardust as the fictional Tangiers Casino.

Ace Rothstein (Lefty Rosenthal) best echoes Meyer II's present sentiments at the movie's end:

> *The town will never be the same. After the Tangiers, the big corporations took it all over. Today, it looks like Disneyland. And while the kids play cardboard pirates, Mommy and Daddy drop the house payments and Junior's college money on the pokers slots.*
>
> *In the old days, dealers knew your name, what you drank, what you played. Today, it's like checking into an airport. And if you order room service, you're lucky if you get it by Thursday.*
>
> *Today, it's all gone. You got a whale show up with four million in a suitcase, and some twenty-five-year-old hotel schoolkid is gonna want his Social Security Number.*

After the Teamsters got knocked out of the box, the corporations tore down practically every one of the old casinos. And where did the money come from to rebuild the pyramids?

Junk bonds.

Proponents of the new Vegas say it's more family friendly, and that may be so. But the easy camaraderie and chance encounters with major celebrities happen less often these days. There are still lots of neon, spectacles, and excursions to attract tourists—and they do—like the Sphere, a high-tech music and entertainment arena designed as a rounded orb whose ever-transforming LED displays can be seen from the nearby Flamingo, which started it all.

With establishments like the Sphere, the pyramidical Luxor, the needled Strat, and the ringed High Roller Ferris wheel on the LINQ Promenade—the second-tallest in the world—the city may look more like a geometry set or amusement park to tourists flying in. A landscape only corporate America could build.

Las Vegas, like everyplace else, has changed. But it still holds its unique spot in American history, thanks to its beginnings with the Mob.

And of course, Meyer Lansky.

It may look unrecognizable to him were he to see it today, but he would understand its evolution, as he did so many things about human nature.

In the end, it was a good bet.

AFTERWORD

By Phil Genovese

I AM HONORED TO HAVE BEEN asked by my friend, Meyer Lansky II, to contribute this afterword. Having reached this page, I'm sure you concur that the authors have penned a standout work wrought from meticulous research and Meyer's revealing inside information inclusive of the Lansky family dynamics, which make for a rich and captivating narrative.

I believe it was 2012 or thereabouts when I first met Meyer Lansky II on social media. After years of poseurs and wannabes making their way to our virtual doorsteps, we both had learned to proceed with the caution one would take testing the thickness of ice on a pond before committing to step further. Thankfully, the ice was strong enough to support a warm and valued friendship all these years.

Our friendship solidified quickly in early conversations. We were, after all, from very similar backgrounds: notorious grandfathers (mine was Vito Genovese, boss of the Genovese crime family); hardworking, honest fathers both born in 1932; and subjected to the interminable suppositions that there were stashes of cash and gold in safe deposit boxes around the world available to us.

In this book, I discovered we were both in bands when we were twelve or thirteen. The name of Meyer's band, the Aphid Blues Band, made me chuckle. I live in Florida now and the aphid insect has been wreaking havoc on my coontie palms the last two years, a novel experience for a guy born and raised in New Jersey. My band's name was the Grains of Sand. I know, pretty groovy, right? We played at the bat mitzvah for my parents' friends' daughter and came in last at a local battle of the bands at the firehouse. We were terrible, but the Beatles got the girls, so we got guitars. Didn't work.

Another experience I shared with Meyer II—and Antoinette Giancana—was the grade-school reveal of our relations' chosen careers. I was in fifth or sixth grade. By then, my grandfather had been "away on business" for five or six years and was someone never discussed in our home.

During recess on the playground, a classmate got in my face, telling everyone that my grandfather was in jail because he was in the Mafia. After a few words, we ended up on the ground—my first fight. The next day, the boy brought a recent copy of *Life* magazine to school. Not much I could say or do except apologize to my friend. I never told my family. You just didn't go there in my home.

I found it interesting that Meyer's father wanted to name him after his father, a man well-known for his notoriety and criminal associations. In Italian families, certainly in the Southern Italy Campania region around Naples, where both sides of my family are from, it was tradition to name the firstborn son after his paternal grandfather. My mother's side has a long line of Gaetano, Giovanni, Gaetano, Giovanni, and after immigration, the English equivalent, Thomas and John. On my father's New York City birth certificate, his first name is Felice (Philip), Vito's father's name. I am the first son, but no one needed another Vito Genovese in the 1950s, so I became Philip A. Genovese, Jr.—and proudly so. My father was my hero and best friend.

I grew up in a small Jersey Shore town with a Revolutionary War legacy where my father established his CPA practice and became a respected civic leader—town councilman at twenty-nine, board of education, zoning board, police commissioner, honorary police chief, Little League coach, fundraiser committee member for our parish church expansion and a new Christian Brothers high school for boys, and chief of our local YMCA Indian Guides Tribe (remember this was the 1950s and early 1960s). My New York

City-raised father even went on the camping trips with us. I'm sure he must have dreaded those woodsy summer weekends at YMCA Camp Ockanickon. He worked very hard to shape a new legacy for *his* family, and because everyone came to know how unlike my father was from his father, he succeeded. One example he and my mother set for us was that whenever asked if we were *related* (to Vito), we would never deny it and trusted that we would be aptly judged by our character and our deeds, and not those of our grandfather.

One other thing Meyer and I have in common is that any "fortunes," legit or not, seemed to have been depleted by the time our grandfathers passed—either lost to the legal paper owners or Mob heirs, or otherwise left to our grandfathers' brothers, who were expected to take care of the family. My father wanted no part of Vito's money. The little he officially inherited, only hundreds of dollars, he donated to the church. My grandfather's brother moved his family from New York to Rome after my grandfather's funeral.

Nonetheless, our grandfathers, along with their notable peers, did amass fortunes and power they likely never imagined possible when they walked away from their families' tenements and the bleak futures of their fathers' immigrant generation. In the streets and teenage gangs of Lower Manhattan, they cultivated their aspirations and honed their given talents, carving lasting relationships that prepared them for the opportunity of their lifetimes—Prohibition.

In 1920, the Eighteenth Amendment made it illegal to manufacture, sell, or transport alcohol. However, it was not illegal to consume it. People from all walks and stations of life still wanted their drink. Soon, small rural illegal distilleries and breweries were supplying locals all over the country. It has been said that George Patton and Dwight D. Eisenhower had a friendly competition with their home basement brews and bathtub gin while they were neighbors stationed at Fort Meade after World War I.

But there were the larger towns and cities with unquenchable thirsts. So, it came to be that the unintended consequence of the suffragette and temperance activists' victory was to create an organized crime bonanza by providing the desirous populace with alcohol from bootlegging and rum-running operations, speakeasies where to gather and imbibe, and illegal gambling halls and street lotteries. And while there were other illegal and not so "victimless" revenue streams, it was without question Prohibition that made the Mob.

It was during these years that disparate gangs learned to organize and use their treasure and muscle to procure influence and sow corruption that would serve them for decades as they transformed and expanded their rackets. Ironically, the most profitable illegal vices of that era—alcohol and gambling, which enriched and propelled those young twentysomething gangsters to their legendary infamy one hundred years ago—are now legal, taxed, and readily available to anyone of age.

Unlike Meyer, though, I had very little time with my grandfather and none of it of any quality. Vito was sentenced to fifteen years in federal prison in April 1959. I was six years old. Before he went "away on business," I do remember the occasional Sunday dinners at his modest two-bedroom, two-bath, 1,200-square-foot rented house on West Highland Avenue in Atlantic Highlands, in Monmouth County, New Jersey, about nine miles from where we lived. This house was a purposeful downsizing from his cliffside mansion in town, which was up on Ocean Boulevard, along a stretch of highlands that are the highest natural elevation on the Atlantic Coast south of Maine. Expansive windows on all floors provided sweeping views across Sandy Hook Bay to Raritan Bay, and on clear days, the New York Harbor and city skyline.

However, Vito's downsizing wasn't for customary reasons: empty-nesting, retirement, or financial concerns. In 1950, my grandmother, Anna, left the mansion and Vito. In 1953, frustrated with Vito's refusal to pay her court-ordered separation payments and Frank Costello's refusal to intervene, Anna secured a lawyer who convinced her that she would need to expose Vito's sources of income in order to secure a judgment for back payments and increased monthly support. In a very well-publicized Freehold, New Jersey, courtroom hearing, Anna testified that Vito ruled the Italian lottery in New York and New Jersey, bringing in over $1 million per year, owned four Greenwich Village nightclubs, a dog track in Virginia, and other legitimate businesses. She also assailed his character and validated his associations with other well-known mobsters of the era. My grandmother had gone where no Mob wife had ever dared venture.

Soon after, Vito auctioned off the furnishings of the mansion and moved into the small house I visited to downsize his public profile. To bolster his new image, Vito invited investigative journalist Dom Frasca from the *New York Journal-American* to visit him in his new home. The resulting book, *Vito Genovese: King of Crime*, included pictures of Vito relaxing at home with his golf trophy, preparing pasta sauce, raking leaves, and checking the oil in his car—an unassuming small businessman settling in for his dotage.

The mansion was later sold to a cooperative buyer. Speculations inside and outside Mob circles questioned the lifespan of my grandmother. Dorothy Kilgallen, the most syndicated newspaper columnist at the time, wrote, "If I were Mrs. Vito Genovese, I'd be awful careful crossing streets." However, as my father told me years later when I asked him about this episode, Vito had a deep, lifelong romantic attachment to Anna, and although they would never be together again after 1950, he made sure nothing happened to her. My grandmother died from a stroke in January 1982. She was seventy-six years old.

Vito sometimes came to our home for Sunday dinners. I have come to believe it was when it suited him to do so. Even at that young age, during his visits, I could feel the heavy drape of palpable tension and resigned tolerance that weighed on my parents. I remember men in suits coming to visit with him after dinner, men he probably didn't want seen visiting his house. He would introduce his three young grandsons and then we would be ushered out of the room. The meetings were never very long and Vito would leave shortly thereafter.

One night, one of the visitors gifted me a large metal fire truck—a bright red and gleaming chrome hook and ladder with working lights, siren, and extendable ladder. The next day, my mother told me that the man who gave me the fire truck was a famous singer. I could guess but probably shouldn't.

I don't remember my grandfather's voice and I don't remember him ever talking to me. It might be true. When my father was failing and in his final months, I would spend long afternoons visiting and talking. One day near the end, he looked up and said, "Ya know, my father never really just . . . talked to me." His eyes were pooled.

In our family, there was an unspoken rule. I'm sure many families have those, the invisible boundaries that partition off awkward events or graceless relations, especially from the youngest generation for as long as possible. We knew there would be no books, no cooperation with writers, reporters, producers, or others wanting our participation in projects about the Mafia, especially those involving my Pop Pop Vito.

I more than once witnessed my father taking a phone call on our kitchen wall phone, his face clouding and firmly stating, "No comment. Please don't call my home again." As you can imagine, this happened from time to time during the 1950s and beyond, whenever there was a salacious event that involved my grandfather or just writers and producers researching their projects.

This is the reason I had to decline Meyer II's invitation to participate in AMC's docudrama *The Making of the Mob*, which aired in 2015. Meyer was one of the noteworthy commentators in the series. I finally met him in person with his wife, Dani, at *The Making of the Mob* launch party, for which he graciously proffered an invitation for my wife and me. The party was held at Sparks Steak House in Manhattan, which is forever etched in Mob lore as the site of the December 1985 assassination of Gambino crime family boss, Paul "Big Paul" Castellano, and his underboss/bodyguard Thomas Bilotti as they exited their limo. Thoughtful choice, I suppose.

The following day, we embarked on an excursion Meyer had requested. Middle Village, Queens is about a thirty-five-minute ride from Midtown Manhattan. My grandfather is buried there in St. John Cemetery along with a long list of fellow mobsters. A short list of notables includes John Gotti, Roy DeMeo, Sonny Franzese, Mike Miranda, Carmine Galante, Salvatore Maranzano, Aniello Dellacroce, Paul Vario, Carlo Gambino, Joseph Profaci, Joe Colombo, and Charlie Luciano.

St. John is the patron saint of many occupations, places, and a variety of other things. One of the occupations is prisoners, which a lot of these guys were at one time or another, and the rest should have been. "Gangsters" is not on his list of patronages, but maybe someone forgot to mention that to the New York Mob, or maybe there's no other place close by that's large enough to hold them all. I took a picture of Meyer standing in front of the Lucania family mausoleum, which is the actual surname and final resting place of our grandfathers' good friend, Lucky Luciano.

I don't think our grandfathers, Meyer and Vito, were good friends. I sense they tolerated each other, at best. While I have only rumors and innuendo, I have suspected that Frank Costello and Lansky colluded to convince Luciano to get rid of Vito when he was appointed acting boss by Luciano when he was imprisoned in the mid-1930s, serving a thirty-to-fifty-year sentence. Vito was, well . . . Don Vitone, and likely flexing his new acting-boss muscles, which may have concerned Costello and Lansky, because thirty to fifty years was a long time. But the rules of the Commission and the fact that they all grew up together probably precluded a violent dethroning.

However, with Costello's political clout, it may not have been difficult to surface a witness to the 1934 murder of Ferdinand "The Shadow" Boccia. In 1937, a New York grand jury indicted Vito for arranging Boccia's murder. My grandfather fled to Italy upon hearing of the pending indictment, where he remained and prospered, first under Benito Mussolini's reign and then with the US Army Military Government in Naples, which was part of the

Allied Military Government of Occupied Territories (AMGOT), which the Allies set up in 1943. In 1945, he returned to New York under arrest for the Boccia murder. As Mob luck would have it, the witnesses died and the case was dismissed.

Most Mob scholars and law enforcement historians concur that Luciano, with Costello and perhaps Lansky and others, conspired to set up Vito for the narcotics conspiracy conviction and subsequent imprisonment in 1959. After all, Vito had been a very disruptive Commission rule-breaker in 1957: ordering Vincent Gigante to take a shot at Costello, conspiring in the murder of Albert Anastasia, and organizing the disastrous Apalachin Mafia summit. The depiction in the 2025 film *The Alto Knights* of Frank Costello torpedoing the summit was likely true and supported by other top hoodlums eager to thwart Vito's power grab.

On rare occasions, as we all grew older, my parents (usually my mother)—and separately, one-on-one with me—would whisper a tidbit or share an anecdote, most of which simply piled on teasers to the growing layers of shadowy secrets that were part of my matriculation in the School of Vito.

On one occasion, I was alone with my mother, having stopped by our family home. I'm not sure what triggered her to tell me the story. Maybe it was June 1975 and the murder of Sam Giancana was in the news. She told me that one day in November 1957, Vito stopped at our house unannounced midafternoon, hoping to see me and my two younger brothers on his way to a meeting. My brothers were napping. I was outside playing in the neighborhood. Vito left after introducing the man with him as "Sam, our friend from Chicago."

The next day, the news media covered little else but the roundup of over sixty mobsters from around the country who were routed from a barbeque in Apalachin, a small town in upstate New York. My mother recognized Sam on the TV news. Maybe Vito and Mooney a.k.a. Sam Giancana had a sleepover and then carpooled to the big party.

I envy Meyer II's possession and sharing of his grandfather's letters. I wish our family had something that allowed us more insight into the person who was our grandfather. Aside from the few gratuitous old newspaper articles describing him as a good neighbor, local Catholic Church benefactor, and a kindly gentleman around town, the preponderance of historical narratives depict Vito as a gangster's gangster. Hard and ruthless—someone I might be afraid to know today.

Apparently, though, he played a lot of golf, tipped his caddies well, and often played alone, sometimes with a couple fellows following him around the course. I know this because, for a period after I returned to Monmouth County, New Jersey, in the late 1980s after five years working in Boston, it seemed that every other time I presented my credit card to an old-timer at a gas station, barbershop, or restaurant, he claimed to have caddied for Vito at Old Orchard Country Club in Eatontown, New Jersey.

Someone who would know told me a story about a foursome of women playing behind Vito. One of the women sank a hole-in-one. Vito waited for them to congratulate the woman. She asked Vito to sign her card as a witness.

Vito chuckled. "I can't do that. I'm wanted in fifty states."

During one of our afternoon chats, I told my father about all the old caddies and asked him if Vito was a good golfer.

He said, "I don't really know, but I'm sure he won a lot."

In fact, I have unearthed archived local newspaper accounts of Vito placing high on the leaderboard in club tournaments, apparently winning him at least the one trophy displayed in the abovementioned picture.

Recently, as I was preparing to write this afterword, I was talking with my middle brother. I lamented that we didn't have any letters or personal items of reference about Vito. He stopped me cold and told me we did—for a while. When he was in grade school, home sick from school one day, my mother left him alone to run an errand. He took the opportunity to sneak a peek into our parents' top dresser drawers—the place you stash valuables and mementos. He found a stack of letters Vito had been writing to my father from prison. They were fatherly inquiries into the status of our family: how my dad was doing with his CPA practice, asking after my mother, how his grandsons were doing in school, and suggesting he was confident he would eventually be released and see us all sometime soon.

He died of congestive heart failure on Valentine's Day in 1969 in the United States Medical Center for Federal Prisoners in Springfield, Missouri. He was seventy-one years old. Sometime after that, my brother checked the drawer again. The letters were gone.

Unable to admit to creeping into our father's top drawer, some years later, he asked my father if Vito ever wrote him letters from prison.

For the first time that I know of, my father lied to one of us and said, "No."

Although he probably waited until he was sure Vito wasn't coming home again, I believe my father destroyed those letters in his unceasing quest to distance himself and our family from Vito's legacy. If we all look back on the worst moments of our lives, they all involve Vito. Little boys not allowed to come to our house to play. Girlfriends' fathers ending relationships. Bloody noses and knuckles when someone wanted teenage bragging rights. Job interviews cut short. And outright approaches by fringe characters who reeked of trouble and desperation.

But make no mistake, my parents made a wonderful life for us. Ozzie and Harriet had nothing on them, and our father *did* know best. My brothers and I had successful professional careers in the corporate world and in government service. We have wonderful children and grandchildren. My parents celebrated their seventieth wedding anniversary in 2021. They are gone now, but they will live forever in the hearts of their children, grandchildren, and future generations. Vito will live long in history, in words and film, but in the hearts of no one.

Meyer's grandfather left somewhat of a different legacy, due largely in part to his gentler nature, and the gambling empire he bequeathed to the world. This book should serve as a final note on his life, which will likewise be long remembered.

This is more than the biography of a mobster. It's a chronicle of a bygone era that left an indelible impact on the ever-evolving American landscape.

Phil Genovese *is the grandson of Five Families boss Vito Genovese and author of the award-winning novel* The Grandfather Clause.

APPENDIX A

Q&A with Meyer Lansky II

Was there a special connection between you and your grandfather?

Yes, not only because I was his namesake, but we had an intuitive connection. When Meyer visited us in Tacoma, Washington, he would stay at the Winthrop Hotel. When I was nine, as I followed him through the hotel's front doors, I heard a voice say, "One day you will be closely connected." I look back now and think I was meant to represent his story and legacy throughout my lifetime as his grandson and namesake.

From a very early age, you noticed that people treated you a little differently when they heard your name. What was that like?

When people hear my name, they either take a step back or ask for my ID.

You never were a part of street life, yet you're very comfortable talking about some of the friends of your grandfather whom you met, like Phil "The Stick" Kovolick, Willie "Ice Pick" Alderman, and Philadelphia's Harry Stromberg. Did they seem different to you, or just like family friends?

I felt Phil "The Stick," who would often babysit me in Miami, "Ice Pick" Willie, and Harry were all good, close family friends. However, when I was introduced to Albert "Tick-Tock" Tannenbaum, I felt apprehensive. I'm not sure why, but the memory remains.

What do you think your grandfather would think of the imposters who try to make money off his name?

He would think the imposters, from the "experts" to the poseurs who claim to be related or had business connections through him, were abhorrent. When Meyer was alive, he was offended by those who he referred to as "writers of fiction who are out to make a buck," and I believe he would be insulted by those who came out of the woodwork after he died to tell tall tales.

Many claim a relationship but fail to get his location or timeline correct, while others miss the mark or neglect to mention him in their research on the history of casinos or how the Las Vegas of the 1940s evolved into the Las Vegas of today.

How do you think your grandfather would feel about this book?

I feel Meyer would be pleased because I'm including most of the letters he wrote to my father, Paul, over a forty-year period, and sharing the stories that he, my father, and Uncle Buddy shared with me. I think he'd be proud knowing I'm coming out more prominently to be the source for legitimate authors and researchers.

Did you ever meet Moe Dalitz?

Yes, I met Moe when I was working in food and beverage for the La Costa Spa in Carlsbad, California, in 1978. One evening, Moe and a handful of his associates came in for dinner. I approached him and introduced myself as Meyer Lansky's grandson. He asked, "Where did your father go to school?"

I replied, "West Point."

The following evening, Moe returned and shared that he had spoken with Meyer, asked if I liked working at La Costa, and if I'd be interested in management training. I thanked him for his offer but decided to take another path.

How did you become friends with Phil Genovese?

After meeting on social media around 2012, in 2015, I invited Phil and his wife, MaryAnn, to a party for the launch of AMC's *The Making of the Mob.* He brought me a signed copy of his novel, *The Grandfather Clause*, and we've been friends ever since. He also contributed the afterword to *The Lansky Legacy.*

Why do you think people are still fascinated with your grandfather to this day?

People who know pieces of Meyer's story are fascinated that his family escaped a Russian czar, made their way to New York's Lower East Side, and how he connected with the Italian and Irish immigrants to create the early 20th-century Mafia, profiting from Prohibition and taking huge financial risks with dozens of modern-day hotel casinos.

Today, Meyer stands as an influential businessman of his era, especially in how he managed his resorts, and his personal style, along with how he co-founded the Syndicate, which all add to that fascination.

The Mafia in modern culture has also burnished his legacy, from Ben Kingsley's portrayal in *Bugsy* and Anatol Yusef in *Boardwalk Empire* to Lee Strasberg in *The Godfather Part II*, Patrick Dempsey in *Gangsters*, and Harvey Keitel in *Lansky*. People come and go, but Hyman Roth is forever! I've been told for decades that Meyer's authenticity is powerful and will be lasting.

Did Meyer Lansky and Lucky Luciano stay in touch after the latter's exile to Sicily? How unique and diverse was the Syndicate they organized in 1931, and how long would you say the organization held its grip on America, operating behind the scenes?

Meyer and Charlie Lucky stayed friends until the end of Charlie Lucky's life. When Meyer visited him in Italy in the late 1940s, the trip made headlines, so they stayed in touch through correspondence. The Syndicate they organized in 1931 was unique in its diversity, bringing in men from Jewish and Irish backgrounds, and at one time totaling three hundred members and one thousand associates. For more than thirty years, they had a stronghold and operated behind the scenes beyond that time.

While Lansky and Luciano were both considered the fathers of organized crime, did Lansky truly helm the entire Syndicate at any point, perhaps in the 1930s before Frank Costello and Vito Genovese stepped onto the scene?

Meyer and Charlie Lucky were nearly equal when the latter went to prison. Before he left for Dannemora, he told the other bosses, "Listen to what Meyer says, that's me talking."

Did anyone in organized crime consider Meyer Lansky a cooperating witness with the US government during World War II, in the investigation of Bugsy Siegel's murder, or in the aftermath of the Cuban

Revolution? How would you say his discussions with lawmen differed from the many "stool pigeons" and "canaries" the Mafia churned out over the years, and why was it permitted, unlike all the others?

Meyer was never a cooperating witness, nor considered to be. The only time he worked with the government, when asked, was with Naval Intelligence during World War II in order to remove the saboteurs from New York Harbor. When Meyer was interviewed following Ben Siegel's murder, he was just as surprised as everyone else. In the aftermath of the Cuban Revolution, there was nothing new to be shared, just the prior confirmation that Fidel Castro was a Communist. Meyer was always sought by the government, never the other way around.

How involved was Meyer Lansky in the operation of organized crime in his later years, namely the 1970s and 1980s? Was he still regarded by its members as a force to be reckoned with?

Meyer stayed involved with the men in his age group in Miami but was never involved with the 1970s mobsters in New York. He was still doing business until his death in 1983.

What happened to Meyer's millions? Where did the $300-million figure originate?

Meyer lost tens of millions in Cuba, having deep investments in its hotels, casinos, restaurants and bars, and other real estate, as well as the marina and airport. He also spent a substantial amount on attorneys' fees and was also a generous philanthropist to many charities during the last twenty-five years of his life. The $300-million figure originated from a struggling journalist looking to make a buck off a story.

What do you envision Bugsy Siegel's future would have looked like had his life not been cut short in 1947? How different do you think Las Vegas would be today had he remained a part of the Flamingo and the city for decades more?

If Ben Siegel had lived, he would have brought Las Vegas into an even more glamorous—and lucrative—era. Ben had the ability to attract visitors to Vegas at the level of Elvis Presley. I think by the end of the 1960s, Ben would have cashed out when the Howard Hughes era began.

Since you know many intimate and unknown details of your grandfather's friendship with Bugsy Siegel, will there be a book about him as well? What misconceptions does the public imagination hold regarding Siegel's relationship with Virginia Hill and the Mafia's purported assassination order against him?

Great question! I have a new book in the works on Ben Siegel. His death was not a Mafia hit, but an assassination that was more personal in nature. With Virginia Hill, I feel they would have always reunited if Ben hadn't been murdered.

APPENDIX B

Cast of Characters

Joe Adonis: Born Joseph Doto, he changed his last name to Adonis to reflect what he felt were his good looks. Adonis quietly rose through the ranks and earned millions. Lansky's intellect impressed him, and he became his business partner in the 1940s. Federal authorities convicted him of violating gambling laws. He moved to Italy in 1956 before being deported.

Vincent Alo: Known to friends as "Jimmy Blue Eyes," he worked closely with Lansky in Florida and Las Vegas. He deeply admired Lansky's business acumen and gentlemanly manner. He was the one who consoled Lansky after he learned that his firstborn son, Buddy, had cerebral palsy. Because they were so close, other mobsters knew his word was good when he was speaking for Lansky.

Albert Anastasia: Born in Italy, he came to the States in the early 1900s and worked on Brooklyn's docks. There, he developed a reputation as a man who relished killing and became the chief executioner of Murder, Inc., earning the moniker "Lord High Executioner" after reputedly eliminating his family boss Vincent Mangano and his brother. His greed was as great as his bloodlust, and he demanded a bigger cut from Lansky's Cuban casinos, which ultimately led to his demise. On the morning of October 25, 1957, he walked into the Park Sheraton barbershop for his regular shave and haircut. Gunmen with scarves covering their faces shot him to death in his chair. The murder remains unsolved.

Frank Costello: "The Prime Minister" of the Mob. A smooth and cunning operator, he rose to the pinnacle of Mob power as the Luciano crime family boss in the interim before it was renamed the Genovese family. Lansky regarded him as a friend but thought he was vain and taken advantage of by politicians. Costello wanted to be seen as a legitimate businessman and even posed for newspaper photos with his wife at their mansion on Sands Point, Long Island. After falling out of favor with the Mob bosses, he survived a shooting by Vincent "Chin" Gigante and stepped aside for Vito Genovese.

Moe Dalitz: He cut his teeth on Prohibition in the 1920s in Detroit. According to his daughter, he reveled in evading authorities with speedboats and secret compartments. He later moved his operations to Cleveland. There, he worked with Sam Tucker and Morris "Moe" Kleinman, who later became close to Lansky. Dalitz and Lansky were friendly until losses in Cuba sparked an estrangement. When Dalitz moved to Las Vegas, he decided to establish himself as a legitimate businessman and cut ties with many of his old friends.

Virginia Hill: Hill fled an abusive childhood in Georgia and married and divorced twice before heading for the bright lights of Chicago. Graced with a freewheeling sexuality and skilled at money laundering, she took up a succession of gangsters. Her most famous relationship was her tempestuous affair with Ben Siegel, whom legend has it called her "Flamingo." Hours before Siegel's murder, they had a violent argument and Hill fled to Paris. After learning of his death, she attempted suicide but survived. She later married an Austrian skier, Hans Hauser. When she died in 1966, it was ruled a suicide, though some have suggested she was murdered.

Meyer Lansky: Born Maier Suchowljansky in Grodno, Poland, in 1902, Lansky immigrated to the US with his family in 1911, meeting Charlie "Lucky" Luciano, Ben "Bugsy" Siegel, and Frank Costello in New York's Lower East Side in his teens. Together they formed the National Crime Syndicate. Considered the brains of the Mafia, Lansky created and built businesses through gains made during Prohibition, including large-scale hotel casino resorts, and has also been credited with inventing modern-day money laundering and offshore banking systems. He died in Miami in 1983 of lung cancer at the age of eighty.

Charles "Lucky" Luciano: He and Lansky met as teenagers on the streets of Brooklyn. Luciano was impressed when Lansky stood up to his gang of toughs. Together, they revamped the power structure of the criminal gangs spawned by Prohibition, creating modern-day organized crime. They remained close even after Luciano went to prison. During World War II, it was Lansky who enlisted Luciano's help from Dannemora in stopping the sabotage of New York's harbors. The phrase "loose lips sink ships" came from this operation.

Willie Moretti: With family ties to Frank Costello, he became a tough enforcer in the New Jersey Mob and made a fortune in rackets he shared with Longy Zwillman. Moretti loved the high life and was close to singer Frank Sinatra. Later in life, he started to deteriorate mentally, which friends blamed on untreated syphilis. His loud and loquacious manner made Lansky uncomfortable. Others, like Vito Genovese, thought he was a threat to the entire organization. On October 4, 1951, he was shot to death in a New Jersey restaurant.

Arnold Rothstein: Known as "The Brain," Rothstein was the ultimate fixer, the go-between for street guys and politicians. He crafted an image of sophistication and genteel wealth, even though his money came from his crimes. He was famous for fixing the 1919 World Series in the infamous Black Sox Scandal. He had an eye for talent. He met Lansky at a bar mitzvah of mutual friends in Brooklyn, and they talked for six hours. He became Lansky and Luciano's mentor for a time. Despite his success, his gambling habit doomed him. After he refused to pay off a gambling debt, he was brutally murdered in 1928 by persons unknown.

Dutch Schultz: Born Arthur Flegenheimer, he started his life in crime by riding shotgun on Arnold Rothstein's whiskey trucks. By the 1930s, he was one of the most prominent gangsters in New York. Admired for his toughness by mobsters like Sonny Franzese, Schultz exulted in his reputation for violence. When crusading prosecutor Thomas E. Dewey announced charges against him, Schultz urged the Mafia Commission to kill Dewey. At a meeting that included Lansky, they considered the idea, but ultimately decided it would attract too much heat. Schultz exploded in fury. Not long afterward, in 1935, two gunmen shot him to death at the Palace Chop House and Tavern in Newark, New Jersey.

Benjamin "Bugsy" Siegel: Exuberant and warm to his friends, he could explode in sudden fits of violent rage. Those explosions led to his nickname, "Bugsy," which he deplored. No one who knew him dared to call him that to his face. He and Lansky met as teenagers and remained lifelong friends. While some so-called Mob experts say Lansky approved Siegel's killing in 1947, family members insist that just isn't true. Siegel's daughter Millicent never would have let Lansky walk her down the aisle if that had been the case. FBI records also show that Lansky cooperated with the investigation into Siegel's murder.

Joseph "Doc" Stacher: A lifelong Lansky friend, he started out as a member of the Bugs and Meyer Mob. He made a fortune running booze during Prohibition. Stacher was at Lansky's side when he paid off Cuban strongman Fulgencio Batista. Later, at Lansky's request, Stacher moved to Las Vegas to represent his interests there. Nailed on income tax evasion charges in the 1960s, he moved to Israel. He quickly developed a network there and tried to help Lansky settle in Israel as well.

Albert "Tick-Tock" Tannenbaum: Tannenbaum got his start as a for-hire leg-breaker and moved up to becoming a contract killer for Murder, Inc. He and Lansky were an unlikely alliance because they were not in business together. Lansky kept him around when he lived in Florida, most likely as a bodyguard. Tannenbaum fit the part. His icy demeanor often rattled people who met him for the first time.

Billy Wilkerson: Wilkerson was the Hollywood nightclub impresario who created the Sunset Strip. Handsome and often charming, he was a heavy drinker and gambler and lover of beautiful women—he married five times. He had a singular influence because of his secret weapon, *The Hollywood Reporter.* When his gambling debts mounted and he needed money to build a casino, he entered a doomed partnership with Ben Siegel, who took over the Flamingo in short order. It was not a sidelining Wilkerson suffered lightly.

Abner "Longy" Zwillman: A close ally of Lansky and Luciano, he absorbed Dutch Schultz's rackets in New Jersey after his death. Adept at bribing politicians, his power was unrivaled in New Jersey. His cachet in social circles was such that he met and had an affair with glamorous actress Jean Harlow. Zwillman attracted the attention of congressional committees investigating organized crime and was charged with tax evasion. Then he ran afoul of Vito Genovese by failing to back him for Mob leadership. Just before he was scheduled to testify, he was found hanged to death in his basement. Although it was ruled a suicide, some suggested it might have been murder.

APPENDIX C

Lansky Family Tree

Benjamin Suchowljansky (d. Aug. 1910)
m. Basha Suchowljansky (d. Oct. 1910)

Max Suchowljansky (1879–1939)
m. Yetta Sandler(1882–1959)

Moses Citron (1876–1948)
m. Sarah Citron (1883–1968)

Meyer Lansky (1902–1983)
m . 1.) Anna Citron (1910–1984), May 1929; div. 1947

Bernard Irving "Buddy" Lansky (1930–1989)
m. Annette Lansky; div. 1975

Paul Lansky (1932–2024)
m. 1.) Edna Shook (1926–2011), 1956; div. 1972

Meyer Lansky II (b. 1957)

Myra Lansky

m. 2.) Kathleen Iverson (d. 1989)

Sandra Louise "Sandi" Lansky (1938–2023)
m. Marvin Rapoport

Gary Rapoport

m. Vincent Lombardo (1935–2014)

m. 2.) Thelma "Teddy" Scheer Schwartz (1907–1997)

Jacob "Jack" Lansky (1905–1983)
m. Anna Lansky

Two daughters, who each had two sons

Esther Lansky Chess (1915–2005)
m. Matthew "Matty" Chess (1907–1977)

Max Chess

Lena Lansky (died young)

Rose Lansky(died young)

APPENDIX D

Fitting the Role: Actors Over the Years

Meyer Lansky

- Lee Strasberg, *The Godfather Part II*, 1974 (as Hyman Roth)
- Brian Benben, *Gangster Wars*, 1981, and *The Gangster Chronicles*, 1981 (as Michael Lasker)
- Joe Pesci, *Eureka*, 1983 (as Mayakofsky)
- James Woods, *Once Upon a Time in America*, 1984 (as Maximilian "Max" Bercovicz)
- Martin Landau, *The Neon Empire*, 1989 (as Max Brower)
- Mark Rydell, *Havana*, 1990
- Patrick Dempsey, *Mobsters*, 1991
- Ben Kingsley, *Bugsy*, 1991
- Marc Grapey, *The Untouchables*, 1993–1994
- Richard Dreyfuss, *Lansky*, 1999
- Joshua Praw, *Lansky*, 1999
- Ryan Merriman, *Lansky*, 1999
- Max Perlich, *Lansky*, 1999
- Edward Asner, *Donzi: The Legend*, 2001
- Dustin Hoffman, *The Lost City*, 2005
- Anatol Yusef, *Boardwalk Empire*, 2010–2014
- Patrick Fischler, *Mob City*, 2013
- Ian Bell, *The Making of the Mob: New York*, 2015
- Julian Mazzola, *The Making of the Mob: New York*, 2015
- Jeffrey Alan Solomon, *The Making of the Mob: New York*, 2015
- James Remar, *Speed Kills*, 2018

- Harvey Keitel, *Lansky*, 2021
- John Magaro, *Lansky*, 2021

Bugsy Siegel

- Larry Blyden, *The Witness*, 1960–1961
- Alex Rocco, *The Godfather*, 1972 (as Moe Greene)
- Harvey Keitel, *Virginia Hill*, 1974
- Clement von Franckenstein, *Lepke*, 1975
- Joe Penny, *Gangster Wars*, 1981, and *The Gangster Chronicles*, 1981
- Marc Figueroa, *The Revenge of Al Capone*, 1989
- Armand Assante, *The Marrying Man*, 1991
- Richard Grieco, *Mobsters*, 1991
- Warren Beatty, *Bugsy*, 1991
- Eric Roberts, *Lansky*, 1999
- Anthony Medwetz, *Lansky*, 1999
- Matthew Settle, *Lansky*, 1999
- Michael Zegen, *Boardwalk Empire*, 2010–2014
- Edward Burns, *Mob City*, 2013
- Joe Mantegna, *Kill Me, Deadly*, 2015
- Jonathan C. Stewart, *The Making of the Mob: New York*, 2015
- David Cade, *Lansky*, 2021

Lucky Luciano

- Eduardo Ciannelli, *Marked Woman*, 1937
- Robert Carricart, *The Untouchables*, 1959–1963
- Telly Savalas, *The Witness*, 1960–1961
- Angelo Infanti, *The Valachi Papers*, 1972
- Gian Maria Volonté, *Lucky Luciano*, 1973
- Vic Tayback, *Lepke*, 1975
- Lee Montague, *Brass Target*, 1978
- Michael Nouri, *Gangster Wars*, 1981, and *The Gangster Chronicles*, 1981
- Mitchell S. Benson, *Gangster Wars*, 1981, and *The Gangster Chronicles*, 1981
- Joe Dallesandro, *The Cotton Club*, 1984
- Nicholas Mele, *The Revenge of Al Capone*, 1989
- Robert Davi, *White Hot*, 1991
- Christian Slater, *Mobsters*, 1991
- Stanley Tucci, *Billy Bathgate*, 1991
- Bill Graham, *Bugsy*, 1991

- David Darlow, *The Untouchables*, 1993–1994
- Billy Drago, *The Outfit*, 1993
- Andy García, *Hoodlum*, 1997
- Anthony LaPaglia, *Lansky*, 1999
- Paul Sincoff, *Lansky*, 1999
- Vince Corazza, *Bonanno: A Godfather's Story*, 1999
- David Viggiano, *The Real Untouchables*, 2001
- Vincent Piazza, *Boardwalk Empire*, 2010–2014
- Rich Graff, *The Making of the Mob: New York*, 2015
- Frank DiNovi, *The Making of the Mob: New York*, 2015
- Giampiero Judica, *Hache*, 2019–2021
- Shane McRae, *Lansky*, 2021
- Amadeo Fusca, *The Alto Knights,* 2025

Virginia Hill

- Dyan Cannon, *Virginia Hill*, 1974
- Annette Bening, *Bugsy*, 1991
- Peggy Jo Jacobs, *Lansky*, 1999
- Kaelan Denali Dickinson, *The Making of the Mob: New York*, 2015
- Samantha Czosnek, *Capone*, 2020

Arnold Rothstein

- Spencer Tracy, *Now I'll Tell*, 1934 (as Murray Golden)
- Robert Lowery, *The Rise and Fall of Legs Diamond*, 1960
- David J. Stewart, *The Witness*, 1960–1961
- David Janssen, *The Big Bankroll*, 1961
- Jimmy Baird, *The Big Bankroll*, 1961
- George DiCenzo, *Gangster Wars*, 1981, and *The Gangster Chronicles*, 1981
- Michael Lerner, *Eight Men Out*, 1988
- F. Murray Abraham, *Mobsters*, 1991
- Stanley DeSantis, *Lansky*, 1999
- Michael Stuhlbarg, *Boardwalk Empire*, 2010–2014
- Hugh Scully, *The Making of the Mob: New York*, 2015

Frank Costello

- Fausto Tozzi, *The Valachi Papers*, 1972
- Feodor Chaliapin Jr., *My Brother Anastasia*, 1973

- James Andronica, *Gangster Wars*, 1981, and *The Gangster Chronicles*, 1981
- Costas Mandylor, *Mobsters*, 1991
- Carmine Caridi, *Bugsy*, 1991
- Kirk Baltz, *Kingfish*, 1995
- Tom La Grua, *Lansky*, 1999
- Anthony DiCarlo, *The Making of the Mob: New York*, 2015
- Paul Sorvino, *Godfather of Harlem*, 2019–present
- Ray Bouderau, *Mob Town*, 2019
- Ron Fallica, *Lansky*, 2021
- Robert De Niro, *The Alto Knights*, 2025
- Luke Stanton Eddy, *The Alto Knights*, 2025

Vito Genovese

- Lino Ventura, *The Valachi Papers*, 1972
- Charles Cioffi, *Lucky Luciano*, 1973
- Robert Davi, *Gangster Wars*, 1981, *The Gangster Chronicles*, 1981, and *Mob Town*, 2019
- Don Carrara, *Bugsy*, 1991
- Robert Miano, *Lansky*, 1999
- Emidio Michetti, *Bonanno: A Godfather's Story*, 1999
- Steven Bauer, *Boss of Bosses*, 2001
- Craig Thomas Rivela, *The Making of the Mob: New York*, 2015
- Steve Przybytek, *The Making of the Mob: New York*, 2015
- Robert De Niro, *The Alto Knights*, 2025
- Antonio Cipriani, *The Alto Knights*, 2025

Vincent Mangano

- Narrazeno Natale, *Bonanno: A Godfather's Story*, 1999 (as Don Vincenzo)
- Daniel Jordano, *The Making of the Mob: New York*, 2015

Albert Anastasia

- Fausto Tozzi, *The Valachi Papers*, 1972
- Richard Conte, *My Brother Anastasia*, 1973
- Gianni Russo, *Lepke*, 1975
- John Aprea, *Gangster Wars*, 1981, and *The Gangster Chronicles*, 1981
- Nick Corello, *Lansky*, 1999

- Maurizio Terrazzano, *Bonanno: A Godfather's Story*, 1999
- Frank Crudele, *Bonanno: A Godfather's Story*, 1999
- Gus Zucco, *The Making of the Mob: New York*, 2015
- Gary Pastore, *The Irishman*, 2019, and *Mob Town*, 2019
- Vincent Minutella, *Lansky*, 2021
- Michael Rispoli, *The Alto Knights*, 2025

Carlo Gambino

- Robert Loggia, *Between Love and Honor*, 1995
- Marc Lawrence, *Gotti*, 1996
- Frank Fontaine, *Bonanno: A Godfather's Story*, 1999
- Al Buscio, *Boss of Bosses*, 2001
- Noah Forest, *The Making of the Mob: New York*, 2015
- Michael Cipitti, *Gotti*, 2018
- Arthur J. Nascarella, *Godfather of Harlem*, 2019–present
- Anthony Skordi, *The Offer*, 2022
- James Ciccone, *The Alto Knights*, 2025

Tommy Gagliano

- Bob Giovani, *Gangster Wars*, 1981, and *The Gangster Chronicles*, 1981
- Guy Kelada, *Bonanno: A Godfather's Story*, 1999
- Salvatore Inzerillo, *Boardwalk Empire*, 2010–14
- Caleb McDaniel, *The Making of the Mob: New York*, 2015

Tommy Lucchese

- Jon Polito, *Gangster Wars*, 1981, and *The Gangster Chronicles*, 1981
- Gregory Cioffi, *The Making of the Mob: New York*, 2015
- Bo Dietl, *Godfather of Harlem*, 2019–present
- Michael Rispoli, *The Offer*, 2022
- Anthony J. Gallo, *The Alto Knights*, 2025

Joe Bonanno

- John Chappoulis, *Mobsters*, 1991
- Ben Gazzara, *Love, Honor & Obey*, 1993
- Tony Nardi, *Bonanno: A Godfather's Story*, 1999

- Bruce Ramsay, *Bonanno: A Godfather's Story*, 1999
- Amadeo Fusca, *Boardwalk Empire*, 2010–2014
- James Kacey, *The Making of the Mob: New York*, 2015
- Chazz Palmintieri, *Godfather of Harlem*, 2019–present
- Claudio Bellante, *Lansky*, 2021
- Sal Landi, *The Offer*, 2022
- Louis Mustillo, *The Alto Knights*, 2025

Joe Profaci

- Joseph Ragno, *Gangster Wars*, 1981, and *The Gangster Chronicles*, 1981
- Joe Viterelli, *Mobsters*, 1991
- Michael A. Miranda, *Bonanno: A Godfather's Story*, 1999 (as Silvio Oliviero)
- Anthony Bisciello, *The Making of the Mob: New York*, 2015
- Joe Bacino, *The Alto Knights*, 2025

Joe Masseria

- Alessandro Sperlì, *The Valachi Papers*, 1972
- Richard S. Castellano, *Gangster Wars*, 1981, and *The Gangster Chronicles*, 1981
- Anthony Quinn, *Mobsters*, 1991 (as Don Masseria)
- Bill Capizzi, *Lansky*, 1999
- Tony Calabretta, *Bonanno: A Godfather's Story*, 1999
- Ivo Nandi, *Boardwalk Empire*, 2010–14
- Stelio Savante, *The Making of the Mob: New York*, 2015
- Louie Lawless, *The Alto Knights*, 2025 (as Joe the Boss)

Salvatore Maranzano

- Joseph Wiseman, *The Valachi Papers*, 1972
- Joseph Mascolo, *Gangster Wars*, 1981, and *The Gangster Chronicles*, 1981
- Michael Gambon, *Mobsters*, 1991 (as Don Faranzano)
- Rob Gilbert, *Lansky*, 1999
- Edward James Olmos, *Bonanno: A Godfather's Story*, 1999
- Giampiero Judica, *Boardwalk Empire*, 2010–2014
- Roberto De Felice, *The Making of the Mob: New York*, 2015
- Jay Giannone, *Lansky*, 2021

Vincent Alo

- Dominic Chianese, *The Godfather Part II*, 1974 (as Johnny Ola)
- Robert De Niro, *American Hustle*, 2013 (as Victor Tellegio)

Joe Adonis

- James Purcell, *Gangster Wars*, 1981, and *The Gangster Chronicles*, 1981
- Lewis Van Bergen, *Bugsy*, 1991
- Sal Landi, *Lansky*, 1999

Dutch Schultz

- Lawrence Dobkin, *The Untouchables*, 1959–1963
- Robert J. Wilke, *The Untouchables*, 1959–1963
- Warren J. Kemmerling, *The Untouchables*, 1959–1963
- John Dennis, *The Lawless Years*, 1959–1961
- Lonny Chapman, *The Witness*, 1960–1961
- Vic Morrow, *Portrait of a Gangster*, 1961
- Vincent Gardenia, *Mad Dog Coll*, 1961
- John Durren, *Lepke*, 1975
- Jonathan Banks, *Gangster Wars*, 1981, and *The Gangster Chronicles*, 1981
- James Remar, *The Cotton Club*, 1984
- Neil Gray Giuntoli, *The Revenge of Al Capone*, 1989
- Dustin Hoffman, *Billy Bathgate*, 1991
- Si Osborne, *The Untouchables*, 1993–1994
- Lance Henriksen, *The Outfit*, 1993
- Tim Roth, *Hoodlum*, 1997
- Christopher Morrow, *The Making of the Mob: New York*, 2015

Frankie Yale

- John Cassavetes, *Capone*, 1975
- Robert Ellenstein, *The Lawless Years*, 1959–1961
- Al Ruscio, *The Untouchables*, 1959–1963
- Joseph Riccobene, *Boardwalk Empire*, 2010–2014
- Andrew Robertt, *The Making of the Mob: Chicago*, 2016

Longy Zwillman

- James Harper, *Lansky*, 1999
- Eric C. Schmitz, *Lansky*, 2021

Moe Dalitz

- Peter Siragusa, *Lansky*, 1999

Moses Polakoff

- Ron Perkins, *Lansky*, 1999
- Chas Rittenhouse Sr., *The Making of the Mob: New York*, 2015

Joe Valachi

- Charles Bronson, *The Valachi Papers*, 1972
- Joe Viterelli, *Jack Ruby*, 1992
- Giancarlo Caltabiano, *Bonanno: A Godfather's Story*, 1999
- Michael Cianciullo, *Bonanno: A Godfather's Story*, 1999
- Erik Decicco, *The Making of the Mob: New York*, 2015

Joe Barbara

- Danny A. Abeckaser, *Mob Town,* 2019
- John Dinello, *The Alto Knights*, 2025

Johnny Roselli

- Sam Grana, *Sugartime*, 1995
- Tony Lo Bianco, *Nixon*, 1995
- Bruce Di Quenzio, *Bonanno: A Godfather's Story*, 1999
- Tony Nappo, *Power and Beauty*, 2002
- Chuck Shamata, *The Company*, 2007
- Michael Wiseman, *Vegas*, 2012–2013 (as Johnny Rizzo)
- Nick Annunziata, *Mafia Spies*, 2024
- John Travolta, *November 1963*, 2026

Santo Trafficante Jr.

- Val Avery, *Donnie Brasco*, 1997

- Roc LaFortune, *Bonanno: A Godfather's Story*, 1999
- Joseph Leone, *Mafia Spies*, 2024

Nucky Johnson

- Steve Buscemi, *Boardwalk Empire*, 2010–2014 (as Nucky Thompson)
- Nolan Lyons, *Boardwalk Empire*, 2010–2014 (as Nucky Thompson)
- Marc Pickering, *Boardwalk Empire*, 2010–2014 (as Nucky Thompson)
- Elan Zafir, *The Making of the Mob: New York*, 2015

Jim Colosimo

- Harry J. Vejar, *Scarface*, 1932 (as "Big Louie" Costillo)
- Joe De Santis, *Al Capone*, 1959
- Frank Campanella, *Capone*, 1975
- Raymond Serra, *The Young Indiana Jones Chronicles*, 1992–1996
- Peter Siragusa, *The Untouchables*, 1993–1994
- Frank Crudele, *Boardwalk Empire*, 2010–2014
- Andre King, *The Making of the Mob: Chicago*, 2016

Johnny Torrio

- Osgood Perkins, *Scarface*, 1932 (as Johnny Lovo)
- Nehemiah Persoff, *Al Capone*, 1959
- Charles McGraw, *The Untouchables*, 1959–1963
- Harry Guardino, *Capone*, 1975
- Guy Barile, *The Babe*, 1992
- Frank Vincent, *The Young Indiana Jones Chronicles*, 1992–1996
- Byrne Piven, *The Untouchables*, 1993–1994
- Greg Antonacci, *Boardwalk Empire*, 2010–2014
- Paolo Rotondo, *The Making of the Mob: Chicago*, 2016
- Al Sapienza, *Gangster Land*, 2017

Al Capone

- Paul Muni, *Scarface*, 1932 (as Tony Camonte)
- Rod Steiger, *Al Capone*, 1959
- Telly Savalas, *The Witness*, 1960–1961
- Neville Brand, *The Untouchables*, 1959–1963, and *The George Raft Story*, 1961

- José Calvo, *Due mafiosi contro Al Capone*, 1966
- Jason Robards, *The St. Valentine's Day Massacre*, 1967
- Ben Gazzara, *Capone*, 1975
- Louis Giambalvo, *Gangster Wars*, 1981, and *The Gangster Chronicles*, 1981
- Robert De Niro, *The Untouchables*, 1987
- Vincent Guastaferro, *Frank Nitti: The Enforcer*, 1988
- Ray Sharkey, *The Revenge of Al Capone*, 1989
- Eric Roberts, *The Lost Capone*, 1990
- Titus Welliver, *Mobsters*, 1991
- Bernie Gigliotti, *The Babe*, 1992
- William Forsythe, *The Untouchables*, 1993–1994
- F. Murray Abraham, *Dillinger and Capone*, 1995
- Lou Vani, *Bonanno: A Godfather's Story*, 1999
- Dominic Capone III, *The Real Untouchables*, 2001
- Julian Littman, *Capone's Boys*, 2002 (*Al's Lads* in the UK)
- Anthony LaPaglia, *Road to Perdition*, 2002 (deleted scene)
- Jon Bernthal, *Night at the Museum: Battle of the Smithsonian*, 2009
- Stephen Graham, *Boardwalk Empire*, 2010–2014
- Umberto Celisano, *The Making of the Mob: New York*, 2015
- Michael Kotsohilis, *The Making of the Mob: Chicago*, 2016
- Milo Gibson, *Gangster Land*, 2017
- Tom Hardy, *Capone*, 2020
- Robert Walker Branchaud, *Lansky*, 2021

Frank Nitti

- Bruce Gordon, *The Untouchables*, 1959–1963
- Harold J. Stone, *The St. Valentine's Day Massacre*, 1967
- Sylvester Stallone, *Capone*, 1975
- Billy Drago, *The Untouchables*, 1987
- Anthony LaPaglia, *Nitti: The Enforcer*, 1988
- Alan Rosenberg, *The Revenge of Al Capone*, 1989
- Paul Regina, *The Untouchables*, 1993–1994
- Stanley Tucci, *Road to Perdition*, 2002
- Bill Camp, *Public Enemies*, 2009
- Owen Black, *The Making of the Mob: Chicago*, 2016

Paul Ricca

- Pierrino Mascarino, *Gangster Wars*, 1981, and *The Gangster Chronicles*, 1981
- Michael D. Russo, *Frank Nitti: The Enforcer*, 1988
- Christopher Valente, *The Making of the Mob: Chicago*, 2016

Tony Accardo

- Maury Chaykin, *Sugartime*, 1995
- Jason Fitch, *The Making of the Mob: Chicago*, 2016
- Nicholas Urzetta, *Mafia Spies*, 2024
- Mandy Patinkin, *November 1963*, 2026

Sam Giancana

- Tony Curtis, *Mafia Princess*, 1986
- Carmine Caridi, *Ruby*, 1992
- Rod Steiger, *Sinatra*, 1992
- John Turturro, *Sugartime*, 1995
- Robert Miranda, *The Rat Pack*, 1998
- Peter Friedman, *Power and Beauty*, 2002
- Serge Houde, *The Kennedys*, 2011
- Emmett Skilton, *The Making of the Mob: Chicago*, 2016
- Al Linea, *The Irishman*, 2019
- Chris Pinto, *Mafia Spies*, 2024
- Thomas Fiscella, *November 1963*, 2026

APPENDIX E

The Lansky Letters

Letters from Meyer Lansky to His Son Paul Lansky, 1949–1972

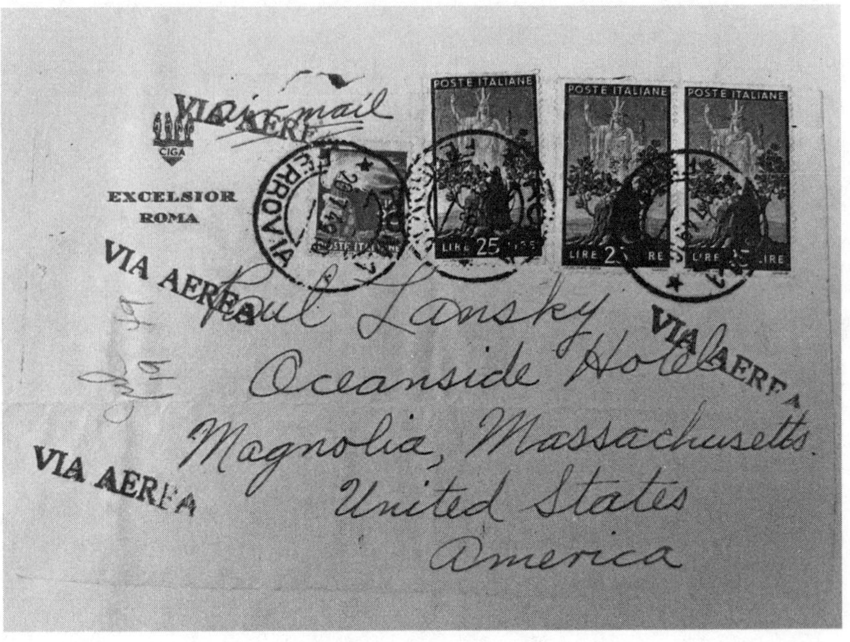

EXCELSIOR
ROMA

July. 19, 1949.

Dear Paul,

Your letter brought a very pleasant greeting.

I am glad to hear that you like your work also that you are in good health. I think it was very wise what you chose to do this summer. Your experience of the sea and land gives you a rounded prospective of life.

I spoke to Bud last week. I also received a letter from Sandra and Esta.

I am glad you are in touch with all of them. I think it is fun for Sandra to send to you for shoe polish.

Paul I can write pages about Rome but this is all the paper I have. They are very short of paper here. I will describe it all to you when I see you, it is simply something beyond anyones imagination. The Vatican leaves you breathless. I would venture to say if it was built to day it would cost $50,000,000,000.

Ted sends you her best.

Love

Dad

Excelsior, Roma
July 19, 1949

Dear Paul,

Your letter brought a very pleasant greeting.

I am glad to hear that you like your work also that you are in good health. I think it was very wise what you chose to do this summer. Your experience of the sea and land gives you a rounded prospective of life.

I spoke to Bud last week. I also spoke to Sandra and Esta.

I am glad you are in touch with all of them. I think it is fun for Sandra to send to you for shoe polish.

Paul I can write pages about Rome but this is all the paper I have. They are short of paper here. I will describe it all to you when I see you, it is simply something beyond anyones imagination. The Vatican leaves you breathless. I would venture to say if it was bult today it would cost $50,000,000,000.

Ted sends you her best.

Love,
Dad

June 23, 1952.

Dear Paul,

I have read your letter a couple of times; thought the matter over carefully and then signed the papers.

The reason I signed it is this. Your thoughts are well worded. I admire you for your attitude. You should make a good officer someday. Second reason, I haven't any right to interfere with any part of your training that may someday save your "Life".

As your Father my heart yearns for your safety. But, there isn't any safety or freedom unless you are trained to fight for it. I know you have the courage and I am proud of your serious endeavor. It is your duty to take it seriously.

My place of business is doing very well. We are sold out for July 4th week end. I left Sandra in Florida. She is having a grand time. She is having more swimming now then she has had all her life. She we will be back June 26th. I will tell you more when I see you. Your Brother is happy with his Yankees. He is also growing more serious about his work.

Roberta has decided to get married sometime this year. The date will be set soon.

We are happy to hear you are well and also that you are doing well in your training. With your determination I have confidence in your well being.

Let me know what time to pick you up. As early as you like.

Love from all of us.

Love
Dad

P.S. Sue has had a baby Girl.

June 20, 1952

Dear Paul,

I have read your letter a couple of times; thought the matter over carefully and then signed the papers.

The reason I signed it is this. Your thoughts are well worded. I admire you for your attitude. You should make a good officer someday. Second reason, I haven't any right to interfere in any part of your training that may someday save your "Life."

As your Father my heart yearns for your safety. But, there isn't any safety or freedom unless you are trained to fight for it. I know you have the courage and I am proud of your serious endeavor. It is your duty to take it seriously.

My place of business is doing well. We are sold out for July 4th weekend. I left Sandra in Florida. She is having a good time. She is having more swimming now than she has had all her life. She will be back June 26th. I will tell you more when I see you. Your Brother is happy with his Yankees. He is also growing more serious about his work.

Roberta has decided to get married sometime this year. The date will be set soon.

We are happy to hear that you are well and also that you are doing well in your training. With your determination I have confidence in your well being.

Let me know what time to pick you up. As early as you like.

Love from all of us.

Love,
Dad

P.S. Sue has had a baby girl.

May. 23 1953.

Dear Paul,

I have received your cheerful letter and was happy to hear how confident you feel about everything. Always keep up your good spirit.

Yes I'm looking forward to that happy day of June 1954. It is quite an extensive program. Paul you are all that a Father hopes to have in a Child. Your deep love and devotion you have shown me since I'm here, made a deep impression in me. Also your humane and charitable deeds toward others makes me proud of you. With your miserly time you get for your self in the City yet you always found time to visit the crippled Children. You have made Mr. Adams very happy, to him it is like a reward for what he is doing. Humane deeds are more important than heroic deeds.

I have ~~finnis~~ finished reading Napoleon; it is very interesting. I ~~had~~ have read history on him before but never an extensive Biography. He really had great principle and vision when he let go of his vanity. I recived a couple of Algebra books from Bud. They have many more formulas but I can't read to much here. It is to hard on the eyes, but the few formulas I looked at refreshed my mind a bit, however I will either mail you those that puzzle me or wait until we get to gether on our vacation.

Hope Jamie's is leg is coming a long, regards to Ed.

Love
Dad

From
Box 175
Ballston Spa., N.Y.

BALLSTON SPA
MAY 23
5 PM
1953
N.Y.

Cadet Paul Lansky
Co. M. I.
U. S. M. C.
West Point, New York

May 23, 1953

Dear Paul,

I have received your cheerful letter and was happy to hear how confident you feel about everything. Always keep up your good spirit.

Yes I'm looking forward to that happy day of June 1954. It is quite an extensive program. Paul you are all that a Father hopes to have in a child. Your deep love and devotion you have shown me since I'm here, made a deep impression in me. Also your humane and charitable deeds toward others makes me proud of you. With your miserly time you get for your self in the city yet you always found time to visit the crippled children. You have made Mr. Adams very happy, to him it is like a reward for what he is doing. Humane deeds are more important than heroic deeds.

I have finished reading Napoleon, it is very interesting. I have read history on him before but never an extensive Biography. He really had great principle and vision when he let go of his vanity. I received a couple of algebra books from Bud. They have many more formulas but I can't read to much here. It is to hard on the eyes, but the few formulas I looked at refreshed my mind a bit, however I will either mail you those that puzzle me or wait until we get together on our vacation.

I hope Jamie's leg is coming along, regards to Ed.

Love,
Dad

Dec. 4, 1956.

Dear Paul,

I received your letter Sat. the 1st I was happy to talk to you and hear that you are well and happy.

It is interesting to read about Alaska climate. I have read a little about Alaska in books but it is never the same as getting information from a person you know.

Holidays usually makes one long for home. It is well when you find good company to enjoy a holiday dinner. My best wishes to Edna, Jamie & Judy. I'm happy to hear that Edna's Mother is well again.

The Hotel is progressing very well, exceptionally fast for Cuba. We hope to have the roof on May 15. If we make and I know we can we will have opening nite Dec. 20th 1957. Then off to the races. These pictures were taken Nov. the 23rd. I will mail pictures to you as we take them to show you how we progress and the same time you will live with it too

Paul, the road building is not all there is to building a hotel. You would be surprise all the detail it takes to get it ready after completion and decorated. Someday I will send you a book on it. After the building comes the staff. The beauty of a Hotel, is one selling point, but service is very important once you get the people in and I'm a stickler for service. I know what it takes to give service and I will have the most modern equipment you can buy to assist in giving good service. It may take a little while, but I assure you I will whip it in shape in little time.

This business is no mystery to me. I don't have to depend on phony managers if they don't suit my idea of ability, and the same goes in the catering department or kitchen. My aim is to go after small conventions. That is a very desirable business from a spending standpoint. I'm lining it up now and will start booking conventions Jan 1957 for May 1st 1958.

I'm in touch with the travel agencies end of the business. As you see I'm not losing any time so that when we open the door it will go off like a clock.

3

This morning I'm having a meeting with the Architect and the Engineers to settle all consructual details and from now on no changes. My decorator arrived this morning and he will start to live with the Hotel and give me a rendering of his plans in a month or he will get the skids. All departments covered well and no time lost. Aim for opening date Dec. 20, 1957 (a must).

Speaking of money, I'm placing $50 in this letter. Two short letters will leave the same time with $50 in each letter for a total of $150 before you arrive from Japan and in time to spend it for Christmas and New Years. Have a good boy.

The letters will be mailed from the States. You can't chance putting money in letters here.

We are all well. I spoke to Sandra since I spoke to you and she is well. I will spend Christmas with her. If you are around telephone us reverse the charges. Her new number is Su 7-7266

Love
Dad

Dec. 4, 1956

Dear Paul,

I received your letter Sat. the 1st. I was happy to talk to you and hear that you are well and happy.

It is interesting to read about Alaska climate. I have read a little about Alaska in books but it is never the same as getting information from a person you know.

Holidays usually makes one long for home. It is well when you find good company to enjoy a holiday dinner. My best wishes to Edna, Jamie and Judy. I'm happy to hear that Edna's Mother is well again.

The hotel is progressing very well, exceptionally fast for Cuba. We hope to have the roof on May 15. If we make and I know we can we will have opening nite Dec. 20th, 1957. Then off to the races. These pictures were taken Nov. the 23rd. I will mail pictures to you as we take them to show you how we progress and the same time you will live with it too.

Paul, the rough building is not all there is to building a hotel. You would be surprise all the detail it takes to get it ready after completion and decorated. Someday I will send you a book on it. After the building comes the staff. The beauty of a Hotel, is one selling point, but service is very important once you get the people in and I'm a stickler for service. I know what it takes to give service and I will have the most modern equipment you can buy to assist in giving good service. It may take a little while, but I assure you I will whip it in shape in little time.

This business is no mystery to me I don't have to depend on phony managers if they don't suit my idea of ability, and the same goes in the catering department or kitchen. My aim is to go after small conventions. That is a very desirable business from a spending standpoint. I'm lining it up now and will start booking conventions Jan. 1957 for May 1st, 1958.

I'm in touch with the travel agencies end of the business. As you see I'm not losing any time so that when we open the door it will go off like a clock.

This morning I'm having a meeting with the Architect and the Engineers to settle all constructural details and form now on no changes. My decorator arrived this morning and he will start to live with the Hotel and give me a rendering of his plans in a month or he will get the skids. All departments covered well and no time lost. Aim for opening date Dec. 20, 1957 (a must).

Speaking of money, I'm placing $50 in this letter. Two short letters will leave the same time with $50 in each letter for a total of $150 before you arrive from Japan and in time for you to spend it for Christmas and New Years. Have a good boy.

The letters will be mailed from the States. You can't chance putting money in letters here.

We are all well. I spoke to Sandra since I spoke to you and she is well. I will spend Christmas with her. If you around telephone us reverse the charges. Her new number is Su7-7260.

Love,
Dad

June. 4, 1957.

Dear Paul,

I received your most welcomed letter and I was happy to hear that both you and Edna are well.

I myself was happy to get away from the constent heat and Sun. The weather in New York was good for the time I was there.

So far the groom doesn't look any the worse of the deal. He seems very happy, infact they both look happy. Very proudly showing off the pictures of the wedding.

In answer to the furniture and business let me say this; whenever you try to rush a job you will always find apparent lack of organization.

A hotel of this size should be on the boards for at least one year. This means that you would have a picture of everything before you put a shovel in the ground but you will find investers aren't interested when you tell them about the great lenght of time so you to do the next best thing.

We have resolved everything since and the furniture will start being manufactured next week. You are right about the lack of organization which caused poor presentation. Decorators usually work on cost plus 15% when you have it financed by them. When you have your own capital you go out in the furniture market after you get all designs from decorator and you have furniture people bid your job on competitive bases. But that is only for the box furniture. The public space you have to contract out. The decorator then will not get more then 10% or less according to the amount involved.

Tariff rates usually run according to the competition of the country. Cuba makes furniture, she does lack assembly line. So you can't depend on time when you get into a big order like ours. Although we are making certain wood pieces for public areas according to our specifications. Such as all bars and large tables in lobbys and places like that.

I would like to hear a little more about your insurance. I don't want you to become a slave to premiums. It can become a burden.

Sandra is really a problem. Marvin visited me and asked if he could help. He was really nice about it and he wants to be helpsful.

I'm trying to do my best to help her and I will keep trying until I see no hope. I made things very plain to her that she will be the only looser if she doesn't correct her-self.

Please send me Ednas birthday date. Events like that if we remember her, will bring us closer to her. The distance keeps us strangers that is why I'm happier to telephone when yourn't there because I want her to know that I don't just call for you.

Everything else is well. Ted sends you her love, she is really fond of you.

Love to both of you.

Love
Dad

June 4, 1957

Dear Paul,

I received your most welcomed letter and I was happy to hear that both you and Edna are well.

I myself was happy to get away from the constant heat and sun. The weather in New York was good for the time I was there.

So far the groom doesn't look any worse of the deal. He seems very happy, in fact they both look happy. Very proudly showing off the pictures of the wedding.

In answer to the furniture and business let me say this; whenever you try to rush a job you will always find apparent lack of organization.

A hotel of this size should be on the boards for at least a year. This means that you would have a picture of everything before you put a shovel in the ground but you will find investors aren't interested when you tell them about the great length of time so you to do the next best thing.

We have resolved everything since and the furniture will start being manufactured next week. You are right about the lack of organization which caused poor presentation. Decorators usually work on cost plus 15% when you have it financed by them. When you have your own capital you go out in the furniture market after you get all the designs from decorator and you have furniture people bid your job on competitive bases. But that is only for the box furniture. The public space you have to contract out. The decorator then will not get more than 10% or less depending on the amount involved.

Tariff rates usually run according to the competition of the country. Cuba makes furniture; she does lack assembly line. So you can't depend on time when you get to a big order like ours. Although we are making certain wood pieces for public areas according to our specifications. Such as all bars and large tables in lobbys and places like that.

I would like to hear a little more about your insurance. I don't want you to become a slave to premiums. It can become a burden.

Sandra is really a problem. Marvin visited me and asked if I could help. He was really nice about it and he wants to be helpful.

I am trying to do my best to help her and I will keep trying until I see no hope. I made things very plain to her that she will be the only looser if she doesn't correct herself.

Please send me Ednas birthday date. Events like that if we remember her, will bring us closer to her. The distance keeps us strangers that is why I am happier to telephone when you're not there because I want her to know that I don't just call for you.

Everything is well. Ted sends her love, she is really fond of you.

Love to both of you.

Love,
Dad

May. 28, 1967.

Dear Paul,

Your letter at hand is interesting. It is wise for you to buy "land," it is the best insurance policy providing you don't become a slave for it. Make sure: your earnings will permit you to make your payments and taxes. Hold the land as long as you can, it has to go up.

I'm happy to hear that Meyer is going to Camp. What will it cost you? what do you need for his clothes? How is Meyer doing at base ball? Did he make the little league? Make a serious try in getting him interested in learning; you should participate in reading with him. Make it sort of a game or conversation.

It was good talking to all of you the other nite I especially got a great kick of listening to Myra. The next time I hope to hear Meyer.

What is the best time of day to call you that you all may be home?

Here is a little added attraction for you vacation time. Another letter will follow with half of this in it you spend it on the Children.

Keep well and happy. Good luck to all of you. Do you want to go to Israel with me? Answer soon.

Love
Dad

May 28, 1967

Dear Paul,

Your letter at hand is interesting. It is wise for you to buy "land;" it is the best insurance policy provided you don't become a slave for it. Make sure your earnings will permit you to make your payments and taxes. Hold the land as long as you can, it has to go up.

I am happy to hear that Meyer is going to Camp. What will it cost you? What do you need for his clothes? How is Meyer doing at base ball? Did he make the little league? Make a serious try in getting him interested in learning, you should participate in reading with him. Make it a sort of a game conversation.

It was good talking to all of you the other nite. I especially got a great kick of listening to Myra. The next time I hope to hear Meyer. What is the best time of day to call you that you all may be home?

Here is a little added attraction for you vacation time. Another letter will follow with half of this in it you spend it on the children.

Keep well and happy. Good luck to all of you. Do you want to go to Israel with me? Answer soon.

Love,
Dad

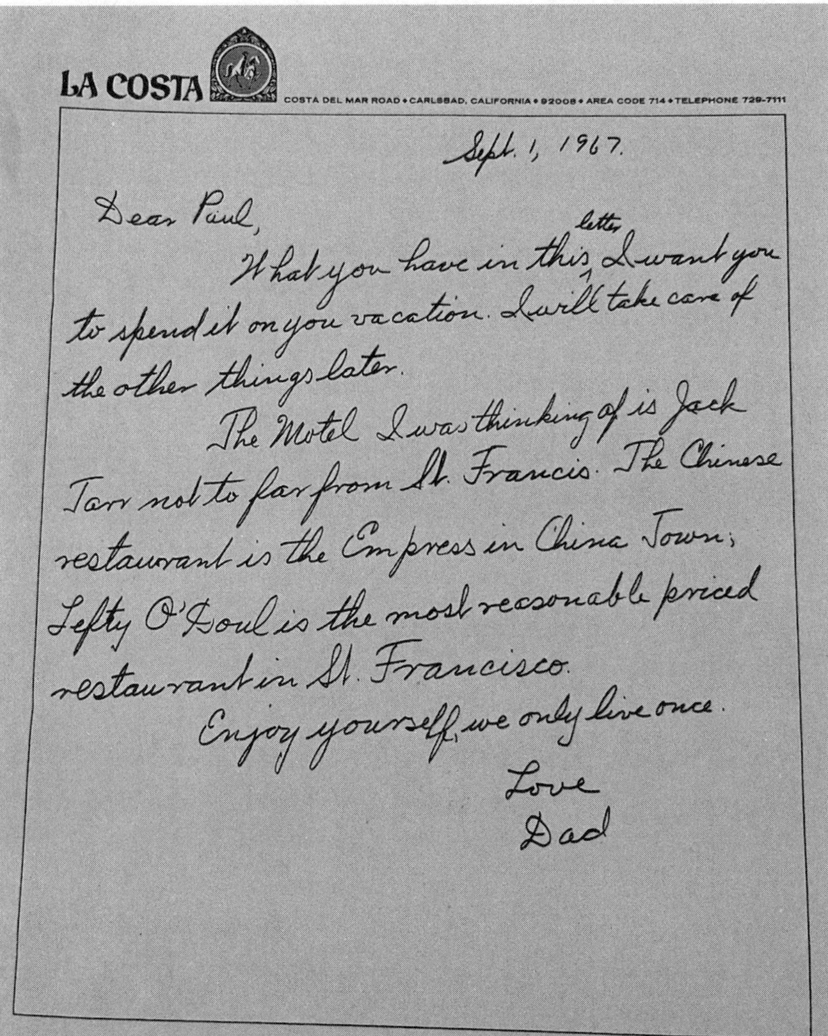

LA COSTA COSTA DEL MAR ROAD • CARLSBAD, CALIFORNIA • 92008 • AREA CODE 714 • TELEPHONE 729-7111

Sept. 1, 1967.

Dear Paul,

What you have in this letter I want you to spend it on you vacation. I will take care of the other things later.

The Motel I was thinking of is Jack Tarr not to far from St. Francis. The Chinese restaurant is the Empress in China Town; Lefty O'Doul is the most reasonable priced restaurant in St. Francisco.

Enjoy yourself, we only live once.

Love
Dad

Sept. 1, 1967

Dear Paul,

What you have in this letter I want you to spend it on your vacation. I will take care of the other things later.

The hotel I was thinking of is Jack Tar not to far from St. Francis. The Chinese restaurant is Empress in China Town; Lefty O'Doul is the most reasonable priced restaurant in San Francisco.

Enjoy yourself, we only live once.

Love,
Dad

אלונות שרון
SHARON HOTELS

Aug. 8, 1970

Dear Paul,

Needless to say, I miss you all and I miss my dog and home. I am really having a rest. To date I haven't any sight-seeing at all; sunday I'm visiting Technion at Haifa.

Technion is the M.I.T. of Israel a friend of mine is executive Vice President of Technion. In 1950 he packt a family of Children and went off to live in Israel. He is sending his car for me Sunday morning and show me most of the Institution and Haifa; Herzlia is 13 Km. from Tel Aviv & about 85 K.M. from Haifa. Good divided highway. I will start sightseeing from now on but I intend to keep this address. If I do leave I will leave a forwarding address. Mail is very slow going & coming usually-6 days.

HERZLIA ON SEA, ISRAEL, TELEX 69112, TELEPHONE 938777 הרצליה חוף-ים, טלקס 69112, טלפון

(2)

So far I haven't had any publicity here; it won't shock me if I get it anyday. The Police visited me and wanted to know how long I intend to stay and that all I can is my visa time which is 90 days. I wanted to know why and on what grounds they set the ruling. They told me of the publicity that I had they (Israel) didn't want to get involved with my presence of being here longer then that time. I asked them if they had knowledge of me being a wanted criminal and what the record was? They said it is true you aren't wanted now but?

We went in to quite a discussion of the inquisition against me and made admit that all that is against me is a racket that made me saleable by newspapermen for their own selfish interest also unscupulous politicians who haven't the ability to propose a platform of the people need.

As of now we will not worry about it. This too shall pass. But if all is well I expect to be away a long time. At present I think of all the embarrassment and lucky that no danger occurred from these write ups. It could have caused ransome to any of us. So for the sake of all of you it is best that I follow this dictate.

Your Brother should be visiting you shortly and he expects to be fed well. I hope his health is good also all of you so you can have a pleasurable time.

Paul, are you in touch with Sandra? It is time you do this! We are a small family. How long I will be around only time will tell; it is time you warm up. You have a good aunt and uncle in Esta & Jack also Matty—you also have a good cousin in Max. Once a time you corresponded today you have grown much neglectful with that. You should also be in touch with good friends like Morris & Jack Rosen. This is all the lecturing for now. Get some good food in the house for the Family. Edna looked a little underfed. Maybe if you gave her a better grade a food you could get her off the starches & desserts.

There is room for engineers here if you are interested It maybe possible to make you a rabinical engineer; with that mustache all you will have to add to it is the beard & you will be home.

I will write again soon. My love to all of You. Keep me informed about Meyer. (his schooling).

Love

Dad

Sharon Hotels
Aug. 8, 1970

Dear Paul,

Needless to say, I miss you all and I miss my dog and home. I am really having a rest. To date I haven't any sightseeing at all; Sunday I'm visiting Technion at Haifa.

Technion is the M.I.T. of Israel a friend of mine is executive Vice President of Technion. In 1950 he packed a family of Children and went off to live in Israel. He is sending his cr for me Sunday morning and show me most of the Institution and Haifa; Herzlia is 13 km. from Tel Aviv and about 8.5 km. from Haifa. Good divided highway. I will start sightseeing from now on but I intend to keep this address. If I do leave I will leave a forwarding address. Mail is very slow going and coming usually—6 days.

So far I haven't had any publicity here; it won't shock me if I get it anyday The Police visited me and wanted to know how long I intend to stay and that all I am can is my visa time which is 90 days. I wanted to know why and on what grounds they set the ruling. They told me of the publicity that I had they [Israel] *didn't want to get involved with my presence of being here longer then that time. I asked them if they had knowledge of me being a wanted criminal and what the record was? They said it is true you aren't wanted now but?*

We went in to quite a discussion of the inquisition against me and made admit that all that is against me is a racket that made me saleable by newspapermen for their own selfish interest also unscrupulous politicians who haven't the ability to propose a platform of the people need.

As of now we will not worry about it. This too shall pass. But if all is well I expect to be away a long time. At present I think of all the embarrassment and lucky that no danger occurred from these writeups. It could have caused ransome to any of us. So for the sake of all of you it is best that I follow this dictate.

Your Brother should be visiting you shortly and he expects to be fed well. I hope his health is good also all of you so you can have a pleasurable time.

Paul, are you in touch with Sandra? It is time you do this! We are a small family. How long I will be around only time will tell; it is time you warm up. You have a good aunt and uncle in Esta and Jack also

Matty—you also have a good cousin in Max. Once a time you corresponded today you have grown much neglectful with that. You should also be in touch with good friends like Morris and Jack Rosen. This is all the lecturing for now. Get some good food in the house for the Family. Edna looked a little underfed. Maybe if you gave her a better grade a food you could get her off the starches and desserts.

There is room for engineers here if you are interested. It maybe possible to make you a rabinical engineer; with that mustache all you will have to add to it is the beard and you will be home.

I will write again soon. My love to all of you. Keep me informed about Meyer. (his schooling).

Love,
Dad

10/28/72
Mr. Paul Lansky
2830 North 27th St
Tacoma, Washington 98407
U.S.A.
AIR MAIL
PAR AVION
ישראל 0.95
ישראל 0.95

Oct. 20, 1972.

Dear Paul,

Your letter is very well put. We will decide at a later date whether to use it for the press or just to show it to him. It is really a strong letter. You sure took him apart on his own statement. It reminds me of a quote by Richelieu: "Let the most honest man write a few lines and I will ruin him for life."

I'm mailing a few articles of interest to read and let me say what is most disappointing is the decision of the court. How they decide on a danger to the state.

Burg himself is a good kind man, it was the Minister of Justice who started out to destroy me, I guess he was looking for a sacrificial goat to cover up his sins. Soon after I went to Court he had to resign because of scandel that involved him for not takin action on a matter that his old law office was handling. Now his son runs it but the Prime Minister got him to come back after a few months and there has been a lot criticism here of this doing.

Don't worry I'm not giving up. I'm not in the habit of giving in easily.

So much for my problems. What about yourself, Edna and the children? I hope you are all well, take care I will be in touch.

My love to all of you. Love from Ted.

Dad

Oct. 20, 1972

Dear Paul,

Your letter is very well put. We will decide at a later date whether to use it for the press or just to show it to him. It is really a strong letter. You sure took him apart on his own statement. It reminds me of a quote by Richelieu: "Let the most honest man write a few lines and I will ruin him for life."

I'm mailing a few articles of interest to read and let me say what is most disappointing is the decision of the court. How they decide on a danger to the State.

Burg himself is a good kind man, it was the Minister of Justice who started out to destroy me, I guess he was looking for a sacrificial goat to cover up his sins. Soon after I went to Court he had to resign because of scandal that involved him for not taking action on a matter that his old law office was handling. Now his son runs it but the Prime Minister got him to come back after a few months and there has been a lot criticism here of this doing.

Don't worry I'm not giving up. I'm not in the habit of giving in easily.

So much for my problems. What about yourself, Edna and the children? I hope you are all well, take care I will be in touch.

My love to all of you. Love from Ted.
Dad

Letter from West Point to Paul Lansky, 1952

UNITED STATES CORPS OF CADETS
West Point, New York

29 May 1952

MEMORANDUM TO:: All Cadets of Class of 1954

SUBJECT: Airborne Training

1. The Superintendent, USMA, has approved the plan of permitting certain cadets to make a parachute-jump from an airplane in flight during the airborne training to be conducted for the Class of 1954, USCC, during the period 16-23 August, 1952, at Fort Benning, Georgia. The following conditions must be met prior to the selection of cadets for jump training.

a. Each cadet desiring to jump must submit a signed request volunteering to engage in special parachute jump training and to make a parachute jump from an airplane.

b. Regardless of age, the cadet desiring to jump must have the written consent of his parent or guardian.

c. Only those cadets exhibiting a marked aptitude for jumping will be selected for jump training. The selection of these cadets will be made by proper authorities at Fort Benning.

d. Even after being selected for jump training and having completed same, conditions at Fort Benning at the time selected for the jump might be such as to cause the authorities at Fort Benning to prohibit jumping by any cadets.

e. Cadets selected will make only one jump from an airplane in flight and no more. No provisions will be made for cadets to perform any additional jumps during his cadet career in order to become a qualified parachutist. Nor can any of this training be expected in any way to replace any future parachute training which the cadet might desire to take after becoming an officer in the U. S. Army.

f. Cadets selected may be required to take approximately eight (8) hours training after hours in addition to the regular training participated in by all members of the class. This training may be conducted in the evening, early morning hours or on holidays, but will definitely come out of the cadets free time.

2. In order to aid cadets in arriving at a decision as to whether or not they should volunteer to jump, the following factors are set forth:

a. In the event of injury as a result of the special training for parachute jumping, or of the jump itself, a cadet, like any other member of the armed services, is entitled to hospitalization. In the event that the injury or disability is permanent and causes his separation because of physical disability, it is a function of the Veterans Administration to determine whether or not any compensation is payable. It is likely that no compensation whatever would be available from the US Government. Therefore, it is entirely possible for a case to occur in which a cadet is permanently injured and disabled as a result of the jump, is hospitalized and then either allowed to graduate without a commission or is discharged from the Corps of Cadets for physical disability with no compensation whatsoever. At the present time there are no retirement benefits for cadets.

-1-
over

b. In the event of death as a result of the special training for parachute jumping, or of the jump itself, the beneficiaries of the cadet are entitled to the sum of $92.90 per month for ten (10) years, under the provisions of the Servicemen's Indemnity Act of 1951, (assuming that no other Government or National Service Life Insurance is in force) and are also entitled to six months gratuity provided by the Act of 17 December 1919 (41 Stat. 367) as amended (400. S.C. 903).

c. For your information the current percentage of injuries incurred by personnel of the 82d Airborne Division is seven-tenths of one percent, which appears to be quite low. However, bear in mind that the members of the 82d Airborne Division are skilled jumpers and have had considerable more training than will be available to cadets at Fort Benning prior to making a jump. But this is not a matter of percentages anyway as far as you as an individual cadet are concerned. It is more a matter of individual desire with respect to your military career. It is possible that a number of cadets might jump with only seven-tenths per cent of injuries in the group. However, you might be that seven-tenths and it might mean the end of your military career and/or the end of your cadet career.

3. Attached are two forms which must be completed and turned in to S1, Hq USCC, by 0800, 30 June 1952, if you wish to be considered for jump training. One is a request to be signed by you indicating that you desire to volunteer to make a jump. The other is a form to be signed by your parent or guardian giving their consent to making a parachute jump and participating in training therefor.

4. Within the next few days the entire class will be called together for further briefing on the subject of this Memorandum, at which time there will be opportunity to ask questions. No cadets will submit any of the completed forms nor send any home to parents for signature prior to this briefing. However, discussion of this matter with parents is encouraged.

BY ORDER OF THE COMMANDANT OF CADETS:

Frank D. Miller
FRANK D. MILLER
Colonel, Infantry
S-1

2 Incl.
1. Request to make parachute jump.
2. Parent's consent

DISTRIBUTION:
1 each 3d Classman
Cmdt.
Asst. Cmdt.
S-1
Asst. S-1 (Adm.)
SSO
S-4
Chief of Staff
G-3, USMA
Aide-de-Camp
JAG, USMA
PIO, USMA
Dean, USMA
A.A.A.
5 1802d Spec. Regt.
16 Hq., 1st Regt.
16 Hq., 2d Regt.
5 Director of MP&L
5 Records
15 S-3
3 Surgeon
3 Director of PE

2

REQUEST TO MAKE PARACHUTE JUMP

1. I hereby request that I be permitted to engage in special parachute training and to actually make a parachute jump from an airplane in flight during the period 16-23 August 1952, at which time the Class of 1954, USCC, will be participating in Airborne Training at Fort Benning, Georgia.

2. I understand that in the event I am permanently injured or disabled in such training or in such a parachute jump, it is quite possible that such injury or disability would compel my separation from the service. Whether or not any compensation would be payable to me on account of such injury or diability, is a matter for determination by the Veterans Administration, upon a review of all the circumstances in any particular case. It is quite likely that I would receive no compensation whatsoever.

I further understand that in the event of my death as a result of injuries received in such training or in such a parachute jump my parents or beneficiary would normally receive $92.90 per month for ten (10) years under the provisions of the Servicemen's Indemnity Act of 1951. In addition, my parents or beneficiary would receive six month's gratuity.

3. I am 19 years of age.

4. Approval of my parents to engage in this parachute training and to make this parachute jump is attached.

Paul Lansky
PAUL LANSKY
(Signature)
Cdt. Pvt., Co. M-1, USCC
Class of 1954

PARENTS CONSENT TO MAKE PARACHUTE JUMP

June, 23, 1952

I, Meyer Lansky, having been informed that my son, Cadet Paul Lansky, has requested permission to engage in special training for parachute jumping, and to make a parachute jump from an airplane in flight during the airborne training at Fort Benning, Ga., given to cadets of the Class of 1954 during the period 16-23 August 1952, interpose no objection thereto.

Meyer Lansky
(Signature of Parent or Guardian)

Letters from Arthur G. Klein to Paul Lansky, 1949–1954

ARTHUR G. KLEIN
19TH DIST., NEW YORK

COMMITTEES ON
EDUCATION AND LABOR
DISTRICT OF COLUMBIA

Congress of the United States
House of Representatives
Washington, D. C.

WASHINGTON OFFICE:
SUITE 401, H. O. B.

NEW YORK OFFICE:
50 BROAD STREET
NEW YORK CITY

January 19, 1949

Mr. Paul Lansky
211 Central Park West
New York City

Dear Paul:

I understand that you are anxious to obtain an appointment to the United States Military Academy at West Point.

I am enclosing herewith a booklet describing the requirements, both physical and mental, for applicants to the Academy. If you desire any additional information you may contact me any weekend, either at my office, Hanover 2-1080, or at my home, Gramercy 5-0026. I will do everything I possibly can for you.

With kindest personal regards, I am,

Sincerely yours,

Arthur G. Klein

Arthur G. Klein, M.C.

AGK:em

ARTHUR G. KLEIN
19th District of New York

Committees on
Interstate and Foreign Commerce
District of Columbia

Congress of the United States
House of Representatives
Washington 25, D. C.

Washington Office:
Suite 1431 NHOB
NAtional 3120, Ext. 1066

New York Office:
50 Broad Street
HAnover 2-1060

November 26, 1952

Cadet Paul Lansky
Co. M-1 USCC
West Point, N. Y.

Dear Paul:

Thank you so much for your kind note of congratulations.

You really are a most unusual boy. Most of the boys that I have appointed to either the Military or Naval Academies have forgotten all about me after they have sent the first letter of thanks, which I believe is somewhat mandatory.

It is a credit to your family and to your upbringing that you go to the trouble of writing now and then, as you have in the past.

Alan Florea's father has told me how helpful you have been. It is simply another indication of your fine character.

Keep up the good work!!

When you next see your Dad, give him my regards.

Sincerely,

Arthur G. Klein

AGK:TR

ARTHUR G. KLEIN
19th District of New York

Committees on
Interstate and Foreign Commerce
District of Columbia

Congress of the United States
House of Representatives
Washington 25, D. C.

Washington Office:
Suite 1431 NHOB
NAtional 3120, Ext. 1066

New York Office:
50 Broad Street
HAnover 2-1080

December 23, 1953

Cadet Paul Lansky
Co M-1 USMC

Dear Paul:

It was nice receiving your recent letter and your usual Christmas Greetings.

I may have told you this before, but you are one of the very few, if not the only boy, whom I have appointed to either of the service academies, who has appeared to be grateful for the appointment and who has corresponded with me.

It is always nice to hear from you and I hope you will continue writing, not only while you are still in the Academy, but after you are out in the Service.

My best to you and your family, and I hope to see you at least at your graduation.

With kind regards, I am

Sincerely yours,

Arthur G Klein

ARTHUR G. KLEIN
Member of Congress

AGK:TR

ARTHUR G. KLEIN
19th District of New York

Committees on
Interstate and Foreign Commerce
District of Columbia

Congress of the United States
House of Representatives
Washington 25, D. C.

Washington Office:
Suite 1431 NHOB
NAtional 8-3120, Ext. 1066

New York Office:
50 Broad Street
HAnover 2-1080

August 25, 1954

Dear Paul:

I was very happy to receive your recent letter and to learn that you are now taking pilot training in Georgia. I am sure you will find your new surroundings as happy as those at West Point.

I wish we had been able to get together while you were in New York on leave, but unfortunately I spent most of my time here in Washington and got up to New York very little. The next time you do get to town, please call me and I shall be very happy to arrange a meeting with you.

I know you will continue the good work and the good record you establised at the Academy and want to wish you all the luck in the world.

With kindest regards, I am

Sincerely,

Arthur G. Klein

Arthur G. Klein
Member of Congress

AGK:em

2/Lt. Paul Lansky
P. O. Box 125
Baibridge Air Base
Georgia

Letter from Moe Dalitz to Paul Lansky, 1955

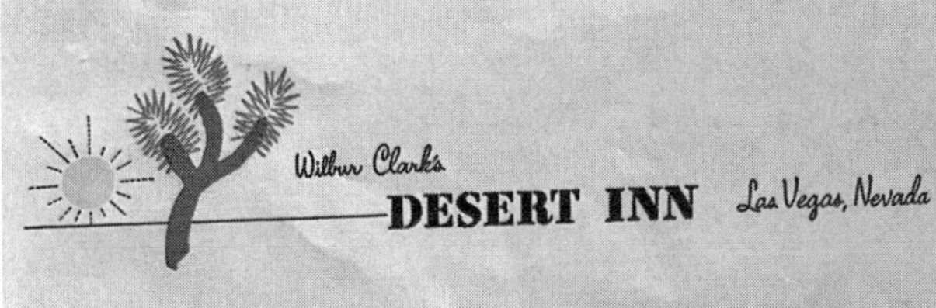

EXECUTIVE OFFICES

July 14, 1955

Lt. Paul Lansky
#26151-A, 55-T
Box 681 SMS
Reese Air Force Base
Texas

Dear Paul:

I am most delighted to receive your letter and very happy to know that you and your friend did enjoy Las Vegas.

I spoke to your Dad on the 'phone the other day, and informed him that you had visited us. I am about to fly to Havana on Monday, so that I can meet him Tuesday.

The purpose of this letter is to tell you that the facilities of the DESERT INN are available to you and your friends at all times, and that should you get a vacation or a spell of leave, we earnestly request you to be our guest.

Enclosed please find a membership card to our championship golf course, and I sure hope that you find an occastion to put it to use.

Always your dear friend,

Moe

Moe

M. B. Dalitz/fjj
Via Air Mail
Encl.

Letter from Dusty Peters to Paul Lansky, 1955

August 18, 1955

Mr. A. E. Loveland
Hotel El Rancho Vegas
Las Vegas, Nevada

Dear Archie:

This letter will introduce Paul Lansky, who is a very good friend of mine and of Beldon's.

Mr. Lansky will be coming to Las Vegas frequently in the future, and I would appreciate your extending all courtesies to him.

Please send his bills to Beldon or myself.

Sincerely,

Dusty Peters

Dusty Peters

DP:nh

AMERICA'S FINEST WESTERN HOTEL

Letter from Sam Tucker to Paul Lansky, 1958

Hotel Nacional de Cuba
HAVANA

September 18, 1958.

Mr. Paul Lansky
704 W. Davis
Ann Arbor, Mich.

Dear Paul:

Thanks for thinking of me, and for sending the photo of your son, Meyer 11.

I hope he grows up to have the wisdom and tolerance, and soft personality of his grandfather.

I hope everything is going well with you, and best regards to your wife.

Sincerely,

Sam Tucker

SAM TUCKER.

INTERCONTINENTAL HOTELS CORPORATION: HOTEL NACIONAL DE CUBA
Carrera SANTIAGO DE CHILE • Del Lago MARACAIBO, VENEZUELA • Tamanaco CARACAS, VENEZUELA
Tequendama BOGOTA, COLOMBIA • Victoria Plaza MONTEVIDEO, URUGUAY • Reforma MEXICO CITY

APPENDIX F

Meyer Lansky II's Husky Orange Cocktail Recipe

The Husky Orange
by Meyer Lansky II

Our great friend Meyer Lansky II, the grandson and namesake of Meyer Lansky, is a bartender. So naturally we asked him to create a new cocktail that would highlight the "Operation Husky" code name during World War II. We named it "The Husky Orange" for the proposed clandestine operation.

1 oz. Orange Stoli
1 oz. Campari
1 oz. sweet vermouth
½ oz. orange juice

Pour over ice in an 8-ounce highball glass and give it a stir with a cocktail spoon.

Churchill in Cuba

A statesman and a mobster, Winston Churchill and Meyer Lansky, had more than a few things in common. They were both fond of Cuba. Churchill first visited the island nation when he was twenty-one, where he developed his lifelong fondness for smoking cigars. They also both enjoyed gambling, although Winston Churchill focused on the play and casino owner Meyer Lansky focused on the profits.

Excerpted by permission of Skyhorse Publishing, Inc. from the book *Churchill: A Drinking Life: Champagne, Cognac, and Cocktails.*

APPENDIX G
Mafia Boss Succession

Five Families

Genovese Family
1890s–1909: Giuseppe “The Clutch Hand” Morello
1909–1916: Nicolò “Nick Morello” Terranova
1916–1920: Vincenzo “The Tiger of Harlem” Terranova
1920–1922: Giuseppe “The Clutch Hand” Morello
1922–1931: Giuseppe “Joe the Boss” Masseria
1931–1946: Charles “Lucky” Luciano
1946–1957: Frank “The Prime Minister” Costello
1957–1969: Vito “Don Vitone” Genovese
1969–1981: Philip “Benny Squint” Lombardo
1981–2005: Vincent “Chin” Gigante
2006–present: Liborio “Barney” Bellomo

Gambino Family
1900s–1910: Ignazio “The Wolf” Lupo
1910–1928: Salvatore “Toto” D’Aquila
1928–1930: Manfredi “Alfred” Mineo
1930–1931: Francesco “Frank Scalice” Scalisi
1931–1951: Vincent “The Executioner” Mangano
1951–1957: Albert “Lord High Executioner” Anastasia
1957–1976: “Don” Carlo Gambino
1976–1985: “Big” Paul Castellano
1985–2002: John “The Teflon Don” Gotti
2002–2011: Peter “One Eye” Gotti
2011–present: Domenico “Italian Dom” Cefalù

Lucchese Family
1920–1930: Gaetano “Tommy” Reina
1930: Bonaventura “Joseph” Pinzolo
1930–1951: Tommaso “Tommy” Gagliano
1951–1967: Gaetano “Tommy Three-Finger Brown” Lucchese
1967–1973: Carmine “Mr. Gribbs” Tramunti
1973–1986: Anthony “Tony Ducks” Corallo
1986–present: Vittorio “Vic” Amuso

Bonanno Family
1890s–1909: Paolo Orlando
1909–1912: Sebastiano DiGaetano
1912–1930: Nicolo Schirò
1930–1931: Salvatore “Little Caesar” Maranzano
1931–1968: Joseph “Joe Bananas” Bonanno
1968–1971: Paul Sciacca
1971–1973: Natale “Joe Diamonds” Evola
1974–1991: Philip “Rusty” Rastelli
1991–2004: Joseph “The Ear” Massino
2004–2011: Vincent “Vinny Gorgeous” Basciano
2013–present: Michael “The Nose” Mancuso

Colombo Family
1920–1927: Salvatore DiBella
1928–1962: Joseph “Olive Oil King” Profaci
1962–1963: Joseph “Joe Evil Eye” Magliocco
1963–1971: Joseph “Joe” Colombo
1973–2019: Carmine “The Snake” Persico
2019–2022: Andrew “Andy Mush” Russo
2025–present: Theodore N. “Skinny Teddy” Persico Jr.

Upstate New York

Buffalo (Magaddino-Todaro) Family
1908–1912: Benedetto Angelo “Buffalo Bill” Palmeri
1912–1922: Giuseppe “Don Pietro” DiCarlo Sr.
1922–1974: Stefano “The Undertaker” Magaddino
1974–1984: Salvatore “Sam the Farmer” Frangiamore
1984–2006: Joseph E. “Lead Pipe Joe” Todaro Sr.
2006–present: Joseph A. “Big Joe” Todaro Jr.

Rochester (Valenti) Family
1950s–1958: Constenze “Stanley” Valenti
1958–1964: Jake Russo
1964–1972: Frank Valenti
1972–1993: Samuel “Red” Russotti

Pennsylvania

Philadelphia (Bruno-Scarfo) Family
1911–1931: Salvatore Sabella
1931–1936: John “Nazzone” Avena
1936–1946: Giuseppe “Joseph Bruno” Dovi
1946–1958: Giuseppe “Joseph” Ida
1958–1959: Antonio “Mr. Miggs” Pollina
1959–1980: Angelo “The Gentle Don” Bruno
1980–1981: Phillip “The Chicken Man” Testa
1981–1990: Nicodemo “Little Nicky” Scarfo Sr.
1990–1995: Giovanni “John” Stanfa
1995–1999: Ralph Natale
1999–2024: Joseph “Skinny Joey” Merlino
2024–present: Unknown

Pittston/Scranton/Wilkes-Barre/Northeastern Pennsylvania (Bufalino) Family
1903–1908: Stefano “Steve” La Torre/Calogero Bufalino
1908–1933: Santo Volpe
1933–1949: Giovanni “John” Sciandra
1949–1994: Rosario Alfredo “Russell” Bufalino
1994–2008: William “Big Billy” D’Elia

Pittsburgh (LaRocca) Family
1888–1914: Salvatore “Banana King” Catanzaro
1915–1919: Gregorio Conti
1919–1925: Salvatore Calderone
1925–1929: Stefano Monastero
1929–1931: Giuseppe “Yeast Baron” Siragusa
1931–1932: John Bazzano
1932–1937: Vincenzo Capizzi
1937–1956: Frank Amato
1956–1984: John Sebastian “Big John” LaRocca
1984–2006: Michael James Genovese

2006–2008: John Bazzano, Jr.
2008–2021: Thomas "Sonny" Ciancutti

New Jersey

Newark/Elizabeth/North Jersey (DeCavalcante) Family
1920s–1956: Filippo "Phil" Amari
1956–1964: Nicholas "Nick Delmore" Amoruso
1964–1982: Simone "Sam the Plumber" DeCavalcante
1982–2015: Giovanni "John the Eagle" Riggi
2015–present: Charles "Big Ears" Majuri

Atlantic City Syndicate
1890s–1911: Louis "Commodore" Kuehnle
1911–1941: Enoch "Nucky" Johnson
1941–1970s: Frank "Hap" Farley

Illinois

Chicago Outfit
1910–1920: Vincenzo "Big Jim" Colosimo
1920–1925: John "The Fox" Torrio
1925–1931: Alphonse "Al" Capone
1931–1943: Frank "The Enforcer" Nitti
1943–1947: Paul "The Waiter" Ricca
1947–1957: Anthony "Joe Batters" Accardo
1957–1966: Salvatore "Sam" Giancana
1966–1967: Samuel "Teets" Battaglia
1967–1971: Felix "Milwaukee Phil" Alderisio
1971–1986: Joseph "Joey Doves" Aiuppa
1986–1996: Samuel "Black Sam" Carlisi
1997–2001: John "Johnny Apes" Monteleone
2001–2006: James "Little Jimmy" Marcello
2006–2010: Michael "Fat Mike" Sarno
2010–2018: John "No Nose" DiFronzo
2018–present: Salvatore "Solly D" DeLaurentis

Rockford (Zammuto) Family
1920s–1957: Antonio "Tony" Musso
1957–1974: Joseph P. Zammuto
1974–1987: Frank J. Buscemi

1987–1994: Charles Vincent "Charlie Vinci" Vince
1994–2000: Sebastian J. "Knobby" Gulotta
2000–2005: Frank "Gumba" Saladino

Madison (Caputo) Family
1940s–1993: Carlo Peter Caputo

Springfield (Zito) Family
1950s–1974: Francesco "Frank" Zito

Missouri

Kansas City (Civella) Family
1912–1931: Joseph "Joe Church" DiGiovanni
1931–1934: John "Brother John" Lazia
1934–1939: Charles "Charlie the Wop" Carrollo
1939–1950: Charles Binaggio
1950–1953: Anthony Gizzo
1953–1983: Nicholas "Nick" Civella
1983–1984: Carl "Cork" Civella
1984–1995: William "Willie the Rat" Cammisano
1995–2006: Anthony "Tony Ripe" Civella
2006–present: John "Johnny Joe" Sciortino

St. Louis (Giordano) Family
1912–1923: Dominick Giambrone
1923–1927: Vito Giannola
1927–1937: Frank Agrusa
1937–1943: Thomas Buffa
1943–1950: Pasquale Miceli
1950–1960: Anthony "Tony Lap" Lopiparo
1960–1980: Anthony "Tony G" Giordano
1980–1982: John "Johnny V" Vitale
1982–1997: Matthew "Mike" Trupiano Jr.
1997–2014: Anthony "Nino" Parrino

Massachusetts/Rhode Island

Boston/Providence (Patriarca) Family
1910–1916: Gaspare DiCola
1916–1924: Gaspare Messina

1924–1954: Filippo "Phil" Buccola
1954–1984: Raymond L. S. "Il Patrone" Patriarca Sr.
1984–1991: Raymond "Junior" Patriarca Jr.
1991: Nicholas "Nicky" Bianco
1991–1996: Frank "Cadillac Frank" Salemme
1996–2009: Luigi "Baby Shacks" Manocchio
2009–2016: Peter "Chief Crazy Horse" Limone
2016–2025: Carmen "The Big Cheese" Dinunzio

Florida

Tampa (Trafficante) Family
1920–1940: Ignacio Antinori
1940–1954: Santo Trafficante Sr.
1954–1987: Santo Trafficante Jr.
1987–2025: Vincent LoScalzo

Miami
Open Territory

Louisiana

New Orleans (Marcello) Family
1860–1869: Raffaele Agnello
1869–1872: Joseph Agnello
1872–1891: Joseph P. Macheca
1891–1922: Charles Matranga
1922–1944: Corrado Giacona
1944: Frank Todaro
1944–1947: Silvestro "Silver Dollar Sam" Carollo
1947–1990: Carlos "Little Man" Marcello
1990–2007: Anthony Carollo

Texas

Dallas (Civello) Family
1910–1930: Carlo Piranio
1930–1956: Joseph Piranio
1956–1970: Joseph Civello
1970–1973: Joseph Ianni
1973–1990: Joseph "Papa Joe" Campisi

California

Los Angeles (Dragna) Family

1922–1925: Rosario “The Chief” DeSimone
1925–1931: Joseph “Iron Man” Ardizzone
1931–1956: Ignazio “Jack” Dragna
1956–1967: Frank “One Eye” DeSimone
1967–1974: Nicolo “Old Man Nick” Licata
1974–1984: Dominic “Jimmy” Brooklier
1984–2012: Peter Milano
2012–present: Tommaso “Tommy” Gambino

San Francisco (Lanza) Family

1932–1937: Francesco “Frank” Lanza
1937–1958: Anthony Lima
1958–1961: Michael Abati
1961–2006: James “Jimmy the Hat” Lanza

San Jose (Cerrito) Family

1940s–1959: Onofrio Sciortino
1959–1978: Joseph Cerrito
1978–1983: Angelo Marino
1983–2009: Emmanuel J. Figlia

Hollywood

Open Territory

Nevada

Las Vegas

Open Territory

Michigan

Detroit Partnership (Tocco-Zerilli Family)

1890s–1913: Pietro Mirabile
1913: Vito Adamo
1913–1919: Antonio “Tony” Gianola
1919: Salvatore “Sam” Gianola

1919–1920: Giovanni “John” Vitale
1921–1930: Salvatore “Singing Sam” Catalanotte
1930: Gaspar “The Peacemaker” Milazzo
1930–1931: Cesare Lamare
1931–1936: Guglielmo “Black Bill” Tocco
1936–1977: Joseph “The Old Man” Zerilli
1977–1979: Giovanni “Papa John” Priziola
1979–2014: Giacomo “Jack” Tocco
2014–present: Jack “Jackie the Kid” Giacalone

Wisconsin

Milwaukee (Balistrieri) Family
1918–1921: Vito Guardalabene
1921–1927: Peter Guardalabene
1927: Joseph Amato
1927–1949: Joseph Vallone
1949–1952: Sam Ferrara
1952–1961: John Alioto
1961–1993: Frank “Mr. Big” Balistrieri
1993–1997: Peter Balistrieri
1997–2014: Joseph “Joe Camel” Caminiti
2014–2024: Peter “Pitch” Picciurro

Ohio

Cleveland (Scalish) Family
1920–1927: Joseph “Big Joe” Lonardo
1927–1929: Salvatore “Black Sam” Todaro
1929–1930: Joseph “Big Joe” Porrello
1930–1935: Ciccio “Frank” Milano
1935–1945: Alfred “Big Al” Polizzi
1945–1976: John T. “John Scalise” Scalish
1976–1985: James “Jack White” Licavoli
1985–1991: John “Peanuts” Tronolone
1991–1993: Anthony “Tony Lib” Liberatore
1993–2004: Joseph “Joe Loose” Iacobacci
2004–present: Russell “RJ” Papalardo

Colorado

Denver (Smaldone) Family
1928–1931: Pete Carlino
1923–1933: Joe "Little Caesar" Roma
1933–1950: Charles Blanda
1950–1969: Vincenzo Colletti
1969–1975: Joseph "Scotty" Spinuzzi
1975–1992: Eugene "Checkers" Smaldone
1992–2006: Clarence "Chauncey" Smaldone

Seattle

Colacurcio Organization (Seattle Family)
1950s–2010: Francis Colacurcio Sr.

Canada

Montreal (Rizzuto) Family
1970s–1980s: Nicolo Rizzuto
1980s–2013: Vito Rizzuto
2013–present: Leonardo Rizzuto

SELECTED BIBLIOGRAPHY

Books

Benson, Michael. *Gangsters vs. Nazis*. New York: Citadel, 2022.

Black, Matthew. *Operation Underworld*. New York: Citadel, 2023.

Bleyer, Bill. *Long Island and the Sea*. New York: Pegasus, 2019.

Conrad, Harold. *Dear Muffo: 35 Years in the Fast Lane*. New York: Stein and Day Publishers, 1982.

Cortland Russo, Carole. *Me and Jimmy Blue Eyes: Growing Up with the Last of the Gentleman Gangsters*. New York: Red Penguin Books, 2020.

Danforth, Harold E., and James Horan. *The D.A.'s Man*. New York: Crown Publishers, 1957.

De Toledo, Zali. *They Called Him a Gangster*. eBookPro Publishing, 2020.

DeStefano, Anthony M. *Top Hoodlum: Frank Costello, Prime Minister of the Mafia*. New York: Citadel, 2018.

Donohue, James A. *Illicit Alcohol, The Chronicle-Express*, May 1965.

Eisenberg, Dennis; Uri Dan, and Eli Landau. *Meyer Lansky: Mogul of the Mob*. New York and London: Paddington Press Ltd., 1979.

English, T. J. *Havana Nocturne: How the Mob Owned Cuba but Then Lost the Revolution*. New York: William Morrow, 2009.

Everest, Allan S. *Rum Across the Border: The Prohibition Era in Northeastern New York*. Syracuse, NY: Syracuse University Press, 1978.

Ferrante, Louis. *Borgata: Rise of Empire: A History of the American Mafia*. New York: Pegasus, 2024.

Gladstone, B. James. *The Man Who Seduced Hollywood: The Life and Loves of Greg Bautzer, Tinseltown's Most Powerful Lawyer*. Chicago: Chicago Review Press, 2013.

Goodman, Oscar, with George Anastasia. *Being Oscar: From Mob Lawyer to Mayor of Las Vegas—Only in America*. New York: Weinstein Books, 2013.

Gooley, Lawrence P. *Bullets, Booze, Bootleggers, and Beer: The Story of Prohibition in Northern New York*. Peru, NY: Bloated Toe Publishing, 2019.

Horne, Field, editor-in-chief. *Saratoga Springs: A Centennial History.* Saratoga Springs, NY: Kiskatom Publishing, 2015.

Karlen, Neal. *Augie's Secrets: The Minneapolis Mob and the King of the Hennepin Strip.* Saint Paul, MN: Minnesota Historical Society Press, 2013.

Kasuga Folk, Amy. *Rumrunning in Suffolk County: Tales from Liquor Island.* Mount Pleasant, SC: History Press, 2022.

Kessner, Charles. *Fiorello H. La Guardia and the Making of Modern New York.* New York: McGraw-Hill, 1989.

Lacey, Robert. *Little Man: Meyer Lansky and the Gangster Life.* New York: Little, Brown and Co., 1991.

Lansky, Sandra, and William Stadiem. *Daughter of the King: Growing Up in Gangland.* New York: Hachette Books, 2014.

Levy, Shawn. *Rat Pack Confidential.* Old Saybrook, CT: Tantor Media, 2019.

Maier, Thomas. *Mafia Spies: The Inside Story of the CIA, Gangsters, JFK, and Castro.* New York: Skyhorse Publishing, 2019.

Messick, Hank. *Lansky.* New York: Berkley Medallion Books, 1971.

Moruzzi, Peter. *Havana Before Castro: When Cuba Was a Tropical Playground.* Salt Lake City: Gibbs Smith, 2008.

Oglesby, Carl. "The Yankee and Cowboy War: The Astonishing Link Between the JFK Assassination and the Deposing of Nixon: Conspiracies from Dallas to Watergate and Beyond." Unpublished manuscript.

Pietrusza, David. *Rothstein: The Life, Times, and Murder of the Criminal Genius Who Fixed the 1919 World Series.* New York: Basic Books, 2011.

Raab, Selwyn. *Five Families: The Rise, Decline, and Resurgence of America's Most Powerful Mafia Empires.* New York: Thomas Dunne Books, 2005.

Reid-Henry, Simon. *Fidel and Che: A Revolutionary Friendship.* New York: Walker & Co., 2009.

Sasuly, Richard. *Bookies and Bettors: Two Hundred Years of Gambling.* New York: Holt, Rinehart and Winston, 1982.

Shnayerson, Michael. *Bugsy Siegel: The Dark Side of the American Dream.* New Haven and London: Yale University Press, 2021.

Sifakis, Carl. *The Mafia Encyclopedia, Second Edition.* New York: Checkmark Books, 1999.

Teresea, Vincent, and Thomas C. Renner. *My Life in the Mafia.* New York: Doubleday and Co., 1973.

Turkus, Burton, and Sid Feder. *Murder, Inc.: The Story of the Syndicate.* New York: Da Capo Press, 1992.

Veitch, Greg. *A Gangster's Paradise: Saratoga Springs from Prohibition to Kefauver.* Manchester Center, VT: Shires Press, 2019.

Wilkerson, W. R., III. *Hollywood Godfather: The Life and Crimes of Billy Wilkerson.* Chicago: Chicago Review Press, 2018.

Reports and Publications

Committee on Governmental Affairs, US Senate, testimony, April 1988

Complete FBI files, Meyer Lansky

Congressional Record, April 1970

Congressional Timeline

Herlands, William B., 102-page report to NY Governor Thomas E. Dewey regarding reasons for commutation of Charles Luciano's prison sentence

Kefauver papers, University of Tennessee, Knoxville, TN

Letters from Meyer Lansky to Paul Lansky

New York State v. Lansky, Meyer, et al., Extraordinary and Special Trial Term of the Supreme Court of the State of New York, County of Saratoga, 1952

New York State v. Luciano, Charles, 1936

Wells, Randy, *Havana Crossing*, High Point, NC: Stanley Furniture

Newspapers

Adirondack Daily Enterprise, 1953

Albuquerque Journal, 1950

American Jewish World, 1937

Atlantic Monthly, July 1970

Brooklyn Eagle, 1928–1952

Chattanooga Daily Times, 1949

Chicago Daily Tribune, 1932

Courier-Journal, 1973

Council Bluffs Nonpareil/The Daily Nonpareil, 1941

Daily News, 1954

Daily News and Evening Sentinel/Fort Lauderdale News, 1948–1958

Daily Notes, 1951

El Reno Daily Tribune, 1957

Enid Morning News, 1950

Evening Star, 1972

Forbes, 1980

Hollywood Sun-Tattler, 1947
Independent Journal, 1973
Inside Labor, September 25, 1972
Jerusalem Post, 1972
Kane Republican, 1950
Knickerbocker News, 1953
Knoxville News-Sentinel, 1949
Las Vegas Sun, 1959–1997
LIFE, 1958, 1967
Los Angeles Herald and Express, 1947
Los Angeles Times, 1971–89
Miami Herald, 1953–2007
Miami News, 1977
Nevada Historical Society Quarterly, 1988
New York Herald Tribune, 1938–1958
New York Journal-American, 1951–1957
New-York Mirror, 1958
New York Post, 1958
New York Times, 1959–1983
Newark Evening News, 1958
Newsday, 1971
News Herald, 1977
Niagara Falls Gazette, 1969
Omaha World-Herald, 1942–1946
Post-Star, 1952
Press-Republican, 1973
Press-Telegram, 1951
Salon, 2016
Saratoga TODAY, August 19, 2011
Saratogian, 1952
Saturday Evening Post, 1955, 1967
Schenectady Gazette, 1954
Sunday Argus, 1977
Terror Spectator, September 2011
Times Leader, 1949
Times-Union, 1952–1953
Wall Street Journal, 1965–1969
Winnipeg Tribune, 1949

NOTES

Chapter 1

1: "He listed his birth date as the same day as the birth date of the United States." Lansky naturalization application.

2: "In fact, he was born on August 28." Interview with Meyer Lansky II.

3: "Homes weren't conducive to spend time in . . . Hot in the summer, cold in the winter." Interview notes with Paul Sann.

4: "He read Shakespeare and . . . memorized *The Gettysburg Address*." Interview with Meyer Lansky II.

5: "Our teachers were strict . . . you could learn very much." Interview notes with Paul Sann.

6: "Nonetheless, he got all As and a couple of Bs." FBI confidential memo, NY 92–660.

7: "But there was something else on his report card: chronic absenteeism." Ibid.

8: "'There were times that food was just enough to exist,' Lansky recalled." Lansky interview with family.

9: "Lansky grimly shut down the line of questioning by saying simply, 'It wasn't nice.'" Interview with Ruth Citron.

10: "One day, he was walking . . . Luciano called Lansky the toughest guy he ever knew." DeStefano, Anthony M., *Top Hoodlum: Frank Costello, Prime Minister of the Mafia*, New York: Citadel, 2018, p. 22.

11: "At my age . . . possible future for a machinist at that time." Lansky family interview.

12: "About a year . . . 'Use your head.'" Shnayerson, Michael, *Bugsy Siegel: The Dark Side of the American Dream*, New Haven and London: Yale University Press, 2021, p. 9.

13: "On hot summer days, they'd swim in New York's Hudson River, often jumping off the piers." Interview with Meyer Lansky II.

14: "Two arrests in 1918, when he was all of sixteen years old . . . a fine of two dollars." FBI file.

15: "Writer Robert Lacey speculated . . . was familiar." Lacey, Robert, *Little Man: Meyer Lansky and the Gangster Life*, New York: Little, Brown and Co., 1991, p. 50.

16: "Bartlett refused to sign the complaint . . . 'I'd like to lock you up for perjury.' " "Robbers' Victim Fails to Identify 3 Held for Crime," *Brooklyn Eagle*, March 8, 1928, p. 22.

17: "The reporter who covered the hearing . . . three men charged with his assault." Ibid.

18: "Rothstein was the ultimate fixer, the go-between street guys and politicians." Pietrusza, David, *Rothstein: The Life, Times and Murder of the Criminal Genius Who Fixed the 1919 World Series*, New York: Basic Books, 2011, p. 134.

19: "I never played with a man I wasn't sure I could beat . . . to making money." Ibid, p. 33.

20: "On November 4, 1928, Rothstein got a call at Lindy's . . . Rothstein refused to say." Benson, Michael, *Gangsters vs. Nazis*, New York: Citadel, 2022, p. 15.

21: " 'You stick to your trade,' he told police. 'I'll stick to mine.' " Ferrante, Louis, *Borgata: Rise of Empire: A History of the American Mafia*, New York: Pegasus, 2024, p. 170.

22: "There is only one way to win, and that is not to play . . . anything else." Pietrusza, p. 352.

23: "He conveniently omitted the fact that he had a criminal record." Naturalization application.

Chapter 2

1: "When Francesco Ioele—commonly known as Frankie Yale . . . his murder." "GANGSTER SHOT DEAD IN DAYLIGHT ATTACK," *New York Times*, July 2, 1928, p. 1.

2: "Joe Adonis's real last name was Doto . . . good looks." Sifakis, Carl, *The Mafia Encyclopedia, Second Edition*, New York: Checkmark Books, 1999, p. 3.

3: "Joe Adonis took over Yale's rackets." Destefano, Anthony M., *Top Hoodlum, Frank Costello, Prime Minister of the Mafia*, New York: Citadel, 2018, p. 93.

4: "Less than four months later, on May 7, 1929 . . . a rabbi officiated." Lansky marriage license.

5: "After Costello finished, Torrio got up and dropped the bombshell: He told Capone he had to go to jail." Ibid., p. 94.

Chapter 3

1: "Luciano and Lansky had taken a train to Chicago . . . the 'mystery trip' in the press." "Seize New York Hoodlums, Here on Mystery Trip," *Chicago Daily Tribune*, April 30, 1932.

2: "Ricca . . . best man at his wedding in 1927." Sifakis, Carl, *The Mafia Encyclopedia, Second Edition*, New York: Checkmark Books, 1999, p. 313.

3: "She believed Buddy's disability was a bad omen . . . marriage." Interview with Susan Citron.

4: "He took refuge . . . crisis." Sifakis, p. 7

5: "One of the first things Anna did was to hire her own interior decorator . . . he prized." Interview with Susan Citron.

6: "For bookends, he had busts of Abraham Lincoln because he had always admired the sixteenth president." Lansky, Sandra, and Stadiem, William, *Daughter of the King: Growing Up in Gangland*, New York: Hachette Books, 2014, p. 24.

7: "The front hallway to the apartment was grand, tiled in black and white." Interview with Susan Citron.

8: "His sons did not get any religious instruction, and the family celebrated Christian holidays like Christmas." Lacey, Robert, *Little Man: Meyer Lansky and the Gangster Life*, New York: Little, Brown and Co., 1991, p. 93.

9: "He and his old friend, Joe 'Doc' Stacher, flew to Havana with the money in suitcases." English, T. J., *Havana Nocturne: How the Mob Owned Cuba but Then Lost the Revolution*, New York: William Morrow, 2009, pp. 15–16.

10: "Lansky replied bitterly, 'I'm not making any money.'" Lacey, p. 99.

11: "One night, he called Anna to tell her that he wouldn't be home for dinner." Ibid., pp. 98–99.

12: "Lansky, for his part, was an emotionally remote husband and father." Interview with Susan Citron.

13: "When we met, he had this little guy with him." Corland Russo, Carole, *Me and Jimmy Blue Eyes*, New York: Red Penguin Books, 2020, p. 18.

14: "His standard suit order was 40 Short, navy, single-breasted." Traub, Alex, "Martin Greenfield, Tailor to Sinatra, Obama, Trump and Shaq, Dies at 95," *New York Times*, March 20, 2024.

15: "Security guards posted at the door ensured that only the right people got in." Interview with Victoria Garlanda.

16: "That wasn't the only place he employed security." Interview with Charles Foesher II.

17: "By 1935, the Piping Rock was the top club in Saratoga." Veitch, Greg, *A Gangster's Paradise: Saratoga Springs from Prohibition to Kefauver*, Manchester Center, VT: Shires Press, 2019, p. 300.

Chapter 4

1: "His own lawyer once said of him." Raab, Selwyn, *Five Families: The Rise, Decline, and Resurgence of America's Most Powerful Mafia Empires*, New York: Thomas Dunne Books, 2005, p. 47.

2: "Enraged, Schultz devised a plot to kill Dewey." Ibid., p. 48.

3: "Kuhn couldn't give his speech." Black, Matthew, *Operation Underworld*, New York: Citadel, 2023, p. 75.

4: "That night, Dewey's assistant, Murray Gurfein, had gone to a long-planned dinner party." Interview with Abby Hellwarth.

5: "Dewey opened up the proceedings . . . 'You are here to mete out justice.'" Dewey's handwritten notes from *State of New York v. Luciano, Charles* court file.

6: "Polakoff and Lansky had both grown up . . . on the other side of the street." Interview with Nancy Nemlich.

7: "Polakoff, for his part, fervently believed . . . but 'not that.'" Ibid.

8: "Costello wasted no time in taking over . . . in the nation." 1988 congressional timeline, "Organized Crime: 25 Years After Valachi," Hearings before the permanent Subcommittee on Investigations of the Committee on Governmental Affairs United States Senate, April 11, 15, 21, 22, 29, 1988.

9: "By January 1937, the Cuban cabinet approved plans to place certain gambling operations under Batista's control." Ibid.

10: "He installed a photo-finish machine and even tested the horses for drugs." Lacey, Robert, *Little Man: Meyer Lansky and the Gangster Life*, New York: Little, Brown and Co., 1991, p. 134.

11: "To run the crap tables, he brought in Al Levy." Ibid., pp. 134–135.

12: "Anna thought, for example, that the family should have liver twice a week." Ibid., p. 88.

Chapter 5

1: "When the city was getting ready for the New York World's Fair, La Guardia . . . Jews were grateful." Kessner, Thomas, *Fiorello H. La Guardia and the Making of Modern New York*, New York: McGraw-Hill Publishing, 1989, p. 403.

2: "He called Lansky. They arranged a meeting." Benson, Michael, *Gangsters vs. Nazis*, New York: Citadel, 2022, p. 50.

3: "'We Jews now have to demonstrate a little more militancy,' Perlman said." Lacey, Robert, *Little Man: Meyer Lansky and the Gangster Life*, New York: Little, Brown and Co., 1991, p. 139.

4: 'You got some boys who might want to punch a Nazi?' he said." Benson, p. 50.

5: "He asked him if he had any influence with the press, particularly the Jewish press." Ibid., p. 51.

6: "Lansky had a box of brand-new hats with American Legionnaires logos on them." Ibid., p. 68.

7: "Top US officials had exhorted American Legionnaires to wage war on Nazism at their convention at Madison Square Garden in New York." "American Legion Told to Wage War on Nazism; F.D.R., Hull, Colmery Warn of Danger to U.S.," *American Jewish World*, September 24, 1937, pp. 1, 21.

8: "The first speaker, Otto Wegener, got up." "Seven Are Injured at Nazi Rally Here When Legionnaires Heckle Speaker," *New York Times*, April 21, 1938.

9: "Shouts erupted in the audience. Several storm troopers . . . interrupted the meeting." Ibid.

10: "The outside group pushed past the guards at the door." "Veterans Fight City's Nazis on Hitler's Birthday," *New York Herald Tribune*, April 21, 1938.

11: "The crowd surged toward the hall, but a detail of police officers held them back." "Seven Are Injured at Nazi Rally Here When Legionnaires Heckle Speaker," *New York Times*, April 21, 1938.

12: "Years later, he described what happened." Feldberg, Michael, "How Jewish Gangsters Fought the Nazis" *Israel Faxx*, May 14, 2019.

13: "They mobilized to fight Nazi propaganda." "N.Y. Mayor Wars on Nazis," *American Jewish World*, May 8, 1938, pp. 1–24.

14: "Ironically, however, the Jewish papers had a little more insight." Benson, p. 78.

15: "He set her up in a luxurious apartment on Ocean Parkway in Brooklyn." Lansky, Sandra, and Stadiem, William, *Daughter of the King: Growing Up in Gangland*, New York: Hachette Books, 2014, p. 43.

16: "He didn't like his younger sister at all." Interview with Susan Citron.

17: "A lot of the Lanskys' friends were sending their sons to military school." Ibid., p. 39.

Chapter 6

1: "The location served another critical need: It allowed his East Coast bookies to take bets." FBI file, 92–2831, section 2.

2: "He and Syms spent between $50,000 and $100,000 renovating the fairgrounds." Ibid.

3: "The daily crowds numbered between 2,500 and 5,000 people." "Continue Racing at Dodge Park," *Council Bluffs Nonpareil*, July 23, 1941, p. 10.

4: "Spectators were allowed to buy options in each dog running a race." *Omaha World-Herald*, July 23, 1941.

5: "On July 22, 1941, just eleven days after the track opened, a local farmer filed suit to stop the track." Ibid.

6: "Although the racing season has been closed a week, nothing but compliments . . . newspaper." Lane, Frank, *Council Bluffs Nonpareil*, September 21, 1941.

7: "By October, True—for reasons that are not particularly clear—dropped his lawsuit." *Omaha World-Herald*, October 28, 1941.

8: "That summer, Lansky and Syms rented the home of Dr. Isaac Sternhill." Interview with Vernon Sternhill, FBI file.

9: "Dog racing in Council Bluffs was profitable for Syms and Lansky for three summers." Keunzer, Kathy, "Meyer Lansky, A Man of Many Faces," *Daily Nonpareil*, August 26, 2018.

10: "The floor of the Arrowhead casino was separated by a walkway from the entertainment area." Interview with Margaret Lynch.

11: "Lansky formed his own distributorship with two former Wurlitzer agents." Lacey, Robert, *Little Man: Meyer Lansky and the Gangster Life*, New York: Little, Brown and Co., 1991, p. 210.

12: "There was violence." 1958 congressional testimony of Milton J. Hammergren.

13: "One night, a guest asked that Arnaz sing 'Quiéreme Mucho,' which he did." Arnaz, Desi, *A Book*, Buccaneer Books, 1997.

14: "US ships were being sunk along the Atlantic Coast." Herlands Commission report, September 1954, p. 4.

15: "The fire started when a spark from a welding torch set fire to life jackets." Hudson River Maritime Staff, "The S.S. *Normandie* Fire (1942)," February 7, 2022.

16: "Not long afterwards, Lansky drove his daughter, Sandra, down to see the wreck." Lansky, Sandra, p. 27.

17: "They worried that it was sabotage by Nazi sympathizers." Herlands report, p. 4.

18: "They feared that enemy agents were working on the New York waterfront." Ibid., p. 17.

19: "US Intelligence suspected the Italians . . . enemy submarines." Ibid., p. 4.

20: "At the time, Lanza was under indictment for conspiracy and extortion." Ibid., p. 12

21: "Through his contacts in the fish market, he was able to place undercover agents." Ibid., p. 35

22: "Lanza said he knew the solution to their problem: They needed Luciano." Ibid., p. 38

23: "Polakoff demurred . . . might attract it." Ibid. and interview with Michael Nemlich.

Chapter 7

1: "'I will be happy to help in any way I can.'" Herlands report, Lansky testimony.

2: "Lansky warned them that Mussolini was very popular with Italians." Ibid., p. 45

3: "On March 12, 1942—just two weeks after their meeting at Longchamps—authorities transferred Luciano to Great Meadow." Ibid., p. 7.

4: "The prison was in a small town, and strangers were immediately noticed." Ibid., p. 45.

5: "Gurfein 'wanted to know if we could trust Luciano,' Lansky later testified. 'I felt we could.'" Ibid., p. 47.

6: "Dear Warden . . . inmate privately." Ferrante, Louis, *Borgata: Rise of Empire: A History of the American Mafia*, New York: Pegasus, 2024, p. 280.

7: "Morhous was also instructed not to record the visits on the usual visitors' record." Herlands report, p. 53.

8: "'What the hell are you fellows doing here?' he asked." Ibid., 61.

9: "Luciano, like Lansky, said he was glad to help." Ibid.

10: "For the next visit, they brought up Lanza." Ibid.

11: "The men were well-funded. They had brought with them $83,000 . . . their mission." FBI confidential memo, June 29, 1942.

12: "When he returned from the visit, he told Haffenden . . . German submarines in the Port of New York." Ferrante, p. 280.

13: "Haffenden would tell Lansky what he needed." Herlands report, p. 63.

14: "Lansky met Haffenden at the Astor Hotel. He assigned Lansky a code number." FBI file.

15: "'There were times I thought I'd die in that desert,' he recalled later." Family notes.

16: "For years, Broward was called the sixth borough of New York . . . so many New Yorkers there." Interview with Bert Nevins.

17: "It was the job of the Hallandale city prosecutor, Joseph Varon . . . each table." Interview with David Bogenschutz and Don Williams.

18: "Luciano was granted clemency in January 1946 for his cooperation." Raab, Selwyn, *Five Families: The Rise, Decline, and Resurgence of*

America's Most Powerful Mafia Empires, New York: Thomas Dunne Books, 2005, pp. 76–78.

19: "Then, on January 3, 1946 . . . clemency for Luciano." "Dewey Commutes Luciano Sentence," *New York Times*, January 4, 1946, p. 38.

20: "Costumes for the floor show cost upwards of $40,000." FBI file.

Chapter 8

1: "On February 3, 1946 . . . been transferred." Lacey, Robert, *Little Man: Meyer Lansky and the Gangster Life*, New York: Little, Brown and Co., 1991, p. 157.

2: "He gave Lansky $2,500 in cash and asked him to turn it into traveler's checks." Ibid., p. 158; and Black, Matthew, *Operation Underworld*, New York: Citadel, 2023, p. 264.

3: "He dispatched several men to shore to get lobster, spaghetti and several bottles of wine . . . Fulton Fish Market." Lacey, p. 158.

4: "He left New York City for a few days just to make sure." Ibid., p. 159.

5: "'According to the FBI . . . West Coast hotel,'" Wilkerson, W. R., III, *Hollywood Godfather: The Life and Crimes of Billy Wilkerson*, Chicago: Chicago Review Press, 2018, p. 311.

6: "The FBI called Siegel in for questioning. He denied making any threats toward Wilkerson." Ibid.

7: "He needed a deep-pocketed investor, and he turned to G. Harry Rothberg." Kefauver Commission on Organized Crime hearing, part 7, 1145–1170.

8: "They warned Lansky and his partner, Syms, that gambling was illegal in Iowa." *Omaha World-Herald*, June 27, 1946.

9: "By the time she was fifteen, Hill got out of there, eloping with a young man who had money." Shnayerson, Michael, *Bugsy Siegel: The Dark Side of the American Dream*, New Haven and London: Yale University Press, 2021, p. 104.

10: "Although Hemingway hated New York . . . Hemingway absolutely hated losing at anything." Interview with Patrick Hemingway.

11: "Lansky liked to take fourteen-year-old Paul to Brown's gym." Interview with Meyer Lansky II.

12: "On August 20, 1946, he and Siegel were speaking on the phone." FBI file.

13: "Nine days later, a man 'involved in construction' got a phone call." FBI file.

14: "Near the end of October in 1946, Luciano . . . arrived in Camaguey, Cuba." Ferrante, Louis, *Borgata: Rise of Empire: A History of the American Mafia*, New York: Pegasus, 2024, p. 315.

15: "He had arranged for Cuba's interior minister, Alberto Pequeno, to grant Luciano an indefinite stay." Ibid.

16: "When they landed at the Cuban airport, Elaine was entranced by the Cuban dolls she saw for sale." Interview with Ruth Citron.

17: "Around Christmas of that year, Lansky secured the top two floors at the Hotel Nacional." Ferrante, p. 316.

18: "The meeting opened with a tribute to Luciano." Black, pp. 275–276.

19: "Siegel had planned to charter planes to fly stars in, but they stayed away." Shnayerson, p. 144.

20: "Worse, the few people who did show up were treated to an unfinished casino." Shnayerson, p. 146.

21: "Siegel flew to New York to see his old friends, and they greeted him warmly." Lacey, p. 193.

22: "He told her he was going to stop paying them and would send them to her father to pay." Ibid.

23: "At the hearing, she testified, 'He's out six nights a week.'" Lacey, p. 171.

24: "The final divorce decree . . . total income." FBI file.

25: "Lansky initially moved in with a good friend of his, William Morris agent George Wood." Lansky, Sandra, and Stadiem, William, *Daughter of the King: Growing Up in Gangland*, New York: Hachette Books, 2014, p. 73.

26: "Then on February 22, 1947, Cuban authorities . . . arrested Luciano." Congressional timeline, p. 307.

27: "A month later, he was deported back to Italy." Ibid.

28: "His activities caught the attention of an American newspaper columnist, Robert Ruark." "CUBA: Hoodlum on the Wing," *TIME*, March 3, 1947.

Chapter 9

1: "PACIFIC TELEGRAM, June 21, 1947." Telegram sent by Meyer Lansky to Sid Wyman at the Flamingo hotel, June 1947.

2: "The pileup of bills tied to the Flamingo hotel . . . everything was on track." Shnayerson, Michael, *Bugsy Siegel: The Dark Side of the American Dream*, New Haven and London: Yale University Press, 2021, pp. 169–170.

3: "That Sunday night, Siegel went out . . . at 810 North Linden Drive in Beverly Hills." Ibid.

4: "A week earlier, she and Siegel had a blowout . . . commit suicide." June 26, 1947, FBI memo to FBI director.

5: "After leaving, she called Siegel . . . never traveled before." Ibid.

6: "After dinner, Siegel picked up a prescription . . . to pull the drapes closed." "Underworld Keeps Its Secrets About Siegel," *Los Angeles Times*, June 28, 1947.

7: "At first, Smiley thought it was firecrackers or some kind of gag . . . everything went quiet." "Crashing Gunfire Told by Smiley at Siegel Inquest," *Los Angeles Herald and Express*, June 26, 1947.

8: "Within minutes, Los Angeles police arrived." "Underworld Keeps Its Secrets About Siegel," *Los Angeles Times*, June 28, 1947.

9: "An informant told the FBI . . . bugged it." June 26, 1947, memo to FBI director.

10: "The next day, on June 21, 1947, Siegel's estranged wife . . . on the West Coast." Ibid.

11: "Police first suggested that it was revenge . . . Siegel had been drawing to himself." "Revenge, gangster quarrel held motives in Bugsy Siegel Murder," *Los Angeles Daily News,* June 21, 1947.

12: "Lansky had his own theory . . . the FBI report says." June 26, 1947, memo to FBI director.

13: "Within ten days of Siegel's murder . . . name is redacted in the FBI file." Ibid.

14: "Meyer II, Lansky's grandson . . . That impressed Lucky." Interview with Meyer Lansky II.

15: "The problem is that the book was bogus . . . of the meetings. Gage, Nicholas, "Questions Are Raised On Lucky Luciano Book," *New York Times,* December 17, 1974.

16: "Some people underestimated him . . . talking about everything." Interview with Meyer Lansky II.

17: "I guarantee your grandfather . . . Billy Wilkerson." Ibid.

18: "Wilkerson started *The Hollywood Reporter* . . . didn't care." Wilkerson, W. R., III, *Hollywood Godfather: The Life and Crimes of Billy Wilkerson*, Chicago: Chicago Review Press, 2018, pp. 89–90.

19: "'Never forget a friend, never forgive an enemy.'" Ibid., p. 207.

20: "Wilkerson knew the Mob guys in Hollywood well . . . Wilkerson owned." Ibid., p. 71, pp. 176–177, 252.

21: "By the fall of 1944 . . . to own a casino to absorb his losses." Ibid., p. 266.

22: "He treated Siegel like an errand boy . . . Wilkerson's orders at every turn." Ibid., p. 288.

23: "Investors approached his attorney, Gregson Bautzer . . . one of the investors." Unpublished 1977 interview with Gregson Bautzer by Dave Offer.

24: "Tensions festered . . . but never did." Ibid.

25: "That same month, reporter Victor Enyart . . . takeover of the Flamingo." Wilkerson, pp. 316–317.

26: "Wilkerson decided not to take any chances. He fled to Europe." Interview with Willie Wilkerson III.

27: "Uncle Buddy talked a lot to Costello . . . led to Siegel's demise." Interview with Meyer Lansky II.

28: "Wilkerson's son Willie . . . had a hand in it." Interview with Willie Wilkerson III.

29: "Ben's family knew, too . . . the Waldorf Astoria Hotel." Interview with Meyer Lansky II.

Chapter 10

1: "He and Costello met with Silvestro 'Silver Dollar Sam' Carollo." Sasuly, Richard, *Bookies and Bettors: Two Hundred Years of Gambling*, New York: Holt, Rinehart and Winston, 1982, p. 128.

2: "He knew, for example, that FBI Director Hoover was an avid gambler." "Magazine Article Tells Of Gambling in Broward County," *Hollywood Sun-Tattler*, April 18, 1947, p. 1 and Interview with Meyer Lansky II.

3: "In December 1947, an attorney who lived in Hollywood, Florida, spoke up at a meeting." Lacey, Robert, *Little Man: Meyer Lansky and the Gangster Life*, New York: Little, Brown and Co., 1991, p. 229.

4: "At the hearing . . . subpoenaed records." Interview with Romney Rogers.

5: “He had the backing of local civic leaders.” “Civic Leaders Praise Rogers,” *Fort Lauderdale News*.

6: “Local deputies were ordered to start gambling patrols.” “Deputies Ordered to Patrol Gambling,” *Fort Lauderdale News*.

7: “Authorities deemed the situation serious enough to assign Rogers a bodyguard.” Interview with Romney Rogers.

8: “He and Alo invited to local press to come in and finish off the food and liquor.” Lacey, p. 232.

9: “It began two years earlier when her husband stole horse race results.” Messick, Hank, *Lansky*, New York: Berkley Medallion Books, 1971, p. 163.

10: “He tapped his waterfront contacts.” Lacey, p. 203.

11: “She worked as a manicurist at the Embassy Hotel.” FBI file.

12: “Teddy and her husband, Philip Schwartz, had lived in the same building as the Lanskys.” Lansky, Sandra, and Stadiem, William, *Daughter of the King: Growing Up in Gangland*, New York: Hachette Books, 2014, p. 81.

13: “‘Reports here indicate that Lansky . . . is considerably peeved.” “Police Tag Luciano Aide to Parlay on Dope Traffic,” *Winnipeg Tribune*, July 15, 1949, p. 9.

14: “Authorities had wanted to tell the Italian police to prevent Lansky from landing.” Ibid.

15: “‘The theory here is that Lansky came to Italy to organize something big with Luciano.’” Ibid.

16: “When nineteen-year-old Buddy came down to Cuba a week later . . . but swore him to secrecy.” Lacey, p. 205.

17: “He took a cab to all the newsstands and bought up all the newspapers.” Lansky, p. 81.

18: “On June 28, 1949, they set sail on the *Italia* from Pier 54 on the Hudson River.” “Lansky Off to Italy at $2,600 One Way,” *New York Herald Tribune*, June 29, 1949.

19: “FBI agents, who grilled him earlier in the day as to why he was taking the trip.” Ibid.

20: “Lansky slammed his cabin door in the reporter’s face.” Lacey, p. 175.

21: “The reporter . . . *Italia* affords.” Malcolm Johnson, “Lansky Sails in Luxury for Italy, Expected to Confer with Luciano,” *New York Sun*, June 28, 1949.

22: "Lansky did, indeed, plan to visit Luciano. They met in the Sicilian village of Taormina." English, T. J., *Havana Nocturne: How the Mob Owned Cuba but Then Lost the Revolution*, New York: William Morrow, 2009, pp. 74–75.

23: "He told the Bureau of Narcotics agents, 'This is just a pleasure trip.' Lacey, p. 219.

24: "Lansky's old friend, George Wood, allowed him to use his apartment for his assignations." Lacey, p. 206.

Chapter 11

1: "Just fifteen minutes before midnight on November 18, 1949 . . . Nevada Club." "Nevada Gambler is Cut Down by Shotgun Blast," *Knoxville News-Sentinel*, November 20, 1949, p. 1.

2: "As he pulled up the garage door, his body silhouetted against the light . . . rushed him to the hospital." "Big Gambler Shot in Back; Fear Scandal," *Los Angeles Mirror*, November 19, 1949, p. 2.

3: "Doctors gave him blood transfusions to keep him alive, but didn't think he'd make it." "Top Reno Gambler Is Shot In Gangland Style Ambush," *Chattanooga Daily Times*, November 20, 1949, p. 1.

4: "Authorities couldn't help but note that the similarities between Fitzgerald's ambush . . . killed Siegel." "Foes Blast Co-Owner of Big Casino," *Brooklyn Eagle*, November 19, 1949, p. 1.

5: "One Florida newspaper noted that Fitzgerald had moved to Reno . . . led by Lansky." "Ex-South Broward Gambler Is Shot in Gangland Assault at Reno Home," *Hollywood Sun-Tattler*, November 25, 1949, p. 3.

6: "He didn't leave the hospital until the following April." "Wounded Gambler Leaves Hospital," *Albuquerque Journal*, April 7, 1950, p. 16.

7: "The Kefauver Committee found corruption everywhere in Miami." "Special Committee on Organized Crime in Interstate Commerce," US Senate.

8: "He was fined $1,000 for illicit gambling activities." FBI file 21 of 26.

9: "On June 19, 1950, barely three weeks after the first hearing in Miami, *LIFE* magazine . . . Kefauver and his allies." Havemann, Ernest, "Gambling in the U.S., Life Presents the Low-Down on Nation's Biggest Racket," *LIFE*, June 19, 1950, pp. 97–121.

10: "It also took pains to point out the societal costs of gambling, particularly on the poor." Ibid., p. 113.

11: "When Broward County Sheriff Walter Clark testified, he tried to be evasive." "Gambling: Big Show in Miami," *TIME*, July 24, 1950.

12: "And by August, Lansky and his brother Jake were indicted . . . paying a $2,000 fine." FBI file.

13: "'Taking Saratoga as Exhibit A . . . a ton of bricks?'" "Dewey Scored for Permitting Crime to Run Rampant at Saratoga," *Kane Republican*, October 12, 1950, p. 1.

14: "He and Polakoff met with Kefauver privately and showed him all the gambling IOUs." Lansky, Sandra, and Stadiem, William, *Daughter of the King: Growing Up in Gangland*, New York: Hachette Books, 2014, p. 100.

15: "He admitted associating with Frank Costello, Joe Adonis, Frank Erickson, and Charles Fischetti." FBI file.

16: "Kefauver, for his part, tried to strike back at Lansky publicly." "Luciano, Meyer Lansky Linked In Crime Probe," *Enid Morning News*, October 13, 1950, p. 14.

17: "On November 20, 1950, he gave a speech to the Economic Club of Detroit." Kefauver papers, University of Tennessee, Knoxville, 1950.

18: "'Did you ever offer yourself to the war services of your country?' he asked Costello." "Costello Defies Quiz on His Net Wealth," *Press-Telegram,* March 21, 1951, pp. 1, 5.

19: "'He no longer indulged in a favorite past time of taking Sandra to musicals on Broadway.'" Lansky, p. 113.

20: "'Make them quit doing that,' she told the committee." Hill's testimony before the Kefauver Committee.

21: "'Like a lot of girls, they started giving me things, bought me everything.'" Ibid.

22: "Told that IRS agents believed that she carried cash for gangsters . . . 'belongs to me.'" Ibid.

23: "'You really want to know why?' she asked." Conrad, Harold, *Dear Muffo: 35 Years in the Fast Lane*, New York: Stein and Day Publishers, 1982, p. 237.

24: "O'Dwyer named the six men who ran the East Coast crime syndicate." "O'Dwyer Names U.S. Crime Ring," *Daily Notes*, March 21, 1951.

25: "To critics . . . 'We didn't expose anyone who didn't deserve to be exposed.'" Walter Cronkite special, 1958.

26: "'Congressman Arthur G. Klein, a friend of Costello's through Tammany Hall, had selected Paul.'" Lansky, p. 81.

27: "'Paul spent a year at the Sullivan School, a prep school in Washington, DC.'" Ibid., p. 81.

28: "Kefauver, the man who . . . 'had placed in him.'" Kefauver papers.

29: "Journalist Hank Messick opined that Lansky . . . avoiding subpoenas from the Kefauver Committee." Messick, Hank, *Lansky*, New York: Berkley Medallion Books, 1971, p. 176.

30: "In a postcard to Paul, he called it 'one of your brother's enterprises.'" November 15, 1953 postcard from Meyer Lansky to Paul Lansky at West Point.

Chapter 12

1: "A conspiracy so vast and overriding in Saratoga . . . 'wielding political power.'" Paul Williams affidavit in James Leary case, part of Saratoga Extraordinary Grand Jury file.

2: "More than $250,000 . . . was paid each year in 'tribute' to politicians." Ibid.

3: "Williams approached the case in a classic prosecutorial fashion . . . public officials." Ibid.

4: "The grand jury indicted Lansky on September 10, 1952 . . . liquor licenses for the Arrowhead." FBI NY-660, NYS Police, Troy, New York.

5: "As Erie County District Attorney, Hagerty had prosecuted a Mob underboss." Interview with grandson Thomas Hagerty.

6: "When Sinatra as a young singer wanted to get out of his contract . . . Dorsey released Sinatra from the contract." Interview with Meyer Lansky II.

7: "Lansky watched the Dewey grand jury . . . his clubs in Florida." Lansky, Sandra, and Stadiem, William, *Daughter of the King: Growing Up in Gangland*, New York: Hachette Books, 2014, pp. 113–114.

8: "It was a glamorous place, with gold-plated faucets in the restrooms." Schanberg, Sydney H., "Dinty Moore's Reflects Opulence of a Bygone Era," *New York Times*, June 4, 1964, p. 44.

9: "The next day, while Sandra was in school . . . and threw up." Lansky, p. 115.

10: "He wanted him to add 'a touch of class' to the Cuba's casinos." Congressional timeline, p. 304.

11: "In June 1952, Hoover sent a request . . . The legal attaché complied." FBI file.

12: "On August 6, 1952, Costello appeared before the grand jury . . . headlines and photos." "Grand Jurors Question Costello," *Times-Union*, August 7, 1952.

13: "A couple weeks after Costello's appearance . . . Lansky's other club with Costello." "Piping Rock Figures Testify At Probe," *Saratogian,* August 21, 1952.

14: "By September 3, Frank S. Hathorn, the Saratoga County sheriff . . . about both clubs." "Sheriff, Who Quit Under Fire, Successor, Before Grand Jury," *Post-Star*, September 4, 1952.

15: "New York State Police arrested Lansky . . . walking out of the courthouse." "Associate of Big-Time Gamblers Posts Bail in Arrowhead Case," *Times-Union*, September 11, 1952, p. 1.

16: "That prompted a nationwide alert for the men and, of course, more headlines." Torrey, Reginald F., "Police Across Nation Put on Alert for 5 of 7 Men Indicted in Arrowhead Probe," *Saratogian*, September 12, 1952.

17: "'The restaurant should be operated on a lavish . . . of the casino.'" Torrey, Reginald W. "Indictment Voted Against Arrowhead, 7 Defendants, Contains Necessary Data for Operating Big-Time Casino," *Saratogian*, September 11, 1952.

18: "Worse, in the case of the Arrowhead . . . 'to provide a cloak of respectability.'" Torrey, Reginald F., "Police Across Nation Put on Alert for 5 of 7 Men Indicted in Arrowhead Probe," *Saratogian*, September 12, 1952.

19: "Williams alleged . . . 'to such a startling degree.'" Williams affidavit.

20: "'Upon being questioned . . . nominee for the defendant Leary.'" Ibid.

21: "In December 1952, US Attorney General James P. McGranery . . . Lansky's naturalization." McGranery press release and "U.S. Acts to Toss Lansky to Russia," *Brooklyn Eagle*, December 18, 1952, p. 1.

22: "In January 1953, FBI agents interviewed him at Polakoff's . . . 'if one wanted to call that illegal.'" FBI file.

23: "He told the agents that he was a West Point cadet . . . he wanted to be an FBI agent." Ibid.

24: "Polakoff was sure they would prevail at trial . . . publicity circus that would arise from any trial." Lacey, Robert, *Little Man: Meyer Lansky and the Gangster Life*, New York: Little, Brown and Co., 1991, p. 208.

25: "Asked his occupation, Lansky said he was an 'unemployed tool and die maker.' Saratoga court record.

26: "As Judge Hagerty prepared to sentence him . . . 'to sympathy in your case.'" "Jail, Fine Lansky in Spa Gambling; Chum of Luciano," *Sunday News*, May 3, 1953, p. 5.

27: "He entered jail with two books under his arm, a Bible and a dictionary." "Bible and Dictionary in Gambler's 'Study,'" *Adirondack Daily Enterprise*, May 14, 1953.

28: "Through his Saratoga attorney . . . to the jail every day." Interview with Margaret Lynch.

29: "When the police came looking for him . . . bag of cash hidden in the grand piano." Interview with Mary Kate Matthews.

30: "He and Lansky were the only inmates in the jail . . . Lansky was never wrong." Lacey, pp. 262–263.

31: "Lansky stuck to regular routine . . . liked airline and steel stocks." Ibid., p. 264.

32: "By July, Lansky was hospitalized for a kidney infection." Saratoga County Jail Journal.

33: "He was seriously ill with diabetes and kidney disease . . . the prospect of deportation." Lacey, p. 212.

34: "Whether it was his illness . . . his dream to be buried in Israel." Lacey, p. 267.

Chapter 13

1: "Floridians loved him . . . lift everyone up." Interview with Meyer Lansky II.

2: "In May 1953 . . . 'degenerates from all parts of the country.'" Miami Crime Commission speech by Daniel P. Sullivan, May 21, 1953.

3: "By August, the US Immigration and Naturalization Service ordered . . . Adonis deported." "Order to Boot Adonis Speeds War on Mobs," *Brooklyn Eagle*, August 6, 1953, p. 11.

4: "By the end of that month . . . Lansky's interests in the Thunderbird and Sands Hotels in Las Vegas." September 25, 1952, letter to the New York and Miami offices of the FBI.

5: "Later, he would also get a piece of casinos in Cuba." Unpublished interview with John Reagan "Tex" McCrary, April 23, 1967.

6: "In late October 1954, the Nevada State Tax Commission opened . . . stake in the Thunderbird." "The *Las Vegas Sun* Daily reports . . . Meyer and Jake Lansky in the Thunderbird Hotel." *Las Vegas Sun*, October 28, 1954.

7: "It was so controversial . . . visit Luciano while he was in prison." "Mobsters' Visits in '42 to Luciano Stir Up Political Furor," *New York Herald Tribune*, January 28, 1958.

8: "Lansky hated the idea . . . could get married after finishing high school." Lacey, Robert, *Little Man: Meyer Lansky and the Gangster Life*, New York: Little, Brown and Co., 1991, p. 276.

9: "Sandra, however, emerged from their talk . . . permission to get married immediately." Ibid.

10: "Lansky talked daily to his brother-in-law, Julius Citron . . . Lansky always laughed." Interview with Susan Citron.

11: "He visited him there twice a month." Lansky, Sandra, and Stadiem, William, *Daughter of the King: Growing Up in Gangland*, New York: Hachette Books, 2014, p. 117.

12: "For the commencement speech . . . following year." Interview with Dick L'Heureux and West Point commencement records.

13: "Though he rarely spoke to friends . . . bond between the two of them." Interview with Dick L'Heureux.

14: "Paul gave his father his graduation ring." Interview with Meyer Lansky II.

15: "Immediately after graduating, Paul . . . got his wings." West Point biography of Paul Lansky.

16: "The irony for Lansky was that he hated Las Vegas . . . an honest game, and he gave it to them." Interview with Meyer Lansky II.

17: "That's why they started the system of comping people . . . cash in their chips and leave." Ibid.

18: "The slot machines required a system of their own . . . removed from the casino." Cook, James, "Casino gambling: changing character or changing fronts?" *Forbes*, October 27, 1980.

19: "Lansky's friend, Doc Stacher . . . was skimmed and not taxed." Ibid.

20: "The Nevada Gaming Commission determined . . . mean revocation of a license." Davidson, Bill. "The Mafia: Shadow of Evil on an Island in the Sun," *Saturday Evening Post*, February 25, 1967, pp. 29–30.

21: "Jimmy Alo turned to Lansky and said . . . set foot in Las Vegas." Interview with Meyer Lansky II.

Chapter 14

1: "Batista wanted to bring Cuba into the modern age, and Lansky was integral to his plans." Interview with Florencio Gelabert Jr.

2: "The employees loved it . . . comfortable place to work and play." Interview with Luis Castaneda.

3: "Lansky liked Trafficante." Interview with Meyer Lansky II.

4: "Anyone wanting to open a casino did . . . Tex McCrary." Interview with John Reagan "Tex" McCrary, April 23, 1967.

5: "He wanted his business concerns kept quiet, and he didn't want his people investigated." Interview with Meyer Lansky II.

6: "It was a place where people of note, like Lansky, could stay and have their privacy ensured." Interview with Bertrand Pellegrin.

7: "They were there to discuss Paul Costello." FBI file, memo to director from New York SAC, October 15, 1956.

8: "A New York gambler named Jerry Ryan was in attendance. He had recently lost $35,000 in a craps game." Ibid.

9: "They set the building on the beach . . . arriving somewhere important." Interview with Randy Wells.

10: "He hired a Spanish architect, Manuel Jose Carrera . . . Lansky to be quiet and polite." Interview with Florencio Gelabert Jr.

11: "The casino had gold-plated slot machines . . . top chef." Interview with Jane Feehan.

12: "Lansky wasn't impressed by Rogers's performance." Interview with Meyer Lansky II.

13: "Batista stopped by." Interview with Florencio Gelabert Jr.

14: "Even though . . . kitchen director." Ibid.

15: "Buddy had met someone . . . take care of each other." Lacey, Robert, *Little Man: Meyer Lansky and the Gangster Life*, New York: Little, Brown and Co., 1991, pp. 329–330.

16: "Trafficante had tried to make his own arrangements . . . but the strongman rebuffed him." Turkus, Burton, and Feder, Sid, *The Story of the Syndicate, Murder, Inc.*, New York: Da Capo Press, 1992, p. 195.

17: "Trafficante immediately reported . . . 'Don't worry about Albert,' Lansky replied." Messick, Hank, *Lansky*, Berkley Medallion Books, 1971, p. 212.

18: "Anastasia's bodyguard had conveniently stepped away . . . shot twenty-nine years earlier." Raab, Selwyn, *Five Families: The Rise, Decline, and Resurgence of America's Most Powerful Mafia Empires*, New York: Thomas Dunne Books, 2005, p. 115.

19: "Police got a tip . . . but couldn't come up with anything implicating him." Raab, p. 116.

20: "A New York State trooper, Edgar Croswell . . . history of bootlegging." Raab, p. 117.

21: "It was Genovese who was stirring up resentment . . . in order to humiliate Genovese." English, T. J., *Havana Nocturne: How the Mob Owned Cuba but Then Lost the Revolution*, New York: William Morrow, 2009, 236–238.

Chapter 15

1: "Batista bowing . . . that surprise me." "Meyer Lansky Back in Cuba Despite Ban," *New York Post*, June 17, 1958.

2: "Dalitz, decided to cash out of Cuba . . . he did just that." Interview with Suzanne Dalitz.

3: "Lansky bought him out, but it ended their friendship." Ibid.

4: "The FBI discovered this . . . Lansky's airline reservations." FBI file.

5: "Lansky told Paul that he spent $120,000 . . . United States, Canada, and Latin America." August 26, 1957, letter to Paul Lansky.

6: "Respected citizens began secretly funneling money and support to the rebels." Matthews, Herbert, "Cuban Rebel is Visited in Hideout," *New York Times*, February 24, 1957, p. 1.

7: "By March 1958, however, *The New York Times* . . . had deteriorated even further." Matthews, Herbert, "Cuba Seen on Eve of Grave Events," *New York Times*, March 23, 1958, p. 10.

8: "On the day of the party . . . the nearly empty ballroom." Lacey, Robert, *Little Man: Meyer Lansky and the Gangster Life*, New York: Little, Brown and Co., 1991, p. 313.

Chapter 16

1: "Castro's rebel underground in Havana . . . friends' homes instead." Dorschner, John, "Havana, 1958–59: The City was Cultured or

Sleazy, Depending on the Point of View," *Miami Herald*, December 11, 1983.

2: "They took off at 2:40 A.M. for Florida . . . asylum." Ibid.

3: "The first thing they smashed . . . could take more for themselves." Messick, Hank, *Lansky*, New York: Berkley Medallion Books, 1971, p. 198.

4: "Lansky, amazingly . . . 'Close the casinos, and fast.'" English, T. J., *Havana Nocturne: How the Mob Owned Cuba but Then Lost the Revolution*, New York: William Morrow, 2009, p. 301.

5: "He and his driver, Armando Jaime Casiellas, scooped up millions of dollars to hide." "Mafia driver's death goes unnoticed in Cuba long after gambling days," *The Tribune, The Miami Herald Bahamas Edition*, May 29, 2007, p. 13.

6: "Within hours . . . Riots erupted, and banks were looted." "Meyer Lansky is Dead at 81, Financial Wizard of Organized Crime," *New York Times*, January 16, 1983. p. 29.

7: "One prominent American, Ernest Hemingway . . . delighted with Castro's victory." Interview with Patrick Hemingway.

8: "He decided to run the Hotel Riviera . . . doing everything from cooking to housekeeping." Lacey, Robert, *Little Man: Meyer Lansky and the Gangster Life*, New York: Little, Brown and Co., 1991, p. 313.

9: "A few loyal employees were willing to help, but most fled." Interview with Luis Castaneda

10: "Lansky hobbled down to his kitchen . . . Teddy mopped the floors." Lacey, p. 314.

11: "Over the next few days, Lansky worked . . . who wanted to leave out of the country." Lacey, p. 315.

12: "Uncle Jack picked her up . . . 'You're getting nothing.'" Lansky, Sandra, and Stadiem, William, *Daughter of the King: Growing Up in Gangland*, New York: Hachette Books, 2014, p. 198.

13: "One reported . . . George Raft, who worked as a greeter at El Casino De Capri in Havana." Teresea, Vincent, and Renner, Thomas C., *My Life in the Mafia*, New York: Doubleday and Co., 1973, p. 220.

14: "After he got a call . . . legal attaché at the US Embassy." FBI file.

15: "The Cuban government held its first court martial . . . The crowd was in a frenzy." R. Hart Phillips, "Cuban Show Trial of Batista Aides Opens in Sports Stadium," *New York Times*, January 23, 1959, p. 1.

16: "He wanted to make it clear . . . he was still in Havana." FBI file, memo to director.

17: "That same day, he gave an interview . . . permit American gamblers to operate." Jarlson, Alan, *Las Vegas Sun*, January 5, 1959.

18: "'No doubt they'll soon be around to talk with me.'" Ibid.

19: "By January 7, he flew from Cuba . . . but the smaller ones had." FBI file.

20: "Lansky didn't know it . . . She even resorted to listening in on his phone calls." Lacey, p. 339.

21: "For their part, the agents thought . . . had his wife committed so he could marry another woman." Ibid.

22: "Two weeks later, he returned to Cuba and opened the casinos to tourists only." Interview with Jane Feehan.

23: "On February 1, 1959, he suffered an attack of pericarditis . . . an oxygen tent." FBI file.

24: "His death came . . . a hung jury three years earlier." Congressional timeline, p. 314.

25: "In April 1959, he left Cuba with his mistress, Carmen." "Mafia driver's death goes unnoticed in Cuba long after gambling days, "*The Tribune, The Miami Herald Bahamas Edition*, May 29, 2007, p. 13.

26: "On May 6, 1959, Cuban authorities . . . demanded their arrest." "Cuba Holds 2 for U.S.," *New York Times*, May 7, 1959.

27: "Trafficante . . . sneaked out the back and went into hiding." FBI file.

28: "He did not know that Cellini's brother . . . had been an FBI informant for the last two years." FBI file.

29: "Agents thought Lansky appeared pale and drawn . . . 'his ability to express himself." Confidential FBI memo, MM 92–102.

30: "He told them he wondered where the rebels . . . the money came from Communists." Confidential FBI memo, MM 92–102.

31: "He admitted that he could lose heavily unless the situation changed . . . national security." Ibid.

32: "The Cuban government freed them . . . should be released." "Cuba Frees 2 Americans," *New York Times*, May 31, 1959.

33: "His attorney, Frank Ragano, won his release by paying a $1-million bribe." Peter Kornbluh, director of the NSA Cuba Documentation Project.

34: "It was located in a private, exclusive community . . . FBI agents noted." FBI file.

35: "Moreover . . . substation there." Messick, p. 223.

Chapter 17

1: "Batista, aware of the plotting against him . . . rebel leader would have none of it." Reid-Henry Simon, *Fidel and Che: A Revolutionary Friendship*, New York: Walker & Co., 2009.

2: "'Dear Capt. Paul . . . important for you to have the cloths, fit properly and look new.'" January 6, 1960, letter to Paul Lansky.

3: "'The judge was most proud to hear from you . . . I apologize for being critical.'" February 28, 1960, letter to Paul Lansky.

4: "Paul's wife Edna thought the relationship . . . she experienced in her family." Lacey, Robert, *Little Man: Meyer Lansky and the Gangster Life*, New York: Little, Brown and Co., 1991, p. 348.

5: "Even though Lansky's own spelling . . . they started corresponding." Interview with Meyer Lansky II.

6: "He approached Bahamian Finance Minister Sir Stafford . . . casinos in the Bahamas." *Jerusalem Post*, January 13, 1972.

7: "He also had extravagant tastes . . . order caviar for 100 people." Karmin, Monroe W., and Penn, Stanley, "Las Vegas East," *Wall Street Journal*, October 5, 1966.

8: "The following month . . . its anti-gambling laws to Bahamas Amusements Ltd." Davidson, Bill, *Saturday Evening Post*, p. 30.

9: "Chesler, too, later admitted that he sought Lansky's advice . . . to help him get started." FBI file and Karmin, Monroe W., *Wall Street Journal*, April 19, 1967.

10: "They were two of the only employees trusted with the nightly count." Karmin, Monroe W. and Penn, Stanley, "Las Vegas East," *Wall Street Journal*, October 5, 1966.

11: "American officials were genuinely worried that the Bahamas . . . 'outpost for US gangsters.'" Turner, Wallace, "Gambling in Bahamas Worries United States Officials," *New York Times*, February 15, 1965, pp. 1, 18.

12: "He greeted guests, signed autographs, and danced with the women." Teresea, Vincent, and Renner, Thomas C., *My Life in the Mafia*, New York: Doubleday and Co., 1973, p. 220.

13: "It became, according to mobster Vinny Teresa, 'the place to be' in London." Ibid.

14: "It was also known for being an honest operation." Renner, p. 218.

15: "'When you wanted to run junkets . . . three to four million bucks a week in action.'" Renner, pp. 217–218.

16: "Parvin, along with partners Raft and singer Tony Martin . . . on a $10.5-million sale." Congressional Record, remarks by Cong. Gerald Ford, April 15, 1970.

17: "Lansky's name didn't show up in any sale paperwork, but he did report the fee on his taxes." Lacey, p. 360.

18: "One night, songwriter Artie Schroeck wanted to see Sinatra . . . to see his idol." Interview with Artie Schroeck.

19: "Patrons had to be dressed . . . No one would be killed in turf wars there." Ibid.

20: "Singer Frankie Vallie marveled . . . pressed $5,000 into his pocket as a thank-you." Ibid.

21: "She didn't know Lansky, but . . . 'It was always Meyer this, Meyer that,' she recalled." Interview with Antoinette Giancana.

22: 'Paul and Edna visited her in New York once . . . appalled at her inattention toward her son.' Interview with Meyer Lansky II.

23: "Buddy told his father that the reason he gambled so heavily . . . Buddy acquiesced." Lacey, p. 337.

Chapter 18

1: "He bragged about reading three books at a time . . . his listeners expressed awe at his knowledge." FBI Airtel to director from New York SAC, June 5, 1962.

2: "He complained that the necessity of making a living . . . how lucky people are who 'fall into it.'" Ibid.

3: "Hoover immediately seized upon it . . . hotel soap contracts in Las Vegas." FBI Airtel from director to SACS in Las Vegas, Miami, and New York.

4: "Unidentified man: 'I kept telling them . . . three against one.'" FBI Airtel to director from NY SAC dated June 11, 1962.

5: "'They're nothing but racketeers, every one of them . . . just a matter of time.'" Ibid.

6: "'Let me tell you something . . . an arrogant punk.'" Ibid.

7: "'That's okay. He loves his wife, he loves his family, and he doesn't want to embarrass them." Ibid.

8: "'Teddy was having trouble with the help.'" Ibid.

9: "Three days later . . . not to jeopardize their informant." Ibid.

10: "They got it done by 1:00 P.M. and got out . . . Lansky and Teddy arrived home." Ibid.

11: "'Subject appeared to have deteriorated greatly . . . Miami agents in April of 1962.'" Ibid.

12: "She even sold her used clothing out of their garage to raise extra cash." Messick, Hank, *Lansky*, New York: Berkley Medallion Books, 1971, p. 223.

13: "He usually had a driver . . . from his days in Brooklyn." Messick, p. 224.

14: "He'd leave home around 10:00 A.M. . . . By 3:30 P.M., he'd head home." Ibid.

15: "He never held business meetings at home." FBI file.

16: "'Blanche stated . . . to be more trustworthy and generous people to work with than the Italians.'" FBI file of SA James J. Kearney, dated December 19, 1962.

17: "That Christmas, Teddy went . . . whenever he came up in conversation." Ibid.

18: "That Christmas Eve, Lansky . . . if she wanted to stay out of a mental hospital." Ibid.

19: "Disappointed agents . . . 'Neither he nor the car has been seen since.'" Teletype to director from Detroit SAC, September 4, 1963.

20: "'NYO (New York Office) advised . . . Armed and considered dangerous.'" FBI teletype to director, October 10, 1963.

21: "Lansky had shared interests in Las Vegas and Cuba . . . Genovese did, too." FBI memo, January 19, 1966.

22: "Then, on December 3, 1963 . . . agents didn't hear anyone speaking." FBI memo to director from Miami SAC, December 6, 1963.

23: "The next day, several people . . . searching Lansky's study." Ibid.

24: "On December 5, 1963, agents removed the bug." Ibid.

Chapter 19

1: "'Lansky today is a very rich man . . . International Credit Bank of Switzerland." Messick, Hank, "Florida Crime 'Money Tree' Widely Rooted," *Miami Herald*, May 23, 1966.

2: "Within a few months . . . Nixon proposed yet another campaign against organized crime." Congressional timeline, p. 322.

3: "'I don't want to take the drama out of your stories' . . . walking away, smiling." Gage, Nicholas, "Underworld Genius, How One Gang Leader Thrives While Others Fall by the Wayside," *Wall Street Journal*, November 19, 1969.

4: "He told a reporter that he moved because he was worried . . . try to kidnap him." Ibid.

5: "In August 1969 . . . seized credit accounts and other records." Savage, James, "Grand Jury in Miami Probes Movement of Las Vegas Funds," *Miami Herald*, June 5, 1970.

6: "That fall, Paul's family visited New York . . . what else they could do." Interview with Meyer Lansky II.

7: "The FBI agents noted that Bernard Sigelbaum . . . 'Meyer wants a breakdown.'" FBI file.

8: "Mike Dupile, one of the bandmates, noticed a short guy to his left who was flanked by two very large men . . . that was the end of the band." Interview with Mike Dupile.

Chapter 20

1: "The agents let Lansky go home . . . The FBI notified Hoover." FBI file, urgent teletype to director from Miami, March 5, 1970.

2: "Within a week, they determined that the pills . . . was no federal crime." FBI teletype to director from Miami, March 10, 1970.

3: "They immediately advised Florida state authorities . . . according to an urgent teletype to Hoover." Ibid.

4: "Three weeks after US Customs . . . having drugs without a prescription." Lacey, Robert, *Little Man: Meyer Lansky and the Gangster Life*, New York: Little, Brown and Co., 1991, pp. 406–407.

5: "It was also Good Friday . . . spend the weekend in jail." De Toledo, Zali, *They Called Him a Gangster*, eBookPro Publishing, 2020, p. 167.

6: "They charged him with a felony violation of the state's barbiturate statute . . . and a $1,000 fine." FBI teletype to director from Miami, March 27, 1970.

7: "'Lansky has been extremely irritable,' the FBI file noted." FBI file.

8: "The prosecutor was so angry . . . before he finished his statement." Levine, Paul, "Judge Orders Lansky Acquitted," *Miami Herald*, June 19, 1970.

9: "Afterwards, a reporter asked Lansky . . . 'I've had them for twelve years.'" Ibid.

10: "He saw the whole thing as a setup." De Toledo, p. 167.

11: "'Extensive favorable newspaper publicity extended by subject's arrest.'" FBI teletype to director from Miami, March 28, 1970.

12: "Meyer Lansky . . . nervous stomach." Savage, James, "Lansky Is Jailed on Drug Charge," *Miami Herald*, March 27, 1970.

13: "Varon argued that Florida law enforcement . . . dismissed the case." DOJ memos, August 10, 1970, and August 18, 1970.

14: "In May 1970, FBI agents reached out to Lansky about a matter of grave importance." FBI file.

15: "Israeli officials immediately dispatched a state attorney . . . police reports." "After Lansky: New Law Likely," *The Jerusalem Post*, April 14, 1972.

16: "On January 25, 1971, the Israeli newspaper . . . intercept his mail." FBI Airtel to director from Legat Tel Aviv, July 23, 1971.

17: "Acting on orders from Interpol, Israel barred three Jewish gangsters from entering the country." "State Tries to Document Lansky's Criminal Past," *The Jerusalem Post*, March 24, 1972.

18: "That same month, the US Department of Justice . . . 'Operation Financier.'" FBI file.

19: "'It is the intention of the department' . . . the teletype to Hoover read." Teletype to director from Miami SAC, January 17, 1971.

20: "On March 4, 1971, Israeli agents . . . testify before the grand jury in Florida." FBI Airtel from Director to SACS in Miami and NY, March 5, 1971.

21: "Worse, from his point of view . . . another former Flamingo employee." "Four Indicted with Lansky Released on Bond," *The New York Times*, March 27, 1971.

22: "Kovolick was called 'The Stick' . . . during the Prohibition years." Interview with Meyer Lansky II.

23: "'When Paul's family visited Florida, Kovolick . . . watch him at the pool.'" Ibid.

24: "Three weeks later, Kovolick's body was found . . . Baxter was convicted." "Body of Gangster Found in the South," *The New York Times*, April 30, 1972.

Chapter 21

1: "*The New York Times* reported that the US Justice Department's special strike force." Gage, Nicholas, "U.S. Investigating Lansky Crime Web," *New York Times*, June 10, 1971, p. 1.

2: "Another paper, *Yedioth Ahronoth*, called Lansky a gangster." FBI file.

3: "This time, Lansky sued the paper for 1 million Israeli pounds." "Lansky Sues Israeli Newspaper That Called Him a Gangster," *New York Times*, July 6, 1971.

4: "'In reply to your letter of May 18, 1971 . . . Sincerely, Meyer Lansky.'" FBI file.

5: "Then he sued *Yedioth Ahronoth* for 1 million Israel pounds for calling him a gangster." "Lansky Sues Israeli Paper That Called Him a Gangster," *The New York Times*, July 5, 1971.

6: "He argued that he was merely an old Jew . . . not forgiven for his Jewishness." Yonay, Ehud, "Lansky Wooing Israel for Keeps," *Newsday*, September 16, 1971.

7: "Vincent 'Fat Vinny' Teresa, a low-level Mob associate of the New England Mafia . . . 'casino gambling business.'" FBI memo, May 9, 1972.

8: "Lansky didn't know it . . . the Justice Department strike force." FBI file.

9: "He didn't know it . . . no Mafia in Israel." Lacey, Robert, *Little Man: Meyer Lansky and the Gangster Life*, New York: Little, Brown and Co., 1991, p. 423.

10: "He received 'a handsome retainer' and . . . because of Lansky's poor health." Goodman, Oscar, with Anastasia, George, *Being Oscar: From Mob Lawyer to Mayor of Las Vegas—Only in America*, Weinstein Books, 2013, p. 48.

11: "The judge, convinced that Lansky's medical condition was serious, dismissed the case in Nevada." Ibid, p. 49.

12: "'This time my client was the biggest name' . . . more phone calls." Ibid.

13: "'After hearing over 500 witnesses . . . New York with Lansky." *Jerusalem Post*, January 13, 1972.

14: "The US Justice Department delivered two suitcases . . . Interpol and British police." *Jerusalem Post*, March 24, 1972.

15: "The prosecutor in the case, Gavriel Bach, met personally with Attorney General Mitchell." Lacey, p. 434.

16: "As described by a reporter . . . 'visibly annoying the bench.'" *Jerusalem Post*, March 24, 1972.

17: "Meanwhile, in June 1972 . . . to gambling junkets to London." "Lansky Indicted in U.S. Tax Plot," *New York Times*, June 7, 1972.

18: "He wrote a letter to Yosef Burg." Lacey, p. 446.

19: "Lansky walked out of court . . . 'A Jew has a slim chance in this world.'" *Jerusalem Post*, September 13, 1972, p. 1.

20: "'On November 5, 1972 . . . election would eclipse the news of his travel.'" De Toledo, Zali, *They Called Him a Gangster*, eBookPro Publishing, 2020, p. 93.

21: "This came even after he offered any country . . . substantial investment in the country." "Lansky Said to Offer A Million to Any Country Offering Him a Haven," *New York Times*, November 1, 1972.

22: "The FBI notified the legal attaché in Bern . . ." Urgent teletype from acting FBI director to SAC Miami. November 5, 1972.

23: "At midnight, he changed to a Swiss Air flight on route to Rio de Janeiro . . . Brazil." FBI file.

24: "He had some reason . . . ulcer medication." Lacey, pp. 454–455.

25: "FBI Agent Kenneth Whittaker arrested Lansky." "Lansky Seized by FBI," *Evening Star*, November 7, 1972.

26: "Lansky told them, 'That's life. At my age, it's too late to worry. What will be will be.'" "Lansky Arrested on Landing in Miami," *New York Times*, November 8, 1972.

27: "A judge ordered him to surrender his passport and restricted him . . . in Florida." FBI file.

28: "A female TV reporter taunted her . . . 'You don't look seventy and sharp!'" Lacey, p. 460.

29: "Teddy spit on her." Interview with Meyer Lansky II.

Chapter 22

1: "All of a sudden, he rolled down his window and spat out, 'Get a haircut!'" Interview with Meyer Lansky II.

2: "One day, Meyer II was playing in the rafters of the family's garage and found some tapes up there." Ibid.

3: "She changed her last name to Mason." Ibid.

4: "They had met at Jerusalem's Dan Hotel." De Toledo, Zali, *They Called Him a Gangster*, eBookPro Publishing, 2020, p. 51.

5: "Later, she described the meeting as being hit by a 'thunderbolt.' De Toledo, p. 50.

6: "'I can't get ham and eggs' . . . he said." De Toledo p. 51.

7: "'Sure, I'll cook you the eggs.'" Ibid.

8: "The next morning, she heard a knock on the door . . . 'I got the eggs, too.'" Ibid.

9: "'My dear, you never kiss a man or a dog on the mouth . . . mouths have been before.'" De Toledo, pp. 52–53.

10: "Women constantly threw themselves at Lansky . . . $300-million fortune." De Toledo, p. 52.

11: "One particularly sentimental gift . . . 'Always in my heart.'" De Toledo, p. 56 and interview with Meyer Lansky II.

12: "'Your father won't meet with Teddy Lansky,' he told her. 'She really wants to talk with you.'" Interview with Suzanne Dalitz.

13: "'They can't hear us.'" Interview with Bert Nevins.

14: "A Bell South telephone repair van was always parked outside the apartment complex." Ibid.

15: "A federal grand jury convicted him of contempt . . . answer grand jury questions two years earlier." "Lansky Convicted of Contempt," *New York Times*, March 1, 1973, p. 38.

16: "He underwent open heart surgery in March." "Lansky Acquitted of Evading Taxes," *New York Times*, July 26, 1973, p. 25.

17: "In July, Lansky appeared in court to plead . . . key witness against him was Vincent Teresa." "Lansky Pleads Not Guilty to Tax Evasion Charges," *New York Times*, July 19, 1973, p. 16.

18: "He was testifying in exchange for a reduction of his sentence for a conviction of securities theft." Fowler, Glen, "Vincent Teresa, 61; Mafia Aide Became Informer and Author," *New York Times*, February 26, 1990.

19: "He testified that he traveled twice to Miami . . . $90,000 in $100 bills." "Lansky Acquitted of Evading Taxes, *New York Times*, July 26, 2973, p. 25.

20: "Confronted with that fact . . . he had been an 'unmitigated liar' in the past." Ibid.

21: "The federal government tells me . . . paid Lansky money from casino profits." Teresea, Vincent, and Renner, Thomas C., *My Life in the Mafia*, New York: Doubleday and Co., 1973, p. 217.

22: "Now, Lansky didn't come to me and say . . . they'd wipe him out in a second." Ibid.

Chapter 23

1: "*The New York Times* published an article . . . errors about the Mafia." Gage, Nicholas, "Questions Are Raised On Lucky Luciano Book," *New York Times*, December 17, 1974, p. 1.

2: "In answer to a journalist's question, Lansky wrote in reply . . . 'trouble for the many.'" Written answers to questions posed by journalist Paul Sann.

3: "'Not 5 percent of the accounts bear any resemblance to reality.'" Gage, Nicholas, "Questions Are Raised On Lucky Luciano Book," *New York Times*, December 17, 1974, p. 1.

4: "In March 1976, he wrote to de Toledo . . . disturbance to the country." March 3, 1976, letter to Zali de Toledo. De Toledo, Zali, *They Called Him a Gangster*, eBookPro Publishing, 2020.

5: "One was the murder of Johnny Roselli." "Lansky and 4 Subpoenaed In Miami in Investigation Into Murder of Roselli," *New York Times,* February 27, 1977.

6: "After Menachem Begin's . . . he reached out to *Jerusalem Post* journalist David Landau." Lacey, Robert, *Little Man: Meyer Lansky and the Gangster Life*, New York: Little, Brown and Co., 1991, p. 491.

7: "'It was a rather sad conversation,' Landau recalled." Ibid.

8: "He called de Toledo and told her, 'Honey, I'm coming!'" De Toledo, p. 96.

9: "The publicity over his coming to Israel would be ruinous to both of them." De Toledo, p. 97.

10: "He shot Teriaca twice in the chest, mortally wounding him. Teriaca died twelve hours after the shooting." "Lansky's Stepson Is Held in Miami On Second-Degree Murder Charge," *New York Times*, July 5, 1977.

11: "He would go to the garage where Lansky parked his car . . . and demand the car." Interview with Meyer Lansky II.

12: "Miami police, however, didn't know about his release." "Lansky's Stepson Charged," *Sunday Argus*, July 3, 1977, p. 7.

13: "Teddy wanted to post bond, but . . . afraid something bad would happen." Lacey, p. 500.

14: "Schwartz's own lawyer warned him . . . 'I'll be careful.' " Merkin, Robert and Williams, Verne, "War of Revenge Feared from Schwartz Slaying," *Miami News*, October 13, 1977, p. 1.

15: "A Bay Harbor Island policeman heard the shot . . . according to a police spokesman." "Lansky Stepson Shot, Killed At Restaurant," *News Herald*, October 13, 1977.

16: "One investigator said the powder burns . . . less than six inches away from him." Merkin, p. 1.

17: "He wrote de Toledo . . . all of the time." De Toledo, p. 153.

18: "In January 1978, Israel rejected him again." LaBrecque, Ron, "Lansky Loses Third Bid to Enter Israel," *Miami Herald*, January 6, 1978.

19: "The reporter noted Lansky's poor health . . . Mount of Olives Cemetery in Jerusalem." Ibid.

20: "By August 1980, the Interior Ministry . . . agree to stay no more than thirty days." Lacey, p. 506.

Chapter 24

1: "He was immediately admitted to the hospital to remove a tumor from his lung." Herald Staff, "Lansky Faces Tests for Pain in Hospital," *Miami Herald*, November 25, 1982, p. 9.

2: "His doctor refused to comment on the rumors, but it was obvious. He had cancer." Ibid.

3: "He'd walk Bruiser—by now blind—along Collins Avenue and nod to neighbors." Whited, Charles, "Meyer Lansky: A Quiet Wizard with Dark Past," *Miami Herald*, January 16, 1983, p. 1.

4: "Barry Neuman ran a car repair business . . . blue Mercedes." Interview with Barry Neuman.

5: "'What are you going to sue them for . . . In real life, he was even worse!'" Lacey, Robert, *Little Man: Meyer Lansky and the Gangster Life*, New York: Little, Brown and Co., 1991, p. 516.

6: "Paul's friend from Boeing, Dick L'Heureux . . . he thought to himself." Interview with Dick L'Heureux.

7: "Lansky's old friend and lawyer, Joe Varon, got his right to vote reinstated." Interview with Dohn Williams.

8: "Citron asked Paul . . . if he would help Buddy financially." Lacey, p. 528.

9: "'Where am I going to get that sort of money from?'" Lacey, p. 511.

10: "'Europe is out. The style I like to travel in is beyond my means.'" De Toledo, Zali, *They Called Him a Gangster*, eBookPro Publishing, 2020, p. 195.

11: "'I miss the country because of my deep feeling for the people . . . caress it all the time."' De Toledo, p. 197.

12: "'If only I had you now . . . I will let you know more definite.'" De Toledo, p. 204.

13: "'At this moment, I'm in the hospital.'" De Toledo, p. 207.

14: "He said it burned his throat." Lacey, p. 532.

15: "Two prominent Miami rabbis arrived . . . 'You didn't want him in life; you're not getting him in death!'" Interview with Meyer Lansky II.

16: "Nondescript white vans and Broward County police cars ringed the property." Interview with Dohn Williams and Bogenschutz.

17: "They held the wake at Sonken's . . . South Florida." Interview with Dohn Williams.

18: "It was confusing and uncomfortable for Meyer II." Interview with Meyer Lansky II.

19: "Jack and Jimmy Alo went to visit Buddy." Lacey, p. 542.

20: "He raised nearly $300,000." Ibid., p. 546.

21: "Her response: 'I blew it.'" Ibid., p. 547.

Epilogue

1: "The Genovese family stepped in to ensure that a favorite actor . . . portray Lansky." Knoelelseder Jr., William K.; Murphy, Kim; Soble,

Ronald L., "Who Plays Lansky? Mob and the Movies: Life or Art?" *Los Angeles Times*, March 19, 1989, p. 1.

2: "At the end of 1988, MCA Inc. suspended him for allegedly funneling money from the company's employee benefit plan to the Bufalino crime family of Pittston, Pennsylvania." Adelson, Andrea, "THE MEDIA BUSINESS; MCA Suspends Executive Named in Corruption Case," *New York Times*, December 16, 1988.

3: "He also bragged about his ties to John Gotti . . . listening in." Knoelelseder Jr., et al.

4: "'If they want war' . . . mobsters flying to Hollywood." Ibid.

5: "Bacow said he knew Lansky personally and that he had his blessing on his script." Ibid.

6: "What they tried to do was become my partner . . . real fast." Ibid.

7: "All the studios are scared to even talk to me now." Ibid.

8: "A few years . . . 'If Hoover won, he got paid, and if he didn't win, they would just forget it,' the man said." Goodman, Walter, *New York Times*, February 9, 1993.

ACKNOWLEDGMENTS

We are especially grateful to our indefatigable and visionary editor, James Abbate, of Kensington Publishing. He conceived this project and shepherded it through the final manuscript with the utmost care. Our savvy and very kind agent, Frank Weimann, of Folio Literary Management, guided us through the entire process with patience and good humor. Special thanks to Antoinette Giancana for sharing her memories with us and to Phil Genovese for his careful reading and addition to the book. And thanks to Dan Pearson, CEO of Dan4 Entertainment, for his unflagging support and encouragement.

This book never would have been completed without the time, energy, and insight of so many people. They include Peter Barbutti, Mark Bauzter (and his father, Gregson, in an unpublished interview before he died), Bill Bleyer, J. David Bogenschutz, Dennis Bruce, Donna and Luis Castaneda, Ruth and Susan Citron, Kenneth Cobb, Suzanne Dalitz Gollin, Mike Dupile, Col. Richard Emery, Jane Feehan, Maryann Fitzgerald, Charles Foesher II, Michelle Isopo, Victoria Garlanda, Florencio Gelabert Jr., Thomas V. Hagerty, Abby Hellwarth, Patrick Hemingway, Neal Karlen, Marc Kristel, Charles Kuenzel, Mary Kate Matthews, Dick L'Heureux, Margaret Lynch, Robin McClintock, Nancy Nemlich, Michael Nemlich, Barry Neuman, Bert Nevins, Bertrand Pellegrin, Glenn Roderman, Romney Rogers, Penny Rosen, Artie Schroeck, Michael Shnayerson, Dr. Vernon Sternhill, Greg Veitch, John A. Vigna, Randy Wells, Willie Wilkerson III, and Dohn Williams.

This book also never would have been possible without Dani Porter-Lansky. Her deep knowledge of the subject, sharp eye, and supreme organizational skills were invaluable, and her passion and humor kept us going. Thank you, Dani.

Lastly, thank you to the many journalists who documented gangster stories over the years, often at their own risk.

INDEX

Italics indicate photos

FURTHER READING

NEW YORK

Five Families

GENOVESE FAMILY

TOP HOODLUM, Anthony M. DeStefano
Frank Costello, Boss

THE DEADLY DON, Anthony M. DeStefano
Vito Genovese, Boss

CHIN, Larry McShane
Vincent Gigante, Boss

GAMBINO FAMILY

LORD HIGH EXECUTIONER, Frank DiMatteo and Michael Benson
Albert Anastasia, Boss

CARLO GAMBINO: BOSS OF BOSSES, Frank DiMatteo and Michael Benson
Carlo Gambino, Boss

MOB KILLER, Anthony M. DeStefano
Charles Carneglia, Soldier

GOTTI'S BOYS, Anthony M. DeStefano
John Gotti, Boss; Salvatore Gravano, Underboss; Gene Gotti, Captain; Angelo Ruggiero, Captain; Charles Carneglia, Soldier; Tony Rampino, Associate

LUCCHESE FAMILY

TOMMY LUCCHESE, Anthony M. DeStefano
Tommy Lucchese, Boss

JIMMY THE GENT, Anthony M. DeStefano
Jimmy Burke, Associate

THE BIG HEIST, Anthony M. DeStefano
Jimmy Burke, Associate; Henry Hill, Associate; Thomas DeSimone, Associate

BONANNO FAMILY

THE BONANNOS, Joe Pistone and Larry McShane
Joe Bonanno, Boss; Philip Rastelli, Boss; Carmine Galante, De Facto Boss; Joe Massino, Boss; Vincent Basciano, Boss; Michael Mancuso, Boss
KING OF THE GODFATHERS, Anthony M. DeStefano
Joe Massino, Boss
THE CIGAR, Frank DiMatteo and Michael Benson
Carmine Galante, De Facto Boss

COLOMBO FAMILY

OLIVE OIL KING, Frank DiMatteo and Michael Benson
Joe Profaci, Boss
JOE COLOMBO, Frank DiMatteo and Michael Benson
Joe Colombo, Boss
CARMINE THE SNAKE, Frank DiMatteo and Michael Benson
Carmine Persico, Boss
LITTLE VIC AND THE GREAT MAFIA WAR, Larry McShane
Vic Orena, Acting Boss
SONNY, S. J. Peddie
Sonny Franzese, Underboss
THE PRESIDENT STREET BOYS, Frank DiMatteo
Joe Gallo, Captain; Albert Gallo, Captain; Larry Gallo, Soldier
MAFIA HIT MAN, Frank DiMatteo and Michael Benson
Joe Gallo, Captain; Carmine DiBiase, Associate

PHILADELPHIA

BRUNO FAMILY

THE DOCILE DON George Anastasia
Angelo Bruno, Boss

PITTSTON

BUFALINO FAMILY

BUFALINO, Charles Bufalino

Steve La Torre, Boss; Calogero Bufalino, Boss; Santo Volpe, Boss; Russell Bufalino, Boss; William D'Elia, Boss

GENERAL

THE LANSKY LEGACY, Meyer Lansky II and S. J. Peddie
Meyer Lansky; National Crime Syndicate; Las Vegas; Cuba
BUGSY AND FLAMINGO, Meyer Lansky II and S. J. Peddie
Benjamin Siegel; Virginia Hill; Las Vegas; Hollywood
OPERATION UNDERWORLD, Matthew Black
Sicily; World War II
GANGSTERS VS. NAZIS, Michael Benson
Meyer Lansky; Benjamin Siegel; Mickey Cohen; Murder, Inc.; World War II
MAFIA SECRETS, Gianni Russo and Michael Benson
Gianni Russo; The Godfather; Hollywood
RED HOOK, Frank DiMatteo and Michael Benson
Brooklyn Mafia
THE FBI'S WAR AGAINST THE MAFIA, Frank Storey
Mafia Commission Trial; Bruno Family; Pizza Connection
THE DON, RJ Roger
Five Families; Mafia Commission; National Crime Syndicate
THE MAFIA'S GREATEST HITS, David H. Jacobs
Mafia Murders; National Crime Syndicate
IN THE GHOST SHADOWS, Peter Chin and Everett De Morier
Chinatown, New York City; Ghost Shadows Gang
MEET THE KELLYS, Chris Enss
Machine Gun Kelly; Kathryn Thorne
DILLINGER'S GIRLS, Chris Enss
John Dillinger